The Fall and Rise of the Market in Sandinista Nicaragua

The Fall and Rise of the Market in Sandinista Nicaragua

PHIL RYAN

McGill-Queen's University Press
Montreal & Kingston • London • Buffalo

© McGill-Queen's University Press 1995
ISBN 0-7735-1347-7 (cloth)
ISBN 0-7735-1359-0 (paper)

Legal deposit fourth quarter 1995
Bibliothèque nationale du Québec

Printed in Canada on acid-free paper

This book has been published with the help of a grant from the Social Science Federation of Canada, using funds provided by the Social Sciences and Humanities Research Council of Canada.

McGill-Queen's University Press is grateful to the Canada Council for support of its publishing program.

Canadian Cataloguing in Publication Data

Ryan, Phil
    The fall and rise of the market in Sandinista Nicaragua
    Includes bibliographical references and index.
    ISBN 0-7735-1347-7 (bound)
    ISBN 0-7735-1359-0 (pbk.)
    1. Nicaragua – Economic conditions – 1979–   2. Nicaragua – Politics and government – 1979–1990.   I. Title.
    HC146.R93 1995   330.97285'053   C95-900610-9

This book was typeset by Typo Litho Composition Inc.
in 10/12 Baskerville.

To my father and my mother, with love

Contents

Acknowledgments

Lynn Mytelka, Laura Macdonald, and Manfred Bienefeld waded through various drafts of this work, and provided invaluable suggestions. I also profited from the comments of Arch Ritter, Fred Judson, Barbara Jenkins, and the two anonymous reviewers of the Social Science Federation of Canada. Joan McGilvray shepherded the book through the McGill-Queen's publication process, and Victoria Grant edited the manuscript with skill and dedication.

This book has been published with the help of a grant from the Social Science Federation of Canada, using funds provided by the Social Sciences and Humanities Research Council of Canada.

Finally, Beth Woroniuk read and commented on countless drafts of this work, and provided constant support to help me see it through to completion. Our discussions over the past decade, both in Managua and here in Ottawa, have done as much as anything to sharpen my understanding of the Sandinista experience.

Phil Ryan
Ottawa, Canada
pryan@ccs.carleton.ca

The FSLN Leadership:
Basic Information

The nine members of the National Directorate are presented in the order in which they entered the Sandinista National Liberation Front. This order of precedence was respected at all formal occasions. Thus, Borge would enter first, Carrión last.

"Tendency" refers to the mid-1970s' faction of the FSLN to which the individual belonged. The three factions were GPP, or *Guerra Popular Prolongada* [Prolonged Popular War], Proletarian, and Insurrectional, also often termed the *Tendencia Tercerista* [Third Way Tendency].

MEMBER	TENDENCY	POST-1979 RESPONSIBILITIES
Tomás Borge	GPP	Minister of the interior, responsible for police and state security
Victor Tirado	Insurrectional	FSLN liaison with most mass organizations, especially unions
Daniel Ortega	Insurrectional	State executive: head of Junta of National Reconstruction until 1984; president thereafter
Humberto Ortega	Insurrectional	Minister of defence
Henry Ruiz	GPP	Minister of planning until 1984; minister for external cooperation thereafter
Jaime Wheelock	Proletarian	Minister of agriculture and agrarian reform

Bayardo Arce	GPP	Party responsibilities, including the FSLN's international relations
Carlos Núñez	Proletarian	Leader of the FSLN delegation to the Council of State until 1984, and to the National Assembly thereafter
Luís Carrión	Proletarian	Vice-minister of the interior to 1987; minister for industry and commerce thereafter

Acronyms Used in the Text

ACRONYM	SPANISH TITLE	ENGLISH TITLE
APEN	Asociación de Profesionales de la Economía	Association of Economists
APP	Area Propiedad del Pueblo	People's Property Area
ATC	Asociación de Trabajadores del Campo	Rural Workers' Union
CACM		Central American Common Market
CAT	Centro de Abastecimiento de los Trabajadores	Workers' Supply Centres
CAUS	Central de Acción y Unidad Sindical	Trade Union Action and Unity Federation
CDS	Comités de Defensa Sandinista	Sandinista Defence Committees
CIA		Central Intelligence Agency (U.S.)
CIERA	Centro de Investigaciones y Estudios de la Reforma Agraria	Agrarian Reform Research Centre

CMEA		Council for Mutual Economic Assistance
CONAPRO-HM	Confederación Nacional de Asociaciones Profesionales, Héroes y Mártires	National Confederation of Professional Associations (Heroes and Martyrs)
COSEP	Consejo Superior de la Empresa Privada	Superior Council of Private Enterprise
CPI		Consumer Price Index
CST	Central Sandinista de Trabajadores	Sandinista Workers' Central
ECLA		United Nations Economic Commission for Latin America
ECLAC		United Nations Economic Commission for Latin America and the Caribbean
ENABAS	Empresa Nicaragüense de Alimentos Básicos	Nicaraguan Basic Foods Company
FBIS		Foreign Broadcast Information Service
FSLN	Frente Sandinista de Liberación Nacional	Sandinista National Liberation Front
GDP		Gross Domestic Product
IMF		International Monetary Fund
INEC	Instituto Nicaragüense de Estadísticas y Censos	Nicaraguan Statistical and Census Institute
JGRN	Junta de Gobierno de Reconstrucción Nacional	Government Junta for National Reconstruction
JPRS		Joint Publications Research Service

MICOIN	Ministerio de Comercio Interior	Ministry for Internal Trade
MIDINRA	Ministerio de Desarrollo Agropecuario y Reforma Agraria	Ministry of Agriculture and Agrarian Reform
MIPLAN	Ministerio de Planificación	Ministry of Planning
OAS		Organization of American States
SNOTS	Sistema de Normación y Organización del Trabajo y Salario	System for the Standardization and Organization of Work and Salaries
SPP	Secretaría de Planificación y Presupuesto	Secretariat for Planning and Budgeting
UNAG	Unión Nacional de Agricultores y Ganaderos	National Union of Farmers and Cattle Ranchers
UNO	Unión Nacional Opositora	National Opposition Union

A Note on Units of Measure and Translations

UNITS OF MEASURE

Though for data on land, crop yields, etc., I have used the hectare as the unit of land area, some direct quotes refer to the "*manzana.*" This is the traditional measure of land area in Nicaragua. It is equal to approximately 0.7 hectares.

The Nicaraguan unit of currency is the *córdoba*, denoted by the symbol C$. All references to dollars denote U.S. dollars.

TRANSLATIONS

All passages directly cited from material which appears in the reference list in languages other than English have been translated into English. All such translations are my own.

The Fall and Rise of the Market in Sandinista Nicaragua

1 Introduction

A warm Sunday afternoon, January 1987. I am doing guard duty with Don Andrés, on a hill overlooking *La Sorpresa*, a state farm with some 140 hectares of good coffee land, about 60 kilometres north-east from the departmental capital of Jinotega. Perhaps to avenge its former owner, an officer of Somoza's National Guard, the farm has been destroyed twice by the contras, in 1983 and 1985. Outside the door of the hut in which we sleep there is a simple wooden cross, in memory of sixteen coffee pickers murdered during the 1985 attack.

Today, though, the farm is quiet below us: people are reading, chatting, or cleaning their rifles. Everyone enjoys the week's one half-day of rest, renewing their energies for the next set of twelve-hour days of coffee picking. In the distance the sun reflects off the sheer white rocks of *Peñas Blancas*, an area that in previous years was the scene of constant fighting.

Don Andrés elbows me: "There are people climbing that hill over there." I strain my eyes at the hill, about a kilometre away, but see nothing. "Don't you see, that fellow in the white shirt just there." Eventually I make out a white speck moving up the hill.

Don Andrés is from this area, and has lived most of his life here. He now works as a gardener in Managua, but promises to return to the mountains as soon as the war is over. "Life can be beautiful here, when you don't have to carry a rifle around everywhere, carry all these bullets, watch every step for mines." And he knows these mountains: whenever our squad has to come down a mountain at 4.00 A.M. after a night of guard duty, I place myself right behind him and keep my eyes fixed on his knapsack, which is the only thing I can make out in the dark. He never falls, and always manages to pick out the obstacles and warn me. No one in my squad knows how old Don Andrés is. He seems old, so we call him "Don" out of respect, but I suspect that this is only because he has lost most of his teeth.

The situation here says much about the subtle ways the u.s.-organized contra war undermined the Nicaraguan economy. We have come from Managua to pick coffee because many of those who have traditionally done so have gone to war. We are not terribly good at the task: most of us are confirmed urbanites, bureaucrats in various government ministries, and our energies are sapped by the hours of nocturnal guard duty. Even if we were master coffee-pickers, yields would be down, because, like the traditional coffee-pickers, many of those who used to tend the coffee plants between harvests have gone to war.

This is a first simple truth about Nicaragua: the u.s. proxy war ground this country into the dust. There were spectacular acts of aggression, such as the attack on Corinto, the country's main port, in late 1983, or the mining of that same port in 1984. But the more common pattern was one of low-intensity mayhem: attacks on state farms and cooperatives, and the murder of rural teachers, health care workers, and agricultural extension specialists.

But there is a second truth about Nicaragua, one that those of us who supported the Sandinista revolution find more uncomfortable. Listen again to Don Andrés: "Look, here you have to take sides. But I tell you, things were better before. The peasant today is really screwed. Before you could work hard, go into a store, and say 'Give me sugar.' And you could buy as much as you wanted. 'Give me batteries,' and there was none of this crap about 'we can only sell you two.' A man would work hard, and he could sell his crop to anyone he wanted, buy from anyone he wanted, buy whatever he wanted. He didn't have to travel miles to buy and sell."

One can judge this lament however one wishes. One might feel that the freedoms whose loss he mourns were empty, that the freedom to buy "as much as he wanted" was the freedom to buy only as much as his miserable earnings allowed, that freedom of commerce was but the freedom to be ripped off coming and going by merchants who sold the fruits of the peasant's labour five times dearer in Managua and gave him goods in return at ten times their real value.

This may well be true, but it is also, at the moment, irrelevant. Don Andrés feels what he feels, his experience has made him sceptical of socialist critiques of market freedom, and thousands of Nicaraguan peasants feel more or less the same. This then is the second simple truth about Nicaragua: the Sandinista project made its contribution to the country's crisis. It alienated a good many people – peasants and others – and it fostered severe economic difficulties.

A third simple truth is that the first two are intimately related. For reasons I cannot quite understand, Don Andrés is here beside me, guarding the state farm. But many people who think much like him are in the mountains around us, carrying guns for the other side. If the farm is attacked, it will be attacked not by the "mercenaries" and "beasts" depicted by the Sandinista media, nor by the "freedom fighters" hailed by Reagan, but by peasants. "Cannon fodder?" Definitely. "Manipulated"? To an extreme. But not without their motives. If the United States provided the material resources for the contras, Sandinista policy helped generate a social base from which the contras could draw human resources. In addition, much government policy helped intensify the economic impact of the war.

After the electoral defeat of the Sandinista National Liberation Front (FSLN) in February 1990, much debate among supporters of the Nicaraguan revolution would revolve around the relative importance of these three simple truths. Thus, Argentine observer Carlos Vilas commented that "we have to recognize that the revolutionary process got stuck in its own internal tensions and ambiguities long before the Sandinistas were defeated at the polls. By then, the rank and file were already weakened and demobilized." He added that "the free and secret ballot became for many voters a means for repudiating specific aspects of the Sandinista administration that were personally irritating: the over-bearing bureaucrat; the illicit enrichment of a Sandinista neighbour; the boss' sexual harassment; the lack of textbooks in the schools while novels, declarations, and speeches by the leaders abounded; dilapidated public buses alongside the manager's air-conditioned car" (1990, 18, 15).

Vilas's remarks were angrily dismissed by two U.S. supporters of the Sandinistas: "The FSLN and the Nicaraguan revolution were the *victims* in an unequal battle with the United States. Vilas' search for 'What Went Wrong?' essentially boils down to a 'blame the victim' argument. Precisely 'what went wrong' is that Nicaragua was forced into the boxing ring with an opponent many times its material and military strength" (Norsworthy and Robinson 1990).

The debate might be seen as a reflection upon one of Marx's oft-quoted phrases: were the Sandinistas brought low by "circumstances not of their choosing," or by the way they sought to "make history"? What must be added to Marx's dictum is that some of the circumstances not of the Sandinistas' choosing were nevertheless of their making. One of Camus's characters says that "after forty, a person is responsible for his face." Similarly, after a few years in power decision-makers are responsible for at least part of the history that weighs like a nightmare upon them.

A. FOCUS OF THE WORK

I lived and worked in Nicaragua from mid-1983 to the beginning of 1988. I taught in the Faculty of Economics of the National Autonomous University of Nicaragua, and in 1986 I moved to Nicaragua's planning ministry, by that point called the Secretariat for Planning and Budgeting. It was clear to all working in the secretariat at that point that Nicaragua was trapped in a crisis from which there was no obvious means of escape. Because I was working in an economic ministry rather than one concerned with defence or foreign relations, a constant theme of discussion was how government policies were implicated in this crisis.

This background explains the general orientation of this book, which will primarily focus on the second of our three "simple truths." The work will examine the contradictions and dilemmas generated by the political and economic project of the FSLN. I draw freely upon hindsight: many of the points made here were by no means clear to me when I was working in Nicaragua.

In choosing this focus, no claim is being made regarding the relative weights of "internal" and "external" factors in the Nicaraguan crisis. The choice of focus is not motivated by any desire to "blame the victim," but by the belief that it is simplistic to view the Sandinistas as purely passive "victims" of U.S. policy. The Sandinistas did, after all, succeed in capturing state power, and held that power for a decade. Though they finally lost the government in 1990, their domestic support remained intact to a surprising degree. As holders of state power, the Sandinistas were "responsible" for everything that happened in Nicaragua during the 1980s, not in the sense that they were to "blame" for everything, but in the sense that Nicaragua, with all its constraints, represented a situation which the Sandinistas had to confront, a situation that demanded choices and actions of them. It is upon these choices and actions that I will focus. Specifically, I will examine the Sandinistas' economic project and its political ramifications. Hence some aspects of the Sandinistas' political project – their view of legislative power, or their understanding of the state's relation to civil society, for example – will be considered only in passing.

At the same time, the book will pay some attention to the other two "simple truths." Chapters five through seven will examine the impact of the contra war, and the interaction of external and internal forces. The Sandinistas' problematic relation with the peasantry, for example, would have played itself out in an entirely different fashion in the absence of the contras.

The book pursues two main lines of argument. First, I will argue that the Sandinistas sought to do much more than merely take and hold state power. Their choices and actions, particularly during their initial period in power, are therefore explicable in the light of their broad project of social transformation. This vision of transformation was heavily influenced by a relatively orthodox Marxism.[1] Second, I will argue that the Sandinistas' project of social transformation contributed to the severe economic crisis from which Nicaragua suffered from the mid-1980s on. Despite the Sandinistas' attempts to modify their economic and political policies after 1984, they never escaped constraints that developed in part from their early policy choices.

Before expanding upon these two arguments, a caveat must be issued. There is an inherent problem in trying to summarize the results of one's investigations in the form of "hypotheses": the exercise often leads to the positing of simple cause-effect relations. But the point of the argument is not to establish a simple causal relation: I am *not* arguing that Sandinista Marxism caused the failure of the Nicaraguan revolution, or that initial policy choices caused all the problems that followed.

Thus, the objective of the analysis is not to establish simple causality but to explore the implications of Sandinista decisions and some of the dilemmas inherent in a Third World socialist project of the type they pursued. This task has to a large extent been ignored by North American writers. As I will argue in chapter two, English-language writings on the revolution have tended to reflect a polarization between supporters of the revolution who generally minimized Sandinista Marxism, and opponents who relied on the demonization of Marxism in order to condemn the Sandinistas and justify the contra war.

My approach, on the other hand, has been to take Sandinista Marxism seriously, and to examine the difficulties that emerge in the attempt to apply a certain vision of socialism in a country such as Nicaragua. I take this approach, not because I want to demonstrate the impossibility of Third World socialism, but because I am a socialist concerned with the viability of socialism in the world, and I believe that this viability cannot be secured without a serious critique of twentieth-century socialist experiences.

To expand upon the first of our two arguments, we may begin by letting the Sandinista leadership speak for itself. In its 1991 report to the FSLN's first party congress, the party's National Directorate proclaimed that "we define the FSLN as the vanguard detachment, which creatively applies Marxist-Leninist principles." Recapitulating the history of the movement, the directorate recalled that "the revolutionary option advocated the overthrow of the Somocista dictatorship, as the starting point for a deeper change, leading to a socialist process" (Dirección Nacional 1991, 10, 6).

The directorate went on to note: "At the beginning of the 1980s, in the *Theses of the FSLN*, we focused on the triumph of the Sandinista Revolution, in an epoch characterized by the transition from capitalism to socialism, which was a world historical tendency. We affirmed that our cause was that of SOCIALISM and that the strengthening of the Popular Sandinista Revolution was our greatest contribution to the cause of socialism in the world." But there are many socialisms in the world. Specifying the socialism of which they spoke, the directorate mentioned "the Soviet Union and Cuba" as two leading representatives of the "socialist countries." Among other "socialist and revolutionary countries," they included "the German Democratic Republic, the Democratic Republic of Korea, Bulgaria, Algeria, Libya, Vietnam" (ibid., 8–9).

The Sandinistas' project of "deeper change, leading to a socialist process" was not fully defined, yet it was marked by certain key elements. Foremost among these was the goal of establishing significant state dominance of the economy: "We sought to gain control, direct or indirect, over the production of wealth, promoting in this way the transformation of social relations, thus developing the role and participation of the workers. With control of the banks, foreign trade, and planning, we managed to obtain the country's most important instruments of economic direction" (ibid., 11).

Apart from state control of the "commanding heights" of banking and foreign trade, the Sandinista project involved significant state productive activity, especially in the agricultural sector. We will see in chapter three the Sandinista project also assumed that the bulk of economic investment would be undertaken by the state. The project also contemplated increasing state influence over prices, and the gradual replacement of market prices with administered ones.

A central anomaly of the Sandinista economic project, relative to those economies that the Sandinistas considered socialist, was the continued survival of the Nicaraguan bourgeoisie.[2] I will argue in chapter three that both political and economic factors led the Sandinistas to decide that the costs of "expropriating the bourgeoisie" would outweigh the benefits. They sought instead to encircle the bourgeoisie, both politically and economically. It is this continued survival of the bourgeoisie that led the Sandinista leaders to distinguish their strategy "leading to a socialist process" from socialism itself. Though they did not define socialism explicitly, various comments suggest that the leaders equated socialism with state expropriation of the major means of production and its attendant social changes.[3] Thus, both their stated commitment to socialism and their repeated comments that the bourgeoisie constituted a transitory ally left open the possibility of an eventual expropriation of the bourgeoisie.

In arguing that the Sandinistas sought to do much more than merely capture state power and hold it, I am arguing that the conception of "political rationality" wielded by many political scientists is not an adequate tool for understanding Sandinista actions. That is, the Sandinistas do not fit the entrepreneurial model of politics described by Downs, who argues that party members seek above all the intrinsic rewards of holding office. They therefore formulate policies as a means to holding office rather than seeking office in order to carry out preconceived policies (1957, 28).[4] But if the Sandinistas do not fit this model, this certainly does not mean that they were indifferent to holding office. There is no reason why some value cannot be both an end in itself and a means to other ends. State power can simultaneously be valued in itself, as a means to the benefits of office of which Downs speaks, as a means to keep future options open, and as a means to transform society.

But we should note the possibility of tension between two dimensions of state power: what might be termed the "generic" dimension, associated with the occupation of government office with its attendant honours and perquisites, may conflict with the "transformative" dimension, associated with the capacity to change society. In the Nicaraguan case, the Sandinistas' decisions to modify their original agrarian reform project, for example, both increased their power in the "generic" sense, by strengthening their hold on the state, and reduced their power in the "transformative" sense, by reducing their capacity to pursue their fundamental vision of socialism.

If one wished to pursue a hypothesis contrary to that put forth here in order to argue, for example, that the Sandinistas were simply run-of-the-mill political opportunists intent on seizing and holding power for its own sake, one would have to address some serious anomalies. The most important of these is the fact that many of the Sandinistas' initial actions upon taking power did not reflect a bare calculus of "generic power" maintenance. Domestically, the June 1979 *Plan of Government* gave the Sandinistas a possible basis for "peaceful coexistence" with the bourgeoisie, which would have allowed the state great latitude for action. Yet the Sandinistas quickly went beyond this program, and did not shrink from repeated confrontations with the bourgeoisie, confrontations that can be explained in light of the Sandinistas' overall economic project. While it is impossible to know for certain whether Sandinista respect for the program would have actually bought peace with the bourgeoisie in the long run, it is significant that whenever respect for the program conflicted with their project, the Sandinistas went beyond the program.

Though the book does not deal with questions of foreign policy, it should be noted that the Sandinistas enjoyed at least the possibility of an understanding with the United States. Clearly, if there was anything that would have been likely to prolong the Sandinistas' hold on state power, it was a tolerable relationship with the United States. Yet, once again, the

Sandinistas did not shrink from a confrontation: they offered material support to El Salvador's Farabundo Marti National Liberation Front, at least until late 1980 or early 1981; they insisted on retaining the phrase about the "Yankee, enemy of humanity," in the Sandinista hymn; they signalled an unmistakable tilt towards the Soviet bloc in early speeches.[5]

The argument is not that the Sandinistas were vague idealists pursuing a grand project at whatever cost. The Sandinistas repeatedly demonstrated a lively sense of political action as a mediation between the possible and the desirable. But the outcome of that mediation cannot be understood without some sense of what was "desirable" for them.

As the 1980s wore on, the Sandinistas faced a marked narrowing of the "possible." Hence the "desirable" became increasingly remote to their day-to-day decision making. As the maintenance of "generic power" became more problematic, less attention was paid to the "transformative" dimension of power. We will see a gradual shift in Sandinista language from talk of economic change to talk of survival, from stress on the need to develop the popular classes to stress on broad "national unity."

This shift has led some observers to stress Sandinista flexibility to the point of questioning whether the Sandinistas really had any grand project of social change at the time they came to power. But – and this brings me to my second argument – the specific nature of the mid-1980s crisis and the ideological/political constraints upon facing that crisis are hard to grasp without understanding the Sandinistas' earlier orientations and actions, which reflected their project of change. The argument thus stresses that political decision making is a trajectory through time. The earlier points of this trajectory constrain, to a greater or lesser extent, those that follow. Early Sandinista price policy, for example, was both an element of the broad project of social change and a means for increasing the popular legitimacy of that project. When they tried to modify that price policy in 1985, the Sandinistas found, like socialist reformers everywhere, that they had become imprisoned by the very instruments of legitimacy they had forged.

Again, the argument that the Sandinista project of social change contributed to the Nicaraguan crisis cannot be isolated from the "simple truths" presented at the outset of this chapter. The Sandinista project might well have succeeded in the absence of u.s. aggression. Nevertheless, I will argue that various elements of the project were problematic in their own right. Further, certain policies increased Nicaragua's vulnerability to external aggression. Early policies towards the peasantry helped give the contras a pool for recruitment. Price and investment policies created a rigid and deficit-ridden state budget that could not adapt sufficiently to the needs of the defence effort. Even if one believes that the United States bears the fundamental responsibility for the Nicaraguan crisis, as I do, the contribution of Sandinista policies to Nicaragua's vulnerability should be understood by socialists throughout the Americas, unless one believes that future socialist projects – of whatever stripe – will *not* have to cope with a hostile U.S. response.

To clarify further the meaning of the two arguments presented here, we may appeal to Weber's view of historical causality (1949, 164ff). To help evaluate the causal importance of a specific phenomenon in history, Weber argued, one should try to imagine to what extent the course of history would have been different in the absence of that phenomenon. The greater the difference suggested by such a thought experiment, the more important is the phenomenon in question. Thus, the arguments presented here can be interpreted to mean that, without the Sandinistas' Marxist ideological commitments, without their initial policies, the history of Nicaragua in the 1980s would have been quite *different*. While counterfactual thought can never establish certainties, let us reflect on this question.

We will see in chapter two that many observers were confused concerning the social base and ideological orientation of the Ortegas' *tercerista* tendency. Leftist observer James Petras dismissed the tendency as "social democratic" (1979, 14), while Shirley Christian argues that the distinction between the Ortegas' *terceristas* and the "social-democratic" Nicaraguan Democratic Movement "was growing fuzzy" by 1978 (1985, 75). It was easy at the time to imagine a take-over of the *tercerista* project by social-democratic tendencies, and in fact Sandinistas belonging to the FSLN's other two tendencies feared this would occur. If this had taken place, and if this "social-democratic" tendency had dominated the new government, Nicaragua might have undergone a modest agrarian reform, expropriation of the Somoza family, various economic reforms, but no real challenge to the bourgeoisie as such, no attempts to organize the majority of the population and transform its ideological orientation, no broad attack upon the sway of the market. Such a moderate reformist government might also have arrived at a *modus vivendi* with the United States.

Thus it is easy to argue that Nicaragua would have experienced a very different decade. But the key word here is "different," not "better" or "worse." For it is just as easy to draw bleak scenarios from our thought experiment: a group of guerrillas arrive in power with few or no ideological convictions, with no deeply rooted vision of social change, with nothing, in fact, but the guns in their hands. While such a situation might have resulted in modest reformism, it is also easy to imagine the government quickly becoming another right-wing authoritarian regime.[6] It is also easy to imagine such a rootless regime seeking simply to replace Somoza as the U.S.'s regional police force.

Thus, the analysis presented here of the difficulties encountered during the Sandinista decade should not be read to imply that some other golden path existed. Though Sandinista Nicaragua experienced a grim economic crisis, few Latin American regimes fared very well in the 1980s. Though the Nicaraguan economic crisis was in many respects the worst in the hemisphere,[7] in no country does the situation today offer great hope to the poor majority.

To recapitulate, then, this book argues that the Sandinistas initially pursued a project of social transformation inspired by a relatively orthodox Marxism, and that this project contributed to the Nicaraguan crisis. Our title, "The Fall and Rise of the Market," encapsulates these two arguments. The Sandinista project can be understood as a broad attack upon the sway of the market in Nicaragua. I will accept Weber's definition of individual markets: "A market may be said to exist wherever there is competition, even if only unilateral, for opportunities of exchange among a plurality of potential parties" (1978, 635).[8] A market economy will be understood as an economy in which most production decisions are mediated through markets, that is, in which decisions are atomistic and competitive. Market society, for its part, will be defined following Polanyi, as a society "shaped in such a manner as to allow [the market economy] to function according to its own laws" (1957, 57). By "attack on the sway of the market," I mean an attack on Nicaraguan market economy and society.

Market society is thus more than a set of economic relations: it sustains and is sustained by diverse political and ideological practices. Decision making to sustain a market society is correspondingly complex. What must be "reproduced," as Althusser pointed out, are not merely the means but also the relations of production (1971, 128). This implies, for example, that market-oriented decision-makers must seek to maintain social toleration of the existing distribution of productive resources, the structures that reproduce a "disciplined" labour force, the typical myths of market society concerning the relation of wealth to "hard work," and so on.

But if market society is a complex reality, so too is the project of overcoming the sway of the market. Thus, the Sandinista project is one with economic, political, and ideological dimensions. This means that the adequacy of specific actions cannot be assessed according to any simple one-dimensional criterion of the sort available, for example, to neo-classical economists. While it is tempting to classify particular policies as "mistakes" in light of the overall Sandinista project, closer examination often reveals the existence of sharp trade-offs that left decision-makers with no unambiguously superior alternative.[9]

Sandinista decision making thus faced a double tension. There was the tension between maintaining their hold on power and using that power to change society, and there were tensions within the project of change itself. The analysis will seek to grasp the complexity of Sandinista decision making. The FSLN leadership was fully aware of some of the dilemmas to be analysed. Others, which I will term "objective" dilemmas, existed independently of the leadership's understanding of them. Examination of these dilemmas is important in order to avoid the easy assumption that a leadership with a different understanding of its situation would have achieved greater success in pursuing its project of transformation.

Thus, for example, chapter three will argue that a fundamental dilemma exists in the construction of socialism between an "accumulation focus" and an "alliance-building focus," a dilemma first articulated in the Preobrazhensky-Bukharin debate during the 1920s. Sandinista leaders, however, did not articulate the dilemma in these terms. While I have portrayed a choice in which both alternatives are consistent with a socialist project, Sandinista leaders were more likely to see the choice as one between "International Monetary Fund" or "technocratic" policies, on the one hand, and "socialist" or "popular" ones on the other. This way of viewing the dilemma has significant implications for its handling. Nonetheless, viewing the dilemma differently would not have made it vanish.

It should be noted that these dilemmas are "objective" only in the sense that the leadership was not fully conscious of them. The existence of such dilemmas depends upon the project chosen by the decision-makers: a different project would generate different "objective" dilemmas. The Preobrazhensky-Bukharin dilemma, for example, exists only if one's economic model requires extensive state accumulation. Hence I have turned to earlier socialist debates in order to clarify some of the dilemmas faced by the Sandinistas, as these are debates among people who had many values in common with Sandinista decision-makers. The debates of socialists are of relevance to socialists.

To focus the study of the Sandinista project, four broad issue-areas will be followed through the life of the revolution:

1 The organization and role of the state sector
2 Price policy
3 Relations with the bourgeoisie
4 Agrarian reform

While other issue-areas could have been examined, the choice is not arbitrary. The interactions between these issue-areas, and between the technical and political contradictions they reveal, demonstrate the complexity of the choices facing the Sandinista leadership. Thus, for example, agrarian reform was influenced both by the desire to maintain tolerable relations with the bourgeoisie and by the desire to develop a state-centric economy, as well as by such more immediately "economic" objectives as the desire to maintain the agro-export sector.

In studying the early years of the Nicaraguan revolution, we will see a partial "fall" of market economy and society, expressed in such phenomena as extensive new state controls on the economy, the autonomization of the state vis à vis the surviving holders of private wealth, the political organization of popular sectors, the project of ideological change involving critiques of wealth and the wealthy, and the rhetorical exaltation of the workers and peasants. Not all these phenomena are in contradiction with markets, narrowly defined, but they all militate against the reproduction of capitalist market relations of production. The latter part of the 1980s, however, saw a resurrection of the market system as the Sandinistas tried to come to terms with a crisis generated in part by the attack on the market. This "rise" of the market was expressed through a relaxation of state controls, through the partial representation of bourgeois interests within the revolutionary bloc, and through an ideological retreat marked by a new emphasis on inter-class unity.

B. OUTLINE

Chapter two will argue that the FSLN came to power shaped by a Marxism much more orthodox than has been recognized or admitted by many observers. Despite their flexibility once in power, this initial orientation had a great influence on their initial policy choices, which in turn influenced the entire course of the Sandinista decade. The chapter will reject the common view that Sandinista ideology was the product of a convergence of Marxism, Christianity, and the nationalism of Sandino. Various orthodox Marxist themes found in the discourse of the Sandinista leadership will be examined, as will the leaders' emphasis on ideological training both within the FSLN and in society at large. The chapter will also argue that even the writings of Humberto Ortega, chief strategist of the allegedly social-democratic *tercerista* tendency of the FSLN, clearly demonstrate an orthodox Marxist self-understanding. Ortega's writings also present a two-stage vision of the revolution, in which an early "democratic-revolutionary stage" would give way to a "socialist" phase. In later chapters, this vision provides an important explanation of some policy decisions in the post-1979 period.

Chapter three will offer a snapshot of Sandinista thinking on the four issue-areas at the moment of taking power, before the dilemmas of holding power had begun to modify that thinking. It will be argued that

Sandinista strategy on questions as diverse as relations with the bourgeoisie, agrarian reform, planning, and price policy was consistent with a state socialist project. The chapter will also examine relevant aspects of the economic legacy that the Sandinistas inherited from the Somoza regime, and will briefly treat some of the dilemmas that have been faced by other regimes on the road to a socialist economy.

Chapters four to seven will follow the four issue-areas through four chronological periods. Though periodization is always somewhat artificial, the periods chosen do provide convenient lines of demarcation. Simplifying somewhat, the four periods can be characterized as follows:

1 Reconstruction and consolidation: 1979–81 (chapter four)
2 Stagnation and policy paralysis: 1982–4 (chapter five)
3 Stop-go adjustment: 1985–7 (chapter six)
4 Radical adjustment: 1988–9 (chapter seven)

In the first period, the economy grew slowly, recovering somewhat from the sharp drop of gross domestic product during the insurrection period. Chapter four's look at the state sector will examine the unsuccessful attempt of the Ministry of Planning (MIPLAN) to gain control over economic policy, the problem of "bureaucratism," and tensions in relations with state specialists. The production-maximizing orientation of state firms and its implications for financial control will also be considered. The examination of price policy will consider the rise of "unofficial market"[10] phenomena in the 1979–81 period, as well as the continuing contradictions in state price policy. Attention will also be paid to the drop in real prices for peasant products and in real salaries. The chapter will argue that the fundamental conflict between the bourgeoisie and the Sandinistas in the period was about power: what the bourgeoisie felt the government must do to guarantee the bourgeoisie's long-term interests was incompatible with what the FSLN felt it must do to consolidate its power and lay the groundwork for change. The frustration of the bourgeoisie's basic long-term objectives will be considered, along with the FSLN's attempts to neutralize the bourgeoisie's political resources. Finally, the 1981 agrarian reform law and the Sandinistas' continued rejection of a small-holder-oriented agrarian reform will be studied.

The 1982–4 period, examined in chapter five, was one of increasing difficulties for the FSLN, difficulties that sharpened the tension between using state power to transform Nicaragua, and merely holding on to that power. Economic growth tailed off, and significant economic imbalances developed. Government policy failed to adapt to these imbalances, a failure whose costs would be felt for the rest of the decade. The contra threat loomed as a shadow over the period, influencing relations with both the bourgeoisie and the peasantry. The FSLN sought to hinder the development of links between the bourgeoisie and the contras, while continuing to channel bourgeois demands in an economistic direction. The Sandinistas were slower, however, to recognize the threat that the contras posed for their relations with the peasantry, a perceptual lag that manifested itself in the agrarian reform strategy of this period. Nevertheless, the transfer of land to the peasantry was accelerated, though the government continued to impose cooperativization on would-be recipients of land.

The 1985–7 period (chapter six) was marked by repeated attempts to address the economic imbalances that had emerged in the earlier periods. Economic adjustment, however, ran into a series of political and technical constraints. The period saw, first, greater realism concerning the existence of markets in Nicaragua, and then a growing "retreat" in the face of market forces. While relations with important parts of the bourgeoisie remained hostile, the growing autonomy of the FSLN's farmers' association led for the first time to the articulation of "bourgeois" demands *within* the revolutionary bloc. Continued pressure from landless peasants, on the other hand, frustrated the state's desire to wind down the agrarian reform, and led to an increasing abandonment of the modernization perspective that had marked the earlier periods of agrarian reform. Towards the end of the period, the Central American peace accord signed in August 1987 began to influence Nicaragua's internal political dynamics.

In the 1988–9 period (chapter seven), economic reforms scuttled most key elements of the state-dominant economy project. Price controls were abandoned, and the market was allowed to determine ever more significant economic variables, including, by 1989, the exchange rate. Politically, the degree to which support for the FSLN had depended upon the containment of market forces became even clearer. The increase in tensions within the Sandinista camp provoked an erratic political strategy on the part of the leadership, with attempts at reconciliation with the bourgeoisie alternating with attacks on that same class. The agrarian reform, for its part, had by and large run its course.

The final chapter will examine various questions raised by the Nicaraguan experience.

C. METHODOLOGY

We must now examine certain epistemological assumptions implicit in this methodology, and some questions regarding the quality of the available information. The attempt to sketch the leadership's broad project and the evolution of its understanding of its situation will require heavy use of the leaders' speeches and writings. The epistemological assumption here is that the leaders' *public words* yield some indicators on their *thinking*. Is this a reasonable assumption?

It would seem that it is not. Successful revolutionaries, like other political actors, are well aware of the need to be careful in their use of language, and to maintain a veil between thoughts and words. Carlos Rafael Rodríguez writes that Castro "told me that one of the defects he found in Communist tactics was that their analyses defined with too much clarity the revolutionary objectives to be pursued and their views on the various classes that would have to be overthrown, which put the enemy on alert and made victory more difficult" (1978, 92). Likewise, Augusto César Sandino, after whom the FSLN was named, once confided to a Basque interviewer that if he declared his true beliefs to people, "they would take me for a madman or a drunk" (Belausteguigoitia 1985, 143).

Near the beginning of his 1974 study of insurrection, Sandinista strategist Humberto Ortega (1981) cited Che Guevara: "War is always a struggle in which each side tries to annihilate the other. Both sides will therefore use, apart from force, every possible dodge, every possible trick, to attain this result" (Guevara 1985, 1:36). Among the "tricks" that the Sandinistas learned early on was to be extremely tactical in their language, evaluating to whom they were speaking, and seeking a vocabulary that would not alienate.

Sandinista poet Leonel Rugama once said that heroes "never said they would die for their country, they just did it." Analogously, the early Sandinistas thought that authentic revolutionaries should not proclaim their ideology, they should just act upon it. Humberto Ortega would later comment that the struggle began "without labels, without proclaiming books that we knew, but did not want to proclaim" (*Bda* 11 December 1979).

The need for discretion emerged from both external and internal factors. Externally, Sandinista founder Carlos Fonseca stressed the need not to "provoke" imperialism (1985, 1:172). Internally, the Sandinistas felt that an openly Marxist language was inadvisable given the long-standing campaign against communism in the country, "that communism that tears babies from the arms of their mothers, burns saints and closes churches, which takes their few cows away from small farmers" (Ramírez 1987, 97).

If observers have been confused by the orientation of the FSLN, and in particular by the nature of its evolution in the late 1970s, this testifies to the success of the movement in cultivating ambiguity in its self-presentation. One can either view this tactic as "dishonest," if one likes to use such categories to evaluate political action, or as an intelligent response to the extremely negative connotations that have been attached to the word "Marxist," in large part through the work of people not notably encumbered with concerns for honesty. Asked whether "Sandinism is the application of Marxism-Leninism to the reality of Nicaragua," FSLN directorate member Bayardo Arce answered: "I would say yes, on the condition that we be clear about the essential problem of arbitrary connotations, the problem of alienated language … When one says 'Marxism' or 'Marxism-Leninism,' people's internal computers set to work – and their computers are of course quite undernourished as far as actual facts are concerned – and in a moment out pops 'Kremlin' " (Ortega, Wheelock, and Arce 1986, 12).

It is clear that the tactical use of language complicates the relation between thoughts and words. But the words of the leadership cannot be dismissed as mere camouflage. In their writings and speeches, leaders must develop an "organizational glue," a set of shared presuppositions that will both enable group members to make decisions in the light of a group ethos,[11] and help dampen intra-group conflicts that may emerge as the group faces new situations. Shared presuppositions help a group approach such situations with a common vocabulary and common assumptions. As FSLN founder Carlos Fonseca put it, Marxism was a "compass" for the organization (1985, 1:141).

It will be argued in chapter two that Sandinista leaders paid great attention to the development of shared presuppositions in the training of party cadres, both before and after coming to power. But this task places certain limits on the degree of discretion with which the leadership may speak. Too clever a rhetoric may confuse the movement's cadres and sympathizers as much as it does the enemy. Thus, though Carlos Fonseca valued discretion, he nevertheless declared in 1968 that "it is necessary that we declare clearly that we wish to put an end to a society divided between exploiters and exploited, between oppressors and oppressed. Let us declare that our overall objective is to return to the workers and peasants, to all workers, the riches which through violence have been stolen from them … [We] are guided by the noble principles of Karl Marx" (ibid.). Fonseca's call for rhetorical clarity came after the FSLN had spent the mid-1960s struggling with its own "reformist" tendencies. Fonseca felt that the FSLN was suffering from "a lack of discipline, audacity, and organization" (1:162), problems that created a need to abandon the more discrete rhetoric of the early 1960s.

Excessive discretion is also a problem for a movement that is seeking to transform political attitudes in society at large. Fonseca commented in 1968 that "our people, who for some time to come will continue to suffer from a low political level, will be confused if we speak in a grey language" (ibid., 1:141). Thus, rhetorical discretion is in conflict with both the need to solidify one's "organizational glue" and the desire to transform political attitudes in general. It will be argued in chapter four, for example, that the desire to transform the political attitudes of Nicaraguans led the FSLN to wage an energetic ideological struggle against the bourgeoisie, a struggle that has puzzled some observers, given the FSLN's apparent desire to enlist the cooperation of that same bourgeoisie.

Because Sandinista leaders sought to consolidate their movement and transform society, their public words could not be entirely divorced from their thoughts. Key elements of their grand vision were communicated through a plethora of speeches and writings. The speeches were often the object of careful collective study and reading by party cadres and by groups of workers within the state and its associated institutions.

If we accept that the public words of the leadership provide an indication of their thinking, the next methodological question concerns the reliability of *access* to those public words. While I will cite from some books of speeches and interviews with the leadership, the principal source will be *Barricada*, the official organ of the FSLN. *Barricada* does appear to have toned down or eliminated some elements from speeches.[12] It should not be assumed, however, that the paper was thereby "censoring" the leadership against the leadership's will. It is more likely that the editors of *Barricada* were given a mandate to exercise "sober second thought," identifying those elements of leaders' speeches better left unpublished. Thus, the public words of the leaders can be considered to have been mildly filtered by the time they reached the pages of *Barricada*. The evidence that this process has not entirely disembowelled the leaders' words is that many printed speeches were anything but anodyne.[13]

Other frequently cited sources of Sandinista speeches are the Joint Publications Research Service and the Foreign Broadcast Information Service, both services of the U.S. government. My comparison of speeches translated in these sources with the corresponding *Barricada* texts shows a general agreement between sources.

Having considered the "epistemology of words," we must now examine the "epistemology of numbers." What is the quality of Nicaraguan economic data? To what degree do the data allow us to reconstruct the economic reality of Nicaragua in the 1980s? The possibility of conscious manipulation of public data has been raised by one observer (Colburn 1986, 6). A former official, now an opponent of the FSLN, echoes this charge, claiming for example that at least three distinct balances of payments were maintained within the government (Alaniz

1985, 117). I have no evidence to support this charge. There are, however, significant inconsistencies in official data, and important errors persisted for quite some time.[14]

One of the most problematic sets of Nicaraguan data is the consumer price index (CPI), which can be considered at best a reflection of the order of magnitude of inflation. Thus, it is possible to say with some confidence only that Nicaragua suffered double-digit inflation from the FSLN's taking of power until late 1984, triple-digit inflation from late 1984 until late 1987, and four- or five-digit inflation after that time.

This means that there is much about the Nicaraguan economic situation in the 1980s that cannot be known with certainty. For example, though there has been considerable discussion of the evolution of rural-urban terms of trade through the FSLN decade, the lack of a reliable urban inflation index, and of any rural index at all, makes such discussions highly speculative. Similarly, measures of "real" salaries are highly dubious, and approach the point of absurdity for the late 1980s.

Whatever the problems of Nicaraguan data, it must be noted that economic data have a dual nature. They both reflect, however imperfectly, a social reality, and constitute part of the reality taken into account by decision-makers. So long as decision-makers treat data seriously, even the worst data yield insight into the economic situation *as perceived by decision-makers*. Thus, for example, whether or not prices actually rose as fast in early 1985 as the CPI indicated they did, the belief that prices had sharply risen affected leaders' perceptions of the economic reform being applied at that time (see chapter six).

A final point: if there is much about the economic situation that cannot be known with certainty, the same is true for the Nicaraguan situation in general. The historian, wrote Marc Bloch, knows of the past "only that with which the past wishes to entrust him" (1989, 16), and any study of Sandinista Nicaragua yields as many puzzles as certainties. I will examine two types of puzzles here, those that will probably never be solved, and those that might be in time.

The first type can probably never be resolved because, if the information necessary for its solution is not already stored away somewhere, it is lost forever. For example, to what degree, and in what way, did the various sectors of the Nicaraguan population support the Sandinistas upon their coming to power? If one were able to answer this question, one might have a better sense of the FSLN's room to manoeuvre upon coming to power. This latter problem has been debated by the Sandinista leadership itself, as it relates to a number of early policy choices. For example, was the FSLN's 1979 base of support strong enough to withstand an initial strategy of economic austerity, or did political consolidation require the FSLN immediately to embark on an ambitious program of social services and to increase the trade deficit in order to import consumption goods? Only if we could answer this question could we say whether or not the large fiscal and trade deficits that the government sparked from the outset were politically necessary.

A second type of puzzle might be cleared up at some point, particularly if the FSLN leadership continues its current policy of discussing the past with ever-increasing openness. One puzzle in this category concerns the career of directorate member Jaime Wheelock. We will see that Wheelock became extremely influential in charting Sandinista development strategy, and that his Ministry of Agriculture and Agrarian Reform succeeded in clipping the wings of MIPLAN, headed by fellow directorate member Henry Ruiz. To anyone familiar with the history of the FSLN, this was a puzzling outcome. Ruiz was one of the most popular of the Sandinista leaders, and had spent more time fighting in the countryside than any of the others. Given the Sandinistas' mystique of the guerrilla struggle, Ruiz's history granted him great prestige. Wheelock, on the other hand, apparently never took up arms, resolutely opposed the insurrectional strategy that brought the Sandinistas to power, and in the mid-1970s was expelled from the movement for disciplinary lapses (Borge 1979, 245). How exactly did Wheelock, whom one might have expected to play a relatively marginal role in the new government, come to such prominence? We do not know, though this puzzle might one day be solved.

2 The Ideology of the Sandinista Leadership

Firearms are essential, but ideology is the very life of the revolution.

Tomás Borge

This chapter will examine the ideology of the FSLN's nine-man National Directorate. I will use Braybrooke's definition of ideology as a "subjectively coherent set of political beliefs" (1967, 4:124). More specifically, the chapter will focus on those aspects of the leadership's ideology that might have affected their *domestic* political and economic policies once in power. Hence it will not examine the ideological roots of the Sandinistas' strategy for assuming power, nor of their foreign policy stance, except where it bears upon the immediate object of study. The central argument of the chapter is that the FSLN came to power shaped by a Marxism much more orthodox than has been recognized or admitted by many observers. Despite their flexibility once in power, this initial orientation had a great influence on their initial policy choices, which in turn influenced the entire course of the Sandinista decade.

The first part of this chapter (A) will argue that any study of the relation between Sandinista ideology and decision making must focus upon the FSLN's National Directorate, since that nine-man body was the undisputed apex of power within the party and the state. Part B will consider the view that Sandinista ideology was the product of a convergence of Marxism, Christianity, and the nationalism of Sandino. I will argue that the contribution of the last two elements of this "convergence" to the Sandinistas' domestic policy decisions was limited.

Part C will examine various orthodox Marxist themes found in the discourse of the Sandinista leadership. I will argue that the presence of such themes as vanguardism and superstructuralism, as well as the leadership's stated positions on such questions as democracy and the market, are all consistent with the view that the leaders were influenced by orthodox Marxism.

Part D will note the stress placed on ideological training both within the FSLN and in society at large. I will argue that this indicates that the leaders did not merely "happen" to be Marxists, but rather that they took their ideology quite seriously, as the epigraph to this chapter indicates.

The fifth part of the chapter (E) will consider the argument that the FSLN tendency led by the Ortega brothers was not orthodox Marxist but "social-democratic." I will argue that the pre-1979 writings of Humberto Ortega, chief strategist of the FSLN victory, clearly demonstrate an orthodox Marxist self-understanding. Ortega's writings also present a two-stage vision of the revolution, in which an early "democratic-revolutionary stage" would give way to a "socialist" phase. This vision will provide an important explanation of some policy decisions in the post-1979 period. Section F will consider objections to the foregoing argument. The final section (G) will consider Sandinista ideology as a "way of seeing," illustrating how the Sandinistas' outlook affected their views on one specific question, relations with the peasantry.

Though it may appear so to some readers, to say that the Sandinistas entered power as orthodox Marxists, or as "Marxist-Leninists," is not an accusation. Rather, it corresponds to many of the leadership's statements on its own ideological background. By "orthodox Marxism" I mean the orthodoxy traditionally promoted by the Soviet Union, and periodically codified in such manuals as the various editions of *Political Economy* issued by Progress Publishers. This orthodoxy is often termed "Marxist-Leninist," though its relation to the actual thought of Marx or Lenin has been the subject of endless debate. It is characterized as much by its form as its content: the systematization of the manuals tends to erase tensions in the original thought of Marx or Lenin. Thus, one can say that, as catechisms are to the Bible, so the orthodox manuals are to the Marxist classics.

Orthodox Marxism has historically been taught to thousands of cadres and millions of students throughout the world. For many, it is the only Marxism they have ever known. As John Saul notes, it has been influential for Third World socialism, "disseminated by the 'eastern allies' of the young socialisms through numerous manuals, teachers and ideological advisors" (1986, 147).

To say, then, that the Sandinista leadership was influenced by orthodox Marxism is to say that they received cadre training based upon the standard manuals, generally in Cuba, and that this training "took" to some degree. Prior to 1979, most Sandinista leaders had extended stays in Cuba.[1] As Bayardo Arce later put it, Cuba "was the only secure land where the Sandinista leaders could heal their wounds in order to continue the battle" (*Bda* 7 January 1984). Many of them received military and political training there.

The fact that the orthodoxy to which the Sandinistas were exposed was mediated through Cuba was of vital importance. The training they received was not hostile to revolutionary voluntarism, to Guevara's view that "one does not have to wait for the revolutionary conditions to be given: the revolutionary group can create them" (1985, 1:31).

To say that the Sandinistas were influenced by orthodox Marxism does not mean that they did not demonstrate flexibility. Ideological commitments need not imply dogmatic rigidity. In fact, the Sandinista leaders demonstrated a remarkable capacity to reflect upon their fundamental project and modify it on the fly. But flexibility must always *start* from somewhere: it is not enough to say that FSLN leaders were flexible, one must also identify the framework within which that flexibility operated. Just as the position of a moving object depends upon the direction and speed of its movement *as well as* its starting position, so too did Sandinista ideology at any given moment reflect not only its "movement" or flexibility, but also its starting point.

In more recent years, Sandinista leaders have been willing to discuss this struggle between flexibility and their original ideological framework. In an interview on 16 May 1988 with the *Wall Street Journal*, Tomás Borge commented that "I'm fighting against my own orthodoxy." Similarly, in an interview with an Italian paper, Borge commented that "for a long time our outlook was orthodox ... Yes, we considered ourselves Marxist-Leninists and had in mind a communist society. We did not like the social democracies" (FBIS 26 February 1988). After the election defeat, former Vice-President Sergio Ramírez would describe the FSLN in power as "trying to get away from theoretical schemes and prejudices, away from the self-proclaimed, eternal truths; struggling to abandon models and create our own path" (1991, 25). Even in 1991, it appeared that this struggle was continuing. Speaking to the FSLN's first party congress in July of that year, Humberto Ortega commented: "It is more difficult to be a revolutionary ... when it is necessary to come together, to find common ground with the classes and social sectors that the Marxist manuals – with which we were trained from very early on – said must be crushed. We had great respect for those manuals, and we were guided by them in the past, but now they are being subordinated to the real dynamic of practice, and obligated to find new positions, and we can no longer, therefore, be mechanically or rigidly guided by them" (1991).

This struggle between flexibility and the leadership's original orthodox framework made Sandinista practice a good deal more "liberal" than many of the statements that will be cited in this chapter might suggest. Despite the leadership's stress on the need for ideological control, *La Prensa* and other opposition media survived, though under restrictions. Much education remained in church hands. My personal experience at the National Autonomous University of Nicaragua suggested that ideological controls at the university level were not nearly as rigorous as the leadership had often suggested they should be. Despite their emphasis on ideological struggle, the Sandinistas left their opponents a great deal of room to act, and Nicaragua was one of the few countries in the Latin America of the 1980s where people were willing to criticize the government publicly.[2] Despite their oft-stated views of formal democracy, and their promise that state power would not be "raffled off" in elections, the Sandinistas held widely respected elections in 1984 and 1990, giving up power in the latter year in obedience to the rules of the formal-democratic game.

A. THE FSLN'S NATIONAL DIRECTORATE

When one inquires into the ideology of the FSLN, exactly *whose* ideology is under scrutiny? The answer to this question will determine what sort of material can be admitted as evidence for the study. Could one approach the question, for example, through a survey of party members? Or through in-depth interviews with FSLN cabinet ministers? Since our purpose is to examine aspects of Sandinista ideology that may have influenced policy decisions, we will focus on the ideology of key decision-makers. For this reason, the study will centre on the National Directorate of the 1979–90 period and its nine "Commanders of the Revolution." Tomás Borge commented in 1984 that "no fundamental decision is taken in this country except by the National Directorate" (1984b, 141).[3] Though the directorate was subject to many influences, Borge's statement is quite accurate: a decision of the directorate was ipso facto a decision of the party.

This does not mean the directorate did not operate under constraints from within the party as a whole. But the FSLN was a democratic-centralist organization. As directorate member Carlos Núñez stressed in 1979, "unhesitating obedience to the orientations of the central and intermediate organizations" is a condition for party membership (*Bda* 11 December 1979). One of the oft-repeated slogans at FSLN rallies throughout the 1980s was "National Directorate, give us your orders." Those on the second level of the FSLN, the Sandinista Assembly, were appointed by the directorate, and had no power of veto over directorate decisions. Thus, in considering the impact of ideology upon decision making, the ideology of the FSLN cannot be equated with the "average" ideology of its members.

As the National Directorate dominated the party, so did the party dominate the government. The June 1979 Plan of Government clearly recognized that the executive branch of the new government, the Government Junta for National Reconstruction, had been formed at the behest of the FSLN (JGRN 1980, 31). The proto-constitution of the revolutionary government, the Fundamental Statute, also noted that the members of the junta were "designated by the revolutionary movement" (JGRN 1979–88, 1:4).

There could thus be little doubt concerning the preeminent position of the FSLN in general and of the National Directorate in particular when the new government took power in July 1979.[4] The government junta regularly recognized this preeminence in its statements. After Humberto Ortega's August 1980 announcement, on behalf of the directorate, that elections would not be held until 1985, the junta ratified the decision, in a communiqué that reaffirmed the fact that junta members were "convoked by the National Directorate of the FSLN to form this executive body of the Government" (*Bda* 16 September 1980).

B.   SANDINISM AS AN IDEOLOGICAL CONVERGENCE?

In reading secondary sources on the Nicaraguan revolution, one is struck by the wide variety of views concerning Sandinista ideology. We may begin with some general impressions, before examining the positions of those who have studied the Sandinistas in more depth.

Conor Cruise O'Brien argues as follows:

Within the Sandinista complex, nationalism and commitment to the cause of the exploited are, as it were, "required" subjects. Marxism and revolutionary Christianity are optional, at least as far as the rank and file are concerned. And even if all the nine comandantes are Marxists, as has been widely believed, their Marxism is still their own homemade version, not one made in Moscow.

I believe that Marxism – even of the homemade variety – is now recessive within Sandinismo, and that the Christian revolutionary element is becoming dominant (1986, 69).

Another visitor to Nicaragua described Sandinista ideology as "the blending of Marxist political thought with the social gospel present in Liberation Theology" (Graham 1987, 35).

There are important differences on this question even among the more extensive studies of the Sandinistas. John Booth, for example, holds that "the Marxist-Leninist vein predominated in the FSLN until the mid-1970s, when the rapid alienation of ever broader sectors of the Nicaraguan people brought many non-Marxists to the FSLN's door." He goes on to note that "the FSLN's rhetoric changed" at that time, and that leaders adopted "an extremely pragmatic program stressing a mixed economy and political pluralism." Thus, he argues, "one must conclude that the ideological evolution of the FSLN was profound. Nicaragua's Sandinistas had developed a new Marxist revolutionary program that retained such Leninist features as a mobilizing vanguard party and profound socioeconomic transformation to benefit the working classes but was also innovative in that it institutionalized political opposition, preserved a large private sector, and established civil liberties" (1985, 146–7).[5]

David Nolan, a Reagan State Department official who wrote the first book-length examination of Sandinista ideology, believes that they were most influenced by "Nicaragua's historical tradition of political violence, the heroic image of the anti-North American guerrilla leader Augusto César Sandino, the Marxism of the student subculture, and the example of Fidel Castro's revolution in Cuba" (1984, 13). But Nolan does not explore in any depth the specific impact of these various elements upon Sandinista ideology. Of Marxism, for example, he writes that it "enabled them to stop wondering why things were the way they were, and to devote their energies to revolutionary action" (19).[6]

Donald Hodges's work on the "intellectual foundations" of the FSLN is a careful study of the thought of Sandino, and of the various Marxist currents that influenced the FSLN. Hodges concludes that "the ideology of Sandinismo is a composite of the national and patriotic values of Sandino and of the ethical recasting of Marxism-Leninism in the light of the philosophical humanism of the young Marx. At the same time it coexists with other independent social and political doctrines" (1986, 288).

Running through these various interpretations are three candidate ideologies that may have helped shape the FSLN's outlook: Marxism, Christianity, and the nationalist thought of Sandino. Some observers have argued that Sandinista ideology is the result of a "convergence" of these three components (Gorostiaga 1986, 52–3). This notion of convergence has occasionally been supported by statements of the leadership. In a 1985 speech Bayardo Arce defined the "political-ideological experience" of the Nicaraguan revolution as a convergence of "three great historic currents of humanity": nationalism, Christianity, and Marxism (1985, 46). I will argue, however, that at least with regard to *domestic* policy issues, the FSLN's outlook was fundamentally shaped by Marxism.

Three points should be borne in mind when contrasting this argument with those put forth by other observers. First, it is possible that an evaluation of Sandinista ideology that did not focus only on domestic policy might give greater weight to the influence of Sandino's nationalism. Second, part of the divergence between this analysis and that of other commentators may reflect my focus on the leadership. Hodges, for example, seems to understand Sandinista ideology as the blend of ideologies held at various levels of the FSLN and its related mass organizations. This allows him to assert that Sandinism has parallel currents, "the one popular and folkloric, the other intellectual and systematic" (1986, 185). While this interpretation is acceptable given the broad implicit definition of Sandinism, it does not distinguish the likely impact on policy of the two currents, nor does it distinguish between the "popular and folkloric" elements that the leadership drew upon instrumentally in order to mobilize grass-roots Sandinistas and the "intellectual and systematic" elements that informed its own outlook. Xabier Gorostiaga casts his net even wider. For him, Sandinism transcends the organizations of the FSLN (1986, 53). With such an approach, one can say pretty much anything one wishes about Sandinista ideology.

Finally, we must remember that much material on Nicaragua was written in a moment that was politically highly charged. The Reagan administration was seeking to destroy the Sandinistas, and one means towards that end was to draw upon the vision of demonic Marxism that dominates the U.S. political mainstream. Faced with this situation, some of those who sympathized with the Sandinistas prudently chose to downplay the Marxist nature of the FSLN. These writers made an understandable choice to present the Sandinista revolution in the best light, by seeking to bypass the "knee-jerk" anti-Marxism of mainstream U.S. political culture.

Bearing these three reflections in mind, we may now examine the possible contributions to the Sandinista outlook of Sandino and Christianity. To what extent did Sandino's ideas permeate the outlook of the FSLN leadership? Would their domestic policy decisions have been affected by Sandino? I would argue not, for two reasons. The first is that Sandino had no clear social program. The section of Fonseca's booklet of Sandino's thoughts entitled "Program for social problems" is exceptionally vague, with statements such as "the worker should not be humiliated or exploited," and "let each person be a brother and not a wolf" (Fonseca 1985, 2:176). Where Sandino expressed opinions on concrete social issues, these were often contradictory.[7]

This does not mean that Sandino was a pure nationalist with no interest in social questions, as claimed by some critics of the Sandinistas (Alaniz 1985). Sandino's nationalist rhetoric was articulated to a strong class rhetoric. He proclaimed his goal to be the "redemption of Nicaraguan workers and artisans" (1984, 1:167). He attacked the "rotting and rancid Nicaraguan aristocracy, comprised of degenerate traitors" (1:167), declared that "capitalists are identified as enemies of our army" (2:205), and dismissed landowners as a "herd of pigs" (1:134). In a phrase that was frequently cited by FSLN leaders in the 1980s, Sandino declared that "only the workers and peasants will persevere until the end, only their organized force will guarantee victory" (2:72). Sandino's army was, emphatically, a force of workers and peasants. Nevertheless, Sandino's social orientation did not translate into a clear program that might have influenced the Sandinistas' domestic policy choices.

Second, the way in which FSLN leaders themselves speak of Sandino suggests that his impact on their social thought was quite limited: Sandino was a "myth," a "symbol" (Borge 1984a, 164, 141). The leaders stress that their *theory* came from elsewhere (Ortega, Wheelock, and Arce 1986, 14; Borge 1984a, 163; Ruiz 1982). When they speak of the "lessons" of Sandino, these are invariably lessons they also learned elsewhere. Thus, Jaime Wheelock holds that Sandino taught them the need for armed struggle, and to depend on workers and peasants (*Bda* 19 May 1980). Tomás Borge attributes the same two lessons to Sandino (1984a, 57–8). Victor Tirado says that Sandino taught the FSLN the need for a vanguard (1986, 49).

If Sandino did not give the FSLN a clear program, he did provide them with a rich rhetoric for mobilization. FSLN founder Carlos Fonseca was the prime force behind the young movement's appropriation of Sandino, fighting to have the word "Sandinista" included in the group's name (Borge 1984a, 25). Fonseca was deeply concerned with finding a national vocabulary within which to express Marxist conceptions. The appropriation of Sandino gave the FSLN a "concrete myth" (Borge 1984a, 164). This myth came with an arsenal of invaluable linguistic resources. Rather than citing Lenin on the importance of a vanguard, FSLN leaders could repeat Sandino's statement that "if Nicaragua had 100 men who loved her as much as I do, our nation would restore its absolute sovereignty" (1984, 1:79). In their endless discussions with Nicaraguans on the need for armed struggle to overthrow Somoza, the Sandinistas could intone Sandino's declaration that "freedom is not conquered with flowers, but with bullets" (2:203).

Fonseca brought together a booklet of quotes from Sandino, analogous to Mao's little red book. The quotes were grouped under such headings as "The anger of the people" and "Yankee imperialism and the U.S. people" (Fonseca 1985, 2:171ff). Study of the booklet was an important part of the political training of FSLN cadres. The legacy of Sandino was an important resource for building a spirit of perseverance within the movement. The legacy would continue to be stressed in the training of cadres during the 1980s.

This does not mean that the FSLN leadership's relation to Sandino was entirely instrumental. For many FSLN leaders, Sandino helped prepare a spirit of rebellion. The father of the two Ortega brothers fought with Sandino (D. Ortega 1987b; Valenta and Valenta 1987, 8). Borge's father was also a friend of Sandino, and gave his son books on Sandino to read (Borge 1989a, 75; 1979, 233).

Thus, Sandino inspired some of the Sandinista leaders to struggle, and the invocation of his spirit and legacy played an important role in the formation of the movement's cadres and in appeals to Nicaraguan society at large. Nevertheless, Sandino's ideas had little influence on the domestic policy decisions the FSLN leadership would make upon taking power.

The case for a Christian influence upon the outlook of the leadership seems even weaker. Though Christianity did influence some of the Sandinista leaders in their youth,[8] none of the directorate members claimed to be Christian when the FSLN took power, though to do so would have been highly convenient in a predominantly Roman Catholic society.

Certainly Christian thought was not a privileged "organizational glue" within the movement: FSLN cadres were never trained in any branch of Christian thought, the way they were trained in Marxism and the thought of Sandino. For a movement that gave great importance to ideological training, this point is significant.

Even those who argue that Christianity was an important influence upon FSLN ideology are quite vague as to the nature of that influence. Basque Jesuit Xabier Gorostiaga identifies the contribution of Christianity to Sandinista ideology as consisting of some vaguely defined "logic of the majority" (1986, 53). This "logic" appears to be little more than a "basic needs" approach: "Our first objective is to satisfy the basic needs of the majority of the population. This creates a new logic which we call the 'logic of the majority,' i.e. the logic of the poor. Instead of organizing the economy from the perspective and interest of the top 5 percent, as was done during the Somoza dynasty, we are trying to organize the economy from the perspective of the majority" ([Ryan] 1982). But to say that the Sandinistas pursued the interests of the "majority" rather than the interests of the "five percent" tells us very little. In what way, for example, did the "logic of the majority" dictate the choice of state farms, rather than that of cooperatives or small-scale production? What Gorostiaga failed to note was that the "logic of the majority" was an "imputed" logic, analogous to Lukacs's "imputed class consciousness" (1971). That is, the Sandinista leadership believed it pursued what the majority would want *if* that majority correctly understood its objective interests. I will return to this point below, in examining Sandinista vanguardism.

Appreciation of the relation between Christianity and the Sandinista leadership has been impeded by two factors. The first is that the FSLN reached out to Christian activists in the early 1970s. Henceforth, religious belief would be no bar to membership in the FSLN, unlike other parties of Marxist-Leninist inspiration. Indeed, priests such as Miguel D'Escoto and the Cardenal brothers formed an important part of the FSLN's public face, particularly before coming to power. This was an important innovation that testifies to Sandinista flexibility, and it may have given some observers an exaggerated sense of the influence of Christianity within the leadership itself.

A second complicating factor was the FSLN's frequent use of religious imagery and allusions. The Sandinistas often made use of religious language, resolutely rejecting Lenin's view that "any flirtation with a God is the most inexpressible foulness" (1969, 40), perhaps because most Nicaraguans were baptized Catholics, and because the Right for its part had never hesitated to manipulate religious symbols.[9] Jesuit priest Peter Marchetti noted that Sandinista leaders "found themselves using the Christian symbol system during the insurrection in order to motivate people to follow them. They found that Christian beliefs were powerful in mobilizing the poor against tyranny" (1982, 51). After taking power, the FSLN continued to blend religious and revolutionary symbolism. An opponent of the FSLN complained of a Christmas poster featuring "a new-born child surrounded by a peasant, a worker, and a militia-member with a gun. The slogan of the poster was 'Christmas – the Birth of the New Man,' and in lower letters 'Christmas in Free Nicaragua'" (Belli 1982).

There was also a religious permeation of revolutionary rhetoric, particularly in the speeches of Tomás Borge.[10] Borge's rhetoric even led some observers mistakenly to speak of his "conversion" to Christianity (O'Brien 1986, 70). Thus, both the use of Christian symbolism and the presence of Christians within the FSLN served to exaggerate perceptions of the Christian influence on Sandinista decision making.

To summarize then, I believe that neither the thought of Sandino nor Christianity was an important influence upon the domestic policy decisions of the FSLN leadership. Sandino's nationalism may have influenced foreign policy choices, and the Sandino legend was an important component in the "organizational glue" through which the leadership maintained unity and commitment. As for Christianity, one can only hold that it influenced "Sandinista ideology" if one wields an extremely broad definition of that concept, as does Gorostiaga.

C. MARXIST THEMES IN SANDINISTA DISCOURSE

The FSLN leadership was well aware of the need for discretion. This made the leaders careful in answering direct questions concerning their ideology. A typical answer was that they were "Sandinistas," and that Sandinism was an ideology *sui generis*.[11]

Nevertheless, National Directorate members were also willing to offer the most fulsome praise of Marxism, indicating an acceptance of Marxism quite unlike their careful and qualified praise of the thought of Sandino or of Christianity. Thus, Victor Tirado termed Marxism "the most advanced thought of humanity" (1987), and ratified Lenin's opinion that Marx's thought "is all powerful, because it is true" (1986, 285). In 1987, Daniel Ortega declared:

The history of Count Dracula is the very history of the exploitation of man by man. Slavery, feudalism, capitalism, imperialism, all prolonging their existence at the cost of the blood of the workers.

The vampires had also made themselves owners of Nicaragua, when the adequate weapon to exterminate them had not yet been invented.

Not until, that is, Marx and Engels discovered the formula, and Lenin efficiently directed its application, driving the spike into the heart of the monster.

Just as Michelangelo penetrated into the depths of human anatomy in order to mould his masterpieces, Marx and Engels penetrated and explored social phenomena from the beginning of humanity, resulting in the masterpiece which gave to the workers the ideological instrument that their class instinct demanded (1987a, 5–6).

These statements are striking because they were made by directorate members who had belonged to the *terceristas*, the FSLN tendency that many foreign observers insisted was *not* Marxist in orientation.

But the foregoing statements tell us little about the *type* of Marxism by which the FSLN leadership was influenced. To clarify this, I will examine certain Marxist themes in Sandinista discourse. These themes are both "symptomatic" of Sandinista Marxism and they also point to some consequences of FSLN ideology for decision making. I will focus on several themes here:

1 Vanguardism
2 Democracy and political rights
3 Superstructuralism
4 The market
5 The just society

These "symptoms" are not symptoms of a "pathology." I believe that all the positions discussed here are, in one way or another, problematic. But so too are the positions contrary to those discussed here. Thus, for example, the critique of formal, or "bourgeois," democracy easily loses sight of the extent to which that democracy can be a valuable achievement, even for non-bourgeois citizens. On the other hand, one cannot deny the oppression that can coexist with formal democracy, or the myriad ways in which that democracy can ignore the needs of the vast majority.

The themes chosen are all relevant to the leadership's policy choices. They are not the central themes of classical Marxism, but all are important in orthodox Marxism, the language of Marxism in power. Because the language of Marxism in power is in part a language of justification, it is fair to ask whether the treatment of these themes in Sandinista discourse really proves that the leaders were *influenced* by orthodox Marxism. Might it not be the case that they merely employed an orthodox Marxist language to *legitimate* policy choices after the fact? I will take up this question below.

Some of these elements are held jointly by Marxists and some non-Marxists. Thus, for example, W.W. Rostow subscribes to a view of historical stages every bit as simplistic as that of orthodox Marxism. Non-Marxist elitism has strong affinities with Marxist vanguardism. Nevertheless, I believe that the overall treatment of the themes presented here is peculiar to orthodox Marxists.

The first theme is *vanguardism.* On 25 July 1979, the very first issue of *Barricada,* the FSLN's official newspaper, declared that "we Sandinista combatants ... have made ourselves the judges and guarantors of the New Nicaragua." Directorate member Bayardo Arce declared that "our workers and peasants know that they cannot have an active and effective participation and cannot be protagonists of the Revolution, without having a solid vanguard like the FSLN" (1980, 35). Though the leadership often declared its interest in "national unity," this unity was to be subordinated to Sandinista vanguardism. On the "Day of Unity," in early 1980, Tomás Borge declared that "there can be no unity with those who wish to maintain the rules of the game of the past, with those who are not aware that a revolution is only possible within the parameters laid out by the vanguard, the Sandinista Front" (*Psa* 11 January 1980).

Vanguardism was necessary because of the backwardness of the Nicaraguan people. As Jaime Wheelock put it, "The worker has a class *intuition,* and knows who his enemies are, but from the point of view of *knowledge* he is in shadows" (*Bda* 5 October 1979). "The people," Bayardo Arce commented, "do not have a real awareness of the limitations of the [revolutionary] process and the national reality" (JPRS 78503).

One of the dangers of this lack of awareness was unrealistic expectations. Reactionary sectors, Humberto Ortega warned in 1980, "will try to confuse the masses, making them believe that the problems, difficulties and errors of our Revolution can be solved in the short run" (*Bda* 5 June 1980). We will see that the leadership was particularly concerned by the problem of "backwardness" amongst the peasantry.[12]

An unusual feature of Sandinista vanguardism, however, was its resolute opposition to the cult of personality. A decree issued by the new junta on its first day in power prohibited "the placing of photographs of officials serving the country in public places, or the use of their names to designate works serving the people" (Decree 2).[13] Veneration was to be reserved for the dead, the "heroes and martyrs."

Marxist vanguardism differs from simple elitism by a proclaimed intention to transform the masses so that the vanguard might be self-extinguishing. Thus, Sandinista vanguardism was tied to a vision of mass transformation.[14] As Daniel Ortega commented, "It is necessary for the people to go through a process of consolidation, transformation and popular democracy" (JPRS 76469). The FSLN, Carlos Núñez commented, used "propaganda, verbal and written agitation, [and] clear and persistent orientation that makes the masses learn and understand the scope of the revolution" (JPRS 75010).

The 1980 literacy campaign was seen as a key element in this transformation. Bayardo Arce declared that "we will be preparing our peasants and workers so that they will be able to increasingly exercise popular power," and junta member Sergio Ramírez commented that "the campaign is the expression of the revolution which aims to change everything" (JPRS 75434). The literacy crusade, Arce noted, "will become the biggest political seminar of Nicaraguan history," adding that "its objective is not only to eliminate the illiteracy of thousands of people but to make them aware of the goals of the revolution" (JPRS 75214). The vanguard was to be the agent of moral as well as intellectual transformation. The local Sandinista Defence Committees (CDS), Tomás Borge urged, should "promote morality" and "eradicate vice" (JPRS 75798).

A key aspect of the mass's development would be its increasing organization. Under the direction of the FSLN, a variety of mass organizations were formed, seeking to give every Nicaraguan at least one point of entry into the structures of the revolution.[15] The vanguard was to lead a people, which, as Tomás Borge put it, is not "an amorphous sum of individuals, but a consciously organized people" (1981a).

As it developed, the people would understand its "objective" or "strategic" interests, and come to pursue these, as opposed to immediate demands. "The workers," Tomás Borge urged, "cannot sacrifice their strategic objectives for immediate demands" (*Bda* 14 September

1981). To do so "would mean going against common sense and against history" (1985d, 25). And the main "strategic objective," as Victor Tirado pointed out, was none other than "the defence and growth of revolutionary power" (1987).

So long as the level of development of the people lagged behind the vanguard, the latter represented something like the "essence" or "soul" of the Nicaraguan people. "We the members of the Sandinista Front," Bayardo Arce declared, "are nothing more than the interpreters of the historic interests of the workers" (*Bda* 2 May 1982). There was thus an immediate identification between the people and its vanguard. Asked in 1980 about elections, Humberto Ortega commented that "our people already voted, on July 19 1979, with its weapons in its hands, and with the blood of 50,000 Nicaraguans. *Our people voted for itself, for Sandinismo*" (*Bda* 11 July 1980; emphasis added). One of the slogans of the FSLN's 1984 election campaign was "The people will vote for the people." In the same vein, Victor Tirado could begin a speech to workers by proclaiming that "the National Directorate has mandated me to speak in the name of the working class" (1986, 117).

This immediate identification of the people and its vanguard meant that the people held power because the vanguard held power. "The workers and peasants are in power," Bayardo Arce declared in 1980 (1980, 29). Victor Tirado commented in 1987 that "since the triumph, the Nicaraguan workers' movement has gained a very important experience, and has consolidated itself as the proletarian class. This class is State, Government" (1987).[16]

The claim of identification between the people and its vanguard had a natural corollary in the leadership's conception of *democracy and political rights*.[17] Defending the suspension of the right to strike in September 1981, Henry Ruiz asked "But strike against whom? Of the workers against the workers? Does not the Sandinista Front represent the interests of the workers?" (*Bda* 14 September 1981). In the words of Tomás Borge, "In a revolution where the exploited have seized power, it does not make sense for them to issue demands" (JPRS 80320). Similarly, in his August 1980 announcement that elections would not be held until 1985, Humberto Ortega told Nicaraguans to "remember that these will be elections to improve revolutionary power, not to raffle it off. Because power belongs to the people, through its vanguard, the FSLN and its National Directorate" (1980). Even during the 1984 election campaign, Jaime Wheelock commented that "sometimes it is said that we are not considering handing over power. Of course we will never hand it over, since we cannot hand over something that is not ours. Power belongs to the people ... and we do not think the people will ever give it up" (*Bda* 14 March 1984).

Not surprisingly, the FSLN proclaimed its rejection of "bourgeois" democracy and freedoms. Daniel Ortega, for example, argued that traditional democracy "gave the privileged the right to exploit children, and gave ordinary people only the right to suffer sickness and hunger" (*Bda* 3 March 1984). The ever-blunt Victor Tirado informed a group of workers that old ideas of democracy were now obsolete, "although you, being workers, are not aware of this yet" (1986, 303).

The vanguard's ability to interpret the people's strategic interests limited the need for traditional forms of political representation. "The government junta," Jaime Wheelock stated in late 1979, "does not need a congress to tell it what problems of the workers and peasants need to be solved" (JPRS 74490). Since the interests of the people were self-evident, those political parties that disagreed with the FSLN must be either "treasonous or ignorant," as Bayardo Arce put it (*Bda* 10 August 1981).

This view of "bourgeois" democracy led the Sandinistas to offer a wide variety of explanations of what democracy meant to them: the ability of people to "participate" in decision making (Borge 1984a, 90); economic progress and hard work (Tirado 1986, 304); the arming of the people (Borge 1984a, 177); mass demonstrations, and meetings where candidates were ratified by a show of hands.[18] When asked by their critics when elections would be held, FSLN leaders would reply with a stock "the people already voted," equating the 1979 uprising with an election of the FSLN over other alternatives.[19]

In fact, democracy seemed to mean for the Sandinistas everything *except* the possibility that the people might throw the FSLN out of power. Carlos Núñez argued that "alternation in power" could not be contemplated, "because we cannot alternate power between the people and the exploiters" (1981).

The directorate's most considered declaration on democracy was read by Humberto Ortega to the rally celebrating the end of the literacy crusade in August 1980:

For the FSLN, democracy is not measured only in the political sphere, nor is it reduced simply to electoral participation. Democracy begins in the economic sphere, when the main social inequalities begin to be weakened, when the workers and peasants improve their standard of living. This is when true democracy begins. Before this, no.

Once these objectives have been attained, democracy is extended to other spheres: it is extended to the sphere of government, when the people influences its government, when the people determines its government, like it or not.

Nevertheless, at a yet more advanced phase, democracy means the participation of workers in the management of factories, farms, cooperatives and cultural centres. In synthesis, democracy is the intervention of the masses in all aspects of social life (1980).

The sequence of the statement is key: the people's control over government begins *after* "the main social inequalities" have been "weakened."[20]

As with democracy, civic freedoms had to be in harmony with, not in opposition to, the revolutionary process. The government would neither "respect nor permit counterrevolutionary freedom," declared Bayardo Arce (*Bda* 31 January 1980). Pluralism does not imply "freedom to exploit," said Daniel Ortega (*Bda* 20 December 1979). This stand had particular implications for press freedom. The government, said Bayardo Arce, "will not permit reactionary groups to use the media to poison our people" (*Bda* 3 October 1980). Tomás Borge, in the colourful language for which he was famous, declared that "freedom of expression to tell lies, to hide the revolutionary truth, to bury the people in anonymity, to put on the front page those who dress up in red ecclesiastical garb: this freedom of expression will never exist in Nicaragua" (*Bda* 20 May 1982). In rejecting a private-sector request for permission to run a television station, Daniel Ortega stated that "here we have totalitarianism in favour of the people, in favour of the small and medium producers" (*Bda* 20 December 1979).

In the place of such "bourgeois" freedoms, said Tomás Borge, the revolution offered "a popular democracy which guarantees the national majority the enjoyment of freedoms that are real, not abstract" (*Bda* 7 September 1979). In the words of a declaration from the FSLN's National Secretariat for Propaganda and Political Education, "Bourgeois liberty has nothing to do with popular liberty, which reflects the objective interests of the people itself, its right to organize and arm itself, politically, militarily, and ideologically" (Secretaría Nacional 1980).

Thus, the content of various freedoms was to be reinterpreted. Traditional "trade union freedom," Tomás Borge argued in 1982, "means the division of the working class ... True freedom for the unions means the freedom to defend the interests of the working class" (Borge 1985d, 30). This view of revolutionary freedom was given some codification in new laws, such as the decree on communications media.

The FSLN leadership's views of democracy and political freedoms were a subset of their broader *superstructuralism*, the tendency to understand in a deterministic fashion the relation between the economic "base" (and its attendant class interests) and the political, legal, and ideological "superstructure" of a society. FSLN leaders frequently displayed such a conception, often in connection with the legal system. Thus, Bayardo Arce asserted in 1980, that "the laws are merely an expression of the political-juridical superstructure which defends and reproduces the economic structures of a society." Arce went on to comment that new laws had not yet been developed in Nicaragua because "we have not yet developed a defined economic structure that would permit the creation of revolutionary legislation" (*Bda* 22 June 1980).

We will see in chapter four that superstructuralism provided the FSLN with an essential code through which it interpreted the bourgeoisie's demands for legal guarantees. Since such guarantees had not been demanded under Somoza, the argument went, it was clear that the bourgeoisie was now furthering its narrow class interests under the guise of concern for legalities and rights.[21]

Such superstructuralism was more than merely rhetorical. The corollary of superstructural analysis was that the assumption of political power by a new class should lead to a conscious attempt to transform the superstructure. Thus, as Bayardo Arce told a teachers' meeting in 1980, the importance of teachers was linked to the importance of "the ideological processes of society." The goal, Arce added, was "to make of each teacher a revolutionary cadre" (*Bda* 5 January 1980). In a 1983 speech, Tomás Borge was more explicit: "Education is the process through which society reproduces the ideas, values, moral and ethical principles, and behavioural habits of the successive generations. All social organization is a function of the class interests that hold state power. Education is a process of forming individuals in ideology, in a complex system of values and ideas that justifies the interests of the class that wields state power" (1985a, 72).[22] In the specific case of Nicaragua, this implied that "through education we must promote revolutionary strength, hatred of man's exploitation by man, loyalty to the revolutionary principles that sustain our vanguard, the FSLN, and open the flood-gates of science so that man's beliefs in fantasies and superstitions, accumulated over centuries, can be washed away" (80).[23] Developing such an education, Borge argued, required transforming teachers themselves: "How can teachers explain to their students the essence of exploitation, exploitation that has stripped part of their own hides, if they don't know how to explain exploitation conceptually? How can they create profoundly anti-imperialist consciousness if they are ignorant of the essence of imperialism?" (72).

The foregoing themes in Sandinista discourse were not mere rhetorical flourishes. We will see in chapter four that many of the points of conflict between the FSLN and the bourgeois opposition centred around Sandinista policies consonant with the ideas examined here. The opposition could not but view these themes in Sandinista discourse with extreme suspicion. The FSLN's vanguardism and conception of democracy seemed designed to give the Sandinistas immunity from criticism, and maintain them in power forever. The nascent mass organizations were viewed as the seeds of totalitarianism and the instrument of a fusion of party and state. Superstructuralism was seen as a way of avoiding the creation of a state of law.

The opposition's reactions to Sandinista actions, on the other hand, served to ratify, from the leadership's point of view, the validity of the orthodox Marxist ideas studied here. Did not the bourgeoisie appear to have discovered a love of democracy precisely when its class interests were threatened? Did not the opposition seem to be using press freedoms merely to confuse the people with rumours and distortions? Thus the Sandinistas and the bourgeois opposition would find themselves in a classic "mirror image" situation, each side armed with an interpretive code that would lead it to interpret the other's actions as a confirmation of its own worst fears.

A fourth theme in Sandinista discourse relevant for policy decisions was *antipathy towards the market* and a belief in the efficacy of centralized planning. The Sandinistas shared the orthodox view that a central aspect of the superiority of socialism over capitalism is its replacement of capitalist anarchy by socialist rationality. In a pamphlet written after his 1957 visit to the Soviet Union, FSLN founder Carlos Fonseca wrote that "there is no competition in the Soviet Union. Production there is planned. Because of this, they never suffer economic crises, nor overproduction. Thus, they have never found themselves forced to throw tea into the ocean, or burn their cotton, or let their apples rot" (1985, 1:62). In its 1969 "Historic Program," the FSLN promised to "plan the national economy, putting an end to the anarchy which is characteristic of the capitalist system of production" (1981, 20).

After taking power in 1979, numerous statements of the leadership indicated agreement with Planning Minister Henry Ruiz's statement that "only a planned, conscious and globalizing action yields the possibility of overcoming underdevelopment" (*Bda* 1 June 1980). Jaime Wheelock commented that "without planning we cannot ensure a sustained and harmonious development which meets, to the extent possible, the social and economic objectives of the Revolution" (1981c). Tomás Borge noted in 1981 that "we must become more mature, we must overcome the adolescence of our Revolution, in order to control the anarchic tendencies of the market economy, to which we are still subjected by a thousand invisible threads" (1981a). In a revealing statement equating socialist planning with rationality, Borge commented, "Mixed economy, yes, but based on a progressive advancement in economic planning. Mixed economy, yes, but based on the idea that irrationality should disappear, or at least tend to disappear, under the pressure of rationality" (FBIS 24 February 1982). Even as the government moved to free up markets in 1987, Luís Carrión commented that calls for market freedom were "nothing more than a formulation of the interests of the rich and of the merchants" (*Bda* 25 May 1987).

At the same time, there would be conflict over the practical meaning of this planning. Ruiz's Ministry of Planning (MIPLAN) would promote the concept of planning presented in the orthodox Marxist manuals, in which the planning ministry directs the overall economic activities of the state and relies upon such techniques as material balances. Jaime Wheelock's Ministry of Agriculture (MIDINRA), on the other hand, would seek to establish a planning relation with the firms under its control, whilst fighting to maintain its autonomy from MIPLAN. We will see in later chapters that the MIDINRA-MIPLAN conflict would be one of the central tensions in the new Sandinista state. The competing conceptions of planning were united on one point: they both involved extensive state involvement in the economy. But they were divided on the implications of planning for the structure of power within the state. By 1982, this question would be resolved in MIDINRA's favour. Thus, the MIPLAN vision of a planning ministry governing the economic activities of both the state and non-state sectors did not advance very far, despite the leadership's apparent commitment to planning.

One final theme is the leadership's *vision of the "just society"* that was to emerge in Nicaragua in the long term. The just society was seen as one without class exploitation. Luís Carrión declared that "in the society which we seek to build, no class will appropriate the labour of another, and work will be an obligation for all, not just for some" (*Bda* 19 April 1982). For Humberto Ortega, "the working class is not struggling for crumbs, but for structural transformations of society, which will lead to a new society in which there will no longer be relations of exploitation and oppression of man by man" (*Bda* 2 May 1982). In Tomás Borge's words, "We are creating a new society in which the individual will not be a commodity, a society in which there will no longer be tigers and lambs, a society in which there are no men who live off the exploitation of other men" (1981a).

In orthodox Marxism, the only "exploitation of man by man" is property-based. Thus, "in the society in which social ownership of the means of production predominates, there is no exploitation of man by man" (Economía Política 1982, 10). The FSLN leaders appeared to view the just society, socialism, and an economy with state-owned means of production as the same phenomenon.[24] But this just society was not attainable in the short run, as the FSLN had to allow the bourgeoisie to maintain its control over a significant share of the economy. As Bayardo Arce would comment in 1982, "In all of the world's countries, the workers want socialism, a more just society where they can be the principal actors ... It is obvious that the present status of the revolution does not satisfy our workers' deepest aspirations" (FBIS 2 June 1982). This theme of tension between the revolution's current status and ultimate goals was, not surprisingly, disquieting for the bourgeois opposition.

To summarize, various central themes in Sandinista discourse clearly reflect themes of orthodox Marxism. I believe that this indicates that the Sandinista leadership's outlook was significantly influenced by this Marxism. Other possible interpretations of this fact will be examined below. First, we will examine the importance that the leadership gave to ideology and to the ideological unity of the FSLN, by examining Sandinista theoretical training.

D. THEORETICAL TRAINING WITHIN THE FSLN

The FSLN leaders did not merely absorb Marxist ideas: they also felt it crucial that others do so as well. Marxism was to be a key ingredient of the movement's "organizational glue." The leadership attributed great importance to the movement's having "correct theory." FSLN founder Carlos Fonseca commented that the "glory and tragedy" of Sandino's movement was its exclusively peasant base: this meant that the leadership as a whole lacked the "political level" that could only come from access to theory (1985, 1:156). Similarly, Tomás Borge commented that the 1950s armed movements against Somoza failed because they lacked "a theory that would allow them to identify the forces in conflict, ranking them in order of strategic and tactical importance." The subjective conditions were developing at the time, Borge said, but there was no "ideology or theory that would order or solidify these conditions" (1984a, 57).

The FSLN had not always been marked by this stress on theoretical clarity. While some early Sandinistas such as Fonseca and Borge had studied Marxism before the FSLN was founded, others came to the movement with less formed political ideas. The movement was formed, as Carlos Fonseca put it, more from "shame" than from "consciousness" (Borge 1984a, 23). In its origins, then, the FSLN was "the union of dispersed ideological and political conceptions" (Borge 1981a). But by the late 1960s there was great dissatisfaction with this state of affairs. The FSLN had little to show for its first years of existence: guerrilla columns were all but exterminated at Bocay in 1963 and Pancasán in 1967, and the years between those experiences saw the FSLN flirt with "reformism".[25]

FSLN leaders came to believe that theoretical weakness was a prime cause of the movement's difficulties.[26] In response to this perception, the following years were marked by a strong formalization of the movement: party statutes were adopted, a general political program was issued, and stress was laid on the theoretical formation of militants. In the words of Humberto Ortega, "the bases for the development of the Marxist-Leninist method of directing the struggle" were laid during this time (1979, 93).

The stress on the theoretical training of cadres would continue to the triumph of July 1979 and beyond. One FSLN member described life in a Managua safe-house in the late 1960s thus: "We spent the evenings in various studies. First, philosophy and politics. Then guerrilla urban tactics" (Guadamuz 1982, 48). When two women joined the cell, their leader decided their hours of "study of politics and philosophy" must be extended, as one of them was in dire need of it (37). A 1977 party program commented that "the organisation of study circles even in the most difficult conditions of repression, such as in prison and on rest stops during guerrilla campaigns, has been a constant preoccupation" ([H. Ortega] 1987, 298). Even in training for specific operations such as the 1974 attack on the house of cabinet minister Chema Castillo, the guerrillas were given courses on the history of Nicaragua (Borge 1989a, 446).[27]

After taking power in 1979, the leadership continued to stress the importance of ideological coherence. Bayardo Arce argued that there could be no ideological pluralism within the vanguard (Ortega, Wheelock, and Arce 1986, 58), and Daniel Ortega defined the FSLN as an "ideologically homogeneous detachment, with a leadership and a militancy based upon Marxism and revolving around Sandinismo as an expression of the Nicaraguan reality" (1987a, 11). Two decades after seeking to forge ideological unity within the movement, the leadership continued to see such unity as vital to the survival of the revolution.

Moreover, the leaders sought to extend this ideological unity to the popular classes as a whole. In response to an interviewer who asked how the Sandinistas could avoid "a return to bourgeois dictatorship of one form or another," Tomás Borge answered that "I think that one guarantee ... is the existence of a revolutionary party which uses scientific analysis to understand the reality of each moment ... Popular organization is another guarantee, organization which permits the arming of the people. But it is not enough to give the people firearms, they must also be given the arms of revolutionary ideology, and these arms are the essence of the defence of the revolution. Firearms are essential, but ideology is the very life of the revolution" (1984b, 148–9).[28]

In the University of Nicaragua's Faculty of Economics, where I taught from 1984 to 1986, this concern for ideological development was translated into a heavy complement of courses on Marxist-Leninist thought at the outset of the university program. Students received five or six "political economy" courses based on Progress Publishers' *Economía Política* (1982), and other manual-based courses on the "history of philosophy," and "socialist economic planning."

E. THE ORTEGAS' "TENDENCIA TERCERISTA"

Much of the confusion surrounding the Marxist nature of the FSLN arose from the manoeuvres of the Sandinista tendency led by Humberto and Daniel Ortega. As the tendency was most often identified as the "*tendencia tercerista*" [third way], many observers concluded that it was a "third way movement, which seeks a middle path between communism and capitalism" (Carl 1984, 116). The tendency's manoeuvres confused even such observers of Latin America as James Petras, who dismissed the tendency as "social democratic" (1979, 14).

The Ortega tendency did much to foster this impression. The Ortegas reached out to broad sectors of Nicaraguan society and toned down their revolutionary rhetoric, at least in public. In the view of John Booth, the tendency "relaxed the original FSLN's requirement for Marxist-Leninist orthodoxy and rapidly increased their ranks with social democratic, social Christian, and bourgeois recruits, although the leaders remained Marxist-Leninists" (1985, 144). But impressions and reality do not always coincide. The Ortega tendency had strong reasons for cultivating confusion, since ambiguity was essential to its political strategy. To appreciate this strategy, and its Marxist inspiration, we must examine the background to the Ortegas' rise to preeminence in the FSLN. This review will also provide a basis for understanding the FSLN's actions in its first years in power, and introduce some of the leading Sandinista personalities and their particular outlooks.

From the mid-1970s on, the FSLN had been bitterly split between two rival tendencies. The GPP tendency, associated most closely with Sandinista founder Carlos Fonseca and Tomás Borge, promoted the strategy of "prolonged popular war." The strategy, called "GPP" after its Spanish name, had been officially adopted by the FSLN in the late 1960s. This strategy, as one FSLN militant would later describe it, "believes in a long period of accumulation of forces, with the creation of liberated zones during the preparation for a long war against imperialism, as in Vietnam" (Habla el Frente 1979, 105). Influenced by Mao and Vietnam's General Giap, the strategy thus postulates that a large segment of the population will have been transformed by its experience in the liberated zones *before* the revolutionary movement assumes power. A smaller faction, the so-called "proletarian tendency," attacked the GPP for its view that Nicaragua was still a peasant society. Led by Jaime Wheelock, this tendency advocated the formation of a mass-based "proletarian party." Wheelock and those of like mind were expelled from the FSLN in late 1975.

But from 1974 on, an alternative approach was being developed by Humberto Ortega.[29] Writing in 1974, Ortega stressed that "the revolution cannot wait for propitious conditions to emerge all by themselves" (1981, 11). Ortega also stressed the need for conjunctural analysis: the principal error, he argued, was to "let the favourable moment pass by"(23). By the early 1970s, even elite sectors of Nicaraguan society were increasingly restive with the corruption and electoral frauds of the Somoza regime. After the December 1972 earthquake, bourgeois discontent with Somoza grew as the president and his associates allegedly stole a large share of international reconstruction aid, and increasingly horned in on private-sector activities. Nevertheless, Somoza was re-elected in 1974 with 95 per cent of the vote, helped by an electoral law that had disqualified nine out of ten opposition parties (Facts on File 1975).

Taking stock of the growing discontent with Somoza in Nicaraguan society, Ortega called for "a flexible policy of temporary and transitory alliances, while always maintaining the guiding principle of the independence and autonomy of the revolutionary vanguard" (1981, 17).

Most importantly, Ortega argued that the FSLN should think less in terms of a prolonged popular war, and more in terms of a rapid insurrection. This would require a change in the FSLN's relation with Nicaragua's popular classes. Rather than simply constituting a recruiting ground for the guerrilla force, as had hitherto been the case, these classes should be mobilized for a mass insurrection. Thus, the Ortega group was also called the "insurrectional tendency."

Ortega was essentially advocating "tacticalism," in the tradition of Lenin and Trotsky. By tacticalism I mean the approach that stresses the possible divergences between long-term strategy and short-term tactics; that appreciates what Lenin called the zig-zags of history; that gives importance to conjunctural conditions, as opposed to those that are purely long-term and "structural." Tacticalism is not "voluntarism." That is, it does not deny the role of "objective conditions" in influencing the success or failure of revolutionary efforts. But, unlike other Marxist approaches, tacticalism lays great stress on objective conditions that are purely conjunctural.

Trotsky in his "Lessons of October" stressed the importance of this appreciation of the conjuncture: "The whole tactical art consists in this: that we seize the moment when the combination of circumstances is most favourable to us. The Kornilov uprising completely prepared such a combination ... Neither the elemental disintegration of the state power, nor the elemental influx of the impatient and exacting confidence of the masses in the Bolsheviks could endure for a protracted period of time" (1971, 39). The Bolshevik right, Trotsky held, responded to Lenin's assertion, "It is now or never!" with a "fatalistic optimism": "No. The party of the proletariat will grow and its programme will become clear to ever wider masses ... And it is only in one way that the party can disrupt its successes, namely, if it should assume the initiative of a rising under the present circumstances" (elision in original). This last statement of "fatalistic optimism" sounds very much like the reproaches which the other two tendencies would level against the Ortega group.

Ortega freely recognized the theoretical roots of his 1974 document, which contains various references to Lenin, Engels, Marx, and Che. He saw his work as an application to Nicaragua of the lessons of revolutions in the Soviet Union, China, Cuba, and Vietnam (1981, 3), and proclaimed that Marxist-Leninist theory was essential for success (15).

In 1977, Ortega and his followers gained an opportunity to implement this "insurrectional" strategy. At the beginning of that year, the FSLN was in a critical situation. Carlos Fonseca and another member of the National Directorate had died in November 1976. Tomás Borge was in jail, and Henry Ruiz's small guerrilla force was isolated in a remote area. Somoza's National Guard was on a rural offensive, destroying much of the FSLN's rural support network, and the guerrilla force spent its time "escaping and escaping," as one combatant recalls (Arias 1980, 114). Thus, by 1977, most foreign and Nicaraguan observers had "written off [the FSLN] as small and of little threat" (Christian 1985, 34).

But with the death, imprisonment, or isolation of half of the National Directorate, Humberto Ortega and those who supported his insurrectional strategy seemed in a position to chart the course for the FSLN as a whole. From mid-1977 onwards, the "insurrectionists" would work to create and maintain favourable "objective conditions." Thus, their military actions were essentially aimed at influencing the political conjuncture.

The October 1977 offensive provides a good example of this approach. In September 1977, under pressure from the Carter administration, Somoza ended the state of emergency that had been in force since late 1974. The FSLN faced the danger that a civilian opposition would be able to organize and gain widespread popular support (H. Ortega 1981, 69). Ortega felt that the FSLN had to act in order to avoid permanent political marginalization. Though the October offensive was crushed in a matter of days, it had a great psychological impact. Just when "[internal] reactionaries and imperialism were convinced that they had annihilated the FSLN, or at least reduced it to its nadir" (66), the movement had launched its largest attack ever. Within days, the bishops and the private sector called for a "national dialogue," and Conservative Party leader Fernando Aguero Rocha commented that the FSLN "has created the best conditions for change in Nicaragua" (FBIS 6 December 1977).

But the October offensive also heightened tensions within the FSLN. The handling of these tensions shows the three FSLN tendencies working within a shared Marxist idiom, which provided each of them with the linguistic resources needed to defend their positions and attack those of the others. Within days of the October insurrection, the GPP tendency issued a communiqué stating that the organizers of the insurrection were not members of the FSLN, and condemning the action as "military coup tactics" (FBIS 31 October 1977). The GPP argued that the Ortega group sought "a simple change in national capitalist personalities within the government machinery which, by its economic and political essence, would always be a tool of imperialist domination." The GPP also held that the call for a national dialogue would simply complicate the work of accumulating forces in preparation for the "prolonged popular war." These were obviously serious accusations. In excommunicating the insurrectionists from the FSLN and charging them with coup tactics, the GPP effectively accused the Ortega group of betraying the FSLN's revolutionary project.

Wheelock's group, for its part, condemned the "foolhardy rightist populist line" of the insurrectionists ([FSLN-Proletarian Tendency] 1987, 162). The "proletarians" feared that the private sector opposition to Somoza would use the violence of the insurrectionists as a lever to force Somoza from power for its own ends. Thus, they argued, the insurrectionists were objectively on the "side of the bourgeoisie, as adversaries of the true interests of the masses" ([FSLN-Proletarian Tendency] 1979, 183). After the September 1978 insurrection, which cost many civilian lives, Wheelock accused the insurrectionists of "scandalous political irresponsibility" (1979, 126).[30]

In an April 1978 "conjunctural analysis," Humberto Ortega sought to respond to the concerns of the other FSLN tendencies that the insurrectionists were merely paving the way for a new "bourgeois government," a "Somozism without Somoza." Ortega recognized that "we are in an open card game with the bourgeoisie, and the strongest and ablest will win ... The FSLN must walk a stretch together with the bourgeoisie, a stretch during which the bourgeoisie and imperialism will try to destroy us and divert the Sandinista liberation process, just as we will try to destroy them and throw their reactionary aspirations into the garbage" (1981, 38, 40).[31]

This is the clearest formulation of Ortega's two-stage vision of the revolution. Bear in mind that those who must be thrown "into the garbage" along with their "reactionary aspirations" were not Somoza and his allies, but the allies of the Sandinistas themselves, the bourgeoisie with which the "FSLN must walk a stretch together." During this alliance, the FSLN, "with international support, and, in due time, with the support of the socialist camp and other progressive forces in the Third World, will try skilfully and gradually to channel the democratic conquests towards worker-peasant power" (1981, 38).

Ortega fully recognized the risks of this "open card game." One critical risk was that the path pursued would foster "reformist" tendencies within the FSLN itself, eroding its will to push the revolution towards its second stage. FSLN leaders had already seen such reformism develop within the party during the mid-1960s. To minimize this risk, Ortega sought to maintain the ideological purity of the FSLN. This concern has been missed by those observers who believe that the FSLN opened its doors to all and sundry during the late 1970s.

In 1977, Ortega stressed that "we are trying to create a *mass* struggle without *massifying* the FSLN." The FSLN must continue to be made up of "the best and most conscious" people (1987, 309). A 1978 internal document of Ortega's tendency once again stressed the "vital work of strengthening the *Sandinista vanguard nucleus* which bases itself on the scientific doctrine of the proletariat and the historical legacy of Sandinism" ([FSLN-Insurrectional Tendency] 1979b, 191–2).

This concern to avoid the "massification" of the FSLN led to the development of a dual military structure, as Carlos Núñez explains:

There were two types of armed organizations, units formed by FSLN militants and mass units. The first were made up of ideologically developed cadres, who shared Sandinista strategy and principles ... On the other hand there were armed mass [militias], broader military organisms. To belong to these it was enough to be anti-Somocista, anti-imperialist, and to be willing to fight ...

Given the great increase in the combative participation of the masses, the militias grew enormously, to the point when one member of the select military units was controlling between 100 and 200 militia members (Núñez, Cuadra, and Ramírez 1985, 66–7).[32]

At the same time, Ortega's insurrectional tendency stressed that the FSLN's rigorous structure not be visible to people at large:

Due to the enormous prestige of our vanguard, the people that in one or another way are aligned with this vanguard feel themselves immediately to be *militants* of the FSLN. This aspect is of enormous importance in terms of morale and should not be curtailed. What is important is to ensure that those elements that are not truly members of [the] vanguard structure – even though they may *feel* a part of the same – not be allowed to assume the responsibilities, duties, rights, etc., of the vanguard's true militants. In time, the people will understand the difference between the vanguard and the masses ([H. Ortega] 1987, 309).

Thus, the Sandinistas sought to coordinate a relatively invisible, ideologically homogeneous nucleus, and a broad mass movement marked by ideological pluralism. Observers who believe the FSLN opened its doors during this period have simply confused the Sandinista nucleus with the broad social sectors which that nucleus organized.

The Marxist lineage of all three tendencies is obvious. All three saw the FSLN as a vanguard ahead of the broad mass. The GPP and proletarians held that only an organized mass consciously supporting a socialist project could give the vanguard the strength it needed to take power and build socialism. The difference between these two tendencies lay in the question of how this mass was to be organized. The insurrectionists, however, held that divisions between Somoza and the bourgeoisie, together with a broad mass with the minimal level of organization necessary to participate in an insurrection in support of its immediate demands, could allow the FSLN to seize power. Once in power, the FSLN would seek to achieve the fuller level of organization and "conscientization" of the masses advocated by the other two tendencies. Thus, Ortega noted in 1977 that the insurrectional strategy did not abolish the need for a prolonged popular war: "PROLONGED POPULAR WAR is the strategy that encompasses the entire process of struggle, including the present phase, the democratic-revolutionary stage, that will take place once the dictatorship is toppled and will be followed by the phase in which the democratic revolution gives way to socialism" (1987, 313). Thus, all three tendencies believed that the achievement of socialism required: (i) a vanguard; (ii) an organized and socialist-oriented mass; and (iii) state power. The essential difference between the insurrectionists and the other tendencies lay in the question of whether or not (iii) might precede (ii).

If I have dwelt on this question at length, it is because so many of the Sandinistas' actions in their first years in power correspond to the Ortega strategy. As noted above, the FSLN in power paid great attention to mass organization and ideological transformation. We will see in later chapters that the leadership frequently hinted that the alliance with sectors of the bourgeoisie would be temporary. The Sandinistas' early actions and statements, as well as the Ortega program presented here, lead to the conclusion that the FSLN initially did hope to deepen the revolution, passing from its "democratic" phase to a "socialist" phase. We will see that this hope was eventually abandoned, though the precise moment when this happened cannot be pinned down.

F. BUT WAS MARXISM ALL THAT IMPORTANT?

I have argued throughout this chapter that the Sandinista leadership was heavily influenced by orthodox Marxism. Orthodox Marxism was consistent with (i) their political rhetoric; (ii) their attraction to a state-dominant economy, and their rejection of the market; (iii) their stress on ideological training within the movement and in society at large; and (iv) the manner in which they debated strategic issues during the FSLN split.

This conclusion differs from that of Donald Hodges, author of the most extensive work to date on Sandinista ideology, who claims that the FSLN leaders were decisively influenced by the "new Marxism" that emerged from the Cuban revolution, and that when they spoke of Marxism-Leninism "they meant the new Marxism rather than the old" (1986, 186). The analysis offered here indicates that, however much "new" Marxism the leaders held, they carried a lot of the "old" Marxism with them as well. Hodges's error, I would suggest, lies in his belief that the "old" and "new" Marxisms are opposites, when in fact they differ only in terms of some specific points. He argues for example that the "new Cuban Marxism was distinguished by its novel conviction that it is not always necessary to know the conditions of revolution in order to make one" (1986, 174). But this difference with the "old" Marxism can coexist with many areas of convergence, including the themes discussed above such as vanguardism and super-structuralism.

At least two objections may be raised to the arguments presented here. The first begins with the fact that many of the themes examined above, such as vanguardism and conceptions of democracy and political rights, are typical components of the self-legitimation of "Marxism-in-power," that is, of state-socialist regimes. Could one not argue that the FSLN leaders merely used orthodox Marxism to legitimate their power without believing in that Marxism?

This objection is consistent with the Downsian view of political rationality, critiqued in the first chapter. For Downs, ideologies are merely "weapons in the struggle for office" (Downs 1957, 96). If ideological themes from orthodox Marxism appear in Sandinista rhetoric, this means only that this Marxism is being used to "legitimate" or "rationalize" positions arrived at for other reasons (Weber 1958a, 117ff).

The weakness of the objection is that orthodox Marxism did not constitute a particularly appropriate vehicle for legitimation in a society in which Marxist ideology was not widely disseminated. Marxist thought had not penetrated Nicaragua as it had other Latin American societies. In fact, given the strong anti-communist propaganda in the Somoza era, to legitimize one's position with appeals to Marxism would have made as much sense as appealing to papal encyclicals in Teheran. If the FSLN leadership were merely seeking a vehicle for legitimation, much more use would have been made of Christian symbolism, and Marxism would scarcely have appeared in their rhetoric.

One could narrow the objection, and argue that orthodox Marxist themes were useful in legitimating National Directorate leadership, not in society at large, but within the FSLN. But for orthodox Marxist principles to serve as vehicles for legitimation within a movement, then that Marxism itself must enjoy support within the movement. That is, it must be more than a cynically used "weapon."

A second objection to the argument presented here is that some of the specific pieces of evidence offered as indications of an orthodox Marxist outlook within the FSLN leadership are consistent with other interpretations. All sorts of political tendencies, for example, have promoted state control of the "commanding heights" of the economy. This of course is true, but it does not weaken the argument, which is that the overall package of words and deeds of the Sandinistas is best explained by the hypothesis that they came to power influenced by orthodox Marxist ideology. Social-democrats or economic nationalists might have proclaimed their desire to control the commanding heights, but I do not think that they would have proclaimed their intention to destroy the bourgeoisie and "throw their reactionary aspirations into the garbage." Thus, the question is not whether each and every phenomenon cited in this chapter proves the hypothesis being argued, but whether that hypothesis constitutes a simple and comprehensive explanation of those phenomena, an explanation superior to the suggested alternatives. This I believe to be the case. The Sandinista leaders came to power talking and acting like orthodox Marxists – not fools who saw no breach between their hopes and their possibilities, but intelligent and realistic orthodox Marxists ready to address the constraints that faced them in July 1979. The best explanation of their words and deeds is that the leadership was in fact influenced by orthodox Marxism.

But what does it mean to be influenced by an ideology? We will examine here just one aspect of that influence: the link between ideology and perception in Sandinista relations with the peasantry.

G. SOCIALIST IDEOLOGY AND
SANDINISTA PERCEPTION

Ideology influences what we want. It also influences what we "see." It is commonplace to observe that human perception is limited, that everyone sees some things and neglects others. It is also common to note that our limited perception is not random, but is structured by our prior assumptions, many of which are not fully conscious, and by our "pragmatic" interests (Berger and Luckmann 1967, 22; Schutz 1970, 75).

Ideology can play an important role in this structuring of perception, focusing our attention on some phenomena and blinding us to others. This is partly an effect of the general pragmatism of perception. In so far as ideology orients us towards "what is to be done," it correspondingly orients our perception. In addition, ideologies, like Kuhn's paradigms, may contain tacit assumptions about which types of phenomena exist in the social world and which do not (Kuhn 1970, 41).[33]

What has been said of individuals applies with perhaps greater force to organizations. There, pragmatic interests and presuppositions will be built into the very structure and standard practices of the organization. As Simon argues, organizations will seek through training to give the individual member a "frame of reference for his thinking" (1965, 16), and will seek, through a division of labour, to focus the member's attention upon matters pertaining to her particular task (102). In addition, the information the leaders perceive directly may be minimal in relation to the information they acquire through "organizational sensors" (Allison 1971, 67). They are thus dependent on information filtered at various points by the pragmatic interests and presuppositions – both organizational and personal – of subordinates.

Using this simple conceptual framework, we may inquire of the information that the Sandinista leaders did and did not possess when they made policy decisions. We will focus here on one issue-area: Sandinista relations with the peasantry. When the Sandinista leaders "gazed out" upon the countryside, what did they see and what did they fail to see?

They certainly saw a countryside divided by class antagonisms. Moreover, their ideological outlook led them to view rural class relations as simply antagonistic rather than as antagonistic yet functional. Thus, rural merchants were viewed by the Sandinistas as super-exploiters of the peasantry. It would become clear over time that these merchants had in fact linked the peasantry with urban markets in a much more complex and satisfactory way than originally believed. The peasantry, in fact, never lost its preference for dealing with private rather than state merchants.

The Sandinistas also saw a countryside marked by backwardness. They shared that hidden lust for modernization held by many leftist critics of modernization theory. Thus, for example, they believed that state farms and cooperatives would serve as agents of both technical modernization and of the ideological or cultural modernization of the peasantry.

These two perceptions combined to give the Sandinistas a particularly negative view of so-called "pre-capitalist" social relations. Thus the 1981 agrarian reform law made non-monetary rental arrangements grounds for expropriation. Because of this, many peasants lost access to land they had worked under these "pre-capitalist" arrangements, and felt themselves worse off for the loss.

But another question must be asked: what did the Sandinistas fail to see in the countryside? They certainly did not see a peasantry differentiated by gender. This blindness may have had an important impact upon the Sandinista project. One must ask, for example, whether the costs and benefits of policies such as cooperativization and villagization might be skewed by gender. Such a question requires some change of focus from the sphere of "production" to that of "reproduction," or domestic work.[34] There we find an extreme concentration of work in female hands: a 1984 study estimated that the average peasant woman spent nine and a half hours a day on household work, while her daughters contributed another six and a half hours. By comparison, her husband and sons together spent less than an hour on domestic work (Woroniuk 1987, 30).[35] Modernization strategies that sought to reduce the physical isolation of the peasant family could have a significant impact upon the domestic workload. A study of women's work day, for example, commented that "creeping deforestation means that an increasing amount of time is spent hauling water and collecting wood. Daily walks of between five and eight kilometres in search of these resources are not uncommon nowadays" (Collinson 1990, 37). Thus, the alleviation of this task through village electrification and potable water projects might have been an important attraction. As those primarily responsible for the care of children, women might also have been more interested in the educational and health services that accompanied the cooperativization process.

The rural modernization promoted by the Sandinistas might have had a more immediate impact upon the sphere of reproduction than the sphere of production. Thus, one can argue that cooperativization and/or villagization could do more to meet the "practical gender needs" of women than of men.[36] One could therefore hypothesize that there was a potential basis of support in the countryside for some of the changes that the Sandinistas sought to promote. This hypothesis might have been tested through different strategies of political interpellation and mobilization. Imagine, for example, that the Sandinistas had made

greater efforts to integrate rural women into their ranks, and in particular into their leadership structure, and had allowed their organization to
be transformed through this integration. Imagine that they had encouraged the development of a relatively autonomous rural women's movement, a movement that could interpellate women as women.[37]

The outcome of such a strategy is not predictable: a vibrant rural
women's movement would have gone beyond questions of "practical
gender needs" to address issues related to "strategic gender needs".[38]
That is, such a movement would have pushed the Sandinistas to address
contradictions of gender alongside those of class. The very autonomy required to make a rural women's movement capable of interpellating
women as women would have posed a range of challenges to the leadership. Thus, a rural women's movement could have both changed the
Sandinista project and given that project greater chances of success.[39]

But this remains an untested hypothesis, as the Sandinistas walked
down the same path that many other socialist movements had walked:
they oriented their appeal to the peasantry around the question of
land, though they knew they could not resolve the land question in the
way that the peasantry hoped it would be resolved. Production was par-
amount; reproduction was irrelevant. The potential interests of peasant
women were never explored, as the appeal to the peasantry was resolutely male-oriented. Omar Cabezas, author of the classic work on the
Sandinistas' rural guerrilla experience, wrote that "the farm animals,
the wife, the children, and the land constitute one element, it is a unit
for the peasant, his indivisible universe. That's why I say that the peasant without land is an incomplete man, a man without a soul" (1982,
242). A political language that lumped "the wife" together with the
farm animals and the land corresponded to a political practice that
sought to work within rural patriarchal structures, rather than question
them. After taking power, the implementation of various rural policies
reflected this same willingness to treat the rural household as an undif-
ferentiated whole of which the eldest male – where one was present –
was the automatic head.

It is important to recognize, of course, that many factors kept the
Sandinistas from seeing rural women as potential partners in a transformation of the countryside, and not all of these factors derived from their
socialist ideological framework. At various points in their memoirs, Sandinistas reveal sexist and "urbanist" attitudes towards rural women.[40] This
raises the question of what independent causal status one should attribute to the Sandinista leaders' ideology: could one not argue that they
were simply drawn to an ideology that privileges contradictions of class
over those of gender because they were men, and that their attitudes
would not have been much different in the absence of this ideology?

While there is much weight in this objection, an ideological frame-work can either strengthen or challenge biases. It is helpful to keep in mind, for example, that Marx often displayed, particularly in his early writings, elitist attitudes towards workers, who were "barbarous" (1964, 123), in a state of "bestial savagery" (169). Nevertheless, this class, pre-cisely because of its "radical chains" (58), had the potential to turn soci-ety on its head. Similarly, one could argue that exposure to a different ideological framework might have helped the Sandinista leadership to glimpse the radical potential of rural women.[41]

In summary, some of these ways of seeing examined here are pecu-liar to orthodox Marxism: for example the view that relations of pro-duction can be neatly categorized into "pre-capitalist" and "capitalist," and that the latter are necessarily superior to the former. Some are shared more broadly by Marxism in general, for example the view that the class relation between merchant and peasant is simply a relation of antagonism. Other elements, such as the desire to struggle against "backwardness," are shared by Marxist and non-Marxist modernists. Fi-nally, the failure to see gender cleavages is typical not just of Marxism but of what has been called "male-stream" thought in general. Thus, even had the Sandinista leadership not been influenced by orthodox Marxism, they might still have held some of the ways of seeing exam-ined here. Yet the specific combination portrayed here was consistent with an orthodox Marxist outlook, and probably with no other.

In examining these "blinds spots" of the Sandinista vision, the re-marks that opened this section should be borne in mind: human per-ception, both at an individual and an organizational level, is inherently limited. Attention may be redirected, but "blind spots" must always re-main. The vision of an all-embracing counter-hegemonic movement that would replace classism with a sensitivity to every social contradic-tion is as ignorant of the limits of human perception and knowledge as was the classical socialist dream of the "perfect plan."

I have argued that the Sandinista leadership came to power influenced by orthodox Marxism. Immediately upon taking power, they had to face the enormous tension between their hopes and the constraints of the situation they faced. That tension is the subject of the next chapter.

3 The Legacy of the Somoza Era and Initial Sandinista Strategy

Lenin commented in 1918 that "the only material we have to build communism with is what has been left us by capitalism" (1971, 72). The legacy that a revolutionary government inherits represents both a series of obstacles to change, and the very medium through which change must be fashioned. While the rhetoric of revolution promotes the myth of total change, the sober reality facing victorious revolutionaries demands that they manage a complex dialectic of continuity and change. For example, economic collapse must be avoided. But in the short run, and perhaps even for a longer period, relative stabilization of the economy will depend upon, or even reinforce, the actors, institutions, and motivations inherited from the previous regime.

This chapter will examine the Sandinistas' first response to the dialectic of continuity and change. It will consider the economic legacy that the Sandinistas confronted upon taking power, and present the thinking of the Sandinistas on certain key questions at that time. The chapter will thus offer a somewhat artificial "snapshot" of Sandinista thinking at the moment of taking power, before the dilemmas of holding power had begun to modify that thinking. The first section of the chapter (A) will present the economic legacy of the Somoza era. Sections B through D will examine initial thinking in our four broad issue-areas: state organization and price policy (B)[1]; relations with the bourgeoisie (C); and agrarian reform (D). For each issue-area, various dilemmas will be presented by drawing on the historical experience of other state-socialist regimes.

A. THE ECONOMIC LEGACY OF THE SOMOZA ERA

The Role of Agriculture

Agriculture is central to the Nicaraguan economy. In the mid-1970s, agriculture itself accounted for 18.3 per cent of the gross domestic product (GDP). Agriculture-related industries represented a further 9.6 per cent of GDP, and 58 per cent of manufacturing value-added.[2] Thus, agriculture and agriculture-related industry accounted for 28 per cent of GDP. In particular, agricultural products dominate Nicaragua's export accounts. In 1976, unprocessed and lightly processed agricultural goods represented $428 million of the country's $542 million of exports (BCN 1978), generating a foreign exchange surplus upon which the rest of the economy depended.

As agriculture dominated the Nicaraguan economy, so did the export sub-sector dominate within agriculture. Nicaragua's traditional agricultural strategy, like those of many other Third World nations, might be termed a "food last" approach. The demands of export agriculture for land, credit, and human resources had priority, with domestic food production repeatedly adjusting itself to the logic of export activity. With the coffee boom of the late nineteenth century, indigenous communities were eliminated and small-holders in general pushed onto poorer land (Wheelock 1978, 17). The post-World-War-Two cotton and beef export booms accentuated two characteristics of Nicaraguan agriculture: the marginalization of food production, and the concentration of land. During the export booms, peasant maize and bean producers were pushed off the Pacific Coast, the region best suited to grain production, first into the central highlands, and then to the agricultural frontier in the Atlantic region of the country, where the land is thought suitable only for perennial crops. The Agrarian Reform Research Centre estimates that in 1977, 63 per cent of soils were being used in ways that did not accord with their best use (CIERA 1984, 21). Geographical marginalization of food production also made it difficult to market output and left small farmers in a weak position vis à vis merchants. Finally, the lack of adequate drying and storage facilities led to high post-harvest losses, estimated at 30 per cent for basic grains and vegetables (60).

Export agriculture also received the lion's share of both bank financing and technical assistance. For the 1977–8 season, cotton and coffee received 85 per cent of short-term agricultural crop credit, while the two main peasant crops, maize and beans, received just 4.7 per cent (BCN 1979). Thus, food production was left with a weak technological and infrastructural base. By the late 1960s, the marginalization of domestic food production had led to the stagnation of output. In the decade prior to the 1979 revolution, growth rates for the major food crops lagged behind the rate of population growth (BCN 1979).

The postwar export booms also contributed to land concentration. By 1978, farms greater than 350 hectares represented 2 per cent of Nicaraguan farms, yet controlled 48 per cent of agricultural land, an increase of 8 percentage points since 1952. Farms of less than 7 hectares represented 45 per cent of farms, controlling just 2 per cent of agricultural land, down from 3 per cent in 1952 (Barraclough 1984). An estimated 60 per cent of rural families had either no land or a quantity of land insufficient to support themselves (Weeks 1985a, 114). The large producers tended to focus on export products – principally coffee, cotton, sugar, and beef – while the small farmers generally produced food for national consumption.[3]

Observers have stressed the symbiosis between landlessness and the labour needs of the export sector. It is estimated that in 1978 almost 80 per cent of the rural economically active population participated in the export harvests. Of this group, 40 per cent had no access to land, and another 50 per cent did not own or rent enough land to survive without supplemental wage labour. Because of the seasonal needs of the export sector, only a fifth of those without access to land could find year-round employment (Deere and Marchetti 1981, 42).

The cotton and beef export booms also drove many rural Nicaraguans into towns and cities. At the end of World War Two, two-thirds of Nicaraguans lived in rural areas. By 1980 that proportion was well below one half. While the rural population grew at an average of 2.3 per cent per year in the 1950–80 period, the population of large urban centres grew at an annual rate of 6.2 per cent (*Bda* 2 January 1984). As the industrial sector demand for labour never kept pace with the influx of migrants, most new urban dwellers moved into petty production or commercial activities.

This legacy would present the new government with numerous problems. Too many people were living in the cities, where there was little socially useful work available. But attempts to stem the rural-urban migration, for example by concentrating the development of social services in the countryside, could conflict with the need to maintain the political support of urban popular sectors. In addition, the vast number of urban dwellers involved in petty commerce would present both technical and political obstacles to the Sandinistas' project of regulating the market.

The agricultural dimension of the legacy of the Somoza years meant that any agricultural strategy would confront a complex set of problems and constraints, among which we can note: (i) the need to generate a foreign exchange surplus; (ii) the stagnation in the production of basic grains; (iii) the lack of fit between an optimal pattern of land use and the inherited pattern; (iv) the large landless rural population; (v) the excessive seasonality of labour demand; and (vi) the concentration of "unproductive" workers in urban commercial activities.

This legacy thus generated a set of objective dilemmas, dilemmas that existed whether or not the leadership was aware of them. This is because the strategy chosen to address any of the problems listed here could have implications for the rest. For example, addressing (ii) by improving current peasant production might reinforce (iii), by rendering more viable basic grain production where it "should not" take place. Alternatively, addressing (ii) by stressing modern production of basic grains could increase the import-intensity of agriculture, thus making (i) more problematic. If one addressed (iv), the supply of labour for the export harvest might dry up, again rendering (i) problematic. One could address this in part by intensifying the mechanization of the cotton and sugar harvests, but this too would raise the import-intensity of agriculture. Problem (vi) offered a possible solution to the labour dilemma, if one could mobilize this sector for the export harvests without high economic or political costs.

One can think of escapes from some of these dilemmas. One can envisage, for example, forms of modernization of basic grains production that need not increase the import intensity of production. Thus, the point here is not to argue that all of these dilemmas were entirely binding, but to suggest the complexity of the agricultural situation facing the new government. This is particularly important to keep in mind now that many Sandinistas believe that their early agrarian policies were purely and simply mistaken.

Dependent Industry

The industrial sector would present the Sandinista leadership with a different dilemma. Unlike agriculture, this sector ran an overall trade deficit. Maintenance and growth of the sector would therefore place pressure on the external balance. To permit the sector to decline, on the other hand, would intensify urban unemployment and could generate political difficulties.

Most of Nicaragua's industry developed in the 1960s under the auspices of the Central American Common Market (CACM), formed in 1960. Under the tutelage of the Alliance for Progress, the Central American nations set about attracting foreign capital: new industries were given an eight-to-ten-year exemption on the payment of duty for equipment and raw material imports, and a six-to-eight-year exemption on taxes on rents and profits. Nicaragua guaranteed foreign investors "the free exit, at any time, of any or all registered capital," and "the free and unrestricted repatriation of net profits" ([Governments of Central America] 1962, Articles 11–13; República de Nicaragua 1955, Article 9).

With these guarantees, the CACM was very attractive for foreign investors. In addition, industrial production inside the market was given tariff protection from outside competition.[4] As a result of tax exemptions and tariffs, industrial companies operating in Nicaragua were able to earn profits that allowed them to recover their investment in just a few years (Gibson 1986, 5).

This import-substitution strategy was an early success, as Nicaragua's manufacturing value-added grew 11.4 per cent per year throughout the 1960s, the seventh fastest rate of growth in the world (World Bank 1982). But the rate of growth dropped to 5.9 per cent in the 1970–7 period (BCN 1979), as the CACM ran into difficulties, among them the withdrawal of Honduras in 1970. New industrial investment in Nicaragua dried up: "Not one important factory opened in Nicaragua in the decade prior to the revolutionary triumph" (Ramírez 1987, 217).

Some observers have attributed the CACM slowdown to the "structural" factor of market saturation, which reflected the absence of reforms to increase the income of popular sectors (Wheelock 1978, 130), while others believe that it was a short-term phenomenon caused by increases in the prices of imported inputs (Weeks 1985a, 64ff). Whatever the cause of CACM's slowdown, critics saw it as proof that the CACM industrialization process was yet another Third World "miracle that led nowhere".[5] The Sandinistas would be strongly influenced by the belief that the industrialization process was fatally flawed.

A key critique of the CACM was that, since its formation had been promoted by the Alliance for Progress, which had been initiated by the United States in the wake of the Cuban revolution, the regional integration process must have fundamentally served the interests of U.S. imperialism. For Jaime Wheelock, the CACM was an integral part of the U.S.'s "global counterrevolutionary strategy" formulated in response to the Cuban revolution (1978, 127; 1983, 108). Thus, the FSLN's 1969 program promised to end the "so-called integration which seeks to intensify the submission of Central America to the United States monopolies and to the local reactionary forces" (FSLN 1981, 35).

It was also argued that the CACM industrialization tended to focus on U.S.-style non-durable consumer goods that only a fraction of the population could afford. Thus, industrialization brought quantitative "growth" but not qualitative "development," in the sense of a "deepening" of the industrial sector. In addition, the tax exemptions and guar antees of unrestricted profit repatriation ensured that a large part of the profits generated in the industrial sector were shipped out of the country, thus weakening the ability of the industrialization process to contribute to overall economic dynamism.

This lack of contribution to overall dynamism, it is argued, was exacerbated by the highly dependent nature of the CACM industrialization. The exemptions offered on import duties for equipment and raw materials encouraged the simple transfer of machinery and production techniques from developed countries, and discouraged the creation of linkages between industry and agriculture. Jaime Wheelock argues that the CACM brought to Nicaragua "more or less obsolete factories with a technology that was no longer profitable in the United States (1981b, 19), and that the whole industrialization process was "simply a fiction" (Wheelock 1983, 109). Thus, a perpetual dependence on imported raw materials was fostered.

There was an element of truth in these critiques, though the picture was probably more complicated than the Sandinistas believed. With respect, first, to the imperialism question, it can be argued that the effects of the CACM were contradictory. While the industrialization process did increase foreign capital's presence in the region, it also allowed for a certain "diversification of dependence." From 1960 to 1977, the U.S. share of Nicaragua's exports dropped from 42.7 per cent to 23.6 per cent, and its share of imports from 52.6 per cent to 28.8 per cent (BCN 1979). This diversification would help Nicaragua survive the U.S. trade embargo imposed in 1985. In addition, the intensification of trade within the region gave industrialists in the other countries an objective stake in Nicaragua's economic well-being in the 1980s, which led to some quiet resistance to U.S. attempts to destabilize the Nicaraguan economy.[6]

Despite its emphasis on non-durable consumer goods, the CACM industrialization process did "deepen" Nicaragua's industrial structure to a limited degree. The share of non-durable consumer goods in industrial value-added dropped from 89.7 per cent in 1960 to 70.3 per cent in 1975, while the share of intermediate goods rose from 7.8 per cent to 17.6 per cent, and that of capital goods and consumer durables rose from a minuscule 2.4 per cent to 8.1 per cent (Dijkstra 1987). Nevertheless, the industrial structure of Nicaragua, and of Central America in general, remained shallow, even in comparison with countries with similar per-capita incomes (Weeks 1985a, 139).

Nicaraguan industry was highly dependent, in the sense that the import intensity for industry was much higher than that for other sectors of the economy. The industrialization that took place under CACM auspices, however, was neither more nor less dependent than Nicaragua's pre-CACM industry: the overall import intensity of the Nicaraguan industrial sector remained stable through the CACM period.[7]

Nicaraguan industry also generated some exports, about three-quarters of which went to CACM partners.[8] Overall, then, Nicaraguan industry may have generated an annual trade deficit of just $8 million in the 1970–7 period (Weeks 1985a, 168), on an average gross output of nearly $200 million. Thus, Sandinista leaders seriously exaggerated the problem of industry when they alleged that the industrial sector imported twice as much as it exported (Wheelock 1983, 109).

It is harder to estimate the impact of CACM industry on the non-trade components of the balance of payments. One indicator is the growth in the repatriation of profits on direct foreign investment. From $1.2 million in 1960, this item rose to $25.9 million in 1976 (IMF 1955–78). While not all of this foreign exchange drain can be attributed to CACM industry, the coincidence between the rise in profit outflows and CACM development suggests that most of this figure can be so attributed.

It is not clear, however, to what extent the incoming Sandinista government should have taken those remittances into account in evaluating the impact of the sector. The new government had a certain room to manoeuvre in its relations with industrial sector transnationals, as shown by the fact that it was able to persuade most transnationals to continue operations despite a suspension of almost all foreign exchange remittances (Austin and Ickis 1986b, 105). Thus, evaluation of industry's foreign exchange impact should note the difference between normal and exceptional periods of operation.

In summary, while there was some measure of truth in the criticisms of the Nicaraguan industrialization process, those criticisms seem overstated. Although CACM industrialization was promoted by the United States, the relation between industrialization and "imperialism" was complex. While it is true that the CACM industrialization process had done little to "deepen" Nicaragua's industrial structure, the quantitative growth of industry was impressive. Industrial value-added rose a total of 327 per cent between 1960 and 1977. The sector was a drain on foreign exchange, yet not to the extent believed by leaders such as Wheelock.

Debt

A final aspect of the economic legacy of the Somoza era was the external debt inherited by the new government, officially estimated at $1.6 billion.[9] The growth of that debt was fairly typical of the Latin American experience in the 1970s. The medium- and long-term external public debt grew 24 per cent annually through the decade (BCN 1970–8), below the Latin American average of 35.2 per cent (Iglesias 1983). As the annual growth rate in the 1960s was also over 20 per cent, the debt grew more than fortyfold over the 1960–78 period.

This growth pattern indicates the extent to which Nicaragua's growth in the 1960s and 1970s was financed, not by direct foreign investment or by local accumulation, but by credit. Mayorga notes that the contribution of domestic savings to investment declined "from around 90% in the early fifties to the 50%–60% range in the sixties and seventies" (1986, 31). From 1960 to 1978, the debt-to-GDP ratio rose from 7.6 per cent to 50.6 per cent. Over the period, the country ran a total current account deficit of just over $1.06 billion, roughly equivalent to the increase in the outstanding debt for the period (BCN 1979). The accumulated debt was used "productively," in the sense that imports of capital goods were consistently greater than the accumulation of debt and the current account deficit over the period.[10] Nevertheless, as elsewhere in Latin America, many externally financed investments through the period were in sectors such as real estate, and could never generate foreign exchange to pay for themselves. Both borrowers and lenders signed loan agreements in the hope that the agricultural sector would continue to generate a foreign exchange surplus, allowing the government to maintain a convertible exchange, and foreign loans to be repaid smoothly.

Also typical of the Latin American experience was the increasing role of private banks in loans to Nicaragua. The private bank share of medium- and long-term external public debt rose from 22.6 per cent in 1970 to 46.3 per cent in 1978 (BCN 1970–8). As these private loans had maturation periods shorter than traditional development loans, and did not have fixed rates of interest, Nicaragua's external accounts, like those of Latin America in general, would suffer from the sharp increase in world interest rates at the end of the decade.

B. STATE ORGANIZATION AND PRICE POLICY

Dilemmas on the Road to a Socialist Economy

The quest for a state-dominated economy involves a number of objective dilemmas. If these are not confronted consciously, choices will be made without a full grasp of their implications. To appreciate these dilemmas, however, we must first examine the specific nature of the socialist economy, as it has existed in the twentieth century. Perhaps the greatest barrier to understanding this economic type has been the wide gap between the language used to legitimize socialist economies and their reality. The language of legitimation was naturally based upon the

Marxian "classics," but this legitimation required that those classics be emptied of much of their content. Social control of the economy was reduced to state control, which in turn was equated with Marxian "planning," whatever the irrationalities that state control provoked. This "planning" was then held to fulfil Marx's promise that socialism would overcome the "anarchy" of market production.

Now, if one begins an analysis of the socialist economy by focusing on its language of legitimation, one can easily miss the critical differences between this economy and capitalism. Analysts have frequently shown that planning has in no way eliminated "anarchy" from the economy: the inability to control investment, the "arrhythmia" demonstrated by "planned" economies, the lack of a significant statistical correlation between the plan's growth targets and actual results, suggest that the planning process may be little more than a time-consuming ritual (Shmelev and Popov 1989, 91). If the difference between capitalism and socialism was thought to be socialist planning, the weakness of that planning could easily lead to the conclusion that socialism is but "state capitalism."

But there is in fact a critical distinction between capitalist and socialist economies, one that can be grasped by beginning at the level of the firm. In the capitalist market economy, firms are in competition, and hence represent parallel, or duplicated, structures. Those at the top of the firm must pursue the search for profit. In the socialist economy, similar firms are subordinated to a common authority. Relations to both suppliers and purchasers will be regulated by that authority. Those at the top of the firm are motivated by the need *selectively to comply or simulate compliance with administrative orders*, in order to pursue personal objectives and/ or those of the firm. "Selectively," because socialist firms found in practice that, since they could not comply with the hundreds of "obligatory" requirements issued by central authorities, they were to a large degree left free to choose which orders they wished to "obey" (Brus 1972). At the same time, the varying ability of the central authorities to monitor compliance with those orders often allowed firms merely to "simulate" compliance.

The situation was not as anarchic as this description suggests, however, because not all orders were created equal. By explicitly or implicitly giving priority to some orders, the centre could lead the firm to respect those orders and indicators understood to be most central for the bonuses of the firm, or for the future careers of management. One criterion of particular importance was that of gross output. The reasons for the stress on gross production are not altogether clear. It may be attributed to an "ideological" factor, the desire to distinguish socialist enterprises (oriented towards "use values") from capitalist ones (oriented towards "exchange values"). This orientation may well have had a "material basis," however, a basis relating to the historical circumstances under which the first socialist economy took shape. While Marx had been the prophet of socialism in advanced industrial societies, of "revolution in the fullness of time," as Schumpeter put it (1976, 58), Soviet socialism emerged under conditions of relative backwardness. In his classic statement on the urgency of catching up with the West, Stalin proclaimed: "We are fifty or a hundred years behind the advanced countries. We must make good this lag in ten years. Either we do it or they crush us" (Deutscher 1966, 328). Thus, the socialist economy that has existed in our time might well be termed "catch-up socialism," to distinguish it from the socialism envisioned by Marx.

But the rapid economic development required by this project was, as Bukharin put it, a process of "constructing buildings with bricks that have not yet been produced" (Ellman 1979, 39). The process was thus inevitably plagued with serious bottle-necks. This may be basis for the focus on use values: the production of bricks – and many other things – has a benefit for economic growth as a whole that the profit-oriented firm will treat as an irrelevant "externality." Thus, an economy-wide system of administration should allow for an "internalization" of externalities, an internalization that apparently found operational expression in an emphasis on gross output.

Yet this is certainly not the whole story. The emphasis on gross production outlived whatever economic usefulness it might have had. Kaser and Zielinsky note that, even after Polish economic reforms had sought to dethrone the gross output indicator, firms found that the indicator continued to play the central role in their evaluation by the state bureaucracy (1970, 104). Writings on the Soviet economy have repeatedly noted the exasperation of reformers who could not understand the persistence of the gross output emphasis despite explicit attacks on it, dating back to 1957 (Shmelev and Popov 1989, 263; Desai 1989, 11). It appears that bureaucrats found this indicator the easiest to wield, and resisted attempts to downgrade it. One could hypothesize that it is easier to monitor the sheer quantity of a firm's output than, for example, product quality, or the calibre of management's response to profit opportunities.

This approach to the distinction between existing capitalism and socialism downgrades the importance of ownership. A privately owned enterprise in a socialist economy can be drawn into an administrative relation with the state, just as a state firm under capitalism can participate in the market like any private firm. Nevertheless, since central authorities have additional resources to encourage compliance from state sector managers, they will find it easier to establish administrative relations within the state sector. Hence, the quest for a socialist economy is also a quest for a state-dominant economy. This state dominance can be expressed through both a dominance of state firms within the economy, and of state authorities over the private sector.

It should not be assumed, however, that the state that dominates under socialism can be viewed as a "unitary actor," nor that the subordination of firms to central state authorities signifies ultimate subordination to a single point within the state. As Michael Ellman notes, "The Marxist-Leninist theory of planning assumes that all the decision makers in an economy form a 'team,' that is, a group of persons working together who have identical goals. In fact the decision makers form a 'coalition,' that is, a group of persons working together who have some, but not all, goals in common" (1979, 76). In socialist as well as capitalist systems, "bureaucratic politics" affect state action. As elsewhere, officials within central state institutions will interpret orientations from above in the light of their own institutional priorities, fully aware that their own career path will probably depend on how their specific area of responsibility is handled, rather than on their overall contribution to the good of the state or society as a whole.

Our point of departure for understanding the difference between capitalist and socialist economies has been the reorientation of the attention of firm managers from the market to administrative orders. Though the order-giver in the socialist economy is no more "sovereign" than the consumer in the market, the shift of attention from market to orders is nonetheless crucial. Competition between firms is replaced by coexistence and shared subordination to state authorities. Of particular importance is the fact that investment decisions are not based upon market signals.

Now Marx held an organic conception of capitalism, in which each element is both result and presupposition (1973, 278). Its central aspects – the competitive market, concentrated ownership of the means of production, the profit motive, pervasive commodification, technological dynamism – were, in Marx's conception, mutually reinforcing. Given this, socialism's negation of the profit orientation and interfirm competition influenced all the other component elements of the complex that is capitalism. For Marx, competition reciprocally flows from and sustains increasing efficiency and technological change, concentration of the means of production, and pervasive commodification. Hence the limiting of markets and competition under socialism means that these other elements would have to be induced by other means, which may or may not be possible. The effort to induce greater efficiency and technological change, for example, was one of the perennial failures of the Soviet economy (Hewett 1988).

Similarly, as competition both directly and indirectly sustains commodification, the attenuation of competition creates the potential for a

"de-commodification" of labour. Since the profit orientation of entrepreneurs in capitalism generates actions that tend towards a levelling of
profit rates across sectors, the absence of that orientation implies the
creation of niches that can easily generate "super-profits" for petty entrepreneurs. Hence there is no tendency within the economy that can
"naturally" eliminate self-employment and sustain the commodification
of labour. Maintenance of a salaried labour force thus requires that "artificial" steps be taken, usually in the form of legal restrictions on the
"second economy."

As the socialist economy described here is fast disappearing from the
face of the earth, it is tempting to conclude that the system was a failure, and that the attraction of Sandinista leaders to many aspects of the
system was simply irrational. But the overall balance sheet is far more
complicated. Socialism's administrative structures allowed central authorities to function as a "spotlight," to use Hewett's simile (1988, 168).
That is, they could bring tremendous attention and resources to bear
upon specific points in the economy. This ability to concentrate energies was manifested in Stalin's 1930s' industrialization drive, a drive responsible for much of the respect for Soviet socialism throughout the
Third World. The socialist economy, it appeared, was indeed the appropriate vehicle for "catching up."

On the other hand, this virtue of the socialist economy presumes that
there are significant unused resources waiting to be "concentrated" by
central authorities. Thus, it is commonly argued that the "fit" between
the socialist economy and the requirements of the Soviet industrialization drive reflected both the relative backwardness of the Soviet economy, and its significant reserves of labour and natural resources. Critics
of existing socialist economies have long argued that such an economy
is unable to manage the transition from this type of "extensive" growth
to "intensive" growth based on increased factor productivity (Goldman
1964; Selucky 1972, 4). Thus, where extensive surplus human and
physical resources are not available, the socialist economy *as it has existed in our time* is probably not the path to catching up.

But this is the reflection of hindsight. The Sandinista leaders were in
fact attracted to the socialist model and thus, whether they knew it or
not, they would eventually have to confront many of the dilemmas of
that model. In considering the specific questions of state organization
and price policy, we will focus on four issues:

1 The problem of prices, accumulation, and political alliances
2 The problem of defining enterprise goals
3 Labour relations and the motivation of work
4 The problem of "specialists"

Some of the most acute dilemmas for socialist policy arise in the area of price policy.[11] Neoclassical economics tends to stress the role of the price mechanism in relation to allocative efficiency. Market-clearing prices signal to producers and consumers alike the relative scarcity of different goods, in relation to society's "effective demand." Neoclassical economists pay less attention to the impact of prices upon distribution, though the question is not altogether ignored.

The question of distribution can be examined at various levels of analysis: between "rich" and "poor"; between "capital" and "labour"; between regions of a country; and so on. Each of these levels of analysis yields different insights concerning the impact of prices, and each may suggest different policy objectives to be taken into account in formulating price policy. Thus, a "rich-poor" analysis can suggest that prices might be manipulated in order to reduce income disparities, while a regional analysis might suggest the use of prices to attenuate rural-urban migration.

A level of analysis that is crucial for understanding the path to a socialist economy is that of distribution between the "state complex" and the rest of the economy. The state complex is defined here as all those institutions whose activities more or less automatically influence the financial situation of the state. The term includes not just those bodies financed from the central government budget, but institutions whose deficits (or surpluses) will almost certainly be covered by (or transferred to) the state banking system. Though the exact boundaries of the state complex may be hazy, the concept illuminates a key dimension of price policy.[12] The state complex that emerged in Nicaragua after July 1979 can be broken down into four basic components: (i) the government proper; (ii) the financial system; (iii) the import-export system; and (iv) the productive and commercial system, comprising state production enterprises and those trade enterprises not included in (iii).[13]

Thus, many prices will affect the distribution of resources between the state complex and the rest of the economy. Of particular interest throughout this work will be the prices paid and charged by state production and trade organizations, including the price of foreign exchange implicit in the state's foreign trade transactions, and interest rates charged by the state financial system.

The issues at stake here can be clarified by a return to a Soviet debate of the 1920s. The two poles in the debate might be termed the "state accumulation" and the "alliance-building" perspectives. Evgeny Preobrazhensky articulated the first position. Socialism depended upon the consolidation of the state complex, which would spearhead the industrialization process, Preobrazhensky argued, and this consolidation depended upon resolving the problem of state accumulation. As the state sector is initially quite small, its growth will depend on resources extracted from the non-state economy. Preobrazhensky termed this extraction "primitive socialist accumulation" (1965, 84), in an imperfect analogy with Marx's concept of primitive (capitalist) accumulation. Preobrazhensky believed that price policy could serve as an efficient instrument of state accumulation since "not a single kopeck [is] needed for any special taxation apparatus" (111). Hence, he advocated "a price policy consciously calculated so as to alienate a *certain* part of the surplus product of private economy in all its forms" (110).

In opposition to Preobrazhensky, Nikolai Bukharin articulated the "alliance-building" perspective. Bukharin argued that the future of socialism depended, not upon rapid industrialization, but upon the maintenance of an alliance between the "worker" state and the peasantry, which made up the mass of the Soviet population. This alliance required that socialism be developed at a "snail's pace," argued Bukharin (Carr 1958, 352). This strategy, Bukharin felt, was threatened by the state accumulation perspective. Hence he subtitled an attack on Preobrazhensky "How to destroy the worker-peasant bloc" (1982). Bukharin jumped on Preobrazhensky's admission (1965, 111) that his approach ignored "the difficulties of a political kind which result from the relations between the working class and the peasantry." To ignore such "difficulties," argued Bukharin, was to ignore the whole essence of constructing socialism (1982, 175–6). Rather than using prices to foster state accumulation, then, Bukharin felt that price policy should seek to maintain political alliances. Instead of raising prices of state products, "we must orient ourselves *toward the lowest possible prices,* toward satisfying the masses" (174).

Both parties to the debate tended to ignore the dilemma they were confronting. Bukharin simply did not take the problem of accumulation very seriously: he suggested that lowered state prices would constitute in and of themselves a significant stimulus to economic growth and accumulation.[14] Preobrazhensky, for his part, demonstrated little interest in sustaining the "worker-peasant alliance," which, he argued, would founder without a stress on state accumulation, through a lack of manufactured goods to exchange for the peasantry's grain (Carr 1958, 316).

Yet there is a dilemma here, one that would confront the Sandinistas in power. The state complex needs resources even for its "simple reproduction," and more so for its expansion. Initially at least, the bulk of these resources must be captured from the private economy, and price policy is an effective tool in this regard. Yet one of the consequences of extensive state intervention in the economy is the destruction of many "fetishes" that accompany the market mechanism. Prices will be robbed of their "naturalness," and will increasingly be seen as the product of government decisions. Price policy may come to be interpreted as an indication of the "class nature" of the state, and shifts in this policy may have serious political consequences. In a sense, broad sectors of the population are freed of their fetishes, only to become thoroughgoing "voluntarists".[15]

It will be seen that this politicization of prices bedevilled the FSLN throughout its decade in power, and the Sandinistas never managed a consistent response to this dilemma. In the early years, one can find traces of a state-accumulation perspective in some planning documents, though government policy as a whole reflected an alliance-building perspective.[16] Later on, the FSLN tried unsuccessfully to address the accumulation problem without destroying its alliances.

Emphasis on state accumulation is but an extension of the emphasis upon financial controls and responsibility. Through its necessary relation to the question of financial controls, the accumulationist perspective comes into conflict with a central aspect of the socialist economy, its "spotlight" capacity to focus resources on specific tasks "at all costs." Though the accumulationist perspective serves the long-run needs of the socialist economy, at any given moment the focus on financial controls will conflict with the short-term logic of that economy.

The debate presented here has implications for the question of monetary emission. Should the state complex not capture sufficient resources through taxation, price policy, or loans, it will have recourse to the "printing press." Preobrazhensky noted that monetary emission "is also one of the methods of primitive accumulation" (1965, 91), and in a pamphlet written during the hyper-inflation of 1920 celebrated the printing press as "that machine-gun of the Commissariat of Finance which poured fire into the rear of the bourgeois system" (Carr 1966, 261). But experience has shown that this weapon can easily backfire. In seizing resources through monetary emission, the state has little control over who actually gives up those resources. The state's political alliances, therefore, may be left at the mercy of the outcome of an inflationary struggle in the private economy. Inflation also vitiates planning and control within the state sector. As monetary emissions continue, the velocity of money will accelerate as people increasingly turn to foreign exchange or non-monetary objects to serve as stores of value. Hence inflation accelerates and the "real yield" from monetary emissions declines, eventually approaching zero (Griffith-Jones 1981, 37; Carr 1960, 31).

Just as revolutionaries must confront the choice between fostering accumulation within the state complex and using that complex to maintain political alliances, so too must they identify the overall objectives of state enterprises. Repeated failures to do so or to translate state objectives into administrative practices have contributed greatly to the problems of state firms. State firms in socialist regimes have traditionally found themselves subject to a wide variety of demands over and above their specifically productive tasks: to contribute to full employment, to undertake political education within the firm, to make workers available for certain local tasks, such as agricultural harvests, and to represent the state in isolated areas.[17]

This multiplicity of tasks is often justified by the fact that the state firm represents social property, and should not be managed according to the narrow criteria of capitalist profitability. The firm must be sensitive to the general interests of society as well (Lange 1965, 12). Maximization and efficiency should be pursued, not at the micro level of the firm as in capitalism, but at the level of the state complex as a whole (Preobrazhensky 1965, 105).

The problem lies not in the multiplicity of goals as such. One could envision an arrangement wherein a limited number of social objectives were communicated to the firm as obligatory parameters, leaving the firm free to maximize one variable.[18] Such a situation would be analogous to a constrained optimization problem in calculus. But the situation observed in socialist regimes is typically quite distinct: a vast number of objectives are communicated to the firm, often in an informal and vaguely articulated manner. The firm's objectives are thus not transparent, and both efficient behaviour and outside evaluation of that behaviour are rendered difficult.

One common expression of the difficulty in clarifying the goals of socialist enterprises is the tension between the goals of gross output maximization and financial efficiency. Output maximization is in contradiction with an emphasis on state accumulation, which requires precisely the attention to "exchange values" to which many socialists are hostile. The emphasis on output at any cost leads to a "productionist" bias in which the state finance system is seen as the handmaiden of the "real" sector.

Triumphant revolutionaries must also address the problem of hierarchy and labour relations within state firms. Once again, precisely because such relations take place within the state complex, they lose the veneer of quasi-inevitability that accompanies capitalist labour relations in their hour of hegemony. After the revolution, labour relations within the state sector reflect back upon the nature of the revolution itself. The drive for productive efficiency can itself injure political alliances. Some optimists, such as Guevara, believed that there is no fundamental dilemma here, that the new regime can generate rising productivity through entirely socialist means: "We affirm that within a relatively short period of time, the development of consciousness can do more to stimulate production than material incentives" (1985, 2: 264). Hence, argued Guevara, there is no real need to attempt to "defeat capitalism with its own fetishes" by relying on material incentives (2:687).

Socialist practice, however, has tended to reflect the pessimism of those such as Preobrazhensky, who argued that "the socialist incentives to labour do not drop from heaven; they have to be developed through prolonged re-education of human nature as it has been shaped in commodity economy, re-education in the spirit of collective relations of production" (1965, 193). Unless Guevara's optimism should some day prove justified, victorious revolutionaries can expect to confront a tension between the goal of increasing labour productivity and that of abandoning "fetishes" of capitalism such as piece-work and Taylorism. We will see in later chapters that the Sandinistas vacillated on the nature of appropriate incentives to work.

The last dilemma to be examined here concerns the relation between revolutionaries and "specialists," that is, professionals and other highly skilled workers. Because they come to power in situations of relative backwardness, catch-up socialists cannot be terribly choosy when staffing the new state. They invariably find that the requirements of the state complex are vastly greater than the supply of politically reliable specialists. The problem is exacerbated by the fact that, even in the midst of such a shortage, the state is expanding its activities into new fields. Thus Guevara commented in 1960 that Cuba needed "specialists, and note that I do not say revolutionary specialists, which would be the ideal. We simply need specialists, whatever their [social] category, whatever mental structure they may possess" (1985, 2:44).

This problem was to a large extent ignored in classical Marxist thought. One finds in Marx's *The Civil War in France*, for example, as in Lenin's *State and Revolution*, a utopian belief that the world can run itself without special expertise. Engels, writing in 1891 to Bebel, expressed the belief that, by the time the German Social-Democrats came to power, "almost absolutely certain" to occur within the decade, the party would have "recruit[ed] enough young technicians, doctors, lawyers and schoolmasters to enable us to have the factories and big estates administered on behalf of the nation by Party comrades" (Marx and Engels 1942, 493).

This, of course, was not the Bolshevik experience. Once the period of War Communism had drawn to a close, managerial positions in the new state were held in large part by "survivors of the former régime" (Carr 1958, 26). A 1922 survey found that only 9 per cent to 13 per cent of bureaucrats supported the Bolsheviks (Griffith-Jones 1981, 70). This state of affairs led Lenin to comment in 1922: "If we look at Moscow with its 4,700 communists in positions of responsibility, and if we compare that to the immense bureaucratic machine, to that great mass, we must ask who is directing whom?" Lenin went on to recall that, often in history, conquered peoples had succeeded in imposing their culture on their conquerors

(1971, 317). By implication, the Bolshevik "conquerors" of Russia were in danger of being overcome by the old bureaucratic culture, a culture intimately related to the interests of the former dominant classes.

The problem of having one's efforts to direct society mediated through a state bureaucracy that is in large part a relic of the previous regime has led socialist leaders to hope that the new regime can produce bureaucrats in its own image and likeness. The FSLN would share this hope. Two key questions are how long such a creation of new socialist bureaucrats might take, and whether "new specialists extracted from the classes of workers and peasants" (Guevara 1985, 2:130) will necessarily be a more pliant medium through which the will of the leadership is expressed.

The Nicaraguan State Complex

The Sandinistas' formation of the "*Area Propiedad del Pueblo*" [People's Property Area or APP] began with Decree 3, issued on the new junta's first day in office on 20 July 1979. The decree confiscated without compensation "all goods belonging to the Somoza family, members of the military and officials who have abandoned the country since December 1977." This measure alone gave the government control of 20 per cent to 25 per cent of both the agricultural and industrial sectors. The entire banking system was nationalized on 26 July. Owners of private banks were to be compensated according to the book value of their holdings, in five-year low-interest bonds. This measure was less significant for the assets seized than for the "commanding height" it gave to the state. In fact the private banking system was close to bankrupt at the time of the nationalization (ECLA 1979, 13). But because of the cyclical nature of agricultural production, Nicaragua's agrarian bourgeoisie was deeply dependent on the banking system. The Sandinistas hoped that this one measure would give it significant control over private production.

Traditional exports, including coffee, cotton, and sugar, were brought under state control in early August.[19] Decree 137 nationalized the mining sector in early November. Though the decree provided for compensation for mine owners, it contained a clause reminiscent of Allende's nationalization of the Chilean copper mines: compensation could be diminished to take into account "the human damage, and ecological deterioration" caused by mining activities and fiscal evasion.[20]

Apart from some other minor sectoral nationalizations, the foregoing measures created the bulk of the APP. Future nationalizations would generally take place on an ad hoc basis. The state sector was therefore an odd beast: while sectoral nationalizations gave the state coherent control in some areas, the blanket nationalization of the

Somoza holdings also gave the government control over a hodgepodge of activities that reflected no grand strategy. This was particularly the case in the industrial sector. As Weeks argues, "While the business empire of the Somoza family was no doubt rationally organized for the purpose of private profitability, it had a structure of little use for purposes of economic planning" (1985b, 289).

It should be noted that, apart from expanding the size of the state sector, the creation of the APP dramatically increased the economy's monopoly sphere, and reduced the scope of competition. The nationalizations in such areas as banking, external trade, and mining monopolized these sectors. The state would also soon move to monopolize imports of basic grains, agricultural inputs, and petroleum.

Goals of state firms. Early statements on the goals of the APP reflected the confusion typical of socialist economies. In early 1980, Minister of Planning Henry Ruiz stated that public firms should meet urgent needs, consolidate new relations of production, promote workers' participation, and "above all, focus all efforts on generating larger surpluses" (*Bda* 20 April 1980). But could firms attend to the first three tasks while devoting "all efforts" to the fourth? Similarly, the 1980 economic plan of the Ministry of Planning (MIPLAN) presented a confused picture. For example, the plan's industrial sector program included among its objectives "maximization of production of food products, popular clothing, medicine, construction materials, and basic inputs for both agriculture and the aforementioned industries; taking into account [the previous objective], maximization of industrial employment; maximization of exports, and rationalization of imports" (MIPLAN 1980, 47–8).

The generation of a surplus was not included among the goals of the sector. This lack of attention to profitability was defended in the name of a "higher" conception of efficiency. As Jaime Wheelock argued, "Efficiency must be social in nature. If, in an effort to obtain surpluses we forget the salaries, the workers' social benefits and the unemployment problems caused by agricultural activities for export purposes, we will be transferring to society an element of instability which represents the cost of social inefficiency" (JPRS 76302).

Throughout the FSLN's decade in power, public statements on the objectives of state firms would continue to have the "wish list" quality of the statements cited here. Even after a shift to greater financial rigour after 1985, planning documents would continue to ignore the tension between financial responsibility and output maximization.

The goals of the state sector would also be confused by what might be termed a "dollar fetish": the view that only objects acquired with foreign exchange are important for economic development. The actions of many state bodies would demonstrate this fetish. Commenting on the lack of profitability of state farms, Joseph Collins wrote:

Some argue that the *volume* of production should be considered more important than profits … For it is the cotton, sugar or coffee (or locally grown food substituted for imported food) that earns the *dollars* or other 'hard' currency that the economy needs. In this view of profitability, the only cost that truly makes a difference is the foreign exchange cost of *imported* inputs such as tractors and fertilizers. Proponents point out that *córdoba* costs are not the same for the state enterprise as for the private enterprise since the government can print *córdobas* (1982, 65).[21]

The statement is an eloquent example of the illusions that control over the "printing press" can foster. Though the 1980 economic plan warned against recourse to monetary emission, Nicaragua would eventually come to suffer one of the worst cases of hyper-inflation since the Weimar Republic.

Contradictions within the new state. Like other socialist revolutionaries before them, the Sandinistas found that staffing the new state was very much a problem of pouring new wine into old wineskins. Tomás Borge commented in 1981 that "our revolution, like others, has the acute problem of scientifically trained cadres. Within the bourgeoisie there are elements who were educated in famous universities, but the contradiction is that those who held the barricades or went to the mountains are not the gentlemen who were educated at Harvard" (1981a).

One observer argues that, in 1979, most "sinecure-oriented bureaucrats simply shifted their loyalty with the change in regime." More skilled administrators, on the other hand, "generally opted to exit." "The result was pulverization of the state apparatus" that left the Sandinistas with a "soft state" (Graham 1987, 19). Though the most highly trained specialists may have left, those who remained wielded significant influence in the new state, according to another observer, since they had more experience than the new cadres placed in the state by the Sandinistas (Bernales 1985, 144).

The Nicaraguan government would soon begin to sign cooperation agreements with various socialist governments that would provide for the overseas training of thousands of Nicaraguan students. By late 1982, there were 700 Nicaraguans studying in the Soviet Union, and Cuba had granted a further twelve hundred scholarships (FBIS 23 December 1982). It was hoped that the return of these students to Nicaragua in the mid- and late-1980s would help create a civil service that combined expertise with loyalty to the revolution.[22] In the mean-time, as one National Directorate member put it, "political and ideo-logical orientation" would seek to guarantee at least the neutrality of specialists, who were "accustomed to high incomes, accustomed to de-veloping values that revolve around the brand of their car, their credit card, the social club to which they belong, or the clothes they wear" (Arce 1980, 8).

I have argued that socialist states did not escape from the problem of "bureaucratic politics," and that these states should be seen as "poly-cephalic," a reality ignored by orthodox writing on planning. Divisions between state bodies were accentuated in the Nicaraguan case by the projection of the FSLN's three tendencies into the new state. The rheto-ric of unity carefully respected by all the members of the National Direc-torate after taking power made it easy to forget the intense bitterness of the splits of the mid-1970s. Indeed, it would become clear after the FSLN's 1990 election loss that the old wounds had never really healed.

Only one member from each of the three tendencies held positions in the first post-victory government, which represented a temporary compromise with the non-FSLN forces that had opposed Somoza. The three were Daniel Ortega for the insurrectionists (member of the gov-ernment junta), Tomás Borge for the prolonged popular war adherents (GPP) (minister of the interior in charge of police and state security), and Jaime Wheelock of the proletarians (ironically, minister of agrarian reform). But by late December 1979, cabinet positions had also been given to Henry Ruiz of the GPP (planning) and Humberto Ortega of the insurrectionists (defence). At the same time, Jaime Wheelock added the agriculture portfolio to his duties.

Thus, by the end of 1979 the three tendencies of the FSLN had marked out their respective "turfs" within the state. A leading Sandin-ista would later comment that "having members of the National Directorate in the government, it was easier to give each a quota of power" (Martínez 1990, 108). The Carter-era U.S. ambassador to Managua, Lawrence Pezullo, commented in a *Wall Street Journal* article of 15 September 1981 that "this isn't a government but a series of fief-doms with a thin veneer covering the anarchy." Since the GPP's Borge built up significant security forces in his Ministry of the Interior, the Sandinistas effectively accepted a situation of dual military power, though the growth of the Ministry of Defence in the mid-1980s would unbalance this initial rough equilibrium. As the rump tendency, Wheelock's "proletarians" placed only one member in the cabinet, and controlled no forces of coercion. Wheelock, however, would make the most of the cards he had been dealt, turning the Ministry of Agriculture (MIDINRA) into an enormous "super-ministry".[23]

It is hard to know to what extent inter-institutional rivalries reflected the prolongation of the tendencies within the state, as opposed to the normal fact that different tasks and bureaucratic locations generate different outlooks. It is safest to say that the presence of the tendencies in the state created a "coincidence of cleavages" that exacerbated problems of bureaucratic politics that would have existed in any case. Thus, MIDINRA's refusal to submit to MIPLAN's bid for dominance within the state probably reflected both the common tension between production and control ministries and the lingering tension between Wheelock and Ruiz.

The Ministry of Planning and Plan 80

One institution that sought to overcome state "feudalism" by gaining control over the economic responsibilities of the new state was MIPLAN, formed on the day after the FSLN took power. Henry Ruiz became minister in late December 1979, and would hold the position until MIPLAN was transformed into the Secretariat for Planning and Budgeting (SPP) in 1985. Days after assuming office, Ruiz declared his hopes that MIPLAN would become the "manager of the entire economy" (*Bda* 30 December 1979).[24] This hope would also be stressed in the 1980 economic plan, which called for a "strengthening of the Ministry of Planning," and a clear identification of ministries such as Wheelock's MIDINRA as "executing institutions" (MIPLAN 1980, 34). This hope would never be realized: MIPLAN never gained control over the state sector, let alone over the economy as a whole.

At the end of 1979, Ruiz presented MIPLAN's "Program of Economic Reactivation for the Benefit of the People" (Plan 80). The plan is the most comprehensive statement of the FSLN's economic strategy upon taking power. Both the broad participation in the drafting of the plan and the diffusion given to the finished document indicate the importance which the leadership gave to the plan. Two qualifications to this should be noted, however. The first is that Plan 80's promotion of MIPLAN control of the state did not enjoy the support of the National Directorate as a whole. The second is that, while the plan promoted a strategy of balanced recovery, it is not clear that the National Directorate ever intended to subordinate other objectives to this strategy. From the very beginning, Sandinista practice diverged greatly from Plan 80's plea for fiscal-financial conservatism.

Plan 80 was an emphatic declaration of the FSLN's commitment to a state-dominant economy. The plan declared at least five times that the state sector would be the "central axis" of the economy (MIPLAN 1980, 13, 20, 22, 33, 67). This state dominance would permit "a gradual transition from a *spontaneous* economic regulation to a *conscious and planned* regulation (both programming and indicative planning) for the whole economy" (25).

The plan sought to lay some of the groundwork for this transition. Among the "urgent measures" proposed for 1980 was the formation of twelve "programmatic coordinating commissions," among which would be commissions for agriculture, industry, finance, and external trade. These commissions would be responsible for making policy recommendations in their areas of competence, and overseeing the implementation of MIPLAN decisions. Each commission would be comprised of representatives of MIPLAN and of the relevant ministries (ibid., 133ff). The plan also promoted the "urgent" tasks of developing planning departments within each executing ministry, whose work would be coordinated with that of MIPLAN, and of developing a centralized statistical system and systems of evaluation to monitor the implementation of the plan.

In examining other elements of Plan 80, we should note that it was primarily concerned with conjunctural, rather than longer-term, questions. Thus, the government was immediately concerned with reactivating the economy after the economic crisis that accompanied the insurrection, and sought to postpone longer-term decisions for a year or two. This strategy is revealed, for example, in Plan 80's investment program, which called for 85 per cent of 1980 investment to be directed towards economic and social infrastructure (ibid., 69). This emphasis allowed the postponement of decisions on how investments would be used to reorient economic production.

Apart from its advocacy of a state-dominant economy, the key question of long-term strategy on which Plan 80 was clear was the need to maintain Nicaragua's agro-export focus. The plan noted that Nicaragua had historically possessed a marked comparative advantage in the agro-export sector, an advantage that derived from both a "productive structure which exploited the work force," and from climate and natural resources (ibid., 55). It was hoped that, even with an attenuation of exploitation in this sector, Nicaragua's comparative advantage would continue to yield significant net foreign exchange earnings.

In its conjunctural strategy, the plan stressed the importance of "three balances": fiscal, macro, and external. The strategy might best be called one of "controlled imbalance." A fiscal deficit equivalent to 13 per cent of GDP was planned, 80 per cent of which was to be financed externally (ibid., 75). This stress on containing the fiscal deficit was joined to repeated pleas to avoid inflation. At one point, the plan argued that "upon tax reform depends the living standards of the masses who are defenceless against inflation. If inflation results from a fiscal deficit caused by an insufficiency of legal taxes, that inflation will effectively represent an illegal tax on the poorest" (129). It was thus hoped that inflation, which stood at 70 per cent in 1979, could be brought down to 22 per cent.

With respect to external balance, the plan projected a trade deficit equal to 12 per cent of GDP (ibid., 120). The plan noted that this deficit "implies postponing the costs of the present process of reactivation. It also implies maintaining our external dependence ... Economic independence is a gigantic and complex task that will be faced by the Nicaraguan people once a basic level of economic reactivation has been achieved" (24). Thus it was hoped that trade could be balanced after 1981, and that Nicaragua could begin paying off its debt in 1983 (89). In a statement that would become prophetic as the decade wore on, the plan stated that the trade deficit of 1980 could not be repeated "without threatening the nature of the Sandinista revolution" (86).

With respect to "macro balance," the plan rejected the strategy of stimulating aggregate demand, despite the existence of excess capacity in the industrial sector. The plan argued that such a strategy would be destabilizing because (i) rigidities existed in short-term agricultural supply; (ii) "the disarticulation of productive and commercial structures" had caused a "series of bottlenecks"; and (iii) in general, the pattern of demand growth caused by a strategy of stimulating aggregate demand would not correspond to the pattern of excess capacity (ibid., 23, 114). Given this analysis of rigidities and bottlenecks, it was expected that services would grow several times faster in 1980 than the goods-producing sectors.

The plan's concern for economic balance led to the rejection of a liberal salary policy. A salary increase, Henry Ruiz warned, would lead to an "uncontrollable increase in prices" (*Bda* 31 December 1979). It was hoped, however, that real living standards would nevertheless improve through the provision of public services, employment generation, and price controls (MIPLAN 1980, 121, 139).

This strategy for improving living standards reflected a fateful political choice. By implementing policies that would benefit a wide range of Nicaraguans, the FSLN was trying to turn the category of "the people" into a political reality, a broad sector firm in its support of the revolution. "The people" would embrace, above all, the urban poor, and hence was a category much broader than that of salaried workers. This sector had played a crucial role in the final insurrection, and the Sandinistas felt that the consolidation of the urban poor's support was crucial for the survival of the revolution.

This focus was not without costs. As Nicaragua's post-World-War-Two development had led to strong rural-urban migration, the country suffered an urban labour surplus and a seasonal labour shortage in rural areas. Unless policies to benefit "the people" were implemented as quickly in rural areas as in the cities, a new impetus for migration into the cities would be created. Increased migration could even nullify the perceived benefits of government policies.[25] The same urban focus could also lead to neglect of the needs of the peasantry.

The stress on "the people" would have serious consequences for salaried workers. It appears that the leadership was fearful of creating a "labour aristocracy" among salaried workers, and was also desirous of channelling workers' energies away from "economistic" demands for salary increases. "Salary," proclaimed Henry Ruiz, "is a trap created by capitalism" (*Bda* 22 December 1979). It would soon become clear, however, that government policies were turning salaried workers into an underclass rather than an aristocracy. The purchasing power of salaries dropped steadily through the 1980s, eroding labour supply in the formal sector and thus working against the consolidation of a socialist economy. Various unsuccessful attempts to reverse this decline would be undertaken in the economic reforms from 1985 on.

Though the strategy of salary restraint and expansion of social services sought to tailor the demand of the popular classes to the foreseeable supply of "popular" goods and services, it is interesting that no similar analysis was applied at the other end of the social spectrum. Both government policy and practice discouraged the importation of non-basic consumer goods. But I have found no discussion in any government document of the tensions that might arise between this practice and the fact that many professionals and bourgeois would be permitted to continue to earn high incomes. This tension would in fact soon contribute to a burgeoning unofficial market.

Stephany Griffith-Jones has argued that Plan 80's concern for economic balance, and particularly its focus on financial responsibility, makes Nicaragua a unique case among socialist revolutions (1983, 596). The actual practice of the government would do much to dissipate this image of uniqueness. The concerns for balance expressed in the plan would repeatedly be dismissed by FSLN leaders as conservative and "technicist," though none of the leaders would ever criticize the plan itself. Indeed, the plan would play a role within the party analogous to that played by the Roman Catholic Church within Nicaraguan society at large: highly respected, but little heeded.

Price policy

In their 1978 political program, the FSLN's insurrectional tendency had promised that "the Sandinista Government will control the prices of all primary necessities: food, clothing, medicine" (1979a, 249). Upon coming to power there was probably no dissent with the high government official who stated that "price controls perform an essential function in the construction of a more humane society" (*Bda* 10 October 1979).

A number of early measures indicated the government's intent to regulate prices. Decree 10, the National Emergency Law issued on 22 July, provided for prison terms of up to two years for anyone changing prices on any good or service whose price had been officially set. The state of emergency declared under this law would last until April 1980. In October 1979, a price freeze for basic products was announced. This was followed by controls on the marketing of basic food products such as beans and maize.[26] In late December, decreases in house rents of 40 per cent to 50 per cent were decreed (*Bda* 20 December 1979). There are numerous indications of difficulties in enforcing these decrees. A communiqué of the Ministry of Internal Trade in January 1980 had to remind people that the penalties for charging excessive prices provided for under Decree 10 are "in effect now" (JPRS 75121). Other reports indicated that few Managua stores were respecting the official price lists (JPRS 75214, 75263).

Plan 80 suggests that the government had not yet confronted the dilemmas inherent in the definition of price policy. The plan declared that "the price level is one of the most visible faces of our Revolution." The fundamental objective of price policy was to be the "defence of the [real] salary of those sectors with the lowest incomes." Yet this must be done without either "disincentivizing production" through low prices to producers, or creating "an excessive cost for the State via subsidies." The plan argued that "under conditions of real shortages, true price controls can only be achieved through rationing," yet declared that such a move "is not desirable under present conditions" (MIPLAN 1980, 96).

The plan then suggested some initial measures: "We must, first of all: guarantee normal supply through a well-organized apparatus of distribution; energetically combat profiteering by intermediaries and speculation; fix official maximum prices, respect for which the State, aided by the mass organizations, will continually monitor, severely punishing any infraction" (ibid.). The plan also stated that prices established by "the organism charged with setting them," which was left undefined, would not be based on the results of "competition," but on a "rigorous analysis of cost," with the application of a determined profit margin for both producers and intermediaries. By abandoning market-determined prices in favour of cost-determined ones, without putting in place a rationing scheme, the plan was essentially opting for "rationing by queues" and its attendant "sellers' market".[27] It is also significant that, while the plan did occasionally mention state accumulation, no such mention occured in the section devoted to price policy. For the time being, the desire to generate popular support by keeping down the prices of basic goods was the prime determinant of policy.

To summarize thus far, the initial questions that had to be addressed by the Sandinistas in their quest for a socialist economy resembled those confronted by other socialist revolutions. As have other revolutionaries, the Sandinistas failed to address clearly some of these issues, such as the objectives of state firms. Like other revolutionaries too, the Sandinistas hoped that specialists trained within the revolution would resolve the tension between expertise and revolutionary loyalty.

However, unlike other cases, the Sandinistas initially created a strategy that proclaimed the importance of financial and other forms of economic balance, and sought to avoid inflation. Yet these concerns would not be translated into practice. Finally, the government's main initial programmatic statement, Plan 80, paid but lip service to the problem of state accumulation, reflecting instead the young government's concern with alliance building.

There were thus similarities between the FSLN's initial situation and that of other revolutionary movements. There were also significant differences. One of the most important of these sprang from the FSLN's decision to seek a long-term *modus vivendi* with the bourgeoisie. This decision must now be examined.

C. THE DILEMMA OF THE BOURGEOISIE

Victorious revolutionaries who pursue "catch-up socialism" find themselves in a complex relation with the bourgeoisie. This complexity is in large part a reflection of the very backwardness within which catch-up socialism is born. One can find three stylized stages in Marx's analysis of the productive roles of owners of means of production.[28] In a first stage, corresponding to pre-capitalist situations and to the earliest manifestations of what Marx calls "manufacture" (1954–9, 1:318ff), the owners of the means of production play either no role or a very limited one in the actual organization of production. Most importantly, they do not monopolize directly productive knowledge, which remains diffused among the direct labourers, because "changes in the methods of production by the subordination of labour to capital" have not yet occurred (180).

In a second stage, the owners of the means of production may monopolize an important segment of productive knowledge, in particular the art of organization. This second stage begins when changes in methods of production leave only the owner with an overall view of the firm's activities. The second stage, in Marx's scheme, slowly passes into a third stage as the owner increasingly hands tasks of supervision and management over to salaried employees (ibid., 3:386). At the extreme, the capitalist comes to be a "coupon-clipper," not far removed from his feudal counterpart, in that he lives off production without taking any direct part in it.

Part of Marx's hope in the long-run ability of socialism to attract support rested on his belief that the evolution of capitalism, by transforming most capitalists into coupon-clippers, would reveal the parasitical nature of private ownership of the means of production (ibid., 3:386ff). He clearly believed that many English capitalists had already reached this third stage. A question that came to trouble some Eastern European theorists is whether this third stage ever really arrives. Even in theory, can the bourgeoisie ever be seen as entirely parasitical? Marx thought so, as he identified the productive activities of the bourgeoisie with "the work of supervision." These activities, obviously, can be delegated to paid management. The troubling question is whether more "entrepreneurial" tasks, those that involve identifying new opportunities for profit and pursuing them, can also be delegated. Some analysts of the economic disequilibria of socialist economies suggest that this entrepreneurial activity provides the capitalist economy with much of the flexibility that socialist economies so conspicuously lack (Kornai 1990; Brus and Laski 1989). Hence, the argument goes, many owners are engaging in a socially useful activity, even if they do not intervene directly in the supervision of production.

This line of argument need not deny that purely parasitical "coupon-clippers" do exist, nor that the "going rate of profit" reflects factors that Marx adduces, such as monopolization of the means of production and compelled surplus labour. But it does hold that entrepreneurial activity can perform a socially useful function, even while it serves to establish the "going" profit rate.[29]

Accepting for the sake of argument that such a third stage might be reached, one can distinguish the distribution of productive knowledge in the three stages. In the first stage, productive knowledge is diffused. In the second, it will tend to be concentrated among the owners of the means of production. In the final stage, productive and organizational knowledge will be concentrated in a group of specialists. If the government wishes to avoid significant economic disruption in the post-insurrection period, in a situation of overall shortage of advanced productive knowledge, it cannot afford to alienate (i) the owners of the second stage, and (ii) the specialists of the third stage. At a purely technical level, it can afford to move against the owners in the first and third stages. This picture becomes more complicated if the different groups examined here are interrelated, for example by family links or by a common ideology. In this case, an attack on the "parasitical" owners of the first and third stages could threaten members of the two groups that one does not wish to alienate. If such links exist, therefore, it will be vital to weaken them before attacking the "parasitical" groups.[30]

Using this three-stage schema, one can hypothesize that revolutions in conditions of backwardness will generally tend to find owners in the first two stages. Hence, while it may be possible for the government to move against first-stage owners, it faces a dilemma in dealing with second-stage owners. The government needs the expertise of these owners, yet it also seeks to consolidate political and economic hegemony.

Victorious socialist revolutionaries have in fact tried to respect this distinction between first- and second-stage owners. While the Bolsheviks were quite willing to have rural landowners dispossessed in the immediate aftermath of the revolution, they were more circumspect in their approach to the industrial bourgeoisie. E.H. Carr notes that extensive nationalization of industry was "no part of the initial Bolshevik programme" (1966, 87), and Nove argues that immediately after taking power, Lenin sought close supervision of private enterprise, rather than nationalization (1969, 42). When the Bolsheviks did nationalize industry in 1918, Carr argues, this nationalization remained purely formal for a time, as the former owners were allowed to continue managing their firms until further notice (1966, 104). Similarly, Kaser and Zielinsky note that much Eastern European industry remained in private hands in the immediate aftermath of World War Two (1970, 21). In the case of Cuba, Carlos Rafael Rodríguez claims that the early policy of the Castro government did not rule out, in principle, the long-term participation of at least part of the national bourgeoisie (1978, 124–5).

Nevertheless, in all of the cases mentioned, the industrial bourgeoisie was to disappear from the scene after a few years, long before it had completed its "historical mission." The dilemma between the need to consolidate control versus the need for bourgeois expertise was in each case resolved in favour of control. Nicaragua is in this respect an unusual case. Let us first examine the situation facing the Sandinistas when they took power in 1979.

The Nicaraguan Bourgeoisie

At a strictly technical level, the FSLN certainly faced productive sectors in the first two stages, and perhaps some in the third.[31] Moreover, the FSLN did face complicating family and ideological links between the different types of owners, and between owners as a whole and the specialists. Traditional cattle ranches owned by absentee landlords or land rented to peasants using traditional technology would be examples of the first stage. The so-called "uncouth bourgeoisie" (*burguesía chapiolla*), medium-scale farmers who participated directly in production, and many owners of small-scale industries, represented second-stage owners. Other sectors of pre-revolutionary Nicaragua are harder to classify. A study of coffee producers in the 1970s found that a majority of medium producers and 67 per cent of large ones did not reside on their farms (Colburn 1984, 504). While it might appear that such absentee landlords probably did not monopolize much directly productive knowledge, it is significant that the technological level of coffee production and yields per hectare varied directly with farm size. Unlike traditional cattle owners who bore a simple rentier relationship to low-yield farms, by the 1970s the coffee bourgeoisie was thus apparently engaged in entrepreneurial tasks: assuring access to credit and to productive inputs, marketing production, and ensuring that a higher technological level of coffee production was sustained. Such was also the case with cotton producers, though many of them also did not directly supervise production. Cotton producers were generally well trained, and observers argue that they wielded valuable technical skills.

Thus, at a purely economic level, had the Sandinistas immediately "expropriated the bourgeoisie," as some leftist critics hoped they would, a serious economic crisis would most likely have resulted. But the FSLN also sought to reach an *entente* with the bourgeoisie for political reasons. Part of the FSLN's success in overthrowing Somoza lay in its tactical alliance with important segments of the bourgeoisie. To have turned on that bourgeoisie immediately after assuming power would have cost the FSLN dearly in terms of both domestic and international support. The FSLN had come into power with the aid of many international forces, some of which were hostile to the party's long-term political project. Humberto Ortega had insisted, as an element of the insurrectional strategy, upon formulating a party program that would garner broad international support, "from the majority of the progressive forces in the world – not just the socialist forces" (1981, 29).

The continued support of these forces was vital for the immediate prospects of the revolution, but that support depended upon projecting a moderate international image. The "progressive" but "non-socialist" international forces that backed the FSLN were watching closely, among other things, the FSLN's relationship to the bourgeoisie. Thus, on 1 August 1979, one of the first editorials of *Barricada* warned against the expression of radical popular demands, since the country urgently required external aid that would only arrive if "normalization" occurred.

Agreement with the bourgeoisie was also helpful in securing aid from sources that could hardly be described as "progressive." The FSLN's caution with respect to the bourgeoisie allowed the *Economist* magazine to comment as late as 1981 that "Nicaragua is not lost yet ... the United States could yet follow Mexico's sound advice to stick a fistful of dollars through a door that remains even a quarter open" ([Ryan] 1982). Jimmy Carter's assistant secretary for inter-American affairs, Viron Vaky, articulated the aims of this approach quite clearly: "If the non-Marxist elements can continue to function and the Sandinista-controlled government can be kept tied into the West's political economy, a Marxist regime can be prevented from consolidating. In time, such an evolution could come about even in spite of the Sandinistas. The implicit conclusion is that it is essential to supply aid to keep the monetary/economic system viable and enmeshed in the international economy, and to support the private sector" (ibid.).

Domestically, there is no reason to believe that the FSLN could automatically count on broad support for an expropriation of the bourgeoisie. The leadership attributed the problematic nature of this support to the underdevelopment of the country's popular classes, which had not yet acquired a sense of their own long-term interests; which is to say that, for the leadership, they were not yet classes in the fullest sense. Thus the very first issue of *Barricada*, on 25 July 1979, proclaimed "the constitution of an active working class" as one of the prime objectives of the revolution.

For both political and economic reasons, then, the Sandinistas decided they would have to pursue their political project in coexistence with the bourgeoisie, at least for a time.[32] But how likely was this class to tolerate the FSLN's attempt to develop a state-dominated mixed economy? There are contradictory indications on this question. On the positive side of the ledger, the Sandinistas faced a bourgeoisie suffering from its own internal contradictions. Foremost among these was the contradiction between the economic interests of the Somoza family and the rest of the bourgeoisie. The disdain of the bourgeoisie not directly linked to the ruling family towards the Somoza sector allowed the triumphant FSLN to expropriate the industrial and agricultural holdings of the Somoza family without significant objections.[33]

The FSLN could also hope to profit from contradictions between medium- and large-scale producers, and between those integrated into "economic groups" and those on the margins. Thus, in August 1979, Daniel Ortega promised that the revolution would promote not just "popular" interests, but also those of sectors "that did not have the opportunity to develop under Somoza" (*Bda* 13 August 1979). The critical question would be whether the Sandinistas could effectively formulate policies that distinguished between these various capitalist sectors.

On the other hand, it has also been argued that the Sandinista project of a state-dominated economy clashed with the "backwardness" of the Nicaraguan bourgeoisie. "Perhaps it would have been easier," commented Sergio Ramírez, "for a less backward, less primitive bourgeoisie ... to understand the rules of the game" (1987, 179). The Sandinistas, argued Argentine observer Carlos Vilas, sought to ensure "the effective functioning of private property as a means of production, not as means of earning a rent. But this implies a state that supervises, through various instruments and channels, the unfolding of this productive function. This is of course a normal aspect of any modern state ... but it was too much for a good part of the Nicaraguan propertied classes" (1984, 238).

It is true that, though the Nicaraguan bourgeoisie had suffered from certain arbitrary actions of the Somoza regime, it had little experience of systematic regulation.[34] A document from the United Nations Economic Commission for Latin America comments that, prior to 1979, "economic policy was characterized by moderation and wholehearted support to the functioning of the market, with few organized social pressures and ability by the Government apparatus to resist such pressures" (ECLA 1979, 5). While the pre-1979 constitution and some laws did proclaim the principle that property must fulfil a "social function" and must be used productively, these principles were not applied to any significant degree.[35]

But to argue that the "backwardness" of the Nicaraguan bourgeoisie was a factor in its eventual conflict with the Sandinistas is to assume that a bourgeoisie accustomed to government regulation in a capitalist environment would be tolerant of the regulation imposed by a Marxist-oriented government. This is in fact a double assumption: (i) that the quality of regulation will not vary significantly between the two types of governments; and (ii) that the bourgeoisie will maintain a "micro" perspective, taking into account only the content of the regulations to which it is immediately subject, and not the broad socio-political situation in which it finds itself. Both assumptions are questionable; the second is particularly problematic, and in fact assumes a bourgeoisie that is "backward" from the point of view of class formation. That is, to believe that the bourgeoisie will maintain a "micro" perspective assumes that this group is mired in an "economistic" attitude that prevents it from acting as a true "class-for-itself." Yet this assumption has been made time and again by observers who claim to be unable to understand why the bourgeoisie reacted so negatively to the FSLN's "generous" policies towards them.[36]

Far from attributing the conflicts between the FSLN and the bourgeoisie to the latter's "backwardness," I believe that the Sandinistas in fact faced a class-conscious bourgeoisie, and that they did their best to make it less so. The thesis of bourgeois "backwardness" is precisely one of those ideas that minimize the dilemmas of "catch-up socialism," since it holds out the hope that a more "modern" bourgeoisie would have acquiesced to the Sandinista project.

The fact that the bourgeoisie as a whole was not fanatically opposed to any new state role in the economy is shown by the support given by much of that class to the Plan of Government issued by the government junta-in-exile in June 1979. The plan was drafted by a group of "40 Nicaraguan experts" convoked by the FSLN, many of who were prominent in the bourgeois opposition to Somoza (NYT 10 July 1979).[37]

The Plan of Government merits careful study as it represented a consensus between the Sandinista and the non-Sandinista opposition to Somoza. Drafted at a time when the Sandinistas were desperate to avoid foreign intervention in Nicaragua, the plan is neither a pure reflection of Sandinista thinking nor a wish list of the non-Sandinista opposition, but a statement of policies that both sides declared themselves ready to accept.

For the non-Sandinista opposition to Somoza, the Plan of Government would come to represent the so-called "original program" of revolution, the original program that some would later claim the Sandinistas had "betrayed".[38] The bourgeoisie, in particular, appealed to the clause that stated that the new government would "advance towards the formation of a mixed economy, in which will coexist: an area of state and social property, of clearly delimited characteristics and scope, whose main elements will be defined beforehand; a private sector and a third sector made up of joint or coordinated public and private investments" (JGRN 1980).[39] Critics of the FSLN would argue that it had failed to define the limits of the state sector, hence undermining the original promise of a mixed economy.[40]

But there was much more to the Plan of Government than the clause just cited, and it is indeed remarkable that much of the bourgeoisie used the plan as the basis for its political activity. The plan vested in the state control over "natural resources, including mines, forests, fisheries, energy, etc."; traditional agro-exports, representing the lion's share of Nicaragua's exports; imports of productive inputs for agriculture; and internal prices, including land rents. The plan also called upon the state to channel foreign financing towards priority sectors, and cited the need for both higher tax levels and a more progressive tax system. Finally, the plan called for a "substantive adjustment" in the banking system, that would promote "the national interest and the common good," and "avoid the concentration of economic power." Thus, the June 1979 Plan of Government, though calling for a clear delimitation of the public sector, also countenanced extensive state involvement in the economy as a whole. Though critics of the FSLN could find in the plan ammunition for their attacks, the FSLN could also invoke the plan to justify its own actions.

An interesting counterfactual question is how the history of the revolution would have been different had the Sandinistas remained within the limits of the Plan of Government. Could the FSLN have avoided conflict with the bourgeoisie and its political allies? Certainly the bourgeoisie would have had much less cause for complaint: it would have enjoyed a greater presence within the state, and greater security of property rights. One could argue, on the other hand, that the post-1979 bourgeoisie spoke so highly of the plan only because it felt the plan was not being respected by the Sandinistas, and that it could therefore serve as a political instrument in the campaign against the FSLN. Had the Sandinistas actually maintained an unwavering respect for the limits set by the plan, it is quite possible that the bourgeoisie would have been less enamoured of it.

One can never know, of course, because the Sandinistas quickly chose another path. However the bourgeoisie might have viewed the actual implementation of the June 1979 Plan of Government, the fact that a significant segment of the bourgeoisie gave even rhetorical support to the plan undermines the image of bourgeois backwardness proffered by some observers of the revolution.

FSLN Strategy towards the Bourgeoisie

For clues to the Sandinistas' strategy towards the bourgeoisie upon taking power, we may return to MIPLAN's 1980 economic plan, which repeatedly declared that the state sector would be the "axis" of the Nicaraguan economy. How did the FSLN hope to attain bourgeois cooperation with this project of a state-dominated economy? The plan simply noted that the private sector must support this process in order to enjoy "state support" (MIPLAN 1980, 32). Given the state's control over financing, this was a significant warning.

A further warning was issued in Henry Ruiz's public introduction to the plan: "If private enterprise does not become active, if it waits to see what is going to happen here, then the Revolution will take the necessary measures, and unproductive large estates will disappear. If private enterprise does not understand that the secret of harmony consists in all of us working for the benefit of the people, it will have made a grave error" (*Bda* 30 December 1979). The threat of eventual expropriation was thus added to that of cutting off access to credit. But carrots accompanied these sticks. Plan 80 promised the formation of permanent corpo-ratist-type bodies for the industrial, agricultural, and trade sectors, with representation from various social sectors to ensure dialogue over sec-toral economic policies. Cooperation with the economic plan would be a "patriotic test" for the bourgeoisie, and a positive response would per-mit a clearer definition of the "rules of the game" so devoutly sought by business leaders (MIPLAN 1980, 14).

In the industrial sector, the plan called for production agreements between the state and private enterprise. Such agreements would guar-antee the necessary inputs and financing to the firm, at fixed prices, in return for guaranteed delivery of final output to the state. The agree-ment would guarantee a "reasonable profit rate" (ibid., 53). Had pri-vate businesses been willing to enter into such production agreements, they would have been left in a position quite analogous to state firms in the traditional socialist economy model: the firm would cede – for the life of the agreement – decision-making power over sources of sup-ply, and over the composition and disposition of its production.

One can also note that the state-private sector relation envisioned in the production agreement strategy left great room for "X-inefficiency" (Liebenstein 1966). To guarantee private firms cost-based prices was to shield them from the "discipline of the market." Had private firms been interested in entering into such production agreements, eco-nomic relations between the private and public sectors would probably have come to be dominated by the same cat-and-mouse games found in socialist economies.[41] In any case, the private sector did not respond to the invitation.[42]

Though the Sandinistas felt constrained to accept the survival of the bourgeoisie, they recognized the potential costs of this decision. Accep-tance of the bourgeoisie meant acceptance of an inevitable opponent of the FSLN's socialist project, an opponent that wielded considerable eco-nomic and ideological influence. The bourgeoisie had close ties to the Roman Catholic Church, and its continued control over economic as-sets and media outlets meant that it could cause the FSLN economic and political damage, through either direct sabotage or mere passivity. We will see in the next chapter that the bourgeoisie would soon prove will-ing to bring these assets to bear in an ideological campaign against the FSLN, and that the FSLN would quickly launch an ideological offensive of its own.

Having no confidence in its long-term relations with the bourgeoisie, the Sandinistas hoped that the bourgeoisie would do out of necessity what it failed to do out of love. It was felt that the state's control over the financial system would give it the leverage to orient the bourgeoisie and divert its resources towards state-determined objectives. As early as 1973,

Sandinista theorist Ricardo Morales had commented on the strategic nature of the Nicaraguan banking system: because of the cyclical nature of
the agricultural economy, Morales argued, producers were highly dependent upon the financial system in order to complete their productive cycle (1983, 138–9).[43]

Jaime Wheelock articulated the FSLN's hopes for the state financial
system in a speech made in early 1981. After the private producer has
paid interest on loans, export taxes, income taxes, and so forth, "he will
retain some amount of money, probably an important amount. This he
will have to keep somewhere, usually in the banks. So this money is also
available to be used for the global economy ... We have not had to expropriate the means of production, though if truth be told, what we are
expropriating are the surpluses" (1981a).

It would soon become clear that this view was mistaken, and that the
FSLN had seriously overestimated the degree to which it could control
the bourgeoisie's disposition of its profits. The error lay in considering
financial systems in the abstract, isolated from their broader socio-political context. For people to deposit their profits in the bank, they must
obviously trust that the financial system will protect the value of their assets, and will return them upon demand. Particularly in the case of a
state banking system, this trust depends upon the trust placed in the
government as a whole. The Sandinista banking system, unlike that
which existed before 1979, simply did not enjoy the confidence of the
bourgeoisie. Over time, the bourgeoisie would discover a plethora of alternatives to placing their money in the state banking system, such as
using material objects as stores of value, or converting *córdobas* into
dollars on the unofficial market. In fact, it will be argued in later chapters that certain government policies would actually create incentives to
do this.

The relation with the bourgeoisie would provide a continual challenge for the FSLN. "Men must either be caressed or else annihilated,"
wrote Machiavelli, "they will revenge themselves for small injuries, but
cannot do so for great ones" (1950, 9). The FSLN leaders felt that the
conditions under which they took power did not permit them to annihilate the bourgeoisie, but neither their own socialist project nor the ideological orientation of their followers would permit a loving caress. This
dilemma would prove to be one of the most serious faced by the FSLN.

D. AGRARIAN REFORM

The evolution of Sandinista policy towards agrarian reform paralleled
the evolution of their overall economic project. Beginning from a position that emphasized state production, the FSLN would gradually be

forced by political factors to accept the growth of "lower" and more "backward" productive forms. Throughout, their policy would reflect the tensions that have historically marked Marxian socialist thinking on the peasant question.

Marx insisted that the perpetuation of small-hold agriculture implied the perpetuation of "universal mediocrity" (1954–9, 1:713–14). As early as 1844 Marx warned against land parcelling (Draper 1978, 406). His arguments against peasant agriculture were based partly on productivity grounds. Marx argued that "proprietorship of land parcels by its very nature excludes the development of social productive forces of labour, social forms of labour, social concentration of capital, large-scale cattle farming, and the progressive application of science" (1954–9, 3:807). Marx thus wrote to Engels that, without socialization of the land, "Father Malthus would prove to be right" (Draper 1978, 407).

But Marx's view of peasant agriculture also reflected his vision of socialism as the realm of "directly social" labour. "Small landed property," he wrote, presupposes "that not social, but isolated labour predominates." Hence "small landed property creates a class of barbarians standing halfway outside of society, a class combining all the crudeness of primitive forms of society with the anguish and misery of civilised countries" (1954–9, 3:813).

The political dilemma arising from this position is clear: how can a socialist revolution triumph if it is opposed to a property form in which much of the population places its hopes? Marx at some point might have hoped that capitalist development would solve the problem by eliminating peasant production before a socialist revolution became a possibility, but his studies of France circa 1848 suggested to him that this might not be the case, and that the peasantry could play an important role in frustrating proletarian aspirations.

Shortly before his death, Engels stated the political problem clearly. "Small production," he confidently declared, "is irretrievably going to rack and ruin." He went on to note, however, that "in the meantime," a workers' party could not take power without a base of support in the countryside. Yet this base must be established "without violating the basic principles of the general socialist programme" (Marx and Engels 1969, 3:458ff). Socialists ever since have sought to square this circle.

Lenin grappled with this dilemma throughout his political life. He wrote in the 1890s that socialists must oppose measures to promote the survival of the peasantry. This view was reflected in early Bolshevik programs (Carr 1966, 26). But the Bolsheviks also knew they were in competition with other parties more sympathetic to peasant aspirations. Thus in early 1917 they sought to wrest support away from the

Provisional Government by calling upon peasants to take over land without hurting production (37).

As would later socialists, including the Sandinistas, the Bolsheviks hoped that the political dilemma could be solved by convincing peasants that their future lay in collective agriculture. Attempts in 1918 to foster voluntary collectivization, however, met with "total defeat" (ibid., 160). The Bolsheviks were thus forced to accept the expansion of peasant production as a price for attaining peasant support during the civil war.

Throughout the early years of the revolution, however, Lenin remained conscious of what he believed to be the long-term costs of this policy. Even as the party was calling upon peasants to seize land, he declared that only "large-scale cultivation for social account" could "deliver mankind from mass poverty" (ibid., 37). As did Marx, Lenin opposed peasant production both on productivity grounds and because of its implications for the project of "directly social" labour. On the basis of peasant production, he argued, "capitalism persists and arises anew in a bitter struggle against communism," fostering "private speculation and profiteering, as against state procurement of grain (and other products) and state distribution of products in general" (1968, 277). Peasant production, in other words, is a barrier to the socialist economy.

This factor would influence much later Bolshevik policy. It is important to bear in mind that when socialist revolutionaries in power debate the best form of agricultural organization, they will take into account not merely such technical data as output per hectare, but also the relative "productivity" of various forms of organization in generating deliveries to the state.[44] A state or collective farm may be preferred on these grounds, though total yields are lower than those of peasant holdings. Thus, despite the drops in harvests owing to the Soviet collectivization drive, grain deliveries to the state increased (Nove 1969, 239).

Like other socialist movements, the FSLN promised peasants an extensive agrarian reform. The party's 1969 program stated that the revolutionary government would "freely transfer land to the peasants in accordance with the principle that the land should belong to those who work it" (FSLN 1981, 21). Small-hold production would be respected, though the voluntary formation of cooperatives would be encouraged. The insurrectional tendency's 1978 program ratified this promise, promising that all lands expropriated from the Somoza family and its allies would be given to "landless peasant families and all those who wish to go work the land" (1979a, 246).

The Sandinistas did not keep these promises, until they were pressured by political factors into doing so. Their initial strategy was to retain all expropriated lands under state control. This strategy was affected by the same views that had influenced other socialist revolutions. There was first a belief within the Sandinista leadership that large state farms would be more efficient and that economies of scale outweighed dis-economies at almost any level of production. Daniel Ortega commented that "it is more profitable for 10,000 peasants to work in a large farm than for each one to work separately" (*Bda* 25 October 1979). For Jaime Wheelock, state production was more efficient than both peasant and large private agriculture: "In underdeveloped societies the scale of production of a local owner can never permit the same possibilities for development, for mechanization, for intensive use of technology as exist in a firm managed by the state" (1983, 92–3).

The quest for a socialist economy also created a bias for large-scale production. As an official of the Ministry of Internal Trade told me in 1983, it was much easier to control the rice market, in which forty farms produce 80 per cent of output, than the bean market, with its 250,000 producers. In this respect, large private farms had an advantage over peasant production, since the former could be "submitted to some planning mechanisms," while small production permitted at best "indicative planning" (ibid., 116).[45]

The leadership saw yet another benefit of large-scale production: its salutary impact upon the peasantry, which was held to suffer from what Jaime Wheelock termed "cultural or ideological weakness" (*Bda* 6 March 1980). Handing out individual plots, Wheelock argued, ran the risk of returning to the "rudimentary and primitive" peasant state those who had already reached the "higher historical stage" of the proletariat (Wheelock 1981b, 21, 23).[46] On the other hand, Wheelock argued, the peasant's participation in "higher forms" of production was part of the process of becoming a "new man" (1986c, 47).[47] Thus, Wheelock felt that the revolution should eventually abolish both large and small private farms (*Bda* 19 August 1979).

These comments indicate a great distance between the Sandinista leadership at the moment of taking power and the "actually existing" peasantry. This distance reflected tendencies in Marxism, but it was also an expression of the social origin and guerrilla experience of the leadership. None of the nine FSLN leaders shared the peasant background of much of Nicaragua's population, nor did the peasantry ever participate directly in the movement to the same extent as other social classes.

Fonseca (1985, 1:118) originally followed Guevara (1985, 1:63) in believing that peasants would make up the bulk of the guerrilla forces. After peasant desertions from the Pancasán guerrilla column in 1967, however, Fonseca concluded that peasants should not participate in regular guerrilla columns (1985, 1:163). Peasant participation was thereafter generally limited to logistical support. Tomás Borge would later comment that before 1979 the FSLN "drew only some sectors of the peasantry into the struggle," adding that peasants "are not yet – nor do I think they ever will be – the principal force in Nicaragua's revolutionary changes" (Borge 1987, 60).

The essential urbanism of the movement and its leadership was obscured by the mystique of the "*montaña*," the place where the "new man" is born (Cabezas 1982), the place where the "honest men, those who are sacrificing all for their people" are to be found (Lang 1979).[48] But the presence of isolated guerrilla columns in remote parts of the country never translated into a close relation with the Nicaraguan peasantry. Thus, there was neither a peasant penetration of the movement's leadership, nor were the leaders able to understand the experience of the peasantry "from the inside," and integrate it with their Marxism. After the triumph they would essentially relate to the peasantry "from the outside." It is not surprising that relations with the peasantry proved one of the most serious problems for the revolution. After losing power, Daniel Ortega commented that "to lose something, you have to have it, and the truth is that we didn't lose the *campesinos*, simply because we never had them" (First FSLN Congress 1991).

This distance between the FSLN and the peasantry created an interesting convergence between the Sandinistas and their opponents on the peasant question. After 1979, the Ministry of Agriculture would promote the physical relocation and concentrations of peasants. This resettlement process, accelerated by the "imperialist military aggression," was seen as promoting "high levels of socialization" (Wheelock 1985b, 90ff). The anti-Marxist opposition, however, also favoured resettlement projects. A 1980 statement of the Democratic Conservative Party declared that such projects would allow rural dwellers to "benefit from the advances of civilization and raise their standard of living" (*Psa* 9 March 1980). Even though the peasantry had displayed much resistance to such projects throughout the 1980s, the opposition's platform for the 1990 electoral campaign promoted the physical concentration of peasants, in order to bring them "the benefits of civilization" (UNO 1989). This convergence points out an affinity between certain aspects of Marxist and non-Marxist modernization tendencies.

Thus, upon coming to power, the FSLN contemplated no "peasant solution" to the problem of landlessness. In a speech to the FSLN-led Rural Workers' Union in December 1979, Jaime Wheelock implied two alternatives for the landless. One was to work on state farms, where each worker was a "Free Person," because the state was not a "new boss," but a "state of the workers and producers."[49] The other was to move to a remote part of the country. Nicaragua did not lack unused land, Wheelock proclaimed, hence agrarian reform should be, not a "distribution of land," but a "distribution of people and an adventure of colonization" (*Bda* 22 December 1979). Wheelock here came perilously close to identifying the new government's policy with that of the ousted Somoza regime.[50]

Initially, the reluctance to distribute expropriated land extended to cooperatives. Upon meeting a worker who asked that a farm be made into a cooperative rather than a state farm, Jaime Wheelock answered: "The state has revolutionary plans that will increase production in a spectacular fashion, and no-one but the state can globally direct these plans" (*Bda* 15 January 1980). By mid-1980 only 7 per cent of the reformed sector was made up of cooperatives, the rest being state farms (Kaimowitz and Thome 1982, 230).

Though the FSLN's views on the disposition of expropriated land has been examined here as a consequence of the Sandinista quest for a socialist economy, and a continuation of orthodox Marxian thinking on the peasantry, other factors also came into play. Given the symbiosis between landlessness and the needs of the agro-export sector, plans to reactivate that sector could have been frustrated by an extensive transfer of land to the peasantry. Jaime Wheelock declared that "handing over land without planning, without a vision of our reality and of our future, would abolish our export economy" (*Bda* 20 May 1980). One could also make the case that turning expropriated agro-export farms over to peasant cooperatives might have led to part or all of those farms being diverted to domestic crop production, at least in the short term. Failing that, agro-export cooperatives may have generated a new rural elite.[51]

Whatever the specific mix of reasons for the FSLN's initial policy on expropriated land, it is striking that the leadership, normally so attuned to the political implications of economic decisions, viewed the land question in extremely economic terms, and tended to give little importance to the peasantry's demand for individual land ownership. The Sandinista preference for state farms was pursued to the extent of forcing cooperatives, formed by landless peasants who immediately prior to the triumph had seized farms belonging to allies of the dictatorship, to be turned over to the state (M. Ortega 1989, 207). Only several years later, when the contra war was at its height, did the government begin explicitly to use the distribution of land to individuals and cooperatives as a key means of weakening the contras' rural support.

In studying the speeches of the nine National Directorate members, I have found only one suggestion during the first year of the revolution that the political implications of the use of the expropriated land be examined carefully. In August 1979, directorate member Victor Tirado commented that "we should use this Somocista land so that when they invade they'll be met by a people united with its army" (*Bda* 12 August 1979). In an apparent answer to Tirado's concerns, Jaime Wheelock proclaimed that "there is no danger of a counterrevolution" (*Bda* 14 September 1979).[52] Years later, with the advantage of hindsight, Tomás Borge would term the failure to distribute the expropriated land to the peasantry one of the greatest mistakes of the FSLN's decade in power (FBIS 16 February 1990).

E. CONCLUSION

The FSLN's initial approach to questions such as the agrarian reform, relations with the bourgeoisie, formation of the state sector, and price policy, was more than a pragmatic response to the needs of the moment. In each case, we find policy choices influenced by the drive for a state-dominant economy. The groundwork was being laid for a socialist economy: a significant share of economic activity was in state hands, and control of the economy's "commanding heights" was expected to yield control over non-state producers. The sphere of the market and competition was being reduced, both through market controls and through the monopolization of key economic activities.

Unfortunately for the Sandinistas, their project was fraught with dilemmas, dilemmas that have manifested themselves in other socialist experiences, and of which the leadership was only partly aware. These dilemmas would not be long in making themselves felt in the 1979–81 period, to which we now turn.

4 Reconstruction and Consolidation: 1979–81

Upon coming to power in July 1979, the FSLN was faced with the urgent and interrelated tasks of economic reconstruction and political consolidation. By the end of 1981, it was clear that the reconstruction had fallen short of its objectives. The 1980 and 1981 economic plans had called for a total gross domestic product (GDP) growth of 45 per cent for the biennium. Such growth would have returned GDP to 98 per cent of its 1977 level, largely reversing the economic collapse of the insurrection period. Instead, GDP rose only 10.25 per cent over the two years, leaving 1981 GDP at just under three-quarters of its 1977 level (ECLA 1979–82; ECLAC 1983–8).

The process of political consolidation appeared more successful, in that the FSLN had firm control of the state. In retrospect, however, one can see that the Sandinistas' chances of establishing a thoroughgoing political hegemony had been seriously reduced, in that the organized bourgeoisie had moved into firm opposition.[1] In addition, the state was itself in turmoil. Finally, rural pressures were preparing the ground for an eventual reduction in the state's influence in the countryside.

Despite the difficulties facing the FSLN by late 1981, the period examined in this chapter would later look like the golden years of the revolution. These were the years of the revolution's greatest triumphs, the most notable of which was the literacy crusade, which taught hundreds of thousands of people basic literacy skills and gave thousands of volunteer urban youth their first contact with the Nicaraguan countryside. This was also a period of rapidly expanding health and education services, including vaccination drives that relied on mass mobilization and won praise from UNICEF.

This chapter will follow our four issue-areas: the state sector, price policy, relations with the bourgeoisie, and agrarian reform. Section A will examine the failed attempt of the Ministry of Planning (MIPLAN) to gain control over economic policy, the problem of "bureaucratism," and tensions in relations with state specialists. The section will also discuss the production-maximizing orientation of state firms. Section B, on price policy, will examine the rise of unofficial-market phenomena in the 1979–81 period, as well as the continuing contradictions in state price policy. Attention will also be paid to the drop in real prices for peasant products and in real salaries. Section C will argue that the fundamental conflict between the bourgeoisie and the Sandinistas in the period was about power: what the bourgeoisie felt the government must do to guarantee the bourgeoisie's long-term interests was incompatible with what the FSLN felt it must do to consolidate its power and to lay the groundwork for change. The section will examine the frustration of the bourgeoisie's basic long-term objectives, and the FSLN's attempts to neutralize the bourgeoisie's political resources. Finally, Section D will focus on the 1981 agrarian reform law, and the Sandinistas' continued rejection of a small-holder-oriented agrarian reform.

A. ORGANIZATION OF THE STATE SECTOR

The Frustrations of MIPLAN

Though MIPLAN's 1981 economic plan spoke triumphantly of the Nicaraguan state having "converted itself into the expression of the popular will" (1981a, 173), MIPLAN's fundamental view throughout this period was that the state was a chaotic beast riven by "institutional feudalism" and characterized by "incoherence, disorganization, [and] lack of discipline" (MIPLAN 1981b). In other words, MIPLAN officials were frustrated by their inability to establish control over the state.

The "programmatic coordinating commissions," which the 1980 economic plan had termed "the principal instrument to control the implementation of the plan" (MIPLAN 1980, 36), and which sought to guarantee each executing ministry's commitment to the central plan, "never quite got off the ground" in the words of one observer (Ruccio 1987, 70). An analysis in *Barricada* on 17 May 1980 noted that state ministers were resisting the commissions, arguing that ministries should be responsible only to the government junta. The National Directorate, acting through the junta, could have ordered ministers to participate fully in the coordinating commissions. But the directorate, while united in its support of planning in theory, was divided on the status of MIPLAN.

The 1981 economic plan repeated MIPLAN's call for "a process of [state] centralization in order to strengthen the unified direction of the economy" (MIPLAN 1981a, 18).[2] More specifically, the plan made a bid to supplant competing ministries in seeking external cooperation, assigning foreign exchange, and authorizing investment (130). Yet, as had happened the previous year, many of the crucial policies of the 1981 plan were simply ignored. One recommendation concerning credit policy was of particular interest because it illustrates the tension between Ruiz's MIPLAN and Wheelock's Ministry of Agriculture (MIDINRA). The 1981 plan insisted that the 1980 policy of giving producers 100 per cent financing of their working and investment capital requirements had been a transitional policy reflecting an "exceptional" situation (40).[3] The plan called for no more than 64 per cent financing of working and investment capital in 1981, and warned sternly that "in no case will 100% of the working capital needed for a production programme be financed" (144). The recommendation was a sensible one, and well within the capacity of the government to implement, but it was not followed. The call for financial prudence – which was also a call to remember the objective of state accumulation – clashed with the "productionist" emphasis of MIDINRA, which felt itself immediately responsible for maximizing agricultural production. The problem of state disaccumulation through credit policies would not really be addressed until mid-1988.

The unpublished summary of an internal seminar held in MIPLAN in November 1981 indicates both the frustrations and the aspirations of MIPLAN officials at this time. The document criticizes the lack of organization in the state, and is highly critical of the lack of coordination of public sector productive activities. Making yet another bid for control within the state and over the economy in general, the ministry called for the "legalization and making obligatory of the economic plans," and the development of a system of "rewards and punishments" that would force all economic sectors to respond to the plan (MIPLAN 1981b).

Events, however, were moving in exactly the opposite direction. MIPLAN's 1982 plan was not approved by the National Directorate (Cabieses 1986), and was never published. Subsequent plans, though approved, were also not published, giving MIPLAN an increasingly low profile within the state, until it was abolished in 1985. MIPLAN's successor, the Secretariat for Planning and Budgeting (SPP), would be given a more modest role from the outset. The National Directorate had apparently decided it would have to live with a "poly-cephalic" state.[4]

It is not at all clear what would have happened had MIPLAN's bid for control been successful. The call for obligatory economic plans represented a striking lack of realism: MIPLAN clearly did not have the information base needed to devise a viable plan, and it was doubtful whether such a base could ever be developed.[5] It is probable that making such plans obligatory would have generated so many evasion tactics among economic actors, including those within the state, that it would have simply cast a heavy "veil" over the economy, rendering it opaque to central planners.

The call for obligatory planning also had to take into account the strong and unpredictable impact of exogenous factors such as international commodity prices upon the Nicaraguan economy. But to this problem the MIPLAN seminar offered what it felt was a viable solution, one that reveals much about the unspoken assumptions of MIPLAN officials: "an increasing integration of the Nicaraguan economy with the centrally planned socialist economies," the seminar participants argued, would allow the planning of export prices and volumes (MIPLAN 1981b).

If MIPLAN's call for obligatory planning reveals a certain lack of realism with respect to the country's economic situation, there were other signs of involution. Union leaders, including those from the Sandinista Workers' Central (CST), criticized MIPLAN for having failed to consult mass organizations while preparing the plan, as had been done for Plan 80 (*Bda* 10 December 1980).[6] Economist Roberto Pizarro would later comment that those at MIPLAN were obsessed with drawing up material balances, and thought that any other approach to the economy was "IMF-ish" (Martínez 1990, 110).

"Bureaucratism"

By late 1980, FSLN leaders were expressing great concern over the growth of the state bureaucracy and the ills of "bureaucratism." Central government employment had risen from 26,000 in 1977 to 52,000 in 1981 (OEDEC 1977, 171; INEC 1986).[7] Thus, an economy that had shrunk by a quarter was supporting a bureaucracy that had doubled in size. Part of this increase reflected the growth of state social services such as health and education. But a portion reflected the desire of some Sandinista leaders to expand their "turf" within the state. Wheelock responded to the fact that his "proletarian" tendency controlled only MIDINRA by turning it into an empire: while most ministries made do with one or two vice-ministers, MIDINRA had five. By 1986, MIDINRA had 4,243 employees on its payroll, twelve times the size of the Ministry of Industry (SPP data).

The National Directorate's Bayardo Arce complained in late 1980 that "a new disease has emerged, 'assistants-ism'. Everybody now has assistants" (Arce 1986, 44). In a speech to CST leaders, Henry Ruiz commented: "You have said that we have a bureaucratic state, and I want to tell you that you are right, we have a state that is pompous and heavy, but it wasn't made this way on purpose. When we took power, everything was undone, and we had to organize the revolutionary State in any way possible. And what we finally did was fill the ministries, give everyone jobs there, because at the time the fundamental goal was to create jobs for the people" (1981).

There were concerns not merely that the state had grown, but that it was hopelessly inefficient. Worries were expressed over "sectorialism," defined as a focus on the specific tasks of one's institution, "while ignoring the goal of consistency with other programs" (*Bda* 7 June 1980). This was linked to the oft-condemned "what-has-that-got-to-do-with-me-ism".[8] Concerns over bureaucratic inefficiency led to what might be called "exceptionalism," allowing specific institutions to bypass the control structures that were being developed.[9]

To a large degree, the FSLN's anti-bureaucratism rhetoric reflected contradictions in its own vision: it wanted the state to do much more than it had traditionally done, yet it did not want state growth. It wanted an economy organized along essentially bureaucratic lines, yet without "bureaucratism." This ill was never clearly defined, and the FSLN critique reflected in part the romantic illusion that activity in the state, as elsewhere, should be "directly social": the bureaucrat should know, without being told, how to harmonize her particular tasks with those of the revolution as a whole. The "big picture" should be self-evident to everyone. A less idealistic view would recognize that no work can get done without a large measure of "sectorialism," and that it is up to the upper levels of the state administration to ensure that the particular focuses of workers in various institutions combine to generate harmonious results. While "sectorialism" within the new state may have become excessive, this was in part an expression of the National Directorate's own inability to resolve its internal contradictions.

Interestingly, Sandinista leaders at times linked bureaucratism with popular input into decision making. Bayardo Arce commented: "Popular participation can lead to bureaucratism. For example, if a company's production plan has to be discussed at various levels, there is the danger that the plan will lose applicability, because it has to go through various filters and discussions which can eventually translate into restrictions on the plans" (Ortega, Wheelock, and Arce 1986, 167).[10]

Sandinista concerns over bureaucratism influenced the relation with state specialists. Following a time-honoured tradition of attributing current problems to the residual effects of the *ancien régime*, Sandinista officials often suggested that problems of bureaucratism reflected the presence of old specialists and old values in the new state. Thus Henry Ruiz criticized those state workers who sought to "maintain the separation, the class differentials, because they have a specialized training" (1980). In a comment typical of the time, one official condemned state workers "who have not wanted to understand that a revolution has occurred in this country" (*Psa* 9 April 1980).

A decade later, one high-ranking specialist would comment that "in the beginning, everyone who was not a guerrilla, who had not participated directly in military actions, was considered a bourgeois" (Martínez 1990, 66–7). Non-Sandinista specialists watched with concern the formation of FSLN cells in state offices, and the increasing frequency of political meetings.[11] Increasing tensions with the bourgeoisie led to heightened Sandinista suspicion of those considered to be the bourgeoisie's real or potential allies within the state (101).[12]

Tensions with state specialists were heightened by the salary question. Though the 1979 budget law had oriented the ministries of planning and finance to devise a salary policy that would "retain within the state an adequate supply of qualified human resources" (Decree 130), the view that prevailed advocated a narrow salary "fan" between low-level and upper-level personnel. This resulted in a ceiling on state salaries that made it hard to compete with the private sector for specialists, and "led to an important exodus of professionals" (Martínez 1990, 59).[13] Though FSLN leaders would later admit that this policy had been costly (Borge 1984b, 152), the standard response to the problem in the early years was to exhort state specialists to be less selfish. Thus, the 1981 economic plan stated that "three-quarters of our country's labour force earns salaries under C$2,000. For this reason the salaries of our specialists will be in accordance with the possibilities of our economy and will not be augmented substantially. This will put to the test their consciousness and patriotism" (MIPLAN 1981a, 178).

Though the policy was costly, it is not clear that there existed an unambiguously superior alternative: offering specialists high salaries at a time when salaries in general were being compressed would have been politically costly, and would also have created tensions with the government's policy of constraining luxury-goods imports.

State Enterprise Behaviour

State firms during this and later periods were generally motivated by a "productionist" rather than an "accumulationist" philosophy. This is attested to by both the inability of many of these firms to repay bank credit and their very lack of concern to do so. Colburn notes that, at the end of the first agricultural season, state enterprises under the control of MID-

INRA "repaid much less than half of the credit they had been extended by the bank" (1990, 45).[14] Colburn's study of state farms also indicates a general lack of interest in financial questions and cost control.[15]

State managers could defend their firms' poor financial performance by citing the wide range of demands being placed upon them by their responsible ministries. In the countryside, it appears that state farms were operating as employers of last resort. Colburn notes that employment on state farms increased 25 per cent within two years of confiscation (1989, 181).

The 1981 economic plan insisted that the productionist orientation of state firms be harmonized with a concern for financial rigour. The plan criticized the "lack of financial discipline in the APP [People's Property Area]" (MIPLAN 1981a, 164). Yet there was an ambiguity in the economic plan's position on accumulation, an ambiguity that would haunt state firms for years to come. All APP firms should be profitable, the plan declared, but this profit should come through efficiency, not through price increases (175). The intention, obviously, was to avoid having state firms take advantage of quasi-monopolistic positions. But the rejection of profits through price increases failed to address the question of how prices should evolve in an inflationary situation.[16] In practice, state-sector prices were allowed to lag behind those of the private sector, which provided a great opening for speculators, and increasingly pushed state firms away from an accumulationist orientation.

The 1981 plan's stress on profitability and financial control was also undermined by credit practice. As Kaimowitz notes, "Faced with the choice between allowing state firms to go bankrupt or giving them more loans, the government chose the latter course, which led to the virtual disappearance of incentives to reduce costs" (1989, 62). Thus, in the early 1980s state firms were subjected neither to centralized financial control, nor to the discipline of the market. To a large extent, the old had died, the new had not been born, and there were increasing doubts whether it ever would be.

B. PRICE POLICY

The young FSLN government took various steps to control prices, yet was hesitant to confront the tensions inherent in that policy. This pattern continued through the 1980–1 period. A number of additional control measures were implemented in early 1980. Decree 216 sought to "make effective the right to housing" by imposing a 40 per cent to 50 per cent cut in housing rents. Decree 323, the first Consumer Protection Law, gave the Ministry of Internal Trade (MICOIN) the right to "fix or freeze" the prices of all products "indispensable for popular consumption," and of all intermediate goods used in the making of such products.[17] The decree also established an "Advisory Council for Consumer Protection," whose composition indicated the political complexity of price controls: the council was to include representatives from five ministries, the police, the Chamber of Commerce, small merchants, and two delegates from popular organizations to represent consumers.

These and other measures reflected the FSLN's belief that essential goods should be made affordable for the entire population. A corollary of this belief was the rejection of the price mechanism to channel consumption. Though the high consumption of beef and other exportables during the biennium lowered Nicaragua's exports, the government limited itself to exhorting "housewives" to be "moderate" in their use of such products (*Psa* 15 March 1980). Advertisements were taken out explaining to consumers how much Nicaragua earned from each pound of exported sugar and calling for a reduction in local sugar consumption (*Bda* 20 January 1981), but domestic sugar prices remained low. The government felt that the alternatives to such moral suasion were unpalatable: higher prices would hurt poor consumers the most; substantial income redistribution, even supposing it to be feasible, would threaten the FSLN's political consolidation. To reduce consumption of exportables through rationing was also thought to have negative psychological and political consequences.[18] Hence, moral suasion reflected in part the unwillingness at this stage to take firmer measures.

Nevertheless, direct state provisioning of goods and quasi-rationing were being tested. In late January 1980, Decree 264 mandated, on an "emergency" basis, the establishment of special stores in all workplaces with more than 30 employees. The stores would sell basic products, in quantities that depended upon the number of the workers' dependents, at official prices.[19]

In a situation in which the state sold products below market-clearing prices, yet did not impose rationing, unofficial-market phenomena were not slow to appear. A Managua radio station complained in late 1979 that "black market speculation with dollars is reaching an unbearable level" (JPRS 74726). *La Prensa* published a picture on 5 January 1980 of people lined up in front of a state supermarket to buy "articles in high demand that they will resell." It was estimated that a 50 per cent spread had already opened between official and unofficial market prices (*Psa* 9 February 1980). These phenomena appeared despite widespread application of the Consumer Protection Law: *La Prensa* reported on 14 March 1980 that 1,000 merchants had been fined under the law.[20]

In a pattern that would hold throughout the 1980s, FSLN leaders attributed phenomena that were a predictable by-product of their own policies to sinister political machinations or psychological pathologies. Bayardo Arce complained of the "psychosis of scarcity" that was leading people to hoard products (*Psa* 18 January 1980), and an article in *Barricada* on 12 April 1980 hinted darkly at an "artificial shortage created by counterrevolutionary groups."

State sales at below-market-clearing prices represented an implicit rejection of an accumulationist strategy. In fact, the state's involvement in distribution was leading to dis-accumulation: in 1980, the government spent C$480 million, over 10 per cent of its total income, on general subsidies (*Bda* 2 January 1981). One observer notes that this came about despite the absence of an explicit subsidy policy. Rather, there were "two conflicting and poorly coordinated price-setting mechanisms, each largely under the control of a different ministry" (Saulniers 1987, 115). Thus, state subsidies were the resultant of decisions on producer prices made by the ministries of agriculture or industry, and decisions on consumer prices made by MICOIN. On the other hand, state policies were providing private traders with "speculative profits" that one estimate put at C$1.5 billion for 1980, the equivalent of 30 per cent of government revenue at the time (Ramírez 1987, 192). An article presented to a national congress of social scientists in 1981 warned that state policies were transferring accumulation from the state to the private sector (Vargas 1981).[21]

As did the 1980 economic plan, Plan 81 indicated that the government was not ready to confront these contradictions. Prices should not outstrip salaries, the plan held (MIPLAN 1981a, 73), and should be cost-based (83). Though the main goal of state domestic marketing should be the "defence of real salaries" (73), the plan rejected state subsidies as a means to this goal, insisting that the subsidies of the Nicaraguan Basic Foods Company (ENABAS) were a "strictly temporary measure" (83). In practice, however, these subsidies would prove anything but temporary. As had the Consumer Protection Law, Plan 81 insisted that a wide variety of institutions be involved in price setting (40). This desire to consult all affected parties would contribute to the paralysis of official price policy during the inflationary years to come.[22]

The plan argued that much inflation in 1980 was due to "high profits" in the private sector (MIPLAN 1981a, 81). Yet this observation did not lead to any questioning of the very possibility of effective price controls in the face of private sector behaviour. Rather, the plan limited itself to moral suasion, calling upon the private sector to avoid "irrational" price increases (177), and pleading for the bourgeoisie to impose austerity upon itself in the name of "National Unity" (26).

Peasant Prices

The desire to counter unofficial-market phenomena while maintaining low official prices for basic products led to an ongoing concern to strengthen "secure channels" through which goods could reach consumers, such as the workplace stores and state supermarkets. It was relatively easy to extend these secure channels right back to the producers, in the case of manufactured consumer goods. For goods produced essentially in the peasant sector, such as beans and maize, it was rather more difficult. Here the state channels would have to be established in competition with long-existing channels running from isolated peasant producers to private urban markets.

The task of creating secure channels running from peasant producers to urban consumers was assigned to ENABAS. Though some observers have argued that ENABAS had a fundamental mandate to improve terms of trade for peasant producers (Collins 1982, 122; Frenkel 1987, 211), the fact that ENABAS prices quickly fell behind those paid by private traders suggests that its actual practice was essentially consumer-oriented.[23] The government responded by seeking to control private traders, and by subjecting peasants to pressures to sell only to ENABAS.[24] The peasantry deeply resented these pressures.[25] Apart from the lower prices paid by ENABAS, peasants complained that the state organization, unlike private traders, failed to supply goods that the peasants could purchase with the receipts from their grain sales. To compound the problem, ENABAS paid with cheques, which forced peasants to make their way to the closest bank, which might or might not have the funds on hand to provide them with cash (Baumeister 1989, 149).[26]

The 1981 economic plan expressed a desire to turn terms of trade in favour of the countryside, a goal that may have been frustrated by bureaucratic politics. When different government agencies sat down to set prices, the interests of urban consumers were represented by the Ministry of Internal Trade, which argued for low consumer prices. The financial interests of the state were represented by the Ministry of Finance, which wanted to keep subsidies down. But no government body spoke forcefully for the peasantry.[27] Perhaps as a result of this "bureaucratic imbalance," consumer prices were kept low, subsidies were kept in check, and official producer prices suffered. It would take some time before this imbalance was rectified.

Salaries

The previous chapter noted that the 1980 economic plan rejected the option of a liberal salary policy. In the 1980–1 period, deflated average salaries dropped 14 per cent. By the end of 1981, they were 27 per cent below their 1977 level.[28]

In late 1979, the FSLN leadership tried to reduce even the nominal earnings of workers by attacking the "Thirteenth Month" bonus. Traditionally, workers received a year-end bonus equal to one month's wages. At the beginning of November, Jaime Wheelock launched a campaign against the year-end bonus, calling it "a scandal" (*Bda* 1 November 1979). With reports that the bonus would be suspended causing dismay among workers whose real incomes had already been eroded, the FSLN retreated, saying that those earning low salaries would not be affected (*Bda* 8 November 1979). In late November, Decree 179 put a cap of c$1,500 on the year-end bonuses. The money saved by this measure was to be dedicated to a fund to combat unemployment. The c$1,500 cap meant that at least half of salaried workers were not affected by the measure, but the FSLN also called on all workers to donate their bonus to the unemployment fund. Tomás Borge declared that it would be "repugnant" for workers not to do so (*Bda* 1 December 1979). It appears that few workers were inclined to part with their bonuses, however, and the whole Thirteenth Month campaign was the first of many excesses of voluntarism in Sandinista salary policy. In late 1980, the National Directorate officially withdrew its call upon workers to donate their year-end bonuses (*Bda* 6 December 1980).

The FSLN's salary austerity policy created an obvious opening for non-FSLN unions. In February 1980, the Communist Party's union federation, CAUS, launched strikes involving 1,700 workers in nineteen factories, demanding a 100 per cent wage increase (*Psa* 9 February 1980). The National Directorate saw the strikes as a direct political challenge. "It is not coincidental," Bayardo Arce declared, that CAUS had called the strike while the "CIA" [Central Intelligence Agency] was trying to "sabotage" Nicaragua in the U.S. Congress.[29] The CAUS strike was part of a broader "imperialist destabilization plan," Arce asserted, playing a role similar to that of U.S.-financed strikes under Allende (*Bda* 1 March 1980). Yet there was some sympathy for the CAUS action within the FSLN unions. CST head Ivan García commented that the demand for a 100 per cent salary increase was "reasonable," but could lead to "contradictions with the reactivation plan" (*Psa* 15 February 1980).

The strikes continued until early March, when striking workers received a wage increase of 10 per cent (*Bda* 4 March 1980). Immediately afterwards, attacks were launched against CAUS officials. The same day that another non-FSLN union launched a strike at a sugar mill, the "masses" seized CAUS offices in Leon (*Bda* 5 March 1980). The following day, the central CAUS offices in Managua were seized by CST activists who chanted "Death to the betrayers of the working class" (*Bda* 6 March 1980).

In mid-1980 the government relaxed its salary austerity somewhat, granting a fixed increase of c$125 to all those earning less than c$1,200 monthly. This measure was said to benefit some 300,000 workers (*Bda* 9 June 1980). The form of the increase indicated a desire to reduce the salary "fan" between high- and low-paid workers. This policy was maintained in the 1981 economic plan, which mandated larger percentage salary increases for lower-paid workers.

The policy of wage austerity was also applied in rural areas, despite the seasonal rural labour shortage, and even though the 1981 economic plan noted that salaried workers in non-agricultural material production earned 88 per cent more than agricultural workers (MIPLAN 1981a, 96). By the end of 1981, the deflated rural minimum wage was one-third lower than in 1977.[30] Nevertheless, it could be argued that the living conditions of rural workers actually improved over this period.[31]

Perhaps more than any other issue, the salary question brought out vanguardist themes in the rhetoric of the National Directorate. In a 1982 speech to workers, Victor Tirado, the National Directorate's liaison with unions, complained that "in the beginning, damage was caused because instead of focusing our energies on consolidating the strategic enterprises and strengthening the working class, we began to discuss things, to demand salary increases, to make demands that the revolution was in no position to fulfill at that time" (1986, 76). The government, Tirado went on, had offered a "social wage" consisting of subsidies on some basic food products, to avoid increases in nominal salaries: "And what was the response of workers? Strikes, factory seizures, work stoppages, absenteeism, labour indiscipline, conflicts between workers, managers, and administrators" (77). "We understand," Tirado added generously, "that this is a legacy of the past." Yet it was not a "legacy" the FSLN was prepared to tolerate for ever. Manifestations of "spontaneity" within the workers' movement, Tirado declared in a 1981 speech, "must be abandoned" (72).

The language is revealing. The National Directorate had declared this a time to rebuild, not to discuss, and workers must act accordingly. Conflicts between workers and managers were all part of the workers' short-sighted response to the government's salary policy. This paternalism was accompanied by a dose of new-speak. "Salary restrictions," Tirado urged in a 1980 speech, "should be seen as a measure adopted freely, voluntarily, and consciously by the workers themselves" (ibid., 63). Whether the salary policy was wise or misguided, it certainly was not a measure adopted "freely" by Nicaraguan workers. But the vanguardist orientation is constantly prone to confuse the views of workers with those of the leaders of the institutions claiming to represent the workers, which institutions are established by ... the vanguard itself. As the 1980s wore on, this confusion would weaken the FSLN's awareness of the political impact of the economic crisis, contributing to its certainty that it would win the 1990 election.

C. RELATIONS WITH THE BOURGEOISIE

We have already cited Humberto Ortega's 1978 statement that "the FSLN must walk a stretch together with the bourgeoisie, a stretch during which the bourgeoisie and imperialism will try to destroy us and divert the Sandinista liberation process, just as we will try to destroy them and throw their reactionary aspirations into the garbage" (1981, 40).

It appeared in the 1979–81 period that this "stretch" had already ended. Through the period, the FSLN's relations with the bourgeoisie deteriorated rapidly, and by the end of 1981 the organized bourgeoisie was fully and openly in opposition to the Sandinistas. With this deterioration in relations went the loss of the early hopes of incorporating bourgeois production into the socialist economy. Henceforth the FSLN's economic project would advance in the face of bourgeois hostility.

Government and pro-government documents occasionally profess surprise at this turn of events. They point to the young government's "generosity" in its dealings with the private sector.[32] But the conflict between the FSLN and the bourgeoisie was not fundamentally about rates of profit, taxes, or interest, though these immediate economic questions did play a role. Rather, the fundamental conflict was about power. To put it simply, what the bourgeoisie felt the government must do to guarantee the bourgeoisie's long-term interests was incompatible with what the FSLN felt it must do to consolidate its power and to lay the groundwork for change.

Ironically, then, the FSLN, which was trying so hard to recreate the popular classes in its own image, to have those classes transcend economism and look to their real or supposed long-term interests, found itself confronting an adversary that was looking to the long term.[33] The elements of the bourgeoisie that coalesced around the Superior Council of Private Enterprise (COSEP), that saw *La Prensa* as its mouth-piece, had all the characteristics of a healthy "class-for-itself." That much of this class-for-itself jumped into the arms of the Reagan administration is proof, not of its immaturity, but of its willingness to behave as Marxist theory has always held it must, by putting its class interests ahead of those of the nation, or (more charitably) by confusing the two. To trace the deterioration of the FSLN's relation with the bourgeoisie, I will focus on the various ways in which the bourgeoisie found its long-term interests threatened by the Sandinistas, and on the latter's efforts to neutralize the political resources with which the bourgeoisie sought to promote its interests.

Many members of the bourgeoisie believed to the last hours of the
Somoza regime that the United States would find some way of dumping
Somoza while preventing an FSLN victory.[34] Even as the Sandinistas entered Managua, leading members of the bourgeoisie were in Caracas
trying yet again for a negotiated solution that would create a "system of
democracy and free enterprise," as the Nicaraguan Chamber of Industries had once put it (FBIS 10 August 1978).

Thus, Sergio Ramírez notes that 19 July 1979 "found the bourgeoisie without arms, without a viable project" (1987, 172). In this situation, how could the bourgeoisie best protect its long-term interests?
One can infer from the actions and declarations of the organized
bourgeoisie[35] three broad objectives: (i) to consolidate the bourgeois
presence in the new state; (ii) to limit the scope of the state through,
for example, the entrenchment of property rights and the promotion
of a "state of law"; and (iii) to overturn or at least to "moderate" the regime through elections.

With what resources would the bourgeoisie pursue these objectives?
Again, the bourgeoisie's actions and declarations demonstrate its reliance on three types of resources: (i) its ideological resources, especially the means of communication in its hands and its alliance with
the Roman Catholic hierarchy; (ii) its ownership of means of production, which lent weight to its call for a "proper business climate"; and
(iii) its external allies.

The FSLN, for its part, sought to convert the bourgeoisie into producers without power, who would "give up their political expectations
and utilize their experience and capabilities to work for the benefit of
production" (Borge 1985d, 26). As Jaime Wheelock put it, "Their
place in the revolution has been that of those who are called upon to
prepare the food at a banquet. They are not invited to the banquet;
they are only the ones who prepare the food. And we want to keep
them hidden away in the kitchen, not to come out. When they do, we
give them a few lashes" (Austin and Ickis 1986a, 785).

The FSLN's strategies and tactics to achieve this objective were almost the mirror image of those of the organized bourgeoisie. Thus,
control over the state should be consolidated and unreliable elements
excluded; the ideology of property rights and of the "state of law"
should be challenged, in order to keep the state's options open; the
bourgeoisie's ideological terrain should be contested; the bourgeoisie
should be dissuaded from using the means of production to extract
political concessions, etc.

The foregoing analysis provides us with six themes through which to
examine the Sandinista-bourgeois relation in the 1979–81 period: (i)
the struggle for control of the state; (ii) the state of law; (iii) elections;

(iv) the media and ideological struggle; (v) the political use of private means of production and the "decapitalization" issue; and (vi) the bourgeoisie's external alliances. After examining these issues, I will conclude with an examination of the final breakdown in relations in late 1981.

The Consolidation of FSLN Control of the State

It was not at all clear in July 1979 that the FSLN had gained the lion's share of state power. One U.S. leftist argued that the new government junta was dominated by "personalities from the nonrevolutionary forces," that the cabinet "appears to be overwhelmingly controlled by liberal professionals," and that only six of the Council of State's thirty-three members were of the left (Petras 1979, 13–14). Another observer believed that the FSLN held only three out of eighteen positions in the first cabinet (H. Weber 1981, 77).

These evaluations misunderstood the correlation of forces in July 1979. The formal Sandinista presence in the state was much greater than Petras or Weber realized. Part of the confusion arose from the fact that figures such as junta member Sergio Ramírez and others in the cabinet had yet to reveal their Sandinista affiliations.

Nevertheless, even had all those affiliated with the Sandinistas revealed themselves immediately, the non-Sandinista presence in the state would have been impressive. In particular, four key cabinet positions were in non-Sandinista hands. Roberto Mayorga, a technocrat and former general secretary of the Central American Common Market (CACM), was minister for planning. Noel Rivas, a former president of the Chamber of Commerce and high Conservative Party official, held the industry and trade portfolio. The agriculture ministry was headed by Manuel Torres, a large landowner affiliated with the Christian Democratic party, while Bernardino Larios, a former colonel in Somoza's National Guard, was defence minister.

Evaluation of the degree of real Sandinista control, however, must bear in mind that the National Directorate never intended to allow the junta, cabinet or Council of State to serve as the state's supreme decision-making bodies. This role was reserved for the directorate itself. In the latter half of 1979, this real structure of power began to reveal itself. Not surprisingly, the confusion over power was clarified most quickly in relation to the armed forces. The Sandinista leadership was determined that the army be "schooled in fidelity to the vanguard of our people" (JPRS 74338). The army's loyalty to the nation would be mediated by its loyalty to the vanguard of that nation. This quickly became clear, in both symbolic and practical terms.

Symbolically, Decree 53 of August 1979 declared that the armed forces would henceforth be named the "Sandinista Popular Army." This title took on greater significance the following month. After an opposition party tried to change its legal name to the "Sandinista Social-Democratic Party," the junta issued Decree 67 declaring that "the use of the label 'Sandinista', in political terms, is reserved exclusively to the SANDINISTA NATIONAL LIBERATION FRONT (FSLN) and the ... organizations of any type that it organizes or that are under its direction." To the opposition, this seemed an open declaration that the army belonged to the FSLN. The question of party control over the armed forces, and of the confusion between party and state in general, would become a central theme in bourgeois political declarations.[36] For the FSLN, however, to complain of the "Sandinista character of the state and of the armed forces" was to "question the unquestionable," as *Barricada* put it on 21 August 1980.

Nor were the armed forces Sandinista in name only. In keeping with the leadership's view of the importance of ideological training, it was announced just three weeks after the taking of power that the political formation of the armed forces had begun (*Bda* 11 August 1979). Luís Carrión noted that this political training would be in the hands of the FSLN, "because these are Sandinista armed forces. That is, the FSLN is not a political party that can be compared to any other party in Nicaragua. So if these armed forces should be educated in the concepts of the New Society, logically the FSLN, as vanguard of the Nicaraguan people, is the most appropriate organization to undertake that task" (*Bda* 4 February 1981).

Two actions, in December 1979 and April 1980, brought the formal distribution of state power into line with the real one, and signalled to the bourgeoisie its marginalization from the state. At the end of 1979, the cabinet was restructured, and the four key non-Sandinista members lost their positions. Henry Ruiz and Humberto Ortega entered the cabinet, Wheelock added agriculture to his agrarian reform portfolio, and the Sandinista character of the executive became much more evident.

The April 1980 action was more explosive. The composition of the Council of State promised in the June 1979 Plan of Government would have left the FSLN and its affiliates in a minority position. In April, however, the three FSLN members of the government junta issued Decree 374, expanding the council from thirty-three to forty-seven members, and granted seventeen council seats to FSLN mass organizations such as the Sandinista Defence Committees (nine seats) and the two major FSLN union federations (three seats each). Though the junta had the authority to make the changes under Article 29 of the Fundamental Statute, the government's quasi-constitution, critics saw the move as a betrayal of pre-triumph agreements between the FSLN and other sectors.

The change in the Council of State was the reason cited by Alfonso Robelo for his resignation from the junta shortly afterwards. Coming just days after Violeta Barrios de Chamorro had stepped down citing health reasons, Robelo's resignation left the junta without any figure enjoying the confidence of the bourgeoisie.

Robelo's resignation, and his subsequent announcement that his Nicaraguan Democratic Movement would not take its seat in the Council of State, created a dangerous situation for the FSLN. Were the bourgeoisie as a whole to follow Robelo's lead and refuse to participate in either the legislative or executive branches, it would have been much more difficult for the government to project the moderate image felt necessary to maintain international legitimacy. The FSLN thus entered negotiations with part of the bourgeoisie, in which the latter was able to wield the external legitimacy question in order to gain some concessions.

Whatever concessions it might win, however, the direction of events was clear to the organized bourgeoisie. Declarations repeatedly complained of the private sector's "marginalization" from state decisions (*Psa* 11 November 1980; 2 March 1980). By mid-1980, it was clear that the bourgeoisie's first long-term objective, that of maintaining its presence within the state, had been completely frustrated. This made the question of limiting the state, of establishing a "state of law," all the more important.

The FSLN and the Rule of Law

The need for guarantees of property rights, and of limits on state action in general, was a constant theme in bourgeois statements during this early period (*Psa* 25 January 1980; 18 February 1980; 26 May 1980; JPRS 74894). The bourgeoisie gave particular importance to the need for a "*ley de amparo*" [law of protection], a law providing for judicial review of administrative actions affecting individuals or their property.

But demands for a state of law ran into the FSLN's superstructural conception of law. The leadership shared Bayardo Arce's view that "the laws are merely an expression of the political-juridical superstructure which defends and reproduces the economic structures of a society" (*Bda* 22 June 1980). FSLN leaders thus regularly expressed scorn for the niceties of "bourgeois legalism" (*Bda* 2 February 1980), which was a "straitjacket" binding the revolution (*Bda* 19 April 1982). Opponents of the revolution might promote such "myths" as equality before the law, Luís Carrión declared, but "we all know that, before the judge, the millionaire and the poor man are never treated equally." Thus the very concept of legal equality is "linked to ideological diversionism." Carrión went on to criticize the equally mythical idea of "three powers": "The State is supposedly divided into three powers, leaving the judicial branch the role of preserving the interests of the exploiting class" (*Bda* 19 April 1982). But it was precisely this "myth," which was an ongoing target of Sandinista speeches, that the demand for a law of protection sought to uphold.

The corollary of the view that laws are but an expression of economic interests is that bourgeois demands for due process and equality before the law were made in bad faith, as a cover for naked class interests.[37] Hence, the superstructural approach, apart from being an ideological legitimation for the FSLN's own disregard for the problem of law, also provided a key for interpreting the demands of its opponents.

Though the FSLN's approach to law reflected its general ideological orientation, the approach did address a real dilemma. Formal legal equality can coexist with substantive class-inequality of access to the legal system. In addition, class biases will permeate many conceptions of justice and civil rights.[38] Hence it is not surprising that, as Weber put it, "formal justice and the 'freedom' which it guarantees are indeed rejected by all groups ideologically interested in substantive justice" (1978, 813). Unless they could rapidly address the class-inequalities of access to the legal system, and generate a whole new legal code to articulate the new rights they were trying to create, the Sandinistas were faced with the dilemma of either tolerating the continuance of the substantive class-inequalities of the legal system, or ignoring that system when necessary. They generally chose the latter option.

When they did try to articulate new rights and duties, Sandinista laws often used a vague language that worried critics. Thus, Article 4 of Decree 5, the "Law for the Maintenance of Order and Public Security," passed on the first day of the government junta's operation, made it a crime to say or write anything that sought to "hurt popular interests or abolish the gains won by the people." Article 17 of Decree 52, the "Statute of Rights and Guarantees" of August 1980 begins with the simple principle that "no person will be forced to do that which the law does not order, nor barred from doing that which the law does not forbid." But the article then exempts from this principle "the duties of action and omission imposed by human solidarity, the duty to behave one's self fraternally, the respect for the rights and freedoms of others, and the necessity of satisfying the just demands of morality, of public order and of general welfare in a democratic society, even when these duties are not expressly established by Law."

The Council of State debate on a law to regulate professionals (Decree 783) indicates the issues at stake in the use of vague language in legislation. An opposition member called for the removal of an article establishing penalties for "those actions or omissions that act against the ethical principles that govern the present law" (*Bda* 11 June 1981). The suggested amendment won enough FSLN support to carry, though the law's language was typical of much legislation being passed. One FSLN member of the council called for the article to stand, stating that "it is necessary to establish the obligation to respect the spirit of the law."

This presents the FSLN position clearly: by including many general principles in their legislation, the Sandinistas were demanding respect for the "spirit" of their laws. They thus eschewed attempts to capture this spirit in infinitely detailed legal codes defining, for example, the conditions under which a firm could be considered guilty of decapitalization. The intention would appear to have been to scare the bourgeoisie, among others, away from a spirit of minimal compliance with the letter of the law. Such an enforced compliance with the spirit of the law is not absent even from capitalist law. Weber notes that "much of the system of commodity exchange ... is possible only on the basis of far-reaching personal confidence and trust in the loyalty of others. Moreover, as commodity exchange increases in importance, the need in legal practice to guarantee or secure such trustworthy conduct becomes proportionately greater. But in the very nature of the case, we cannot, of course, define with formal certainty the legal tests according to which the new relations of trust and confidence are to be governed" (1978, 884). The problem from the bourgeoisie's point of view, then, was not so much the inclusion of vague terms in legislation, but the structure of power within which those terms would be interpreted. It was no longer a case of a judge from an upper-class background deciding which of two parties had not exhibited good faith in a contractual relation, but of the spirit of Sandinista legislation being interpreted in a new judicial framework hostile in many respects to the bourgeoisie as a whole.

For the articulation of new rights and duties was accompanied by the development of judicial and quasi-judicial structures in which many traditional guarantees were suspended. Decree 5, for example, established special emergency tribunals to try those accused of offences against public order. Though the tribunals had the power to imprison people for up to ten years, the decree stipulated that those accused be given just two days to prepare their defence, that the trial last no more than three days, and that the tribunal's sentence be inappellable.

A key example of new quasi-judicial structures were the agrarian tribunals, established to hear appeals of decisions taken under the Agrarian Reform Law of July 1981. The decisions made by the tribunals were inappellable. In one of the clearest expressions of the class orientation of Sandinista legislation, Decree 832 barred from sitting on the agrarian tribunals any person who had ever "taken part in judicial proceedings against a peasant on matters relating to land, either as a party, attorney, witness or in any other way."

Thus, Sandinista legislation clearly indicated that the FSLN leaders' belief in the superstructural nature of law was not going to remain at a purely philosophical level. That belief guided, or at least had a strong affinity with, their approach to law and to bourgeois demands for legal guarantees. There was much in the Nicaraguan reality that supported both the superstructural view and the practice that accompanied it, but this practice had its costs. As E.P. Thompson argued, the view of law as a "pliant medium to be twisted this way and that by whichever interests already possess effective power" can lead one to forget that "if the law is evidently partial and unjust, then it will mask nothing, legitimize nothing, contribute nothing to any class's hegemony" (1975, 262–3). Whatever the motives sustaining the FSLN's approach to law, that approach fostered the view among many Nicaraguans that the FSLN constituted just one more de facto regime, like so many others that had plagued the country through its history.

As the Sandinistas rejected the idea of a "state of law" in general, they were also cool to property rights in particular. This attitude at times reflected the leadership's attempts to deal with pressure from the FSLN's mass organizations and its broad social base.[39] An example of how the mass organizations could complicate the handling of property questions came in early 1980, around the issue of "intervened" property. Decree 38 of August 1979 had given the government the power to "intervene" – temporarily seize – the property of persons accused of being allies of the dictatorship, to prevent the deterioration or sale of such properties while investigations were being carried out. MIDINRA had also intervened a number of private farms that had been seized by workers, or where workers were in a severe conflict with the owners.

Anxious to end a situation in which the state was acting as a temporary manager for scattered holdings, the government in early February 1980 passed Decree 282, which outlined procedures for the definitive confiscation of intervened properties, or their return to their owner in cases where the owner "is not subject to confiscation according to relevant legislation." But the decree led the FSLN's Rural Workers' Union (ATC) to organize a mass march on Managua, demanding that "not one inch of land" be returned to owners (*Bda* 17 February 1980). The government accepted the demand, passing Decree 329, which expropriated all properties currently under MIDINRA intervention. At the same time, Decree 329 outlawed land seizures, ordering that all future expropriations be undertaken only by MIDINRA.

COSEP protested strongly against what it termed a "legalization of arbitrary actions," and warned the government that "a crisis is at the doorstep" (*Psa* 6 March 1980). One could not expect the bourgeoisie to be grateful for the provision of Decree 329 outlawing private land seizures: stealing property had always been illegal, they might reason, why was it necessary to pass a law forbidding that which was already forbidden? For many bourgeois, the real message of the law was that the FSLN, however much it might proclaim its respect for private property rights, was willing to legalize violations of those rights.

Interestingly, the government was much more cautious with the property rights of the urban bourgeoisie. Some factories had been seized by workers prior to Decree 329 (*Bda* 15 November 1979; 14 December 1979), but the decree led to a rush of seizures by workers demanding that factories be nationalized just as land had been (*Psa* 28 February 1980). Though the government was willing upon occasion to expropriate factories, it refused the demand for a blanket nationalization of all factories seized by workers. Moíses Hassan of the government junta called upon workers to exercise "patience, cautiousness, serenity, sacrifice, and political clarity," warning them that "there are certain limits that cannot be passed, without endangering the Revolution" (*Bda* 12 March 1980).[40] Thus the FSLN was making a clear distinction between urban and rural capital. This may reflect an awareness of the different "stages" of the two types of capital.

The Election Question

Having been frustrated in its attempts both to maintain a strong presence within the state and to establish a "state of law," the bourgeoisie found by mid-1980 that its hope for imminent relief from Sandinista rule through elections was also not to be realized. In the wake of the resignations of Violeta Chamorro and Alfonso Robelo from the junta, COSEP negotiated an accord with the Sandinistas through which it agreed to participate in the Council of State in return for certain concessions. An element of the May agreement between the FSLN and COSEP that was not made public at the time was that a date for national elections would be set on 19 July, the first anniversary of the revolution. In late May, it was reported that Borge was indicating that municipal elections would be held in 1981, and national elections in 1982–3 (*Psa* 26 May 1980). The first anniversary came and went without an election announcement however. COSEP immediately complained, saying the May agreements had been violated (*Bda* 22 July 1980).

In late August, COSEP got its election announcement, though not the sort that it had anticipated. In a speech at the end of the literacy crusade, Humberto Ortega read a National Directorate communiqué stating that elections would not be held before 1985. The long delay was necessary, the communiqué stated, to overcome "the backwardness and the economic, social and moral destruction of the country".[41]

Thus far, the communiqué arguably remained within the bounds of the FSLN's pre-revolution understanding with other sectors, as codified in the Plan of Government.[42] In his own addendum to the communiqué, however, Ortega told the crowd to "keep in mind that these elections will be held to improve revolutionary power, not to raffle off power, because power is in the hands of the people, through its Vanguard, the Sandinista Front for National Liberation and its National Directorate" (1980). COSEP interpreted this addendum as a declaration of the FSLN's "intention of remaining in power forever" (1987, 237). The FSLN's cultivated ambiguity on this point would not be abandoned until 1989, when the Sandinistas made it clear that they would leave power if they lost the 1990 elections.

Ideological Struggle

As the FSLN frustrated the bourgeoisie's pursuit of its long-term objectives, it also sought to counter the bourgeoisie's political resources. This was most evident in the area of ideology, where the FSLN and the bourgeoisie wrestled for the hearts and minds of Nicaraguans. Sergio Ramírez would comment in 1981 that "because of the strength of the contradictions that come to the surface after the revolution, it is impossible *not* to have an aggressive verbal war against the bourgeoisie" (1987, 175). The central theme of this ideological offensive was the absence of the bourgeoisie from the struggle to overthrow Somoza. "In the trenches and on the barricades," proclaimed Tomás Borge, "we never saw those pretty people, those perfumed people. What we saw instead were the workers, the peasants, the great protagonists of the insurrectional and revolutionary triumph" (*Psa* 14 April 1980). Even the progressive elements in the private sector, argued Daniel Ortega, "never played a firm role within the process of liberation," and always sought a negotiated solution with Somoza (*Bda* 8 September 1979). Members of the FSLN, on the other hand, had run the risks and paid the price of liberation with their blood. They had paid the piper, now they would call the tune. Asked by what right the new government had closed a Marxist opposition newspaper, Bayardo Arce proclaimed that "revolution itself is the source of right" (*Bda* 25 January 1980).[43] One can question the connection between making a revolution and having the right to hold power afterwards, but it should be stressed that, in a country with no history of democratic legitimacy, the FSLN's grounding of its legitimacy on its role in overthrowing Somoza carried much weight. The FSLN's argument that participation in the overthrow of Somoza was a key source of political rights was implicitly accepted even by the Catholic bishops, who based their case for "freedom to organize political parties" on the fact that "various forces have contributed generously to the historic process" (Conferencia Episcopal 1981, 77). Similarly, a typical speech by COSEP head Enrique Dreyfus began with a history of the revolution, showing the private sector's resolute opposition to Somoza (*Psa* 2 March 1980). Only then did Dreyfus move on to the bourgeoisie's complaints with the Sandinistas. Thus, the bourgeoisie countered the FSLN's history of the revolution with one of its own.[44] In this version, a broad range of social forces had cooperated to overthrow Somoza, hence "the revolution has no owner," as opposition leaders often put it.

A second theme of the Sandinista ideological offensive was consistent with Humberto Ortega's vision of a two-stage revolution: the FSLN leadership continually hinted at the transitory nature of the mixed economy, and insisted that the bourgeoisie subsisted at the pleasure of the FSLN. "When we have more power," declared Carlos Nuñez, "the workers and peasants will decide what they want this country to be" (*Bda* 25 September 1979). "The Revolution will put an end to freedom of exploitation," promised Tomás Borge (*Bda* 29 October 1979). Calls upon popular sectors to cooperate with the bourgeoisie were generally phrased in the form "our friends, at least for the moment, are the democratic bourgeoisie."[45]

This type of rhetoric is extremely puzzling, unless one sees it as a means to prepare Nicaraguan popular sectors for an eventual expropriation of the bourgeoisie. Talk of transitory alliances was not aimed at inducing more friendly behaviour from the bourgeoisie, since it suggested that large private enterprises would eventually be nationalized whatever the behaviour of their owners. The Sandinistas were repeatedly warned by bourgeois leaders that such rhetoric was hurting "business confidence," yet they continued to combat the idea that the existence of the bourgeoisie was natural or eternal.

In their ideological struggle with the bourgeoisie, the Sandinistas sought to contest the latter's ideological resources. This can be seen with respect to the media, religion, and education. After the fall of Somoza, the bourgeoisie controlled the newspaper *La Prensa* and twenty private radio stations. The government, for its part, controlled the country's only two TV stations, and thirteen radio stations (Nichols 1982). These media were acquired through the decree expropriating the belongings of Somoza and his allies. In addition, the physical assets of the Somoza-owned newspaper, *Novedades*, ended up directly in FSLN hands, rather than being transferred to the state. These assets formed the basis of *Barricada*, the official party newspaper. The Sandinistas saw the media under their control as instruments of ideological transformation. An editorial in *Barricada* on 13 August 1979 announced that "the task of we journalists is to contribute to having no Nicaraguan remain outside the mass organizations. Our work should be oriented through discipline, through the full identification with the process being traced out by our leaders." "Rather than simple journalists," the paper declared, "we are Sandinistas" (*Bda* 7 September 1979).

The Sandinistas hoped that the state's television monopoly would prove particularly effective, especially in urban areas.[46] They thus rejected opposition demands for a private TV station. "In our country," Daniel Ortega stated, "means of communication, such as television, will not be placed in the hands of political interests whose intention is not exactly to support the Popular Sandinista Revolution." Junta member Sergio Ramírez added that "in Nicaragua there will only be state television, so as to channel the culture and education of our entire people" (*Bda* 20 December 1979).

For its part, it soon appeared that the bourgeoisie was seeking to turn the media under its control into a unified voice of opposition. In December 1979, Radio Corporación cancelled all its newscasts and fired its reporters, who were apparently considered too progressive (*Bda* 1 December 1979). The Union of Radio Journalists of Managua claimed that a broad campaign was under way to marginalize progressive reporters (*Bda* 3 December 1979). The most dramatic evidence of this came in April 1980, at the *La Prensa* newspaper.

An outspoken opponent of the Somoza regime, *La Prensa* had represented since the FSLN's victory an uneasy mixture of pro- and anti-government journalists. In April, however, the paper's owners, the Chamorro family, opted to transform *La Prensa* into a unified opposition paper, and replaced editor Xavier Chamorro with his nephew Pedro Joaquín Chamorro Jr. The staff, which opposed the action by an estimated three to one majority (Christian 1985, 154), closed the paper in protest, accusing the Chamorro family of wanting to turn *La Prensa* into "the spokesman of minority, privileged and anti-popular sectors" (FBIS 22 April 1980). The paper reopened a month later, after the family agreed to give Xavier the capital necessary to open a competing paper, *El Nuevo Diario*, to which the majority of *La Prensa*'s former staff transferred. The FSLN would henceforth be faced with an opponent that enjoyed great domestic and international prestige, yet that was increasingly rabid in its opposition to the revolution and everything it stood for, and clearly aligned with the most right-wing sectors in the United States.[47] *La Prensa* would repeatedly confront the FSLN with insuperable dilemmas: as the war intensified, *La Prensa* seemed like a Trojan Horse in the heart of Nicaragua, yet every action against the paper damaged the prestige of the regime.

As the Sandinistas and the bourgeoisie vied for control over the media, so too was the Roman Catholic Church contested terrain. The organized bourgeoisie enjoyed close relations with much of the church hierarchy, relations that had been established during the last years of the Somoza regime. In August 1978, business sectors were proclaiming an alliance between "true capitalists and the Church" (FBIS 3 August 1978). Shortly after the FSLN took power, a wire-service story noted the formation of a business-church opposition, seeking to reduce FSLN control of the government (FBIS 10 August 1979). While touring the United States in late 1979, a group of business people told a reporter that "the private sector allied with the Catholic Church will not allow extremists to dominate Nicaraguan politics" (FBIS 6 November 1979). As conflict between the new government and the bourgeoisie intensified, the latter continued its increasingly successful overtures to the bishops. Junta member Alfonso Robelo alluded to threats to the "sacred principle of freedom of religion," and continually invoked God and religion in his speeches as he began to distance himself from the government (FBIS 19 March 1980).[48]

Political interests in Nicaragua traditionally tried to wear the cloak of religious legitimacy, and both the Sandinistas and their opponents relied on religious imagery in the post-1979 situation. The conflicting attempts to link Christian beliefs to specific political projects led also to attempts to change the internal structure of the Nicaraguan Catholic Church in accordance with those projects. Thus, *La Prensa* sought to magnify the stature of Managua Archbishop Obando y Bravo, a hard-line opponent of the Sandinistas, while ignoring more moderate bishops and the grass-roots of the church. The paper in effect tried to make a sort of "local pope" out of Obando. He was continually referred to as "pastor of the Nicaraguan flock," though he was only in charge of the archdiocese of Managua (*Psa* 5 September 1982). He was the "illustrious Nicaraguan prelate" (*Psa* 1 August 1982), the "father of his people" (*Psa* 10 August 1982), the "representative in Nicaragua of our God-Man" (*Psa* 24 December 1987).

Other bishops did not fare as well. When Carlos Santi was consecrated as bishop of Matagalpa in July 1982, *La Prensa* omitted his first sermon as bishop, in which he thanked "the Lord … Saint Francis … Pope John Paul … and the representatives of the government, with whom I wish to have a cordial, friendly, and respectful dialogue" (END 2 August 1982; *Bda* 1 August 1982). Instead, the paper carried a speech by Obando in which he spoke of the "difficult and heroic task" of being a bishop (*Psa* 1 August 1982). When Julian Barni, another moderate, was consecrated bishop of León, *La Prensa* failed to report the event altogether.

The FSLN, for its part, tried to support progressive clerics and grass-roots communities, sectors that came under attack from the right as the Nicaraguan political situation polarized. Typical in this respect is Tomás Borge's comment, speaking to a group of children: "Have you heard about the Inquisition? No? ... Well, the revolution does not persecute the church. Sometimes we believe a high-ranking church sector is persecuting the revolution and the Christians. In the times of Somoza, progressive priests and those identified with the people were persecuted by the Somozist tyranny. Now there is a church sector persecuting these same priests and nuns ... they are doing the same thing Somoza did" (FBIS 23 June 1981).[49]

The opposition's overtures to the church were clearly more successful than those of the Sandinistas. Managua's Obando y Bravo remained one of the most popular figures in Nicaragua – and a strong opponent of the Sandinistas – throughout the 1980s, while by 1982 the base communities established to counter the power of the hierarchy in the church were already moribund.

The Sandinistas were more successful in other areas of ideological struggle, however. The vast majority of students were in state schools and, as with the media, the Sandinistas saw education as a process of "forming individuals in ideology," as Tomás Borge put it (1985a, 72). Just one month after the Sandinista victory, the new vice-minister of education announced a plan to shift education from "Somocista and bourgeois knowledge" to "scientific knowledge" (*Bda* 15 August 1979).

The Decapitalization Question

One of the swords hanging over the heads of leftist governments that seek to coexist with a bourgeoisie is the danger of an implicit or explicit "capital strike." The Sandinistas gave early notice that they would counter any perceived attempt to extract political advantage from privately owned means of production. In January 1980 Attorney General Ernesto Castillo announced that some "capitalists" were "determined to carry out a process to withdraw the capital of the country's industries and businesses, thus sabotaging our reconstruction process." Castillo called on workers to "report all these cases because the government is willing to adopt harsh measures against the unscrupulous capitalists" (JPRS 75121).

In March 1980 the government decreed a law against decapitalization, which aimed to block the transfer of resources out of the country.

In announcing the law, Luís Carrión called for "strict worker vigilance to guarantee the implementation of the decree" (*Bda* 3 March 1980). This call for workers to enforce controls on capital made the bourgeoisie predictably nervous. Both before and after the decree, workers seized factories charging decapitalization.

The FSLN did not feel that the decapitalization law had overcome the problem. In the first half of 1981, there were repeated charges from mass organizations and FSLN leaders that urban and rural entrepreneurs were allowing their capital to run down, and that exporters were using transfer pricing to ship profits out of the country (*Bda* 3 March 1981; 12 March 1981; 2 July 1981). These accusations were not fanciful. On 16 August 1981, the *New York Times* cited a "young executive" saying "I've collected $80,000 abroad since the revolution. Why shouldn't I? If I'm being called a bourgeois, an exploiter, a counterrevolutionary all day long on radio and television, I have to be prepared for what might happen tomorrow. The Government gives us economic incentives, but what we want is a climate of political confidence."

On 19 July 1981, the second anniversary of the revolution, the FSLN responded to the decapitalization problem and to demands within the party and the mass organizations for tough action against the bourgeoisie. Fifteen companies were confiscated (Decree 759).[50] Other tough measures were decreed, including an agrarian reform law, and Decree 760, which "appropriated" the property of all persons who had been, or would be, absent from the country for six months without "justified reasons."

Daniel Ortega referred to these measures as the definition of the "rules of the game" that the bourgeoisie had so frequently demanded: "The rules of the game are imposed by the people. Those who wish to play are welcome to do so. Those who don't, they should get out of here or the people will crush them." In a clear expression of the FSLN's desire to push the bourgeoisie into an economistic mould, Ortega declared that "in this country we are guaranteeing [the property] of anyone who wishes to produce without acting against popular power" (1981).

External Allies

The FSLN had to some degree succeeded in countering the bourgeoisie's ideological resources and circumscribing its ability to use ownership of means of production for political leverage. Weakening the bourgeoisie's external alliances, particularly with the U.S. government, would be a more difficult matter. The bourgeoisie saw U.S. pressure as a crucial element in its relations with the Sandinistas, and one can argue that the points of inflection in bourgeois strategy during the 1979–81 period mirrored changes in the U.S. political climate.

Once the Carter administration had failed in its attempt to forestall a Sandinista victory, it opted for a path of conciliation and modest economic aid, hoping that "the Sandinista-controlled government can be kept tied into the West's political economy," in the words of U.S. official Viron Vaky ([Ryan] 1982). Thus U.S. officials repeatedly signalled that aid would be used to demand Sandinista respect for "human rights" (*Bda* 23 August 1979), to "bolster private business" (*NYT* 17 March 1980), and to prevent "Nicaragua being abandoned to Marxism" (*Psa* 8 June 1980).

This situation gave great leverage to the bourgeoisie: were it to signal that Nicaragua was "lost" to the Marxists, U.S. aid would have dried up. This leverage was evident in May 1980, in the wake of the departure of Robelo and Chamorro from the government junta. Arguing that Robelo's party "does not defend the interests of private enterprise, since it is just one of many parties in Nicaragua" (*Bda* 30 April 1980), COSEP took it upon itself to negotiate with the FSLN on behalf of the bourgeoisie. COSEP entered the negotiations with a long set of political demands, including the passage of the Law of Protection, stronger guarantees for private property, the separation of the FSLN and the state, and the formation of a constituent assembly through free elections. Indicating its concerns over tensions in the workplace, COSEP also called upon the FSLN to "foster attitudes that reconcile social classes."[51] COSEP's minimum demands for taking its five seats in the Council of State were the promulgation of the Law of Protection, an end to the state of emergency that had been in place since July 1979, and the resolution of the *La Prensa* conflict (*Psa* 26 May 1980).

The Carter administration's proposed loan of $75 million formed the backdrop of these negotiations. The loan was meeting tough opposition in Congress, and the Democrats' Tip O'Neill linked the passage of the loan to the appointment of two "moderates" to the junta to replace Robelo and Chamorro (*NYT* 25 May 1980). Approval of the loan was critical for the Sandinistas, as it would provide a green light to other potential donors and lenders.[52] Without that green light, the Sandinistas' reconstruction program would have been strangled.

It is thus not overly speculative to suggest that U.S. pressure contributed to the willingness of an FSLN normally so hostile to the political demands of the bourgeoisie to meet many of those demands in May 1980. The Sandinistas initiated passage of the Law of Protection, moved to resolve the *La Prensa* crisis, and restored the government junta to its original size of five members with the naming of Arturo Cruz and Rafael Córdova Rivas.[53] COSEP, for its part, agreed to participate in the Council of State, signalling an end to the government's first major political crisis. The U.S. Senate approved the $75-million loan a week later (*NYT* 25 May 1980).

The rise in Congress of a determined opposition to Carter's relatively conciliatory approach to the Sandinistas was one shift in the U.S. political situation of which the Nicaraguan bourgeoisie took note. A more dramatic shift, obviously, was the election of Reagan in November 1980. Just days after the election, COSEP and three conservative parties left the council. Two "free" trade union federations followed meekly one day later. The timing of their withdrawal does not seem to make sense in terms of the domestic situation. There had been no particular provocations since the August election announcement. Thus, it is easy to conclude that the shift in COSEP policy reflected the changed international situation. The Republican Party platform had judged Nicaragua lost to the Marxists, and declared support for future efforts to overthrow the Sandinistas.[54] Given the Reaganite position, it was natural for COSEP and various conservative parties to seek to establish themselves as an "authentic" opposition, and to distance themselves from any hint of "collaboration" with the FSLN. A COSEP official would later comment that "Reagan's rhetoric produces the triumphalism of the hard-liners. It means you abandon strategy" (Gutman 1988, 240).

The bourgeoisie's new hard-line stance was evident in another event of November 1980. Just days after the Council of State walk-out, COSEP's Jorge Salazar was killed by police near Managua. Though Salazar had been involved in a quixotic plan to provoke a coup against the FSLN,[55] COSEP's once-conciliatory Enrique Dreyfus spoke of Salazar's behaviour as having been "heroic and exemplary," and other members of COSEP called him a "martyr for the motherland" (*Bda* 19 December 1980). From this point on, bourgeois leaders would find themselves torn between pursuing the "civic struggle" and working for the overthrow of the FSLN.

Whether or not the bourgeoisie's actions in November 1980 were externally motivated, the FSLN certainly interpreted them this way. Daniel Ortega commented that "minority groups have gained heart, thinking that the FSLN has lost force and that the President-elect of the U.S. is going to support them in attacking Nicaragua" (*Bda* 15 November 1980). The walk-out from the Council of State and COSEP's reaction to Salazar's activities brought strong warnings from the FSLN. Bayardo Arce stated that the FSLN's commitment to a mixed economy and political pluralism was being sorely tested.[56]

But the bourgeoisie was not to be scared off from its alliance with the United States, as this alliance was the only secure political card it retained. The bourgeoisie might own various media outlets and enjoy the firm support of various bishops, but media could be closed and bishops expelled. Nevertheless, Reaganism would make the alliance with the United States more complicated for some bourgeois leaders.

It would soon become evident that the Reagan administration was promoting a polarization of Nicaraguan society. This left bourgeois leaders with a difficult choice between leaving the country to join the contra leadership, or running the risk of being on the receiving end of an eventual Sandinista crack-down. One can assume that at least some of those with immobile capital must have resented this choice tremendously. Thus, while many bourgeois leaders would tie themselves ever more closely to the Reagan project, others would occasionally express frustration with the u.s. strategy.[57]

The final break-down in relations between the Sandinistas and the organized bourgeoisie came in late 1981. In September the government issued Decree 812, declaring a "state of economic and social emergency." The decree promised prison terms of one to three years for taking part in strikes or land seizures, disseminating "false news" on the economy, engaging in "speculation" in the market, and a variety of other offences.[58] Charges under the state of emergency would be heard by the emergency tribunals established by Decree 5. The decree also suspended the application of the Law of Protection to administrative actions linked to the implementation of the state of emergency. In conjunction with the state of emergency, the government also called for a 5 per cent cut in current government expenditures and other austerity measures,[59] and sought to gain tighter control over the parallel market for dollars.

The government declaration of the state of emergency referred to a series of "factors that have impeded the attainment of production and investment goals, such as: the decapitalizing attitude of some entrepreneurs, who have transferred their assets outside the country; the lack of state control on the parallel market for dollars, which has now grown to an intolerable level; fraud in the payment of taxes and duties ... and, on the other hand, the seizure of factories, strikes, and labour indiscipline" (*Bda* 10 September 1981).

Interestingly, the declaration of a state of emergency enjoyed initial support from the bourgeoisie. COSEP's Enrique Dreyfus commented that "the measures are definitely positive," and added that "now we really will have social peace" (*Bda* 10 September 1981; 11 September 1981).[60] Though one could point to previous decrees banning land seizures, it seemed that this time the government was truly determined to suppress rural and urban class tensions.

The bourgeoisie's initial acquiescence to the state of emergency raises interesting questions about its overall motives. It appeared that the bourgeoisie had found a form of authoritarianism it could understand and live with. It is possible that sectors of the bourgeoisie were considering a tacit pact with the FSLN, in which the bourgeoisie would refrain from challenging "popular power," so long as that power maintained peace and quiet in the workplace, and protected property rights.

The FSLN, however, was not ready to transform itself into a neutral arbiter between the bourgeoisie and popular classes, and its actions under the state of emergency gave notice of this. The government twice suspended publication of *La Prensa* for two-day periods for violations of the state of emergency, and Humberto Ortega made highly threatening statements.[61] In late October, COSEP published an open letter criticizing the FSLN for having abandoned the "original project" of the revolution, and claiming the FSLN was leading Nicaragua towards a "Marxist-Leninist adventure." "We are approaching," COSEP declared, "the threshold of the destruction of Nicaragua" (*Psa* 20 October 1981). The government responded by arresting most of the COSEP leaders. At the same time, it cracked down on the Communist Party and its union federation (*Bda* 22 October 1981).[62] Those arrested were charged with violations of Article 4 of Decree 5, which forbade actions that "hurt popular interests." The COSEP leaders were sentenced to seven months in jail, and the arrested "ultra-leftists" to three years (*Bda* 30 October 1981).[63]

A long road had been travelled between late 1979, when COSEP leaders were willing to praise the 1980 economic plan, and late 1981, when those same leaders found themselves imprisoned. There is much room for debate on the particular points of inflection of this road, but the direction of the road is clear: while the FSLN had originally hoped that moral suasion and a blend of carrots and sticks would guarantee both the political neutrality of the bourgeoisie and its incorporation into the state-dominant economy, by 1981 the organized bourgeoisie was in clear opposition.[64]

The FSLN would confront this evolution with various strategies. It would attempt to use "economic incentives" to induce the bourgeoisie to continue to produce; it would also continue to take bourgeois producers into account in formulating economic policies, and seek to reach private understandings with bourgeois elements that had remained aloof from COSEP, such as Alfredo Pellas, who owned the largest sugar mill in the country.

The Sandinistas also sought to strengthen links with small and medium private producers. This strategy led to the formation of the National Union of Farmers and Cattle Ranchers (UNAG), the FSLN's mass organization for private agricultural producers.[65] At the same time the FSLN sought to prevent the development of alliances between this sector and COSEP forces. The fact that UNAG was formed to contest a key social sector with the bourgeoisie led the FSLN to grant it more autonomy than other mass organizations.

Some FSLN leaders were now coming to see that political conditions demanded a greater acceptance of peasant production, despite their initial hostility towards it. This insight developed unevenly among the FSLN leaders, but from this point onwards there would be a gradual retreat from certain objectives of the state-dominant economy, in the name of preserving the revolution, in whatever shape possible. This retreat can be traced most clearly in the evolution of the agrarian reform.

D. AGRARIAN REFORM

The FSLN approach to the land question immediately upon taking power was statist. There was no explicit provision in that approach for addressing peasant land hunger. Rather, it was hoped that employment on state farms, perhaps in conjunction with some colonization projects in marginal areas, would attenuate land hunger without fostering the "historical regression" of peasant production.

Peasant land seizures throughout 1980–1 were in part a response to the Sandinista strategy, a response that at times was encouraged even by members of the FSLN's ATC. The government reacted to these seizures in statist fashion: land seized was generally incorporated into the APP. This had the effect, observers have noted, of discouraging land seizures without returning land to private owners towards whom peasants often felt great animosity.

In early 1980, the government did try to address land hunger through a quasi-agrarian reform. Decrees 230 and 263 set maximum rents for cotton and basic grain lands, maxima that were well below market levels at the time, and authorized MIDINRA to intervene any land that was neither cultivated by the owner nor rented out.[66] It appears that some land seizures represented an attempt to enforce compliance with these decrees. An ATC official commented in July 1980 that "hundreds" of large producers were refusing to rent out land. The ATC would routinely visit the local bank to "investigate" whether an owner had taken out a loan to cultivate a plot of land that was not being rented out. If not, the ATC official said, the land was seized, and the owner was paid the legal rent for the land (*Bda* 7 July 1980).[67]

On the first anniversary of the revolution, in July 1980, Daniel Ortega promised that an agrarian reform law to nationalize all idle lands and address peasant land hunger was imminent (*Bda* 20 July 1980). Yet the decree was not issued. One observer argues that the law was delayed for technical reasons, citing a MIDINRA official's comment that "we need time to get our own act together first" (Collins 1982, 88).[68]

It is more likely that the law was delayed by concerns within the FSLN over the possible impact of an agrarian reform upon both bourgeois behaviour and the future of the state-dominant economy.

The agrarian reform law (Decree 782) was finally presented on 19 July, 1981. The law has been analysed as "anti-feudal," as opposed to anti-capitalist. Article 1 of the decree declared that "this Law guarantees the landed property of all those who work it productively and efficiently." The decree thus provided for expropriation of land that was idle, underused (criteria for defining which were spelt out), or abandoned. Except in cases where the land was abandoned, no person owning less than a total of 350 hectares in the more advanced agricultural departments of the country, or less than 700 hectares elsewhere, was to be affected. No ceiling was placed upon the amount of land an individual could own, so long as that land was worked efficiently.

The central provisions of the law were in fact strikingly close to those of the agrarian reform law of 1963, which provided for expropriation of lands "which do not fulfill their social function because they are idle or uncultivated, or because they are not exploited in an efficient manner, or because the owner does not make use of them" (Tijerino and Palma 1978, 172). Thus, in large part the Sandinistas' agrarian reform law simply called for the enforcement of a law from the era of the Alliance for Progress. Jaime Wheelock argued that the law gave producers a double protection, because it guaranteed their right to land, and because lands distributed to peasants under the terms of the law would put an end to land seizures (*Bda* 22 July 1981).[69]

Yet one section of the law undercut the guarantees to efficient production. Articles 24 to 26 gave MIDINRA the right to turn localities into "agricultural and agrarian reform development zones" for purposes of implementing "a plan or special project of production, of territorial reordering, and/or of population resettlement." Within such zones, which MIDINRA could identify at its discretion, land tenancy could be transformed notwithstanding the limits and guarantees of the rest of the law. As Jaime Wheelock commented, "if we run into any of the limitations which the agrarian reform imposes, when we make the decision to trace out a territory on the map – and there is no limit on the territory that a zone can comprise – then we could make within this zone all the changes that are necessary, including changing property ... be it small, family, or medium and large farms" (1981b, 4). Wheelock went on to note that "we have an instrument that allows us in, shall we say, a discretional manner, to make whatever reforms are necessary to transform agriculture in Nicaragua. The law is drawn up in political terms, in terms that make the law an instrument for the revolutionary alliance, for the national alliance. That is why its application is discretionary. Under the law, everything can potentially be affected ... [N]othing is automatically affected, but everything is potentially affected."

The implication of the law's flexibility was suggested in late 1981 when Wheelock announced the expropriation of land in southern Nicaragua, "some of it idle, the rest of it belonging to Somocistas" (*Bda* 12 December 1981). As the contra war heated up, political expropriations would become an important instrument of government retaliation against suspected contra collaborators.

Land titles acquired under the agrarian reform law were not alienable, and were indivisible for inheritance purposes. Thus, the government sought to withdraw agrarian reform land from the land market. The law gave priority in the granting of land to peasants organized in production cooperatives, although some provision was made for the granting of titles to individual producers. Jaime Wheelock commented in late 1981 that he envisaged a Nicaraguan countryside in which 20 per cent of land was in state hands, while 40 per cent to 50 per cent of the land would be in the hands of "a solid cooperative movement which transforms the broad, variegated, dispersed and primitive peasant smallhold economy into production units that are modern and increasingly technified" (1981c). More than a transferral of land from the modern to the peasant pole of a "bimodal" countryside (Johnston and Kilby 1975), then, the agrarian reform law sought to adjust ownership within the advanced pole, and prevent the "regression" of land to the peasant pole.[70] It was believed that cooperatives could be subjected to central control almost as completely as state farms. In fact, the cooperatives "were initially included in the material balances of the state plans" (Kaimowitz 1989, 71).[71] As Marvin Ortega notes, the state tried to force cooperatives "to sow the products it stipulated, to use the technology it stipulated, to sell at official prices in controlled markets, [and to adopt] the system of organization that it stipulated, independently of the wishes of cooperative members" (1989, 200–1). Ironically, Ortega notes, the cooperatives that were most successful in the long run were those that managed to escape state verticalism (219).

Thus, the orientation towards cooperatives was perfectly consistent with the state-dominant economy. But this orientation would weaken the ability of the agrarian reform process to solidify the FSLN's relation with the peasantry, as shall be seen in subsequent chapters.

E. CONCLUSION

In 1984, Jaime Wheelock would refer to 1981 as "the year in which all our forecasts collapsed" (1985a, 77). Forecasts of an easy recovery of pre-revolution levels of production, forecasts of balanced and popularly oriented economic growth, forecasts of a multi-class alliance developing the economy under FSLN hegemony: all these were dead or dying by the end of 1981.

This is not the verdict of hindsight. The MIPLAN seminar of late 1981 listed among the problems facing the economy "the external breach, which continues to increase; the strong dis-accumulation of the APP; the enormous external debt which now involves debt service payments in the order of 50% of the total value of exports, not including short-term debt ... the failure of material production to meet targeted levels; the excessive expansion of the tertiary sectors and of the state apparatus, which is provoking an unmanageable fiscal deficit; the enormous idle capacity." Together, these elements were "provoking a situation which is now taking on the characteristics of a crisis" (MIPLAN 1981b).

Apart from these economic factors, the U.S.-organized counterrevolution was getting into gear, and would dominate the attention of FSLN leaders in the coming years. As will be seen in the next chapters, the same counterrevolution that made an adjustment of economic direction so necessary also made it politically difficult.

5 Stagnant Economy, Paralysed Policy: 1982–4

The 1982–4 period was one of increasing difficulties for the FSLN, difficulties that sharpened the tension between using state power to transform Nicaragua, and merely holding on to that power. The contra threat loomed as a shadow over the period, influencing relations with both the bourgeoisie and the peasantry. The FSLN sought to hinder the development of links between the bourgeoisie and the contras, while continuing to channel bourgeois demands in an economistic direction. The Sandinistas were slower, however, to recognize the threat that the contras posed for their relations with the peasantry, a perceptual lag that manifested itself in the agrarian reform strategy of this period.

Economic growth tailed off: real gross domestic product (GDP) suffered slight drops in two out of three years, increasing only in 1983. Total GDP growth for the three-year period was just 2.1 per cent, leaving 1984 real GDP at 76 per cent of its 1977 level. This modest growth compared to a total planned growth of 14.6 per cent (Cabieses 1986). GDP per capita dropped 7.6 per cent in the 1982–4 period, and by 1984 stood at just 61 per cent of its 1977 level.[1]

In addition, significant economic imbalances developed. The 1982–4 period saw an average annual current account deficit of $640 million, much higher than average annual exports.[2] Nicaragua could finance such deficits owing to continued high levels of external financing. This financing, and the need to renegotiate earlier loans,[3] led to a 70 per cent increase in the external debt during the 1982–4 period. The fiscal deficit crept up from its 1980–1 level of 10 per cent, reaching 14 per cent of GDP in 1982. In 1983, the deficit exploded, reaching 30 per cent of GDP. This occurred despite an increase in the tax burden, from 19 per cent of GDP in 1981 to 26 per cent in 1983. Government spending rose from 33 per cent of GDP in 1981 to 61 per cent in 1983. Though the deficit fell to 25 per cent of GDP in 1984, it had come to represent a major factor of disequilibrium in the economy.[4] Partly as a result of the fiscal deficit, inflation crept slowly upwards, measuring 22 per cent, 33 per cent, and 50 per cent for 1982, 1983, and 1984, respectively. As unofficial-market prices increasingly diverged from official ones, the consumer price index (CPI) became increasingly suspect. In general, government policy failed to adapt to these various imbalances, a failure whose costs would be felt for the rest of the decade.

A. STATE-SECTOR ORGANIZATION

In contrast to the great fanfare that accompanied the publication of the 1980 economic plan, and to a lesser extent that of 1981, the planning process became invisible during the 1982–4 period. The National Directorate did not approve the 1982 economic plan, and the 1983 plan, though approved, was classified as confidential. Subsequent plans enjoyed only limited circulation. In 1984, the government established the "Economic Council," which was made up of various cabinet members. The council was to be the "highest organ of consultation" of the government junta on economic matters (Decree 1359), and the status of the Ministry of Planning (MIPLAN) seemed to be downgraded to that of a "secretariat" for the council. Observers noted that the junta was increasingly relying on specialists who had been affiliated with the Ortegas' insurrectional tendency (JPRS LAM–84–079). These specialists would assume a more visible role in establishing economic policy from 1985 on.

The disappearance of planning from public view corresponded to MIPLAN's loss of prestige within the FSLN. In August 1983, Daniel Ortega criticized the planners for consistently setting unrealistic growth targets, the first such public criticism that I know of (*Bda* 14 August 1983).[5] In September 1983, an "economic cell" was quietly set up to examine the general direction of economic policy. The cell, most of whose members were skeptical of MIPLAN and its conception of planning, would help formulate the new economic policy adopted in early 1985 (Martínez 1990, 123).

Though FSLN leaders were increasingly aware of the fact that intensified military aggression and the state of the economy in general "made it practically impossible to plan anything" (Cabieses 1986, 14), they continued to endorse certain policies typical of a catch-up socialist economy. Daniel Ortega, for example, endorsed the main objectives of Plan 83, which included the "maximization" of material production, and the intensification of state control of the circulation of goods (MIPLAN 1983; *Bda* 6 May 1983). MIPLAN targets continued to be set in splendid isolation from the economic realities facing most Nicaraguans. Thus, the 1984 economic plan called for a real increase of 27 per cent in investment spending, and a 0.1 per cent drop in private consumption, despite the 46 per cent fall in the latter category since 1977 (MIPLAN 1984a, 155, 177).

MIDINRA's Bid for Control

MIPLAN's quest for domination of the economy was blocked above all by Jaime Wheelock's Ministry of Agriculture (MIDINRA), which had its own views on the proper organization of the state. These views were clearly articulated in a 1982 document from CIERA, MIDINRA's research centre. CIERA started from a frankly "productionist" premise: "Whereas under capitalism those areas of state activity that have to do with circulation (sales, financing) are privileged ... in Nicaragua today, as in all systems that are struggling to free themselves from capitalism, social emphasis should restore material production and reproduction to its true status" (1983a, 11). This productionist orientation, however, was being threatened by "institutional feudalism":

When the revolutionary government set forth the intent to direct social services in accordance with the needs of production, it was moving in the right direction. However, institutions reconstructed on the base of preceding state structures are developing particularistic features that distort that clear vision; they are beginning to assume an autonomous existence and are attempting to impose their own objectives on the whole of the state apparatus. Unless policies are spelled out on the basis of and in conjunction with the growth of basically agricultural production, agro-industry, and the extractive industries, etc., the effectiveness of the state will be reduced (ibid.)

Thus, like MIPLAN, MIDINRA was advocating a centralized, hierarchical state structure. The difference between the two visions, of course, was the question of which institution should occupy the apex of the state pyramid. CIERA argued that "the revolutionizing of our economy entails in great measure the revolutionizing of the nation's agriculture. This responsibility falls essentially on the shoulders of [MIDINRA]" (ibid., 14). The CIERA document went on to lament the fact that "although it is responsible for the agricultural sector, MIDINRA is unable to embrace the entirety of the instruments and means of action that define an agricultural policy" (12).

Taken together, the foregoing quotes indicate a clear desire for control over many elements of the state: MIDINRA should be able to influence policies relating to "circulation" (i.e., the banking system, and the internal and external trade ministries), and it should be able to curb the "autonomous existence" of the social ministries.

These goals were to a large degree realized. MIDINRA, for example, was able to place representatives on the banks' loan approval committees. These representatives, argues Biondi-Morra, were often the most powerful members of the committees (1988, 354). One thus had MIDINRA-dominated committees approving loans to MIDINRA. This penetration of the banking system was a key factor in the spread of a productionist orientation throughout the state.

MIDINRA's bid for power may have been more successful than that of MIPLAN because of the attractiveness of MIDINRA's long-term vision. While MIPLAN's quest for detailed central planning struck many Sandinistas as quixotic, MIDINRA's project had the virtue of at least apparent plausibility. This vision was articulated by MIDINRA head Jaime Wheelock: "The revolution is beginning to develop a new economic model, based on the search for a new role in the international division of labour. We can continue to be producers of consumer goods, but it is not the same thing to produce unprocessed consumer goods as it is to produce processed goods. We wish to be an industrial country, that sells manufactured goods, by processing our own agricultural goods, packaging our food, making furniture out of our wood ... This is the profound national sense of the revolution" (1983, 110; elision in original).

Apart from promoting the processing of agricultural goods, the MIDINRA vision called for a significant modernization of agriculture. The country faced a choice, Wheelock argued: "Do we take as our principal path the use of technical assistance, land, credit, etc. to affect the universe of 200,000 *manzanas* of traditional [maize] production, which now yields eight to ten quintals per *manzana*? Or do we follow the path of giving priority to compact high-technology projects?" (1985a, 60). Yet Wheelock believed that this choice was no choice at all: the high-technology path was the "only viable one" (ibid., 109), the only way to produce food and export products simultaneously (1983, 94), the only way to get milk to Nicaraguan children (1984b).

This view would exercise a tremendous influence on Nicaraguan economic strategy, yet at no time did Wheelock ever feel compelled to justify his position. He was aware that the path chosen involved significant difficulties. In a 1984 interview, Wheelock noted that "intensive technology involves, because of the need for chemicals, more dependence upon imported inputs; to some extent, sowing three times a year can intensively deplete the natural resources of the land and can hurt the soils.

There is not the sufficient technical force in the country to support the vigorous level of growth that is planned" (Ortega, Wheelock, and Arce 1986, 246). Yet he repeated that this path was the "only viable one."

Part of his belief that the high-technology path was viable stemmed from a remarkable view of the workings of international capitalism. Asked "Where will the money come from?", Wheelock replied: "From the world crisis ... The generalization [of the crisis] has left equipment companies in Europe, North America and even in Latin America with large inventories that they cannot sell. And so there is a tendency on the part of states, instead of subsidizing these companies, to help them economically by granting them lines of credit. So Nicaragua ... has sought these lines of credit for capital goods" (ibid., 250).

This assessment was offered when it was quite clear that Nicaragua's access to lines of credit from the developed capitalist countries was disappearing.[6] Wheelock was, in short, a "techno-utopian": advanced technology could solve Nicaragua's main development problems, would descend on the country at little or no cost, and had no side-effects worth considering.

This vision began to be implemented in a great investment push during the 1982–4 period. The push reflected Wheelock's advocacy of agro-industry and agricultural modernization. A survey of Nicaragua's main investment projects in the 1979–85 period indicates that the agricultural and agro-industrial sectors accounted for over 70 per cent of the total value of these projects, ten times the share of the industrial sector (Spoor 1987).

Apart from reflecting Wheelock's vision, however, these large investment projects reflected typical features of catch-up socialism. Feasibility studies had not been completed for the majority of the projects launched during this period (Argüello, Croes, and Kleiterp 1987, 31). A high government official told me in 1987 that many of those making investment decisions in the state simply did not believe in cost-benefit analyses of any stripe. An atmosphere in which projects were promoted "at any cost" was prevalent during this period.[7] The logic of decision making seemed to be based on the need to generate production that was easily captured by the state sector.[8]

A project that reveals much about the thinking underlying the decisions of MIDINRA strategists was the TIMAL sugar refinery. The refinery was the largest single agricultural investment project, and MIDINRA officials claimed it would be the largest refinery in the world. Financed by loans from Cuba and as many as eight other countries, the project involved building a 12-square-kilometre artificial lake. Water from the lake would travel several miles in a cement canal, to be used in sophisticated centre-pivot irrigation systems. Sugar would be harvested mechanically. The bagasse would generate power, making the refinery self-sufficient in energy, and even allowing it to contribute electricity to the national grid.

The level of mechanization of TIMAL and other MIDINRA projects suggests that MIDINRA's operative assumption was that labour would be a scarce resource in Nicaragua for some time to come. War, emigration, and salary controls did generate a wage-labour shortage in the mid-1980s. Yet this shortage should have been considered conjunctural, not made the basis of a long-term technological strategy. Nicaragua's GDP had dropped substantially since 1977, while its rate of population growth was the second highest in Latin America. These are not conditions that make for a long-term labour shortage. Predictably, as the contra war wound down, Nicaragua was faced with severe unemployment. In addition, two of the conditions that generated a labour shortage, emigration and low salaries, created an even more severe shortage of *skilled* labour that was necessary for the success of a high-technology strategy. It was reported in early 1986 that 75 out of 300 technicians trained in Cuba for the TIMAL project had quit, citing frustrations over wages and a lack of possibilities for advancement (*Bda* 8 January 1986). Twenty per cent of construction workers on the project had also left, most of them heading into the commercial sector.

One project that symbolized MIDINRA's willingness to marginalize peasant production was the "Contingency Plan" for maize production, launched in 1983. The principal peasant crop would now be grown on irrigated Pacific Coast cotton land, both publicly and privately owned, between cotton seasons. The plan would require over $18 million in imported capital goods, mostly the same sophisticated irrigation equipment used in the TIMAL project.

The plan sought to respond to the perceived failings of peasant production, to the long-term goal of moving basic grain production out of the central highlands, and to the intensification of military conflict in those highlands. In the first year, MIDINRA officials projected yields of 93 quintals of maize per hectare; actual yields were 50 quintals per hectare (Zalkin 1987, 973). Undeterred, they projected maize and sorghum yields of 101 quintals per hectare for 1984 (*Bda* 24 March 1984). Actual yields appear to have been closer to 57 quintals per hectare (Spoor 1987). Though yields were lower than expected, they were much higher than the national average, and the Contingency Plan began to make a substantial contribution to national maize production. But at what price? Costs of production were higher than the norm (MIDINRA 1984), and at a more realistic exchange rate, the cost gap between MIDINRA's import-intensive maize production and traditional production would have been even wider. Defenders of the strategy maintained that it was essential to increase grain production "whatever the cost." This is a weak argument, as a strategy of promoting peasant maize production "whatever the cost" instead of lowering real producer prices might have produced more favourable results at lower cost than did the Contingency Plan.

It is also argued that the strategy cannot be evaluated merely in economic terms, since the concentration of production outside the central highlands was a military necessity. While it is true that the war was interfering with highland agricultural production, it is also true that the focusing of human and material resources on the Contingency Plan may have intensified the alienation of small producers and increased their cooperation with the contras. Indeed, while Contingency Plan maize output was increasing, peasant maize and bean output was dropping, leading to a net decrease in production of the two main food crops (Spoor, 1987). Import-intensive production was replacing low-import production.[9]

In conclusion, the viability of MIDINRA's development vision was more apparent than real. The strategy ignored the foreign exchange constraint on the Nicaraguan economy, naively assuming that foreign donors would indefinitely finance the low-cost transfer of capital goods; it was informed by a "techno-utopianism" that ignored Nicaragua's concrete technological needs; and it ignored the political implications of economic strategy, in particular the implication for relations with the peasantry. As the utopian nature of the MIDINRA project became clearer, the government sought to modify its development strategy. Nevertheless, the very scale of the projects initiated in the 1982–4 period, and the predictable delays in the implementation of these projects meant that MIDINRA's development vision dominated government investment for the rest of the decade.

Bureaucratism Revisited

The greater involvement of the state in the economy during the 1982–4 period rendered problems of administration ever more visible. Attempted cures for these problems were often worse than the disease. Thus, to avoid "sectorialism" and "anarchy" in the assignment of foreign exchange, a complex mechanism was established in which all requests for imports had to pass through reviews and two commissions, one of which included a member of the government junta, the minister of external trade, and the head of the Central Bank (Maxfield and Stahler-Sholk 1985, 255). Such a structure ensured that "everyone" was consulted on import decisions, but also led to long delays in foreign exchange allocations. A 1987 analysis reported delays of up to two years between the time that imports were requested and then finally approved (Pizarro 1987, 18). Uncharacteristically, MIPLAN argued for a decentralization of import decisions (1984a, 167), but in a situation in which foreign exchange was increasingly scarce, the government chose to maintain tight control.

FSLN leaders continued to attribute problems in the state apparatus more to the problem of "bureaucratism" than to the overall project of a state-dominant economy. Typically, problems in the state were seen as leftovers from the *ancien régime*.[10] This analysis was not merely rhetorical, and had real consequences. The view that problems within the state reflected the political or moral deficiencies of bureaucrats carrying within themselves the spirit of the Somoza regime fostered the belief that greater direct involvement of the FSLN in the day-to-day affairs of government would cure or at least attenuate bureaucratism. While the party had been active within the state since July 1979, party-state links were intensified with the regionalization of some government activities initiated in 1982 (*Bda* 20 July 1982).[11] By 1985, the same individuals headed both the party and the state apparatus at the regional level. Though aimed at "Sandinizing" the state, some observers feel the intensified party-state link served instead to bureaucratize the party, as cadres found an increasing portion of their time occupied by governmental tasks.

Behaviour of State Firms

During this period, the output-maximizing orientation of state firms continued, to the detriment of their possible contribution to state accumulation.[12] The view of Henry Ruiz is typical of the period: "We are interested in getting goods to the people, not in profits" (JPRS LAM–84–131). This orientation, along with an accommodating financial system, naturally gave the state sector greater productive dynamism than other economic sectors. Jaime Wheelock stated in 1986 that the output of state farms rose from 16 per cent of national agricultural output in 1980 to 26 per cent in the 1984–5 cycle, despite a reduction in the size of state holdings. He added that this proved the state farms were more "efficient" than the Somoza farms out of which they had been formed, since the latter had only accounted for 16 per cent of agricultural output (Wheelock 1986c, 42). The inference is interesting, as it presumes that "efficiency" is measured only in terms of yields per unit of land, and by extension, that land is the only scarce factor of production.

This conception of "efficiency" predominates in planning documents prepared by both MIDINRA and MIPLAN: table after table presents targets and results for total output and yield levels, yet one is hard pressed to find any mention – much less actual targets – of efficiency in the use of other factors of production, such as labour and imported inputs. This silence is linked to the lack of mention of financial performance. It is thus not surprising that, from 1979 to 1985, only 4 of 102 state farm complexes were profitable (Colburn 1990, 24). Far from being the "engine of accumulation," as the 1980 economic plan had envisioned, the People's Property Area was becoming an increasingly costly burden upon the state: by 1984, transfers from the government to state firms reached 7 per cent of GDP (Kleiterp 1989, 97).[13]

These poor financial results, it should be noted, occurred in a world of topsy-turvy prices. State firms, much more than their private counterparts, were constrained to respect official prices, which were diverging ever more rapidly from market-clearing prices.[14] Thus it would be unfair to cite financial losses as proof that state firms were inefficient in some overall sense. The argument is rather that state firms were not even oriented towards financial efficiency. In the words of a state manager cited by Biondi-Morra, "Eventually management had to accept the fact that the rules of the game had changed, and that to have a company in a state of virtual bankruptcy no longer mattered. Once this conclusion was reached, nobody in the company had any more qualms about borrowing" (1988, 350). State firms were thus exhibiting the disdain for the profit motive typical of firms in a socialist economy.

B. PRICE POLICY

The government was reluctant to supplement its policy of setting official prices and establishing "secure channels" with actual rationing. In late 1981, however, Internal Trade Minister Dionisio Marenco commented that the setting of official prices was having little or no effect on actual prices. The government was faced with two alternatives, Marenco stated: either "saturate the market" with goods in order to bring market-clearing prices down to their official level, or implement rationing (*Bda* 11 June 1981). The first option being impossible, the government chose the second.

Rationing may originally have been seen as a means to regulate the consumption of exportables. The first affected product was sugar, rationing of which was gradually developed in January and February 1982. But rice was added to the "consumer card" in late 1982 (*Bda* 13 October 1982), and laundry soap and cooking oil in early 1983 (*Bda* 23 March 1983). In addition, gasoline rationing was imposed in August 1982, with private vehicles being limited to 20 gallons per month (*Bda* 1 August 1982). As each product joined the rationing scheme, the state nationalized its distribution, making it illegal for private traders to market the product.

There appear to have been heated debates within the government around the decision to begin rationing. Alejandro Martínez, then minister of external trade would later blame foreign advisor E.V.K. Fitzgerald for the decision, claiming Fitzgerald, one of Daniel Ortega's most trusted advisors throughout the 1980s, treated the Nicaraguan revolution "as an experiment" (Martínez 1990, 106). If Fitzgerald was influential in the decision, he had much logic on his side. Once the government had decided to get key products to consumers at controlled prices, something like rationing was inevitable: to sell official products without such control (as was done for many products deemed non-essential) simply handed a source of accumulation to the "resellers" who lined up to buy products at official prices in order to resell them in the unofficial market.[15]

During the time I lived in Nicaragua, opinion on rationing seemed divided. Some did complain that it limited their freedom to purchase various products, but many Nicaraguans expressed to me the view that the rationing scheme was fundamentally fair, and that it ensured that everyone received a certain supply of key products at affordable prices. Opposition rhetoric notwithstanding, I do not believe the FSLN paid a serious political price for the rationing per se, so long as the "secure channels" continued to deliver the goods.[16] Nationalizing the distribution of some products, however, suspends the capitalist "naturalness" of supply problems, just as official prices suspend the "naturalness" of capitalist prices. Rationing thus increased the political impact of reductions in the supply of consumption goods.

In comparison with subsequent years, the unofficial market had a relatively low profile in 1982. Margins between official and free market prices were relatively low. The spread between the unofficial-market rate and the highest legal rate of the dollar (the "parallel" rate), however, increased throughout 1982 from 1.4:1 to 2.8:1 at year's end (Spoor 1987, 30). The unofficial-market dollar rate governed the price of a large number of imported products in the unofficial market. By the end of 1983, the exchange rate spread would reach 6:1, and a year after that it had hit an astonishing 16:1.

Much more public alarm was expressed over the unofficial market in 1983. Not only were price spreads increasing, but many more people were shifting from formal sector work to unofficial market activities, which were regarded by the government as socially noxious. Though the analysis of the unofficial market continued to be highly politicized, the phenomenon was in large part the result of government policies: the increasing attraction of unofficial-market activities reflected a combination of ever greater profits to be made there, as the gap between official and market-clearing prices widened, and the drop in real salaries in the formal sector.[17]

Throughout 1983, the mass organizations pushed for stricter controls on marketing. "Speculators," commented a Sandinista Defence Committee official, "are as damaging as armed counterrevolutionaries" (*Bda* 24 March 1983). In his speech on the fourth anniversary of the revolution, Daniel Ortega decried "the problem of the monopolizers, of the speculative hoarders, of those who have a Somocista mentality and continue making money on the hunger and needs of the people ... We must punish with real severity the speculative practices of monopolization and, generally, all trafficking in the hunger and necessities of the people. The laws are there. The decisions are there. But we need the energy of everyone to force compliance with these decisions" (1985, 208).

Such rhetoric would become quite frequent in subsequent years, but it always outstripped the actions taken against the unofficial market. While Sandinista rhetoric attempted to depict the "speculators" as a small class of enemies of the people, this was not the perception of most Nicaraguans, who found many of their neighbours or family members involved, in one way or another, in unofficial-market activities. A 1983 study warned that attempts to encourage mass participation in the enforcement of price controls were creating divisions in popular neighbourhoods (CIERA 1983b, 80). By 1984, as the Sandinistas confronted the unofficial market, they were forced to say, like the old Pogo cartoon, "We have met the enemy, and he is us." While many of those engaged in unofficial-market activities passionately hated the Sandinistas (as anyone could confirm on a trip through Managua's Eastern Market), there were also many who supported the FSLN on most issues yet ignored its discourse on economic morality. As Carlos Vilas commented of the urban informal sectors, "There does not seem to be for them any particularly acute contradiction between ideological adhesion to the Revolution, and even participation in some of its tasks, and fiscal evasion, price gouging, and the hoarding of basic products" (1984, 417–8).

Thus, firm action against the unofficial market in the name of the state-dominant economy could have threatened the FSLN's urban political base – just as its attempts to foster the state-dominant economy in the countryside was eroding its rural base. Hence, while willing to engage in certain attacks on the Eastern Market, the government generally limited itself to merely rhetorical assaults on the unofficial market. This made the discourse of economic morality increasingly utopian and irrelevant for people. To an increasing degree, "material" and "moral" stimuli were pointing in contradictory directions. Many quite pro-Sandinista Nicaraguans of my acquaintance, though willing to risk their lives fighting against the contras, nevertheless saw respect for economic laws as naivety.[18] Thus, the "moral substratum" of the new economy was being destroyed by policies that made it simply too costly to obey the law, and too easy to do otherwise.

While price policy was favouring accumulation within the unofficial market, it was also leading to disaccumulation within the state complex. This disaccumulation was laying the basis for the inflationary spiral of the second half of the 1980s. The irony is that policies aimed at controlling inflation contributed to one of the worst cases of hyperinflation in history. We noted the 1980 economic plan's concern that inflation would hurt popular sectors. Inflation was also viewed as a threat to the stability and predictability required for a state-administered economy. Various policies were designed to dampen the inflationary impact of increased government spending. Costs were controlled by the cheap credit policy, by the government practice of selling imported inputs to producers applying the c$10:$1 official exchange rate, and by salary controls, which also served to dampen demand-pull inflation. When all else failed, price controls were used to suppress inflation.

But these measures, with the exception of salary controls, limited the income of the state complex. The banking system was lending money at negative real interest rates.[19] Thus, the state banks were collecting less real purchasing power if and when loans were repaid than they had originally issued.[20] The banks could not merely roll over purchasing power when they extended new credit; rather, they had to create new purchasing power, and thus fuel inflation. This problem was not addressed until mid-1988, and the manner in which the government addressed the problem carried a significant political cost.

Price controls and the exchange rate policy worked in the same direction. Price controls were more easily imposed on public sector production, but the policy of "reasonable margins" applied to such production frustrated the hope that the public sector would be a source of state accumulation. In the extreme, if the profit margin applied to arrive at the selling price is lower than the rate of inflation for the period of production, the public company ends up with less purchasing power than it started with. To continue producing, it must seek further credit.

In addition, unless it can be ensured that state-produced goods stay within the secure channels until they reach the consumer, the price restraint exercised by state companies will not benefit consumers. Private agents who succeed in coming between the public company and the consumer, to the extent that they can sell the product at a near-market price, become the main beneficiaries of the state pricing policies.[21] An example of this phenomenon is that of beef: by late 1984, the state slaughterhouses were offering c$6,000 per head to producers, while clandestine houses offered c$15,000. As a result, only the state producers sold to the state houses. Yet the same state slaughterhouses turned around and sold a large part of their production to private merchants at c$17 a pound, only to have it show up in the Managua market at c$50 (Wheelock 1985b, 18).

For some products, inflation was also widening the gap between prices paid to producers and subsidized consumer prices. By late 1984, the state was paying bean producers c$8 a pound, putting out c$2.75 for storage and transport costs, then selling the pound of beans to consumers at c$4, leading to the extreme of producers selling all their beans in order to repurchase them more cheaply from the state marketing agency.[22]

The fixed exchange rate also caused state disaccumulation. The government sold imported inputs to producers applying a c$10:$1 rate of conversion. This kept price increases for these imported inputs below 10 per cent per year over the 1980–3 period, while domestic inflation as registered by the CPI was 26.6 per cent per year. Initially, the government tried to apply the same rate of exchange in calculating the prices at which it bought export output from producers. Thus, producer prices were tied to world prices by a fixed rate, despite the differential between domestic and world inflation. This meant that nominal producer prices for coffee and cotton for the 1981–2 agricultural cycle were lower than those for the 1977–8 cycle (Spoor 1987), despite an accumulated inflation of 173 per cent between December 1977 and December 1981.

In January 1982, the Sandinista Assembly recognized that the c$10:$1 rate could no longer be applied rigidly to exports. Producer prices were effectively freed from world prices, and a cost-plus logic came to be used.[23] Thus, various product-by-product implicit rates of exchange were created, all higher than the official rate. These implicit rates ranged from about c$20:$1 for cotton in the 1983–4 harvest to c$100:$1 for sugar at the beginning of 1985.[24] In effect the state, which was "selling" dollars through its imported input policy at c$10:$1, was "buying" them through its producer price policy at much higher rates.

Thus began "exchange rate loss." The state complex had to throw more *córdobas* into circulation to buy exportables than it withdrew from circulation through its sales of imports. Exchange rate loss quickly became a major source of monetary expansion, rising from an estimated 5 per cent of nominal GDP in 1982 to nearly 14 per cent in 1984 (Arana, Stahler-Shock, et al. 1987, 22).

To summarize, the interaction of anti-inflation policies, in a situation where inflation was inevitable owing to the fiscal deficit and expansive credit, turned many of these policies into their opposite, that is, into inflation-generating policies. At one pole of the economic system were private producers and merchants reaping inflation-based profits and taking advantage of the gap between official and market-clearing prices to earn large trading margins. A large part of the profits earned by this sector entered the unofficial market for dollars, in a search for either foreign exchange itself or for luxury imports that the official imports policy had tried to reduce.

At the other pole of the system was a state complex continually resorting to monetary emission to cover its government and credit activities, yet continually transferring purchasing power to the other pole of the economy, through its negative real rates of interest, exchange rate loss, and the "reasonable margin" pricing policy that restrained state-sector prices. These initially anti-inflationary measures impoverished the state complex, leading to a choice between cutting back on social services and other government spending, reducing real wage levels, "printing money" to resolve the contradiction, or applying all three responses in varying degrees. To the extent that the state resorted to creating new purchasing power, a vicious circle was created: as the rate of inflation rose, the transfer of purchasing power from the state complex to the opposite pole was intensified, in so far as real interest rates became ever more negative, and the public sector's "reasonable margin" policy became ever more self-defeating.

While it impoverished the state, government price and distribution policy also contributed to the alienation of the peasantry. In June 1982, the government's Managua Market Corporation prohibited the selling of basic grains at higher-than-official prices. With official consumer prices below prices being paid to producers, the policy was designed to give the state marketing agency a monopoly on basic grains (*Bda* 3 June 1982). This objective was never realized, and peasants continued to sell at least part of their marketed output to private traders.[25] Yet in so doing they continued to meet with state harassment.

Without directly questioning the objective of state marketing of peasant products, officials of the FSLN's National Union of Farmers and Cattle Ranchers (UNAG) warned of the dangers of the current price policy. Official prices, UNAG head Wilberto Lara commented in early 1984, "are the victim of tortoise-ism," always being set too late (*Bda* 12 March 1984). In late 1984 UNAG argued that official prices had fallen below the cost of production (*END* 12 September 1984).

An ironic aspect of all this is that, just as the pricing policy applied to state-produced goods often benefited private agents more than final consumers, so too did the peasant price policy. For example, most maize bought at official prices from peasants was not sold to consumers, but to private urban tortilla makers whose prices to consumers were generally uncontrolled.

Official statements during the period indicate a confused awareness of the problem of peasant prices. In a 1983 interview, Jaime Wheelock boasted of the "advantageous prices for maize and beans" (1983, 89). Yet in the same interview he commented that "at a certain point, we and some sectors of production and [state] regulation wanted to make the law of value disappear. But what disappeared instead were nearly all the basic grains. We tried to set a price for beans and force everyone to sell at this price, even the peasants, so that there would be a supply of low-price beans. But what happened? Not only did prices rise even more quickly because of shortages, but these products disappeared" (117). Despite this comment, attempts to suspend the workings of the "law of value"[26] for basic grains were to continue for some time yet. Baumeister and Neira argue that a response to the problem of peasant prices was blocked by state-production advocates in the government, who felt that price increases would only strengthen their enemy, the large private producers (1986, 296).

An additional irritant for the peasantry was the disarticulation of trade created by the state purchasing agency's failure to supply goods that the peasants might purchase, a problem whose importance was now being grasped by government officials. In May 1984, Internal Trade Minister Dionisio Marenco stressed that getting manufactured products out to the countryside was at least as important as increasing prices for peasant products (1984). In late 1984, Jaime Wheelock admitted that this problem had "tremendously decomposed the peasant economy" (1985b, 34).

By 1984, there was widespread awareness in official circles of the problems being generated by price policy in general. The 1984 economic plan urged that inflation be used to "recover surpluses for the State," and noted various negative consequences of low official prices: deliveries of milk to state channels were dropping, clandestine lumber production was rising, among others (MIPLAN 1984a, 140, 19). But the official response to the problems created by the pattern of economic control was to propose more control. The main objective of price policy, the 1984 plan insisted, should still be the "defence of real salaries" (136). In May, the Sandinista Assembly declared that "it is necessary to exercise resolute control over products that are important for popular consumption" (*Bda* 19 May 1984). This was interpreted as a call for a "war on speculation," which became the watchword for a while.

In this spirit, the long-promised new Consumer Protection Law was introduced in the Council of State in May 1984. The law gave police, not just the courts, the power to apply penalties (*Bda* 25 June 1984). It also gave the Ministry of Internal Trade (MICOIN) the power to intervene "any firm or distribution channel" it thought necessary in order to control the flow of any particular product (Marenco 1984). In introducing the law before the Council of State, Minister of Internal Trade Dionisio Marenco warned that "either we break the hands of the speculators or they will break us." But he also warned that "an indiscriminate campaign against merchants will cause many problems, distorting the existing distribution networks and causing absolutely unnecessary political discontent."

Marenco also struck a new note, indicating a shift in thinking that he and a few others had been developing over the previous year. Part of the problem, Marenco argued, was that official prices were "laughable" relative to other prices in the economy, and the government was "killing the possibility of using money as a means of economic stimulus and of economic control" (ibid.). He also announced that consumer subsidies would be eliminated, a decision that would take several years fully to implement. The elimination of subsidies, Marenco acknowledged, "is not a decision that will win applause or win a popularity contest, but a very difficult decision. That is why it has been considered in great depth, as it has very serious implications, but it is the only alternative we can see at this time."

Marenco's speech is significant, as it presaged the major change in economic policy implemented in early 1985. The new thinking led to increases in official consumer prices for twenty-five products in August 1984 that narrowed the gap between these and unofficial-market prices (*Bda* 3 August 1984).[27] In late September, MICOIN announced the opening of a "parallel market" for goods moving through official channels, in which one could buy unrestricted quantities of goods at near-market-clearing prices. The parallel market strategy, which reflected a concern to shift accumulation from the unofficial market to the state complex, angered many Nicaraguans, as MICOIN was suddenly able to fill supermarkets with all sorts of goods, after proclaiming for weeks that everything was in extremely short supply. The new strategy was also announced after weeks of newspaper advertisements proclaiming the importance of the "secure channels," and left many people confused about the direction of government policy.

The increases in official prices and the opening of the parallel market created great resentment towards MICOIN. In my economics classes, Marenco was the only government official my Sandinista students felt comfortable attacking by name. If MICOIN's new policies were a foretaste of the new economic policy, the political response could hardly have been encouraging for the government, and explains in part why the broad reforms, when they finally came in 1985, moved forward in fits and starts.

Salaries

The government policy of salary austerity continued in this period. Deflated by the CPI, average real salaries in 1984 were 23 per cent lower than 1980, and 44 per cent below their 1977 level.[28] The FSLN leadership continued to counsel patience on the matter. In his 1982 May Day speech, Tomás Borge warned against "economistic errors," and declared that the working class would be "going against history" to struggle primarily for economic demands (1985d, 25).

The FSLN's Sandinista Workers' Central (CST), generally docile throughout the 1980s on salary matters, showed some short-lived restlessness during this period. Through 1982, the CST toed the line. But the National Council of the CST that met in July 1983 was in a more belligerent mood. Workers had previously called for price controls instead of salary increases, CST head Lucío Jimenez declared, but price controls had not been effective. Now both controls and salary increases were necessary. He noted that low wages were hurting production, giving the example of a local textile factory that was short on workers (*Bda* 6 July 1983).

The CST proposed increases in minimum wages, asking for example that the industrial minimum, frozen since June 1981, be raised by 70 per cent (*Bda* 10 July 1983). Interestingly, this proposal was made in the face of direct criticism from the National Directorate's labour liaison, Victor Tirado. Tirado met the CST demands with a confusing speech, which proclaimed, among other things, that "salary is one of the basic categories to carry out the law of unceasing and continuous development of the productive forces. Thus its handling should be done in a serious and responsible fashion, so that it can play an important role in the struggle for the fundamental interests of the working class" (1986, 93). Tirado argued that salary increases should only reflect productivity increases, and he promoted piece-work, which would become an important element of policy in the coming years.[29] Tirado finished by counselling workers to "work as hard as possible without asking for anything; thus should be the working class, the vanguard class" (97). After this confrontation with the National Directorate, the CST leadership retreated. By August 1983, Jimenez was calling for a brake on salary increases until the problem of salary "anarchy" had been addressed (*Bda* 12 August 1983).

Thus, salaries were not adjusted, even though the Ministry of Labour itself was calling for a 50 per cent increase in minimum wages (*Bda* 28 July 1983). Official documents recognized the negative consequences of the salary policy. The 1984 economic plan stated that "employment and salary policy should seek to stem the flight of qualified workers from the industrial sector" (MIPLAN 1984a, 56). The National Directorate, however, was concerned that compensating for the accumulated decline in real salaries would trigger a sharp rise in inflation. In his 1984 May Day speech, Jaime Wheelock commented: "In the present situation, it is worthless for the union to go to the company and demand a salary increase ... If we increase salaries, prices will increase faster. Because if we increase salaries, what happens? Salary is a cost of production for beans, for cotton, for maize, for sugar, for everything" (1984a).

This simple analysis, which had been the stock-in-trade of the leadership since the post-insurrection months, was increasingly diverging from reality. First, as real salaries decreased, they became an ever less significant component of total costs. Second, inflation during this period was essentially demand-driven. This is demonstrated by the wide gaps between official prices set using a cost-plus logic, and market-clearing prices.[30] Salaries were adjusted upwards in late 1984, and they would be readjusted periodically with the shift of economic policy in 1985. But the view that salary increases were to be avoided to the extent possible continued for several more years.

While many workers were concerned about the erosion of their purchasing power, the government was more concerned with "anarchy" in salary administration, which was leading to the "pirating" of workers between state institutions, and a consequent high rate of mobility of skilled personnel. Attempts to limit movement within the state sector appeared in the 1982 budget (Decree 917). By 1983, the government was resolved to address the issue. Victor Tirado noted that the new government had inherited a salary structure that was a "faithful reflection of the anarchy and injustice of the Somocista dictatorship." Salary differentials had not taken into account the varying "complexity of work" and "worker dedication" (1986, 90). It was now necessary, Tirado argued, to impose the principle of equal pay for equal "quantity and quality" of work (94).

In July 1983, discussion began in various state institutions on the implementation of the "System for the Standardization and Organization of Work and Salaries" (SNOTS). The SNOTS system, whose first phase was gradually implemented through 1984, sought to classify all salaried work in the country into one of twenty-eight categories, according to the degree of "complexity" of the work, level of training required, etc.[31] All workers in any given category would receive the same basic salary. Where it was possible to set quantitative goals for a certain job, that job would be "standardized," and the worker's salary would depend on meeting a basic "norm." Such workers would also receive bonuses for overfulfilment of their norms. Essentially, therefore, they would be doing piece-work.[32]

The plan also contemplated a variety of other bonuses, which could be applied even to workers whose output could not easily be quantified. Among the other forms discussed and/or implemented were bonuses for seniority and educational level, bonuses for working in a region to which the government was trying to supply workers, and bonuses depending on the evaluation of work by one's supervisor.[33]

Predictably, workers who had been rebuffed in their search for general salary increases now focused their attention on the job classification procedure. In late 1984, the first legal strike in several years broke out at the Victoria beer factory, as workers demanded that they be reclassified at a higher point in the SNOTS scale (*Bda* 21 August 1984). The classification process did allow for some upward salary drift. In June 1984, a Ministry of Labour official claimed that implementation of the SNOTS scale had led to an average 40 per cent increase in salaries (*Bda* 4 June 1984).

Overall, government officials felt that the SNOTS policy had dampened conflicts over salaries. A satisfied minister of labour would declare in 1987 that SNOTS "has allowed the union movement to focus on its main task, which is to raise productivity. Thus, a series of economic demands have been left behind. This type of struggle would have increased labour indiscipline, and would have led to an increase in strikes because of continuous salary demands" (*END* 5 May 1987).

It was originally hoped that the bonus system could be developed soon after the implementation of the basic salary system. In practice, however, bonuses other than those for "overfulfilment" were slow in coming, and employers frequently complained that SNOTS had become a strait-jacket that prevented them from rewarding their best personnel. Later in the 1980s, the rigidity of the SNOTS system was to have a serious side-effect: the attempt to address salary "anarchy" meant that the government found itself announcing simultaneous salary increases for some 300,000 workers. Each such increase thus became a signal for prices to increase. A complicated new relation between salaries and prices was thus created, in which salary increases sparked inflation through a mechanism that was neither cost-push nor demand-pull.

C. RELATIONS WITH THE BOURGEOISIE

While not bending to the bourgeoisie's political demands in the 1982–4 period, the FSLN did make more effort to avoid a sharp class polarization that would drive the bourgeoisie as a whole into the arms of Reaganism. Occasionally, FSLN leaders would warn that the Reagan administration could threaten the bourgeoisie's own survival.[34] Upon other occasions, however, Sandinista leaders promised that they would not be provoked into taking rash measures, and gave the mixed economy a renewed vote of confidence.[35] There was also relatively little pressure exerted on the bourgeoisie by the Sandinista mass organizations during this period. As the war intensified, the FSLN tightened its control over its mass organizations, and this control was used in part to minimize open class conflict with the bourgeoisie. This section will first examine the bourgeoisie's political activities, and then the economic "incentives" offered by the government to the bourgeoisie, and the latter's response to those incentives.

With the intensification of the contra war and other forms of U.S. pressure, the organized bourgeoisie both brought its agenda into closer alignment with that of the Reagan administration, and sought to capitalize on U.S. pressure in order to pursue its interests. The Superior Council of Private Enterprise (COSEP) and the right-wing parties would invite the U.S. ambassador in Nicaragua to their meetings, meekly visit the embassy whenever they were convoked, and make no apologies for the ever-clearer convergence between their political rhetoric and that of a foreign power that was trying to destroy the Nicaraguan government.[36]

A March 1982 declaration of the "Democratic Coordinator" provides a good illustration of the attempt to link an internal agenda with that of the United States. The Coordinator, formed in 1981, was comprised of all the component organizations of COSEP, a few right-wing opposition parties including Robelo's Nicaraguan Democratic Movement, and two U.S.-backed labour federations.[37] In March 1982 the group presented its proposals for a solution to political turmoil in Nicaragua and Central America. The Coordinator called for a non-aggression pact between Nicaragua and the United States, similar pacts with Central American neighbours, the end to outside assistance of all armed insurgencies in the region, and the resumption of U.S. economic aid to Nicaragua. Up to this point, there was nothing that FSLN centrists would find particularly objectionable. The document then called for a "gradual process of regional disarmament, whose ultimate objective would be the reduction of military forces to the point that only police forces would remain." The sovereignty of these disarmed countries would then be "firmly guaranteed" by the Organization of American States (OAS).

The Coordinator also called for negotiations within each country of the region. In the Nicaraguan case, these negotiations would lead to such goals as "effective political pluralism," "a clearly defined mixed economy," and the review of all laws to ensure their compliance with the "Original Program" of the government. All internal negotiations "would be obligatory and would be subject to the supervision of an international committee of representatives of American states which, with the assistance of the OAS, would ensure compliance with agreements" (*Bda* 25 March 1982).

The Democratic Coordinator thus sought to use U.S. pressure to win support for a "package deal" that would offer something for everyone. Contra pressure would be called off in return for a regional disarmament that, for the Sandinistas who had little faith in the capacity of the OAS to restrain the Reagan administration, would essentially ratify Central America's traditional status as a U.S. protectorate. The call for obligatory negotiations with the opposition under international supervision in effect denied the government its status as the legitimate sovereign government of Nicaragua. This denial of legitimacy, a new twist in the bourgeoisie's position, coincided with the interests of the Reagan administration, as it justified U.S. backing of the contras.

The organized bourgeoisie would attempt to capitalize on every escalation of U.S. pressure throughout the coming years. On the day after the United States invaded Grenada, a group of opposition parties declared that "it is indispensable that Nicaragua ... promote immediate actions of national reconciliation, which will only be possible through the fulfilment of the Original Program of the Revolution" (*Psa* 26 October 1983). As the FSLN denounced such proposals as thinly veiled treason, various members of the bourgeoisie abandoned the "civic struggle" and joined the contras. Former government junta member Alfonso Robelo took this step in mid-1982, Conservative Party leader Adolfo Calero early the following year. Others would follow.

Given its rejection of the legitimacy of the Sandinista government, the organized bourgeoisie was presented with a dilemma when the FSLN called for national elections to be held in November 1984. To participate, or to refuse to participate without a credible excuse, could serve to legitimate the government internationally. Participation did hold out the possibility of weakening FSLN power, either by capturing a significant number of seats in the National Assembly or, less likely, by capturing the presidency itself.

Consistent with its denial of the government's legitimacy, the Democratic Coordinator called for elections to be supervised by the OAS or some other international body. When the FSLN rejected this proposal, COSEP called on rightist parties to boycott the elections (*Bda* 23 March 1984). This position represented a problem for the Democratic Coordinator, however. A rightist electoral opposition to the FSLN was forming, and the Coordinator ran the risk of being marginalized as an opposition force.[38] In July, the Coordinator named Arturo Cruz, former member of the government junta, as its presidential candidate. Cruz sought to position himself as a mediator between the FSLN and the contras. He announced that he would not register to run in the election unless certain prior conditions were met, such as a pardon for all imprisoned members of Somoza's National Guard, and the initiation of direct talks with the contras (*Bda* 26 July 1984; 4 August 1984). In negotiations with the FSLN, Cruz even implied he had the power to have the contras agree to an immediate cease-fire.

In the end, negotiations broke down, and Cruz did not run. The Sandinistas felt that the Democratic Coordinator, which had tied its future so closely to the Reagan administration, was following the latter's orders that it not participate in elections. Years later, Cruz would comment that his decision not to run had been a mistake, and admit that he was on the payroll of the U.S. Central Intelligence Agency (*NYT* 8 January 1988).

The FSLN won two-thirds of the vote, while the rightist parties that did participate won most of the rest, which most observers considered a surprisingly respectable showing.[39] Nevertheless, COSEP and the Democratic Coordinator were successful in convincing many external observers that they were the only "true" opposition to the FSLN, and that the elections were a sham.[40]

Though the FSLN sought to contain the bourgeoisie politically, in January 1982 the Sandinista Assembly extended to part of the bourgeoisie an economic carrot to accompany the stick of nationalization: "incentives" in the form of increased prices for export production. The bourgeoisie welcomed the new policy as a sign of increased Sandinista pragmatism.[41] *La Prensa* saw in the policy an indicator of a "rightward shift" in the revolution. The policy caused tension within the FSLN, however, and was opposed by Henry Ruiz, who argued that it would merely give the bourgeoisie a windfall profit (Cruz 1989, 142). Throughout the coming years, these "incentives" would be seen by some as a partial capitulation to the bourgeoisie in the class struggle taking place in Nicaragua.

FSLN leaders frequently referred to the special prices paid to the export bourgeoisie as "political prices" (Ramírez 1987, 212). The implication was that it was worth paying these prices, and incurring "exchange rate loss," whether or not private production actually responded to the incentives. Carlos Vilas argues that "with the intensification of external military aggression, the economic measures adopted by the State on behalf of entrepreneurial groups – above all agro-exporters – objectively took on the character of economic stimuli of their political behaviour, more than of their investment behaviour" (1985, 21).

One hopes that the economic policies taken with respect to the bourgeoisie were politically oriented, for the truth is that as incentives of productive behaviour, they were quite ill-conceived. The import and export price policy, though provoking "exchange rate loss" on the part of the state complex, did not thereby automatically transfer purchasing power to the *productive* bourgeoisie. The same set of policies could thus correctly appear to elements in the FSLN as a give-away to the bourgeoisie, and to the productive bourgeoisie as a severe limitation on their earning capacity. Such a contradictory evaluation occurred because of the conflicting logics of the two sectors.

The FSLN could point out to agro-exporters that the state was selling them imported inputs at a 10:1 rate of exchange, and that it was paying them a guaranteed price calculated on a cost-plus logic, which meant that it was buying their production at an implicit rate of exchange much higher than that of 10:1. How could the bourgeoisie complain, when faced with such generosity?

Because the export bourgeoisie had a very different view of things: by keeping input prices low and applying a cost-plus logic, not only producer prices but also producer profits rose more slowly than the rate of inflation. Many producers changed their *córdoba* profits into dollars on the unofficial market or bought imported luxury goods there, and thus measured their profits against this unofficial-market rate. This rate rose at an average of 121 per cent annually during the 1981–4 period (Spoor 1987, 30). By this measure, entirely consistent with the logic of a dollar-oriented bourgeoisie, producer profits diminished radically over the period.

But if government policies led both to a great loss of state resources and to a reduction in the profits of the productive bourgeoisie, who profited from these policies? As argued above, the policy of importing and selling goods at a rate of exchange that increasingly diverged from a market-clearing level created a great opportunity for arbitrage profits for anyone who could straddle the official and unofficial markets. No doubt many bourgeois producers profited in this manner, but in their capacity as "speculators," not in their capacity as producers. That is to say, government policy may have handed to the bourgeoisie as arbitrageurs what it took away from them as producers. Even if the bourgeoisie thereby "came out even," however, such policy was not neutral in its consequences, as it discouraged precisely the behaviour it should have encouraged, and vice versa.

Much the same can be said of credit and interest rate policies. The high levels of working costs covered by bank credit allowed producers who had economic surpluses left over from previous production cycles to dedicate these to other activities, often speculative or unofficial-market-oriented. Had they been tempted to deposit their profits in the state banking system in order to be able to apply them to the next productive cycle, as FSLN leaders had naively assumed they must, the negative real rates of interest paid on deposits would have brought them to their senses. Since the banking system also charged negative real rates of interest on its loans, it was forced to generate new purchasing power to cover working costs that many producers could have met themselves, had the state offered them the appropriate financial instruments to protect their revenue from inflation.

Hence, if policy bought the political neutrality of part of the bourgeoisie, it did so only because it allowed and even encouraged that bourgeoisie – along with a host of petty arbitrageurs – to engage in behaviour that was increasingly undermining economic stability. This, for some, was too high a price to pay. In a revealing phrase, the 1984 economic plan called for a system of export incentives that "actually stimulates exports" (MIPLAN 1984a, 168). But such a system could not be devised without addressing all the price disequilibria that policy had generated.

All this must be kept in mind when evaluating the productive behaviour of the bourgeoisie. Ryan (1986) presented data that illustrated the greater productive dynamism of both the state sector and of small private production, relative to that of medium and large private production. Between 1980 and 1983, for example, the share of total agricultural production generated by medium and large private producers fell from 63 per cent to 33 per cent, while that generated by the state sector grew from 14 per cent to 25 per cent.[42]

The question is what this productive performance on the part of the bourgeoisie proves. Many Sandinistas and observers took it as a symptom of systematic bourgeois sabotage of the revolution, of an organized campaign of "clandestine war" against the FSLN (Weeks 1985, 290). This evaluation may be correct, but it is important to note that bourgeois economic behaviour can be explained without reference to such an organized campaign. The problem is that total output statistics judge the bourgeoisie by the criteria of the socialist economy. The bourgeois enterprise, unlike the typical socialist one, seeks to maximize profits, not output. When policies drive a wedge between productivity and profitability, as government policies did during this period, it is not surprising that bourgeois production stagnates. Thus, one should ask whether bourgeois performance reflects a deliberate ignoring of opportunities for profit, or whether the bourgeoisie was not simply following its own good sense.[43] Underlying many Sandinista complaints about the bourgeoisie lay the ever-frustrated hope that the bourgeoisie would behave as something other than a bourgeoisie. Advocates of future state-dominant mixed economy projects will have to consider whether the success of their model depends upon the leopard changing its spots.

D. AGRARIAN REFORM

The July 1981 agrarian reform law represented a retreat for the proponents of state agriculture: events had proven that peasant land hunger was not going to be satisfied by the offer of employment on state farms, and some compromise was necessary to contain anarchy in the countryside. By favouring production cooperatives, however, the law sought to limit the scope of the retreat. The reversion to "primitive" peasant production would be contained, and land would be maintained within the modern pole of the bipolar agricultural system.

It appears that officials within MIDINRA were slow to accept even this partial retreat from the statist vision. As Gilbert notes, "the state sector continued to dominate the ministry's budget, consuming resources which might have gone into organizing and supporting the cooperatives" (1990, 93). For two years after the declaration of the agrarian reform law, change proceeded at a snail's pace. By the end of 1982, a mere 1.6 per cent of Nicaragua's agricultural land had been transferred. Of this, over 80 per cent had been used to form production cooperatives.[44] MIDINRA seemed much more adept at expropriating land than at transferring it to peasants: by mid-1982, five times as much had been expropriated under the agrarian reform law as transferred (*Bda* 15 June 1982). Those with more patience than landless peasants argued that such things take time, that all must be done scientifically. The land transfer was proceeding slowly, Jaime Wheelock insisted, only because the government was "carefully seeking out the best land" to transfer to peasants.

MIDINRA apparently had little intention of modifying this approach. Salvador Mayorga, vice-minister in charge of the reform, announced in January 1983 that the coming year would see the transfer of 140,000 hectares – about 2.5 per cent of all agricultural land – to cooperatives. Mayorga added that during 1983, MIDINRA's attention would be focused upon a "selected group of cooperatives," which would receive benefits such as special technical assistance and training in accounting (*Bda* 30 January 1983; FBIS 8 February 1983). Jaime Wheelock declared in a 1983 interview that "we have achieved a rather acceptable process of transformation," and held that the agrarian reform would now enter a phase of "consolidation and rationalization of that which has been achieved" (1983, 85, 88).

But politics imposed an abandonment of this gradualist approach to the agrarian reform. I believe that the U.S. invasion of Grenada in late October 1983 marked the point of inflection in the reform process. Contra attacks had been stepped up, key oil-storage facilities had been destroyed on both coasts, and many believed there would be a decisive attempt to overthrow the Sandinistas before Christmas. Up to this point, the reform process was following the languid rhythm predicted by Mayorga in early 1983. But just two days after the invasion, Jaime Wheelock announced that 160,000 hectares would be transferred before year's end (*Bda* 28 October 1983).[45] In addition, the government began to transform de facto possession of land into legal title for thousands of peasants.[46]

Thus, as noted in early 1984, "30 per cent of the land given to *campesinos* since October 1981 was granted in the last 41 days of 1983 ([Ryan] 1984). For 1984, MIDINRA planned to either transfer or give legal title to some 490,000 hectares of land. As Jaime Wheelock noted at year's end, "political conditions" forced a near-doubling of this pace (Wheelock 1985b, 21).

This represented more than merely a quantitative acceleration in the agrarian reform. Land was now being transferred at a pace that would inevitably undermine MIDINRA's vision of an agrarian reform dominated by modern, well-organized cooperatives maintaining close links with the state. For the first time, the FSLN was accepting that the survival of the revolution would require at least a partial abandonment of the vision of a state-dominated countryside, as well as a "regression" of some land into the "primitive" pole of the bipolar agricultural economy.

Nevertheless, government resistance to the transfer of land to individuals continued. Though the transformation of de facto possession into legal title represented a significant support for small-hold production, by the end of 1984 only 8 per cent of land actually transferred had been granted to individuals. In addition, some peasants had lost access to the land that they had previously worked.[47] A 1982 document of MIDINRA's research centre, CIERA, celebrated the fact that "the individual peasant economy is being channeled into higher forms of organization" (CIERA 1983a, 71). The document discussed the need to "utilize the political space accorded by the will of the peasant community to move ahead in the socialization of our economy and our society. Such an effort will necessarily have to rely on the mobilization of thousands of cadres in the countryside to provide political and ideological support in the difficult task of collectivization" (13).[48]

The peasantry was not enamoured of this strategy.[49] As one observer put it, the production cooperatives represented "an unwelcome toll necessary to gain access to land" (*Envío*, June 1987). Both FSLN and UNAG officials attributed the resistance to cooperatives to ideological backwardness. Victor Tirado noted in late 1981 that "it is not easy to eliminate from the minds of many *compañero* peasants the established system of individually working the land. We must all fight against that system. We have to eliminate from our minds the individualistic ideas because it has been proven that collective exploitation of land favors peasants more than individual work in a plot which perhaps will never get him out of misery and backwardness" (JPRS 79359).

But peasants could legitimately argue that the cooperatives were more trouble than they were worth. Many cooperatives suffered from serious problems of internal organization. In some cooperatives, small groups of members – often belonging to the same extended family –

tried to force out other members, thus reducing the number of members among whom profits would be shared.[50] Such ousted members would be replaced by salaried workers.

The war gave the peasantry another reason to resist production cooperatives, which were a favoured target of contra terrorism. In late 1983, the government reported that nearly 400 cooperative members had been killed by the contras (*Bda* 24 November 1983).[51] Despite the peasant resistance to collective production, by late 1984 there was no plan to modify the focus on production cooperatives. As we shall see in the next chapter, however, political conditions once again imposed a shift in the direction of the agrarian reform.

Unlike the 1979–81 period, FSLN handling of land questions now demonstrated greater concern not to frighten the rural bourgeoisie any more than was necessary. Restrictions on land seizures were apparently more effective than previously, and the government used some state land for the agrarian reform in order to cushion the tension between peasant land hunger and the desire to pacify the bourgeoisie. Thus, though the transfer of land to peasants accelerated in 1984, expropriations declined by nearly 60 per cent (Wheelock 1990, 118). By late 1984, the state share of agricultural land had declined from 23 per cent to 19 per cent. The FSLN repeatedly expressed its desire to protect producers "who are efficient and are not involved in counterrevolutionary actions" (*Bda* 2 June 1984). By late 1984, Jaime Wheelock was promising that expropriation of land for reform purposes would soon be suspended in entire regions of the country, though "counterrevolutionary" producers would still be vulnerable (Wheelock 1985b, 33–4). This promise could not be kept, as will be seen.

E.   CONCLUSION

By the end of 1984, Nicaragua had entered into a political and economic crisis. The most serious political problem for the Sandinistas was no longer the relation with the bourgeoisie, which had occupied so much attention since 1979, but the relation with the peasantry. The Sandinista leadership was slowly realizing that, whatever the "objective class nature" of the contras' overall project, the peasantry had become the contras' effective social base. While members of the bourgeoisie might root for the contras from Managua, or join the contra leadership in Miami, those who fought and died with the contras were, by and large, peasants. This does not mean that the peasantry had gone over to the contras en bloc. But enough peasants had turned to the contras to give the United States the basic human resources it needed to wage its war against the Sandinistas.

At different points in this chapter, we have noted the various bases of peasant disenchantment: the state was trying to force peasants to sell their output at low prices; rural trade had been disarticulated; MID-INRA was focusing its energy on large modern projects rather than peasant-oriented extension services; the agrarian reform was forcing peasants into cooperatives, and ending "pre-capitalist" rental relationships that had been the only access to land for many peasants.[52] These factors help explain the willingness of many peasants to participate in, or collaborate with, the contras.

It was difficult for the FSLN leadership to understand the roots of peasant disaffection. Jaime Wheelock commented in 1983 that "if the revolution has benefitted any social sector in the country, that sector is the peasantry" (1983, 92). The leadership could point to the tremendous increase in credit granted to peasants, and to the extension of health and education services in the countryside. It could also point to the same agrarian reform that had frustrated so many peasants: the reform, after all, was reducing the concentration of land ownership, even if cooperative ownership was not the first choice of many peasants.

Unable or unwilling to identify the economic roots of peasant alienation, the leadership took refuge in its long-held concept of "peasant backwardness." The contras were directing propaganda towards the peasantry, Luís Carrión argued in 1983, because the peasantry has an "almost fanatic religious mentality" (Gilbert 1990, 97). Phenomena such as the peasantry's impatience with the agrarian reform were viewed as a symptom of peasant "individualism," which could be addressed through the "mobilization of thousands of cadres" advocated by CIERA.

Despite its belief in peasant backwardness and its tendency to underestimate the peasantry's grievances, however, the FSLN was able to change course from 1985 on. We will see in the next chapter that many of the specific grievances of the peasantry were addressed through shifts in policy. These shifts, however, also imperilled the FSLN's overall political project, and made the socialist economy an ever more distant dream. The FSLN had to sacrifice elements of its project in order to secure its hold on power.

While the FSLN was thus able to address its central political problem, the economic crisis proved more intractable. After the FSLN lost power in 1990, there was much debate within the party on where things had begun to go wrong. Though it was certainly not obvious at the time, I believe that during the 1982–4 period the policies outlined here created an economic mess from which the FSLN was never able to extricate itself. Just as its early anti-inflationary policies had been converted by the logic of the situation into spurs to inflation, so every attempt at stabilization implemented from 1985 on seemed to increase economic instability.

It is possible, though by no means certain, that economic reform would have been more successful had the government attempted to implement a change of direction sooner. Why did it not do so? Certainly many within the government were aware of the problems being caused by the increasing economic imbalance. As has been noted, MIPLAN stressed from the beginning the need for balance in the economy. Perhaps the chief weakness of official economic policy was that it advocated an "economics of balance," but failed to articulate a contingency plan, an "economics of imbalance." When severe fiscal-financial imbalance emerged in 1983, there was simply no coherent policy response. Policy was paralysed.

Timing played a role in this: the depth of the economic crisis became apparent only slowly, even for those of us who were living through it. In 1982, the government deficit in relation to GDP was up only mildly from the previous year, and December-to-December inflation had fallen for the third consecutive year. The tax system was improving, and it was reasonable to assume that the fiscal-financial imbalance would continue to be manageable.

It was in 1983 that everything went off the rails. Yet it was also in 1983 that Nicaragua enjoyed the highest GDP growth in Latin America and the Caribbean (CEPAL 1985). The FSLN celebrated the results: Jaime Wheelock proclaimed that "we are now following a more solid and firm strategy, that will improve the quality of life of the entire people" (*Bda* 25 January 1984).

By the time the economic crisis became visible to all, Nicaragua was involved in a serious war, a war that threatened all of the fundamental objectives of the revolution. The government could see no way to restore economic balance without policies that were bound to erode its political support, at least in the short run. Thus, despite the difficult economic situation, the FSLN's economic platform in the 1984 election essentially promised to stay the course: "centralized planning" would "continue to be strengthened," as would the "defence" of the prices of basic consumer goods (FSLN 1985, 316).

But the political cost of changing course was not the only barrier to change. Equally serious was the fact that within the FSLN leadership itself there was simply no consensus on where to go. Should there be an intensified control of the economy? Or should a restoration of market mechanisms be attempted? There was an awareness that control was proving contradictory, yet the history and instincts of the leadership militated against a turn to the market. The National Directorate was divided on these options, and there was probably no single person in the country who fully understood the implications of each path. Alejandro Martínez would later comment that officials were worried that a clear discussion on the economic crisis and the available options would threaten the "extraordinary unity" that the National Directorate had thus far maintained (1990, 113).

By the time Nicaragua's long election period was finished in November 1984, the government could no longer delay a major revision of policy. In a December 1984 speech, Jaime Wheelock referred to the problems of inflation, the foreign exchange shortage, and food shortages, and commented, "We can now say that these tendencies have become factors of extraordinary gravity for the national economy and for the revolution" (1985b, 16). In an indication of the coming change of policy, Wheelock blamed the situation on external factors and on the "wearing out of the economic policies that we adopted."

The economic distortions generated by the interaction of the legal and unofficial markets were reaching the point of the ludicrous. A company given access to foreign currency could buy a new tractor for c$150,000, but $300 worth of spare parts for an old tractor, which had to be sought on the unofficial market, cost just as much. People mocked the "so-called secure channels," and were ever more dependent on the unofficial market, with its mark-ups of up to 500 per cent over official prices. New occupational categories developed accordingly. A few blocks from my place of work, women and children slept on the sidewalk in front of a shoe store that sold at official prices, in order to buy, first thing in the morning, footwear that showed up across the street in the Eastern Market by mid-morning, with prices having undergone a rapid mark-up of 400 per cent.

The economic situation gave a new tone to the language even of those who supported the FSLN. An article in the pro-government *El Nuevo Diario* on 31 December 1984 began: "A worker was saying to me the other day that it seems that the Revolution is being made on behalf of the new rich, the import-export traders, the hoarders, the black marketeers, those who, without serious obstacles, grab up the toys, the spare parts, the food, all the little that we have in this country through our great sacrifice."

Thus, the FSLN was forced to act. But it did so without internal consensus, and this was to prove decisive in the coming period. With each sign that its new policies were not working as well as expected, it would back off, and policy would be frozen once again. The 1985–7 period would be a time of spasmodic economic reform.

6 The Hesitant Turn to the Market, 1985–7

In his famous funeral oration, Thucydides has Pericles say of the Athenian empire: "It may have been wrong to take it; it is certainly dangerous to let it go" (2.62–4). Much the same could be said of the Sandinista state's relationship to the Nicaraguan economy from 1985 on. After a multifaceted attempt to "take hold" of the economy by substituting state administrative action for the mechanisms of the market, Nicaragua entered a chaotic period of "letting go," in which the FSLN sought to extricate the state from its administration of the economy without destroying its bases of support.

In this attempt, the FSLN repeatedly confronted the fact that the instruments one forges often become shackles. The Sandinistas had implemented such policies as price controls, subsidies on basic goods, and cheap credit, partly as instruments to help legitimize the revolution. In the latter half of the 1980s, they saw the dialectic of such instruments: the legitimacy of the revolution was tied up with policies that were no longer sustainable.

Over the period, the effects of policy changes and other factors such as the war destabilized the economy. Real gross domestic product (GDP) fell in all three years. The total decline over the period was 5.8 per cent. Per-capita GDP fell by 14.8 per cent, ending the period at just 52 per cent of its 1977 level. In addition, both external imbalance and inflation escalated to levels unprecedented in the country's history. Nicaragua's export sector continued its collapse. Goods exports, valued at $385 million in 1984, reached a nadir of $247 million in 1986, recovering slightly to $300 million in 1987. Current account deficits were in the neighbourhood of $800 million each year. The 1986 current account deficit was over *three times* the value of goods exports.[1]

The current account deficit naturally led to a continued rise in external public debt. Much of the increase in the debt, however, was due to rising arrears. By the end of 1985, the country had $959 million in overdue obligations (SPP 1986b, 17). Of the $837 million increase in the external debt in 1986, $548 million represented rising arrears (ECLAC 1986). By the end of 1987, the external public debt stood at $6,270 million, over twenty times the level of exports.

For many Nicaraguans, the most notable aspect of the 1985–7 period was the escalation of inflation, which jumped from 50 per cent in 1984 to 334 per cent, 747 per cent, and 1,347 per cent in the three subsequent years. In large part, this result represented a dynamic set in motion by the government's own attempts at economic adjustment.

The structure of this chapter differs slightly from that of the two previous ones. As changes in price policy were closely related to changes in the organization and role of the state, these two themes will be treated together in section A. Sections B and C will examine relations with the bourgeoisie and the agrarian reform.

A. PRICES, THE MARKET, AND THE STATE

In late 1984 the National Directorate lacked consensus on the best response to Nicaragua's economic situation. The two broad options were understood to be an intensification of state control, or some form of "turn to the market." The draft economic plan for 1985 of the Ministry of Planning (MIPLAN), which never saw the light of day, advocated the first option. Prepared in October 1984, the plan recognized the severe problems facing the country. The state of the external sector was "extremely delicate" (MIPLAN 1984b, 1). Inflation was being stimulated by a "shortage of basic goods," the cost of defence, the "uncontrolled growth of the state apparatus," and by exchange rate loss (2–3). Basic consumption had fallen to the point that "the very social base of the revolutionary process" was endangered (8).

The plan recognized some of the negative effects of the pattern of economic controls. Price policy had discouraged basic grains production (ibid., 18), and the "distortion of relative prices" had contributed to the growth of the informal sector (96). Nevertheless, MIPLAN recommended an intensification of control. The state must be reformed to guarantee "centralization, verticality, consistency, uniformity and harmony in the execution of policies and plans" (11). In general, MIPLAN argued, the government "should adopt measures that clearly ratify the popular nature of the revolutionary process and its indestructible commitment to the poor and humble of our country." In an expression of impatience with policies thought to favour the bourgeoisie, the plan declared that "national unity must be understood in eminently popular terms." The "popular" orientation for which MIPLAN was calling signified a rejection of greater reliance on market mechanisms.

This approach enjoyed the support of at least two influential members of the National Directorate, both former leaders of the Prolonged Popular War Tendency. Planning Minister Henry Ruiz was one. The other was Tomás Borge, perhaps the most popular Sandinista leader among the general population. In an October 1984 speech to the Sandinista police force, Borge argued that "we have to take the reins firmly and put on our spurs if we intend to ride that runaway horse – the law of value – under the present conditions of our economic system" (1985b, 379). Calling for an organization of "production and distribution with an unequivocal policy of justice and democracy," Borge warned that the "greatest of errors would be to transform a tactic into a strategy," that is, to respond to the economic crisis in a way that lost sight of the revolution's "final objective" (379–80).

Borge reiterated these concerns in a letter to his fellow National Directorate members in December 1984, in which he advocated an intensification of economic control on several fronts: state marketing needed strengthening, private merchants should be limited, state enterprises should be subject to a more centralized direction, the FSLN's presence within the state should be intensified, and MIPLAN's leadership of planning must be recognized to overcome "profound inconsistencies in the management of economic policy" (1984c).[2]

But a shift in power was occurring within the National Directorate, through which both Borge and Ruiz would lose ground. The occasion of the shift was the choice of a presidential candidate for the 1984 election. The FSLN's option for a presidential model inevitably placed a strain on the National Directorate's collegial style of leadership, as one of the nine leaders would become sole head of state.

The directorate chose Daniel Ortega. There were repeated reports of tensions within the directorate over the decision. These reports suggested that Borge, as the "only living founder of the FSLN" and the most charismatic member of the directorate, had felt that he was the logical choice for president (Alaniz 1985, 261; Cruz 1989, 183). A comment of the ever-blunt Humberto Ortega suggested that the very reasons for which Borge might have thought himself the natural choice created an obstacle for him: asked why Borge had not been chosen as the FSLN's candidate, Ortega spoke of the need to "combat *caudillismo*," and avoid the error of the original movement of Sandino, in which "a whole revolutionary movement fell apart because it was founded exclusively upon one person" (Ortega, Wheelock, and Arce 1986, 87). The directorate thus apparently feared that collegial leadership would founder altogether under a President Borge.

Upon his inauguration as president, Daniel Ortega announced a government reorganization in which MIPLAN was abolished and replaced by the Secretariat for Planning and Budgeting (SPP), under the direction of Dionisio Marenco, who had entered the FSLN through the Ortegas' insurrectional tendency, and who had most recently served as minister of internal trade.[3] The SPP was to be allowed no illusions of becoming the dominant body within the state: it was constituted as a secretariat to the president and to the new National Planning Council, henceforth the main economic policy-making body in the state.[4] This change in status led to the departure from the SPP of many MIPLAN veterans who felt that "planning should be planning," as one official told me.

The new SPP came complete with its own 1985 economic plan, prepared in late 1984 by a team of advisors working independently of MIPLAN. As this plan's analysis and policy recommendations formed the basis for new economic measures announced in early February 1985, we can examine the plan and the policy shift together.

As did MIPLAN's economic plans, the SPP's 1985 plan began with a recognition of various problems facing the Nicaraguan economy: a drop in the supply of goods and services, the deterioration of means of production and transport, inflation, and a growing "speculative commercial sector," among others (SPP 1985, 2). Unlike the MIPLAN analysis, however, the new plan had a much stronger "financial" orientation, manifested in policies to attack the sources of monetary emission, and a greater respect for the importance of relative prices. We will examine these two aspects in turn.

Controlling Monetary Emission

Among the problems facing the economy, the 1985 plan identified "the accelerated decapitalization of the National Financial System, which is linked to exchange rate loss, unrecoverable credits, and Central Government deficits" (ibid.). Government deficits, in turn, were caused by "high defence spending, and an expansionary spending policy which does not correspond to the country's productive base." The plan stated: "We have wanted to do more than what is possible, but now reality is imposing a readjustment of goals compatible with our possibilities" (6).

This theme of coming to terms with reality was predominant in Sandinista presentations of the new economic policy. The government's "principal economic error," the National Directorate argued, "was that we wished to do too many things at the same time" (Dirección Nacional

1985a, 3). The revolution had tried "to overcome poverty from one day to the next," commented Jaime Wheelock (1985c, 12). Whether or not the country's economic problems were due to an excess of revolutionary romanticism, the new rhetoric of realism signalled the leadership's belief that the "eminently popular" policies advocated by MIPLAN could no longer be sustained.

The plan thus recommended, and the government implemented, a number of measures to address monetary emission and reduce demand at a macro level. Subsidies were eliminated on food and reduced on public transport.[5] "State subsidies," the National Directorate declared, "which initially were so useful to defend the interests of the working people, now, because of shortages, only serve to increase the profits of speculators" (1985a, 3). A freeze was to be put on central government hiring, and the public investment program was to be "rationalized" (ibid.).[6]

The plan also called for a "rationalization of credit and exchange rate policy" (SPP 1985, 11). To address exchange rate loss, a devaluation was undertaken, which established multiple exchange rates.[7] All but small agricultural producers would see the share of working costs covered by credit reduced from 100 per cent to 80 per cent (Cuadra 1985). Yet here a new policy contradiction was generated, one which Sandinista decision-makers never quite grasped during their decade in power. The contradiction emerged from a serious lacuna in the 1985 economic plan's analysis. Though it examined several causes of monetary emission, the plan did not touch on the question of negative real interest rates. Thus, the February 1985 measures called only for a minuscule increase in interest rates.[8]

Negative real interest rates constituted a double problem: they contributed to monetary emission, and they made it impossible for agricultural producers to finance their own working costs by depositing their surplus in the banking system at the end of the agricultural cycle, since the real value of those deposits would be eroded before the next cycle began. As inflation accelerated from 1985 on, it would become increasingly difficult for producers to finance even a small portion of their own working costs, unless they had a non-cyclical source of income outside the agricultural sector itself. Thus, the policy of reducing the share of production costs financed by bank credit, which the 1981 economic plan had first demanded, continued to be unenforceable. The government would have another go at this in early 1988, once again without addressing the interest rate problems, with disastrous results.

Correcting Relative Prices

The SPP's 1985 economic plan identified "a situation of anarchy in the price system which provokes irrationality in the destination of products, discourages production and foments speculation and contraband" (1985, 2). The plan noted that official prices for producers were often lower than costs, and had not been adjusted with the required speed. It also noted that the wide gap between official and unofficial prices was making it hard to keep goods within the "secure channels" (8). The plan expressed particular concern over the relative deterioration of peasant prices, which had "discouraged peasant production, interrupted the normal interchange between the city and the countryside, and, politically, weakened the worker-peasant alliance" (9). The plan also noted the decline in real salaries, which had "encouraged the transfer of salaried workers to non-productive sectors," and led firms to use a variety of non-salary mechanisms to retain their work force, leading in turn to "distortions in the work relationship" (10–11).

The plan thus called for "correction of the system of relative prices" (ibid., 83). The devaluation was one element in this correction. In addition, producer prices would be increased, to "guarantee a reasonable margin of profit to productive activity" (Hüpper 1985). Real salaries would also be protected. The plan called for a preliminary salary increase to make up for 1984 inflation, followed by a 64 per cent increase to compensate for the predicted effects of the first round of economic measures (SPP 1985, 85). In early February, salaries were raised between 47 per cent and 60 per cent for workers at the lower end of the national wage scale (SNOTS), and 13 per cent to 25 per cent for those at the upper end. In March, there was an across-the-board 20 per cent increase. These two increases left real salaries close to their early 1984 level.

With the introduction of the new measures, there were repeated promises that real salaries would henceforth be stabilized.[9] Salaries would be adjusted to compensate for price increases, and commissaries for "productive" workers would be strengthened (Cabrales 1985a). The adjustment in relative prices was thus presented as a shift from a policy of "indiscriminate subsidies for all" to decent salaries for productive workers and for "all who are making a working sacrifice for the Revolution" (Wheelock 1985c; Dirección Nacional 1985a).

This phrase captured the orientation of the new measures, which sought to protect the formal economy and material production from the perceived threat of a growing urban informal economy, and of unofficial commercial activities in particular. In the many official speeches and interviews that accompanied the new policies, there was not always a clear distinction between these two "threats," between the informal sector as a whole and unofficial-market "speculators." According to the new analysis, the previous economic imbalance had transferred purchasing power to the "informal sector" (Hüpper 1985), and it was now hoped that the new policies would "reorient wealth, which is now being left in the hands of speculators, towards the workers and producers, who are those who create this wealth" (Dirección Nacional 1985a).

While various leaders attacked the "speculators" in their presentations of the new measures, many of the new measures would hurt the entire urban informal sector. Therein lay a key political risk of the new economic policy. While the 1985 economic plan called for a "broad campaign against the informal sector" (SPP 1985, 82), the non-salaried sector in poor urban neighbourhoods represented an important part of the FSLN's constituency. There was thus a conflict between the economic goal of consolidating the formal economy, which was consistent with the overall project of a state-dominant economy, and the political history and base of support of the FSLN.

The new economic measures affected the non-salaried urban poor dramatically. Official meat prices were more than doubled, and the official prices of beans, rice, and sugar rose 200 per cent, 110 per cent, and 243 per cent, respectively, in the same week. For some products, the increase in official prices did not affect consumers greatly, as it had been next to impossible before the price increase to find the product at the official price. Nevertheless, many Nicaraguans complained of being subjected to an economic "shock treatment".[10] While salaried workers were being fully or partially compensated for the costs of the measures, those in the informal sector wondered how they would make do.

It should be recalled that the FSLN's original option for price controls and subsidies on basic goods to promote popular interests, rather than salary increases, reflected its view that the "people" was a political reality much broader than the salaried sector. It now seemed that the FSLN was turning its back on this broad conception of its political base in order to focus on a narrower group. This appearance was somewhat deceiving, as the new policies were less designed to create a "privileged" group of salaried workers, than to help a group that had lost ground in relative terms. Nevertheless, much government and FSLN rhetoric left the impression that the non-salaried sector as a whole was being condemned.

Perhaps because of the political delicacy of the new measures, members of the National Directorate who were uncomfortable with the new policy direction refrained from public criticism. Though he had been a staunch defender of MIPLAN, Tomás Borge commented in February 1985 that the economic plans generated by MIPLAN prior to 1985 "were developed on the basis of our old dreams, not on the basis of a consistent project" (END 25 February 1985), indicating his acquiescence to the new rhetoric of realism.

Nevertheless, both the political costs associated with the change of economic direction and the initial lack of consensus within the directorate would soon lead to a softening of the new economic logic, and then to its eventual abandonment. Before examining this evolution, we will consider the question of the extent to which the new measures represented a "turn to the market."

Strictly speaking, a turn to the market would signify greater acceptance of the interplay of atomized demand and supply forces in setting prices, determining production priorities, etc. In this sense, the 1985 measures do not represent a turn to the market. In the public presentation of the new measures, government and party officials reiterated their determination to attack those forces that were weakening the state's capacity to guide the economy. The charging of higher-than-official prices, the transfer of goods out of the "secure channels," unsanctioned competition with state marketing agencies: all these phenomena were condemned under the loose heading of "speculation," which was to be confronted with renewed force.[11] Failure to defeat this foe would mean that "the economy will lose the popular orientation that the Revolution has conferred upon it," as Jaime Wheelock put it (1985c).

Similarly, the new policy on producer prices aimed to re-establish "a reasonable margin of profit" (Hüpper 1985), rather than to allow the market to determine price and profit levels. Thus, as Wheelock stated, the new measures sought to promote "containment and rationalization, order and control," virtues dear to the heart of all proponents of a state-dominant economy (1985c).[12]

At the same time, however, the new policies indicated much greater respect for the existence and power of the market. The Nicaraguan economy, Wheelock declared, is "governed by the laws of the market" (1985c). This apparently simple statement reflected a heightened awareness among state and party decision-makers of the limits of state economic controls. Thus, in its presentation of the new measures, the National Directorate admitted that prices would rise, but argued that this would increase supply, "which is what, in the end, will allow prices to be stabilized" (Dirección Nacional 1985a). Despite all the rhetoric on attacking "speculation," it was now recognized that the forces of supply and demand could overwhelm price controls.

Greater recognition of the market's power was also present in the types of measures being proposed to contain that power. Analogously to the "parallel market" for basic goods established in late 1984, the new "parallel market" for foreign exchange sought to confront the unofficial market by displacing it. This new currency mechanism would deal with "all transactions that cannot be handled by the controlled official market" (Cuadra 1985). That is, foreign exchange that the government could not capture directly through its control of goods exports could now be traded in government exchange houses at a rate to be "determined by supply and demand." This rate, in the original conception of the parallel market, would be adjusted daily (SPP 1985, 74).

This measure, as well as the increases in producer prices and elimination of subsidies, reflected in part the belief that the unofficial market should fundamentally be attacked by squeezing its profit margins. Success in attaining this objective would make formal sector employment attractive again, by reducing the incomes that could be earned through arbitrageur activities (ibid., 113).

Thus, rather than a "turn to the market," the economic policies of early 1985 represent recognition of the power of market phenomena in the Nicaraguan economy, and recognition of the importance of the price mechanism. The new strategy called for, not a capitulation to the market, but a new strategy for confronting it, one that sought to attack unofficial-market profits by decreasing the margins between official and market-clearing prices, and sought also to contain state disaccumulation. The measures were a partial shift towards an "accumulationist" perspective, away from the "alliance-building" that had hitherto dominated policy.

When the measures were announced however, many observers had a different view of the matter. Distinctions between reliance on the market and recognition of the market's power, between increased concern for financial performance and a "monetarist" orientation, or between economic adjustment and an "IMF recipe," were not clearly drawn in the minds of many observers, and perhaps not even in the minds of all decision-makers. However loose the conceptual categories wielded by many observers and decision-makers, these categories were much more politically influential than the sorts of distinctions presented here. With the introduction of the measures, Sandinistas heard their leaders speaking a hitherto shunned language: the main economic problems of the country were suddenly being analysed with the concepts of "supply" and "demand," and even the recognition of the power of the market in Nicaragua seemed to many to mark an ideological retreat.[13] Thus, it is not surprising that one local magazine felt the need to publish a long and detailed explanation of the difference between the new economic measures and IMF-type stabilization recipes (*Pensamiento Propio*, March 1985).[14] The perception that the new measures did in fact represent a "turn to the market" would add to the political problems associated with the measures in the coming months.

Crisis of the 1985 Plan

For the measures quickly did run into difficulty. FSLN and mass organization activists working in the popular *barrios* warned that actions aimed at weakening the informal sector were also weakening support for the government among the popular classes. Such a development was dangerous at a time when the popular neighbourhoods were expected to contribute a significant number of young men to the military service.

A key economic concern for decision-makers was that the rate of inflation triggered by the measures was much higher than anticipated. The SPP's economic plan had recognized that devaluation, increases in producer prices and salaries, the reduction of subsidies, and the attempt to reduce margins between official and unofficial prices would generate some immediate inflation, but had expressed the hope that this would be contained by a reduction in "the fiscal-financial deficit, which would begin a trajectory leading towards greater stability and control over the price system" (SPP 1985, 83). Inflation would be pushed via costs, but restrained via demand. The plan thus projected an overall jump of 84 per cent in the consumer price index (CPI) (103–4).

But this projection assumed that the compression of demand would be so significant that the overall price system would be relatively "inelastic" with respect to changes in such variables as the exchange rate or salaries. It was thus assumed that it would be a relatively easy thing to overcome the price distortions that had been allowed to develop over the previous years. That is, it was assumed that those prices that were not officially controlled would stand still long enough to allow official prices to catch up, a real devaluation of the currency to take place, and real salaries to recover somewhat.

But this optimistic forecast was not borne out, and it quickly appeared that an "adjustment spiral" in the level of prices was being generated. In the February-April period, the CPI rose 51 per cent.[15] At the beginning of May, salaries were increased 45 per cent to compensate for the inflation, in keeping with the logic of the 1985 plan. But inflation wiped out this increase within thirty days. The 46 per cent increase in the CPI in May brought the total increase since February to 121 per cent, and led decision-makers to fear that they were on the verge of triggering hyper-inflation. At this point, the brakes were put on the adjustment program.

The inflationary impact of the adjustment had much to do with the fact that it was undertaken in 1985 rather than one or two years earlier. The government was trying to rectify substantial distortions brought on by stagnant salaries and an increasingly overvalued *córdoba*. Had those distortions been tackled earlier, they would have been much less severe, and the resulting "adjustment spiral" could probably have been avoided.

By the end of 1985, there were ample signs that the logic of the 1985 plan had been abandoned on several fronts. Salaries had not been increased since May, despite a 150-per-cent increase in the CPI in the June-December period. The official exchange rate was also stagnant, allowing exchange rate loss to escalate and price distortions to re-emerge. The parallel market for foreign exchange, which was originally conceived as a replacement of the unofficial market, was not performing this function: while the unofficial-market rate for the dollar was roughly equal to the parallel rate in May, by December it was 33 per cent higher (Spoor 1987, 30).[16] Not surprisingly, the parallel market became relatively marginal: in December 1985, it traded a little over $500,000, a small fraction of the amounts thought to be moving in the unofficial market (*END* 21 January 1986).[17] By way of comparison, in the second half of 1990, when the parallel rate was almost identical to the unofficial-market rate, the exchange houses purchased an average of $12.6 million monthly (*Análisis*, January 1990, 24).

Similarly, the gap between official and unofficial prices had widened rather than narrowed. In December 1984, open market prices for food products were 105 per cent higher than official ones. By April 1985, this gap had closed to just 10 per cent. But by the end of 1985 the gap stood at 218 per cent (SPP 1986b, 36). Instead of gaining ground, official prices for agricultural production were rising more slowly than the CPI. The official prices of peasant crops such as beans and corn had dropped nearly a third when deflated by the CPI (40). According to SPP data, average prices paid to manufacturing sector producers fell by 25 per cent in relation to the CPI in 1985. They fell a further 35 per cent in the first half of 1986, thus suffering a cumulative drop of 51 per cent relative to December 1984.

In early 1986 there was an attempt to renew the process of adjustment. In January, salaries were increased an average of 89 per cent, and the *córdoba* was devalued through the establishment of a unified exchange rate of C$70:$1 for almost all goods imports except petroleum. These measures were not accompanied by a sharp increase in the CPI: the annual rate of inflation during January-February was 269 per cent, slightly below the 1985 rate. In March, salaries were increased 50 per cent, official prices on a range of consumer goods were raised, and the exchange rate for petroleum imports was raised to the C$70:$1 level. Whether because of these measures or not, the CPI jumped violently,[18] and, as in 1985, the government reacted by quietly suspending the adjustment process.

Basic Grains and the Peasantry

But if the overall logic of the 1985 economic plan had been abandoned, there had not been a simple return to pre-1985 economic policy. Sandinista leaders had become concerned about the problem of peasant disaffection and its contribution to the contras' strength. It was thus believed that changes in policies affecting the peasantry would contribute to the defence effort. Despite the slow movement of official prices for peasant crops through 1985, important steps were taken to address peasant alienation. The improvement in the supply of goods to the peasantry at official prices, in which the farmers' association (UNAG) would play a crucial role, sought to rectify a critical error in early Sandinista policy.[19]

Equally important was the government's decision in March 1985 to liberalize basic grains trading, beginning in the regions most affected by the contras. Jaime Wheelock commented that "the State could not fight with everyone, taking the maize and bean harvests from peasants while we were fighting a counterrevolution" (1986c, 53).[20] This policy met with some resistance on the part of those government officials responsible for urban questions, and would fluctuate somewhat in 1986–7.[21] While it relaxed formal controls on the basic grains market, the government maintained informal pressures on production cooperatives and the peasantry in general to sell to the state.[22] Nevertheless, from this time on the state was generally unable to supply beans to individual consumers.[23]

The sequence of policy shifts on the question of grain trading exemplifies a sequence that would occur with economic policy in general. The pre-1985 period was characterized by a policy of coercive administrative controls on grain trading, with official prices that were stagnant and quite unrelated to market-clearing levels. The 1985 economic plan called not for a use of the market mechanism in grain trading, but for the setting of higher official prices in recognition of the power of the market. These higher prices would make state-administered trading both more effective in capturing grain and less coercive from the peasantry's point of view. But this policy was soon abandoned for one that assigned a much greater role to market competition.

In fact the approach of the 1985 plan hid a policy dilemma. If the higher official prices called for under the plan were meant simply to restore a "reasonable" margin of profit, then official prices could well continue to lag behind market-clearing ones, particularly if key elements of the cost structure of production such as interest rates or the exchange rate were being held well below market levels. But in this case the state would either have to continue to use coercion to capture grain from the peasantry, or fail to capture it altogether. On the other hand, had official prices tracked their market-clearing levels, official consumer grain prices would have had to jump with every deterioration in the market situation, thus increasing urban discontent.[24] Given these options, it would appear that decision-makers saw liberalization of grain markets as the least politically costly option at the time. It removed a source of tension in relations with the peasantry, and, by sending urban consumers into the unofficial market in search of beans, might make them more liable to blame "speculators" than the government for high prices.

Market liberalization did not remove the state from the beans and maize business altogether. It still captured the two products from state farms, cooperatives, and peasants who were willing to sell part of their harvest to the Nicaraguan Basic Foods Company (ENABAS). The state continued to receive foreign donations of the two products, and the "Contingency Plan" was beginning to produce basic grains that were immediately captured by ENABAS. An increasing share of the domestic and imported grains captured by the state, however, was required for various forms of "institutional" consumption. ENABAS was responsible for supplying basic grains to the armed forces, government, and industrial cafeterias, and agro-export farms, particularly during the harvest period.[25] A significant share of national basic grains production remained entirely within the state sector: produced on state farms under the Contingency Plan, marketed by a state agency, and ending up in the bellies of state workers and soldiers.

Calls for Renewed Control; Attacks on "Speculation"

Despite the overall abandonment of the logic of the 1985 economic plan, then, Sandinista leaders could point to positive elements in the year's policy shifts. In particular, the leaders felt that changes in price and distribution policies affecting the peasantry, as well as changes in agrarian reform policy, had contributed to what was being termed the "strategic defeat" of the contras.[26]

Nevertheless, with the abandonment of the 1985 plan, there appeared to be no clear overall economic policy. The contradictions generated by the 1985 plan's strategy of respecting the power of the market prompted, not surprisingly, calls for an intensification of state control over the economy. In a confidential speech in July 1985, Internal Trade Minister Ramón Cabrales lamented that "the mixed economy policy keeps us from laying the bases of a new society." Cabrales called upon the state to "neutralize the politically vacillating class of large merchants," arguing that his ministry should take over all wholesale trade in the coming years (1985b). A national assembly of the FSLN unions called in September for a "reinforcement of economic centralization," and for the "reduction and control of the prices of basic products" (Asamblea Nacional de Sindicatos 1985). Given these sentiments, and the political concerns generated within the FSLN and in the population at large by the 1985 plan's perceived "turn to the market," the situation was ripe for implementing the plan's call for a resolute attack on "speculation." Under the state of emergency declared in October 1985, many private merchants and importers were arrested for alleged links to the contras (Cabrales 1985c; *END* 19 October 1985).

The government also launched its most resolute attack yet on Managua's Eastern Market, heart of the unofficial market, an attack that had been debated within the government and popular organizations for three years (Cabrales 1985b). Both to increase the effectiveness of the attack and to reduce its political cost, the government applied a policy of divide and conquer, by seeking to force out of the market only those merchants who had been there less than five years. The police and the Ministry of Internal Trade (MICOIN) set about expelling thousands of merchants, and reducing the market's physical space substantially. By early 1986, the Eastern Market had been physically reduced from a space of some 35 hectares to under 3 hectares (*END* 19 February 1986). All terminals for rural buses that used to end in the Eastern Market were transferred to other points in Managua, to disrupt links between rural intermediaries and urban "speculators" (*END* 31 January 1986). Overall, the government claimed that the number of merchants in the market had been reduced from 20,000 to just 3,000 (*Bda* 23 February 1986).

While these measures were undertaken with great fanfare, and did change the face of the Eastern Market for a time, it is not clear that any serious reduction in "speculation" resulted. Containing the unofficial market proved somewhat analogous to picking up liquid from a broken thermometer: activity was dispersed more than eliminated. Thus, the shrinkage of the Eastern Market was accompanied by a significant increase in the range of products sold by mobile vendors on the streets of the popular *barrios* of Managua. In any case, by early 1987 it was reported that some 3,500 illegal merchants had returned to the Eastern Market (*END* 21 January 1987).

Tensions in the 1986 and 1987 Economic Plans

Pressure for renewed state control was manifested in the SPP's 1986 and 1987 economic plans, although in an erratic fashion. The 1986 plan was a rather incoherent document that manifested the general policy vacuum that had arisen in the wake of the abandonment of the 1985 economic measures. The plan recommended that exchange rate loss be reduced, yet failed to propose a policy that would accomplish this objective. It ignored, once again, the problem of negative real interest rates. On the question of price policy, the plan returned to the sort of incoherence typical of the economic plans of MIPLAN: price "distortions" should be reduced, prices should stimulate production, yet price policy should also aim at protecting real wages. Essentially, the plan simply listed all the desiderata of price policy, rather than confronting the need to choose among them. The plan declared that "consumer prices should rise in proportion with producer prices," without providing a strategy for attaining this result, offering only the cryptic promise that inflation would be controlled by establishing "profit levels in accordance with the economic reality of the country." The section on price policy urged that the "secure channels" be broadened, while the section on distribution policy urged that they be reduced to a few key products. Reflecting the constituency promoting renewed state control, the plan called for a greater centralization of import decisions, and the use of material balances to determine import needs in each sector (SPP, 1986a).[27]

Similar tensions were manifested in the 1987 economic plan. In August 1986 the National Directorate and the Sandinista Assembly had issued an internal party document that called for, among other things, greater state control over production and distribution. The state productive sector, the document declared, should become the "articulating and hegemonic force" for all production (Dirección Nacional y Asamblea Sandinista 1986). The SPP's 1987 economic plan explicitly took this FSLN document as its basis. The plan called upon the state to increase its "directive capacity" over the economy (SPP 1987, 2), and promoted an "organic centralization" of state decision making, in which all key economic decisions would be made only in consultation with the National Directorate (11).[28]

On the other hand, the plan also called for better treatment of non-state producers, and greater participation of those producers in the planning process (SPP 1987, 9–10). It also recommended greater autonomy for People's Property Area companies (8). In the area of prices, the plan was sceptical of the possibility of controlling prices in what it called the "commercial" market until the fiscal deficit had been brought under control. Rather than advocating strict price controls, the plan recommended that prices for all but essential goods move to market-clearing levels, and that the state use indirect taxes to capture the margin between costs (plus "reasonable" profit) and market prices (200–1).

State Enterprises

One of the areas manifesting the tensions of the new economic policy was that of state enterprises. We have noted the generally "productionist" orientation of state firms, to the detriment of a more "accumulationist" orientation that would be sensitive to the problem of financial returns. The 1985 policy shift sought to address this imbalance. State firms, declared the National Directorate statement introducing the 1985 plan, "must become examples of efficiency, saving and productivity" (Dirección Nacional 1985a). Jaime Wheelock called upon state companies to "measure the results of their economic management just like any private company" (1985b, 28), and in March 1985 he warned directors of state companies that they would be shut down if they did not show a profit in 1985 (*END* 7 March 1985). Like many threats issued by the directorate, this one was not actually implemented, but it served to indicate a shift in policy towards state firms.

The new focus on financial results did bear some fruit. In 1986, the electrical and phone companies operated without deficits, and the latter even generated a surplus (ECLAC 1986).[29] In early 1987, Jaime Wheelock claimed that "the majority of State companies – with a few exceptions – are now profitable" (*Bda* 27 April 1987). Transfers from the government to state firms thus declined from 7 per cent of GDP in 1984 to just 1 per cent in 1987 (Kleiterp 1989, 97).

To a great extent, however, these profits were illusory, reflecting a highly distorted cost structure and problematic accounting practices. Firms were calculating depreciation costs based on the original *córdoba* value of their equipment. As inflation escalated, this meant that firms effectively stopped including the cost of replacing machinery in their total cost calculations. In addition, the import costs of state firms were depressed by the overvalued *córdoba*. Thus, part of the profits of state firms simply reflected the exchange rate loss of the state complex as a whole. A third factor depressing costs was the sharp reduction in real salaries since late 1984.

In 1987, two of my students from the National Autonomous University examined costs and profits in five state textile companies. Applying shadow depreciation and import costs, the study concluded that the total profits of the five companies in mid-1986 were reduced by approximately 65 per cent (Avilés and Amaya 1987). Had the firms also had to pay nominal salaries that maintained real earnings at their December 1984 level, total profits would have disappeared altogether.

Thus, the fact that state companies were earning profits did not mean that the state complex was being strengthened at the expense of the unofficial market, as the 1985 plan had intended. While the state textile companies were content to earn a profit of c$40 per yard of cloth, the gap between the official consumer price for cloth and the unofficial-market price was over c$4,000 per yard. Thus, if only 5 per cent of state-produced cloth "escaped" to the informal market – a very conservative assumption – unofficial-market intermediaries would earn over five times as much as the state companies (Ryan 1987, 25).

However illusory state profits may have been, the focus on financial results did call for new forms of behaviour on the part of state managers. This call was ratified in the 1987 economic plan, which promised that the state firms would be "self-financed, and freed of all tutelage on the part of the [state] institutions with which they are associated" (SPP 1987, 8). The companies, the plan promised, would operate on the basis of "liberalized prices," and seek greater profits (194).

But the government and the National Directorate had not really faced the problems related to the stress on financial results. Signalling the new focus, Jaime Wheelock had exhorted at the end of 1984: "From the Director of the company to the workers: let everyone be concerned, let each one be like a little capitalist, concerned about the labouring society. The socialist mode of production is really this worker with great awareness of the need for profit, but in a collective form, a non-contradictory form" (1985b, 29). Wheelock was articulating the ever-frustrated hope of state-socialist leaders everywhere that state firms could focus on profits, just like "capitalists," whilst selflessly promoting a series of other objectives identified with the common good of society.

But there were numerous signs that state companies were responding to the stress on finances by engaging in forms of behaviour that frustrated other state objectives. Because the government had not been willing or able to close the gap between official and unofficial prices, the easiest way for a state manager to increase profits was to slip a certain portion of production out the back door into the unofficial market. Internal Trade Minister Ramón Cabrales complained in July 1985 that agricultural firms under the control of the Ministry of Agriculture (MIDINRA) were breaking marketing agreements with his ministry in order to sell in other markets. Other state companies, he charged, were holding back produce in order to force the government to increase prices for producers (1985b).[30] Thus, the pressure on state managers to produce profits was in conflict with the policy of using the state firms to keep the "secure channels" supplied.

As has occurred in various socialist reform experiences, the conflicts between profit and other objectives, as well as the irrationalities generated by profit-maximizing behaviour in the presence of a distorted price system, led the government to engage in interventions that contradicted its policy of increasing company autonomy and encouraging state profits. These interventions frustrated company managers who had been promised autonomy: the director-general of a state textile firm complained that "I am nothing more than a messenger" (D. Ortega et al. 1987b). One crucial intervention concerned state trading companies. Despite the new orientation, "profit" remained a dirty word for many FSLN cadres. Marketing profits were especially transparent, since FSLN unions could identify the prices at which products were leaving state production companies. In September 1985, the FSLN unions criticized the Ministry of Internal Trade for its alleged 35 per cent mark-up on products sold in the Workers' Supply Centres (CATS) (*END* 26 September 1985). Within days, prices in these centres, which were already but a fraction of unofficial-market prices, were dropped 25 per cent (*END* 1 October 1985). The unions' position was soon ratified by the National Directorate, which stipulated that companies run by the Ministry of Internal Trade should earn little or no profit (Dirección Nacional 1985b).

The political sensitivity of price increases by state firms led to other interventions. When salaries were increased by 58 per cent to 100 per cent in January 1986, Jaime Wheelock, who by this point had gained significant authority within the National Planning Council,[31] ordered state industries to absorb the increase without raising prices (*Bda* 3 January 1986). The 1987 economic plan's statement on producer prices manifested the same tension between encouraging state profits and avoiding the appearance of state profiteering. Prices, the plan declared, should allow for "a reasonable profit (not less than the rates of interest on bank deposits applicable to the sector)" (SPP 1987, 35). But with real rates of interest increasingly negative, this statement suggested that state companies were not really going to be allowed to earn much in the way of profits, and would in fact continue to represent a drain on the state complex.[32]

Finally, though there was a severe shortage of labour throughout the formal economy as a whole, the profit orientation was not allowed to threaten employment in any specific sector. Daniel Ortega admitted in mid-1987 that many industries were working at 60 per cent capacity, but promised that this would not lead to lay-offs, as the government did not wish to create unemployment (*Bda* 19 July 1987).

Thus, a series of tensions remained in government policy towards state enterprises, despite the greater focus on financial results that emerged from the 1985 economic plan. Many of these tensions would be resolved in favour of an intensified financial orientation in the 1988–9 period.

Salary Policy

If the handling of state enterprises was an area of tension for the government, salary policy was one of grave crisis. Despite the 1985 economic plan's promise to protect real salaries from the effects of inflation, nominal salaries were frozen after May 1985. After two increases in early 1986, salaries were frozen again for the rest of that year. By the end of 1985, salaries deflated by the CPI were at just 50 per cent of their December 1984 level. By the end of 1986, they had fallen to just 16 per cent of that level.

This state of affairs raised the discourse of the National Directorate to an ever more voluntarist pitch. In a speech to workers in mid-1986, Victor Tirado commented: "Why, if you work eight hours today, can't you work ten tomorrow? Let's not turn it into a question of salaries, but of ideology. If we look at salaries, the workers have a 100-year-old tradition ... All the strikes that have occurred in Latin America in the last three years have been around salary demands; in those countries such demands can be just, but in a revolution they pass into history" (1986, 143–4). Jaime Wheelock criticized the "conservative, economistic and reactionary view that the worker can only be brought to the workplace through money, through mercantile mechanisms, and not through revolutionary demands." Such a view, Wheelock proclaimed, "is based on an erroneous tendency to underestimate the revolutionary role of the people" (*Bda* 27 October 1986). National Directorate members called upon workers to think of the soldiers off fighting the contras before they lamented their own situation: "Our combatants don't ask for higher salaries, or better houses or more food. They have a high consciousness, and a political understanding of their role within this great revolutionary process" (Tirado 1987).

Yet the leadership was aware that this proclamation of the revolutionary potential of the people, of its capacity to transcend mere economic concerns, was to a large extent whistling in the dark. Everywhere there were signs of the impact of declining real salaries. An internal SPP evaluation of 1985 noted that production in the major state textile companies had dropped 15 per cent, due in large part to "resignations and a drop in productivity because of disagreement with salary policy" (1986b, 59). SPP data indicated that the government and state companies were losing and trying to replace over one-fifth of their labour force each semester. The labour turnover was as high as 40 per cent per semester in the textile sector, which was expected to play an important role in the defence effort. Workers who might have gone to the coffee harvest in earlier years now preferred to stay in provincial towns, running their petty commercial activities (*Bda* 10 October 1985).

Asked why the government had compressed real salaries so severely, Daniel Ortega admitted that salaries represented the only variable over which the government still had much control (D. Ortega et al. 1987b). But salaries were more easily controlled in part because the various FSLN unions of salaried workers, unlike FSLN activists working in the popular *barrios* and in other FSLN organizations such as UNAG, showed little interest in defending their constituency's "immediate interests." In August 1986, the National Directorate had assigned the FSLN unions the task of "strengthening labour discipline [and] raising productivity" (Dirección Nacional y Asamblea Sandinista 1986).

The unions took to the task with gusto, but ignored the task of defending their constituency in the give-and-take through which policy was being formulated. Union leaders in fact opposed salary increases, preferring to call for price controls, despite the clear evidence that such controls were losing all effectiveness. In 1988, Daniel Ortega would comment that "since 1985, we have been waging a large-scale battle against the policy of increasing wages, a battle in which the CST [Sandinista Workers' Central] and the ATC [Rural Workers' Union] have stood out" (1988c).

Despite the acquiescence of the FSLN unions, government control over salaries was somewhat illusory. Government and enterprise managers did what they could to hold on to workers. Despite repeated prohibitions of the practice, payment in kind was a key tactic for evading salary controls in productive enterprises.[33] Firms also compensated by such measures as increased social benefits (Sullivan and Delgado 1988) and increased overtime (Biondi-Morra 1988, 292).

Another compensating mechanism, while legal, to some extent frustrated the aims of government policy. Throughout the 1985–7 period, the SNOTS system was made more flexible with the introduction of a number of bonuses supplementing the base salary. These included bonuses for above-norm production, seniority, training, and education level, and for work quality. Originally meant to encourage productivity and help retain strategic workers, there were increasing concerns within the government that managers were using the bonus system to increase indiscriminately the earnings of all their workers. Data collected in 1987 by the Employment and Salaries Department of the SPP suggested that bonuses represented approximately 100 per cent of the basic salaries of productive sector workers and 30 per cent for other workers. Concerns over the indiscriminate nature of bonuses would lead to a sharp reduction in the bonus system in the 1988 economic reforms.

The compensating mechanism upon which the government had rested its hopes were the "secure channels" dedicated to formal sector workers. When the 1985 economic measures were announced, Internal Trade Minister Ramón Cabrales had promised that commissaries for productive sector workers would play a central role in protecting real salaries (Cabrales 1985a). In February 1985, the government signed an agreement with the CST in which it promised to establish workplace commissaries for over 300,000 productive sector workers (*END* 18 February 1985). In June 1985, CATs were set up in urban supermarkets for "non-productive" workers (those in the central government, health, and education sectors), offering a variety of consumer goods at official prices. It was hoped that the commissaries and CATs together would compensate formal sector workers for nominal earnings lower than those available in the informal sector.

As with the 1985 measures in general, however, the government and FSLN found it hard to resist political pressures from outside the formal sector. In October 1985, Ramón Cabrales complained that the CATs had given access to many who were not formal sector workers, such as retired workers, families of mobilized soldiers, and veterans (Cabrales 1985c). Given the large number of people allowed access, it was not surprising that the CATs became increasingly chaotic. While it was originally hoped that each worker would visit the CAT once a month, the intermittent nature of supply to the stores made repeat visits necessary. This in turn made such visits more time-consuming: in mid-1987, one CAT manager estimated that the average shopper required four hours to pass through the store (*END* 2 July 1987). A memorandum prepared in the Ministry of Labour in early 1987 suggested that visits to the CATs were one of the major causes of "labour indiscipline" in the state sector.

The difficulties associated with shopping in the CATs may help explain the fact that in September 1987, the CAT cards that gave access to the stores were selling on the unofficial market for just C$40,000 (*Bda* 8 September 1987). This represented just 32 per cent of the average worker's base salary at the time. This figure suggests that the CATs, while playing some role in workers' survival strategies, were not a major compensation for low nominal salaries.

Even had the CATs been models of efficiency, it was increasingly difficult for "secure channels" to compensate for low nominal salaries. A variety of factors, such as liberalization of the grain trade, the practice by state companies of diverting part of production to the unofficial market as a response to pressures to show a profit, and the general "leakiness" of the secure channels inspired by the increasing spread between official and unofficial markets, made attempts to protect real earnings without raising nominal salaries increasingly ineffective. Such attempts were anachronistic, given the increasing power of market forces, and the decreasing relevance of the administrative mechanisms that had been established in the early years of the revolution.

In late 1986, however, government and FSLN decision-makers remained loath to accept this analysis. The Employment and Salaries Department of the SPP, in which I worked, submitted a draft chapter of the 1987 economic plan that called for a salary increase of 100 per cent, and warned that each month that passed without adjusting nominal salaries would make that adjustment, which must inevitably occur, more catastrophic. The recommendation was rejected, though the government reversed course soon afterwards.

Advance of the Market in 1987

Since the abandonment of the adjustment logic of the 1985 economic plan in mid-1985, policy statements had revealed an ongoing tension between the need to recognize the power of the market and a desire for the reassertion of the state's capacity to direct the economy. Around April 1987, this tension was resolved in favour of market liberalization, as the government abruptly reversed itself on several matters.

In the matter of basic grain trading, the 1987 plan had reaffirmed the policy of "regional price liberalization" (SPP 1987, 200). Under this policy, grain could be traded freely *within* the country's six main regions, but the state was to control the interregional movement of grain. To this purpose, MICOIN established roadblocks to impede the illegal movement of grain, in particular into Managua. The government held that the policy sought "to prevent having those peasant regions where the war was taking place, and where the bulk of the population was being displaced, being left without food" (Cabrales 1987, 42). On the other hand, the policy could also have been aimed at restoring controls over basic grain distribution without risking a direct confrontation with peasants, since the roadblocks would directly affect only intermediaries seeking to move grain between regions.[34] Interregional controls, if effective, would allow ENABAS to compete more effectively with unofficial intermediaries, since the prices that those intermediaries could pay peasants would be restricted by their loss of access to the higher-priced Managua market. In late February 1987, MICOIN announced a strengthening of the roadblock system (*Bda* 25 February 1987). Yet a little over a month later, the roadblocks were suspended altogether (*Bda* 4 April 1987). Henceforth, the state would accept a free market in basic grains, while still trying to persuade producers to sell part of their output to ENABAS.[35]

A similar reversal occurred in the policy on private merchants. In February, MICOIN announced a plan to reduce the number of legal merchants by 60 per cent (*Bda* 25 February 1987). Within months, however, the government announced that commercial licences would be granted to anyone who applied (*END* 18 July 1987). It was hoped that this measure would generate significant income for the state, as merchants would pay roughly 1 per cent of their sales for their licences (*Bda* 29 September 1987).

A third significant reversal concerned salaries and official prices. The official "line" since the freezing of salaries in early 1986 was that real wages should be protected by such essentially anti-market measures as the "secure channels" established for salaried workers, and price controls. On the same day that MICOIN announced the suspension of its roadblock policy, however, the government announced a new policy of "periodic adjustments in prices and salaries, in accordance with indices of inflation and with changes in the structure of costs" (*Bda* 4 April 1987). The policy shift recognized the government's inability to protect real incomes through the policies hitherto applied. Base salaries were increased an average of 58 per cent in April, and would be adjusted five more times before the end of the year, for a total increase of 810 per cent, more or less keeping pace with accelerating inflation.

More than the 1985 economic measures, the 1987 shift in policy represented the state's retreat in the face of the market. There was even a willingness to experiment with the use of competition rather than direct control as a means of attaining policy objectives.[36] Signs of what can fairly be called a market ideology began to appear in the pro-FSLN newspapers, and in the statements of some government officials.[37]

There was conflict within the National Directorate over this change of direction. Henry Ruiz told an assembly of his ministry's staff that he disagreed with the current direction of the National Planning Council, but that he was a minority voice there. Even as the government was implementing measures to increase market freedom, Luís Carrión commented that the call to free markets was "nothing more than a formulation of the interests of the rich and of the merchants" (*Bda* 25 May 1987).

But these concerns were outweighed by a sense of the urgent need to change course. This need was articulated by an interministerial working group headed by Finance Minister William Hüpper, whose recommendations formed the basis of the policy shift. In a study completed around March 1987, the group warned that "the increasing gap between the official price system and other prices is producing a systematic disaccumulation of the formal sector of the economy, in favour of the informal sector, which is leading to the reduction and decomposition of the former, a situation which contradicts the strategic objectives of the revolutionary project" (Hüpper 1987). Thus, as in 1985, the new policy sought to protect the formal sector of the economy. Now, however, more concessions to the market were necessary to attain this objective. The working group stressed that the "artificial containment of a set of prices" had not been effective in controlling inflation, and recommended that all but a few prices should be set "in terms of the market."

Apart from the strictly economic erosion of the formal sector resulting from government policy, the FSLN leadership was deeply concerned by the moral erosion that accompanied it. While there was room for debate on the exact degree of collapse of real salaries since December 1984, there was no doubt that the fall was extreme, leading those workers who remained in the formal sector to make ends meet with a variety of legal or illegal tactics. The 1987 economic plan had commented that, "in the majority of cases," Nicaraguan families engaged in "speculation" (SPP

1987, 133). In March, Luís Carrión expressed alarm at the "extremely dangerous situation of social decomposition," manifested in increasing thefts from schools, hospitals, and supermarkets. Carrión warned that these symptoms were leading to "disorganization and anarchy," and were "seriously impeding the country's development projects, and corrupting the consciousness of workers themselves" (*Bda* 22 March 1987). A wide variety of economic crimes, Internal Trade Minister Ramón Cabrales warned, were becoming "normal in the eyes of both the people and the institutions that represent revolutionary power" (*Bda* 15 July 1987).[38]

Reports of theft from state institutions increased over this period. A director of state banana plantations allegedly conspired to steal bananas from his own company (*Bda* 23 March 1987). The CST charged that one-fifth of bananas and maize production was being stolen from state farms, one million plastic bags a month were disappearing from the plastics factory, etc. (*Bda* 31 July 1987). Perhaps more than any other factor, this perceived "decomposition" led Sandinista leaders to reverse salary policy.[39]

More generally, an "informalization" of the state complex was taking place, eroding the clear distinction between the formal and informal sectors that had underlain much economic policy. The majority of Managua families were engaging in a combined survival strategy, in which they straddled the two sectors (*Envío*, December 1986). This combined strategy was introduced into the state sector itself: in the ministry in which I worked, one could increasingly find workers engaging in buying and selling during the work day, using phone lines – an extremely scarce resource outside the formal sector – to close deals.

The interaction between the state complex and the unofficial market also operated at another level. Together, the ministries and companies of the state represented the biggest customer in the unofficial market. This is easy to understand if one considers the logic and operation of the catch-up socialist economy. Both ministries and state firms were regularly given "top priority" tasks that must be accomplished "at any cost".[40] But at the same time, access to dollars and imported goods was quite controlled. A ministry or company had to present an estimate of its need for dollars long before each year began. Given the extreme shortage of dollars, the requests of a specific institution were almost never met fully.[41]

This meant that a state industrial company, for example, could never meet its production goals if it had to rely only upon official imports. Its salvation was the fact that its *córdoba* budget was not very tightly controlled. Many of the largest state textile companies, for example, maintained financial records that were months out of date and bordered on fiction (Avilés and Amaya 1987). Under these conditions, one of the costs of performing tasks "at any cost" was the entry into the unofficial market to find whatever could not be obtained through formal channels. This activity naturally became more common as foreign exchange became more scarce, and as the proportion between foreign exchange captured by the state and that circulating in unofficial channels shifted to the detriment of the state.

This entry into the unofficial market both required and perpetuated lax financial controls. As Colburn points out, such receipts as one could come by in the unofficial market were but "hastily written slips of paper" (1990, 108). Thus, in contrast to the original vision of the state-dominant economy, in which order and control would slowly spread out from the state sector to cover the economy as a whole, one saw the chaos typical of the unofficial market imposing itself upon the state sector. Ironically, this phenomenon resulted precisely from the logic of the catch-up socialist economy, in which tasks are to be performed "at any cost." From the bending of rules required to perform such tasks, it is often a small step to personal corruption, since both one and the other are sheltered by the lack of financial and other controls.

The Adjustment Spiral

The decision to adjust salaries was based on the assumption that this would not significantly increase inflation. As Jaime Wheelock put it in May 1987: "If we don't increase salaries, inflation continues. It is not salary increases that are provoking inflation. Obviously, they can affect inflation a bit, but what produces inflation is the fiscal deficit" (*Bda* 28 May 1987). The analysis of those of us who supported this position was quite simple: real salaries had declined to such an extent that they no longer represented a significant source of demand, nor a significant factor in the cost structure of firms and the government. Given the extremely low level of salaries, their increase should not contribute much to the fiscal deficit, nor to cost- or demand-induced inflation. A similar analysis could be applied to the adjustment of official prices: these were lagging so far behind unofficial-market prices that their increase should not contribute much to increases in the overall price level.

But in fact inflation did accelerate rapidly from April 1987 on. While the CPI had crept upwards at a rate of just 1.4 per cent per month in the first trimester of 1987, it jumped 1287 per cent, or 33.9 per cent per month, from April to the end of the year.[42] Nicaragua had entered a hyper-inflationary period of four- and five-digit annual inflation. In what way did the adjustments in salaries and official prices contribute to this result? One explanation can begin with the hypothesis that, despite the common view of the unofficial market as an anomic chaos, various state pressures on "speculation" had in fact created a practice among many unofficial-market sellers of limiting themselves to "reasonable" price increases. Their definitions of reasonableness differed widely from that which the government wielded: some macro-economic event that had no impact upon the seller's cost structure could be seen "reasonably" to justify a price increase. Whatever their flexibility, I believe that tacit norms of reasonableness were in effect in much of the unofficial market.[43]

Such a phenomenon is quite consistent with a maximizing-behaviour hypothesis. Sellers in the unofficial market knew that keeping price increases "reasonable" would avoid problems with their customers, problems that could easily escalate into conflicts with the state or with the FSLN's mass organizations. Thus, following a policy of "reasonableness" can be seen as a strategy to maximize a value dependent upon two dimensions: profit and security.

One could then argue that the 1987 salary and official price increases constituted a major signal validating "reasonable" price increases in the unofficial market. It was common to find vendors who said they had raised prices "because of SNOTS," though their own cost structure in no way depended upon the level of salaries. Part of the problem was the very massiveness of the SNOTS system, which now comprised over 300,000 workers. Nicaraguans – both buyers and sellers – could believe that an increase in SNOTS meant "everyone's" nominal income was going to rise. This belief validated the "reasonableness" of price increases in the unofficial market. Thus, a system designed to bring order to the salary system seemed to have a tremendous unforeseen cost: it appeared to make it near-impossible for real salaries to recover lost ground.[44]

Thus, Nicaragua entered an "adjustment spiral": despite the deeply depressed level of salaries, each increase sparked great inflation, probably through its impact on expectations concerning "reasonable" price increases. This spiral could not have been maintained had macro-demand been constrained: in theory, there was no reason why increases in depressed salaries should generate the increase in nominal purchasing power necessary to sustain an overall increase in unofficial-market prices. Once again, however, the poorly understood interaction of the state and the unofficial market played a key role. So long as state officials continued to enter the unofficial market seeking to fulfil their objectives "at any cost," that market had a key source of demand willing to put up with "reasonable" price increases. Higher prices charged in the unofficial market simply increased the nominal fiscal deficit, which, along with the money supply, played a relatively passive role in adjusting to new prices.

If this reconstruction of the dynamics of 1987 inflation is correct, the adjustment spiral had become the prime cause of inflation. Thus, even a relatively low ratio between the fiscal deficit and nominal GDP was now compatible with almost any level of inflation, depending on how fast the government was willing to try to "adjust" relative prices. This fact would be amply demonstrated in 1988.

The salary question now confronted the government with a no-win political dilemma. While freezing salaries had not won the workers' love, neither did adjusting them under conditions of hyper-inflation. Workers had good cause for feeling they were worse off than before: announcements of wage increases were made early in the month, but the actual increased pay was usually not received until month's end. In the meantime, workers had to confront the price jumps that resulted from the announcement of the salary increase, with only the previous month's salary in their pockets. The salary increase at best sought to protect workers from the previous month's inflation, yet left them de-fenceless against current inflation, a significant problem with inflation running between 20 per cent and 30 per cent per month.[45]

Thus, by late 1987, there was probably much sympathy for the decla-ration by various opposition unions that, since neither salary freezes nor salary increases under the SNOTS system could protect real earn-ings, SNOTS itself had to be abolished (*END* 8 October 1987). This move was under consideration in the government, but involved serious problems. It was risky to end salary controls when many workers and employers would not be in an oppositional relationship: in a situation of rapid inflation, managers in the government and the productive sec-tor could rely on the Ministry of Finance and the market, respectively, to ratify any decisions they made concerning nominal salary levels.[46] Hence, an end to salary controls could reasonably be expected to trig-ger an ever more rapid wage-price spiral. This dilemma was but one of several that were making themselves increasingly felt by year's end.

The Problem of Specialist Salaries

In a situation in which real salaries in general were deteriorating, those of "specialists," professionals, and other highly skilled workers pre-sented a particular problem for the government. The evolution of the government's handling of the problem illuminates the interplay be-tween political pressures from the FSLN's various constituencies, the FSLN's own interpretation of its class nature, and economic problems that urgently required attention.

We have noted the dilemma which the FSLN – like all Marxist move-ments in power – faced with respect to specialists: their expertise was required, but their politics and ideology were mistrusted. The leadership, like other revolutionary leaderships before it, placed its hope in a new generation of specialists that would be produced by the Revolution itself, and thus freed from the "deformations" of the *ancien régime*.[47] In the meantime, the "old" specialists were to be tolerated, though closely watched.

This outlook made itself felt in the design of the SNOTS system. In a country where there had never been government controls on maximum salaries, the first SNOTS scale imposed a "fan," or ratio between the highest and lowest salaries, of 8.82. The various salary increases of early 1985 lowered the salary fan to 6.42. But by late 1985, the government was aware that this approach to specialists was running into a fundamental barrier: emigration. According to SPP data, specialist emigration in 1985 alone was just slightly below the total for the 1979–84 period. Though persons classified as specialists comprised only 6.7 per cent of the economically active population, they accounted for 16.5 per cent of emigration from that population in 1985. This reflects in part the fact that specialists found it easier to gain entry to other countries. Coupled with the movement of specialists into the informal sector, emigration created a crisis for the government's approach to this social sector. More specialists were leaving than the educational system was producing, and in any case there were grave doubts concerning the level of expertise of the newly graduated specialists.

The leadership thus sought to change course, and to sell this change to the popular sectors within its constituency. In a strong repudiation of the earlier hope that specialists would respond to "moral" incentives, CST leader Lucío Jimenez declared that "no one would want to be a doctor if he wouldn't earn any more than a machine operator, so the economy would not develop." This fundamental principle that more "complex" work should be better paid, said Jimenez, had been violated in the 1985 salary increases: "This deviation, rather than reflecting inexperience, was a political error based on the demand of workers who were not in agreement with higher salaries for specialists" (*Bda* 6 January 1986).[48] The January 1986 salary increase was skewed in favour of the upper level of the SNOTS scale, and the salary fan was widened to 8.23. Later in 1986, the number of SNOTS categories was increased from twenty-eight to thirty-nine, allowing many specialists to be classified at a higher level. This led to a further widening of the salary fan, to 11.17.

But all this had little impact. Given the low level of real salaries in general, tinkering with the salary fan could have little impact on specialists' living conditions. When deflated by the CPI, the salary of the top level of SNOTS in December 1986 was just 90 per cent higher than the *minimum* wage of two years earlier. Thus, the exodus intensified. In 1986, the emigration of specialists rose by 51 per cent over 1985. Emigrants in such critical categories as doctors and agronomists doubled in one year. In 1986, specialists made up nearly a quarter of economically active emigrants.

This situation led the government to decide that it could not "protect everyone the same," as SPP Minister Dionisio Marenco put it in early 1987. Sandinistas must eschew "egalitarian theses," declared Daniel Ortega, since without material incentives, no one would wish to train themselves (D. Ortega et al. 1987b). In April 1987, Jaime Wheelock told a meeting of FSLN cadres that "of the 300,000 salaried workers covered by SNOTS, there are only 1,450 high- and medium-level specialists, and we have decided to improve their living conditions. The working class possesses the clarity necessary to understand the importance of putting professionals in a special situation" (*Bda* 27 April 1987).

The FSLN's organization of professionals (CONAPRO-HM[49]) was itself becoming more aggressive in pressing the claims of its constituency. Professionals, declared one CONAPRO-HM leader in May, "have proposed, planned and carried out all that has been done in this Revolution" (*Bda* 7 May 1987). A "mechanical egalitarianism," complained another, had reduced specialists' access to such "essential articles" as electric appliances (*Bda* 21 October 1987).

Learning the lessons of 1986, the government's attempts to improve the living conditions of key specialists no longer relied on the salary mechanism. Instead, the government sought to create non-salary privileges. One of these was a special CAT for specialists (*Bda* 8 October 1987; *END* 23 October 1987). Other perks, in use before 1987 but whose application was now being extended, included the "sale" of imported Ladas to key specialists on terms that more or less made them gifts.

These practices provoked concern in many quarters. One contributor to *Barricada* asked, "Does not the political strategy of attracting professionals to the Revolution through material incentives dangerously open the door to opportunism? Does this strategy guarantee that they will not demand even more goods in the future if they are to continue their support, under threat of accepting a better offer elsewhere?" (*Bda* 21 October 1987). After CONAPRO-HM demanded an exemption from the SNOTS scale and a variety of other privileges for specialists (*Bda* 3 October 1987), one Ministry of Labour official angrily commented that "professionals need to reflect, because in the end it is the people who have subsidized their learning" (*Bda* 12 October 1987).

But these concerns did not affect the overall shift in party policy in favour of material incentives for specialists. An editorial in *Barricada* on 22 October 1987 called for the "necessary deference for those who organize and mobilize the bulk of the labour force," and declared the principle of distribution according to "capacity, and the quality and quantity of work." Another reminded readers that "egalitarianism" was a "populist" concept, rather than a revolutionary one, and that those who promoted it were "demagogues" (*Bda* 28 October 1987).

The magnitude of the shift in the FSLN's rhetoric is startling: "egalitarianism," one of the central pillars of early revolutionary rhetoric, was now rejected as mere populism and demagogy. Faith in moral incentives was now seen as recklessly idealistic: moral appeals to the specialists had fallen on deaf ears, as evidenced by the large number of doctors and engineers sweeping floors in Miami or Toronto. Appeals to heroism and attacks on "economism" would henceforth be limited to the "fundamental classes" of the revolution, the workers and peasants.

It is a measure of the importance of Marxist ideology within the FSLN that this shift in policy and rhetoric was articulated as a shift between variants of Marxism. In the earliest years of the revolution, the Sandinista leaders had spoken to specialists in much the same tone that Che had used when he toured Cuba to meet with university students or professionals: a formerly privileged group was asked to forget the past and generously play a key role in building the future. The revolution was a Promethean force that would soon level the peaks and valleys separating the poor from the privileged in the new Nicaragua. The 1987 attacks on "egalitarianism," appeals to the principle of distribution according to "capacity, and quality and quantity of labour," and the rejection of other possible principles as mere "populism," on the other hand, all sounded very much like the salary chapter of any Soviet textbook on political economy.[50]

Summary: The Dialectic of Market and Administration

The 1985–7 period had seen a number of concessions to the continued power of the market, and even a willingness to let certain dimensions of economic life, such as the distribution of private grain production, revert to the market sphere. But this reorientation of policy had brought the Nicaraguan economy no apparent relief, and seemed instead to have plunged the economy into chaos. Part of this appearance is illusory, as it reflects the coincidence between the timing of the economic reforms and the accelerated crumbling of the economy under the impact of several years of war. Nevertheless, the hesitant "turn to the market" of the 1985–7 period, and the uneasy interaction between the spheres of market and administration that resulted, had left the economy with as many fundamental irrationalities as had existed in late 1984. In essence, the government had failed to find a policy mix that would permit a stabilizing "turn to the market." Three problematic areas will be examined briefly here.

First, there had been an acceptance of the market in handling peasant *output*, but peasant *inputs* continued to be managed by the state. The peasantry was still able to buy production inputs at low official prices. In fact, because peasants were given bank loans to finance their purchase of inputs, and these loans carried deflated interest rates that were swiftly moving towards -100 per cent as inflation accelerated,[51] agricultural producers in general were receiving inputs from the state for next to nothing, with no corresponding obligation to deliver part of their output to the state. Even the most inefficient of producers could earn a profit, and the state complex lost money in its relations with agricultural producers, which undermined the objective of price stabilization through macro-demand containment. Thus, one saw a credit and input policy that reflected a "productionist" bias, and militated against the price stability the government sought, but which generally failed to generate production for the secure channels themselves.

This odd mix of policies seemed to beg for a resolution in one of two directions: either the government should use its control over credit and inputs to extract some output from producers, which would allow it to strengthen the "secure channels," or something approximating market prices should be applied to the provision of credit and input services. But the government was reluctant to address the problem. The question was whether relations with agricultural producers in general and the peasantry in particular could be altered without disturbing either production or the FSLN's rural alliances.

The leadership thus limited itself to pleading with producers. Jaime Wheelock declared in May 1987 that "the peasant has received land and inputs: machetes, files, boots, tractors, lighters, from the efforts of the people, who have produced these goods and brought them to the peasant. So he has to direct his production towards other producers, towards the workers ... towards the nurses and doctors" (*Bda* 28 May 1987).

But at this point the leadership could have had few illusions on the efficacy of such pleading. The mix of policies towards rural producers was accepted for the time being by FSLN leaders as a price for the revolution's "alliance with the countryside." When the leadership finally decided in 1988 to abandon this policy mix, it would do so in a particularly catastrophic fashion.

A second highly problematic area of policy was the exchange rate. While the 1985 economic plan had sought to reduce both exchange rate loss and the price distortions resulting from an overvalued *córdoba*, the stop-go pattern of adjustment had led to precisely the opposite result. The ratio between the unofficial and official rates of exchange had stood at 50:1 in late 1984; by the end of 1987 the unofficial rate was at least three hundred times higher than the lowest official rate, and there was even a 200:1 spread among *legal* exchange rates. The government feared that devaluations would accelerate the adjustment spiral, and that it might prove as impossible to achieve a real devaluation as it had proven to increase real salaries. At the same time, however, it was clear that economic stabilization would require policies to address the problem of exchange rate loss.

The third and final area of concern was that of salaries. Events had shown that neither stable nominal salaries, with reliance on "secure channels," nor salary adjustments under the conditions prevailing in the Nicaraguan economy, could protect the real earnings of Nicaraguan workers. As almost no one believed in the government's capacity to control prices by late 1987, there were increasing pressures to allow a full-fledged market for labour, though such a strategy would also entail serious difficulties.

Agricultural credit and inputs, the exchange rate, and salaries: these three policy areas would be crucial points of focus in the policy shifts of 1988. The depth of the dilemmas facing the government in these areas, and the general exasperation with the country's "adjustment spiral" and its associated hyperinflation, were creating a belief in the need for some form of "shock therapy." The coming years would see several applications of such shocks, until, one February day in 1990, Nicaraguans would respond in kind, giving the FSLN a shock from which it has yet to recover.

B. RELATIONS WITH THE BOURGEOISIE

As 1985 brought signs of greater respect within the FSLN leadership for the staying power of the market, so too was there more acceptance of the long-term role of the private sector in general and the bourgeoisie in particular. As with the recognition of the market, the shift in thinking with respect to private producers was politically delicate, and the National Directorate sought to express the shift within a framework of Marxist language and analysis.

A key example of this timid and highly "coded" shift in the view of private production came in a speech by Victor Tirado, days before the announcement of the new economic measures:

Free enterprise was tried in Nicaragua, and it brought us backwardness, misery, dependence, dictatorship; maybe it was good for other countries, maybe it was just or correct, but it has been shown that in Nicaragua it failed. But it is not a question, as is often affirmed, of wiping private enterprise off the map, of eliminating private enterprise; we don't think so. We believe that the private sector performs and should perform an important role in the mixed economy. Some sectors of private enterprise understand this, others do not.

According to the latter, those who do not understand, the mixed economy means that the Sandinista Front should abandon the leadership of the government ...

Sometimes for economic or political reasons, because of a lack of cadres, or because of spiritual and material backwardness, the State cannot take on the administration of the entire economy, and this is where the private sector plays an important role ...

On the other hand, this revolution is well defined for us; it would be hasty and hare-brained to try to push reality, to try to skip stages and take on tasks for which the society is not yet ready. And so the mixed economy, the existence of a strong state sector and a vigorous private sector are objectively necessary and destined to last through a long historical stage (1985, 125–6).

The speech indicated the shift in FSLN thinking that had taken place since 1979: from the talk of transitory, "tactical," alliances often heard in 1979–80, to talk of a "long historical stage." A rhetoric stressing the historical "mission" of capitalism to develop the means of production to an advanced stage, and recognizing the impossibility of "skipping stages," was now spreading through the National Directorate, serving as a vehicle by which the directorate expressed the need to put statist aspirations on the back burner for the foreseeable future.

Even the more resolutely statist elements within the directorate appeared to accept the change in orientation. Tomás Borge commented in mid-1985 that "we are not an island like Cuba ... This geopolitical factor has obliged us, independently of our will, to develop political pluralism and a mixed economy. The development of this tactic has been converted into a strategy and today the mixed economy, for example, is not a tactical option or a camouflage. It is a strategy." Borge went on to note that "this makes the conduction of the revolutionary process among the masses much more difficult" (1985e).

In another expression of the new political mood within the FSLN leadership, Daniel Ortega held a nationally televised meeting with a wide range of private producers, including leaders of the Superior Council of Private Enterprise (COSEP), days after the announcement of the new economic measures. The tone of Ortega's remarks to the producers was generally conciliatory, recognizing, for example, that injustices had occurred in the application of the agrarian reform (*Bda* 18 February 1985).[52] In the same meeting, however, Ortega ratified the Sandinista strategy of pushing the bourgeoisie into an economistic mold: Ortega responded to a harsh speech from COSEP head Enrique

Bolaños by stating that he had come to discuss "economic," not "political," questions with producers.[53] The FSLN was to be more open to the specific economic concerns of producers, including bourgeois producers, but it was not about to "abandon the leadership of the government," as Victor Tirado had put it.

Greater recognition of the need to address the concerns of the bourgeoisie led to an attenuation of class rhetoric. A new category was invented, that of "patriotic producers": those who continued to produce, who did not cooperate with the contras or with the politicized bourgeoisie within COSEP, who accepted the FSLN's political dominance, be they ever so bourgeois in strictly economic terms, were absolved of the historic sins of the bourgeoisie.[54] Jaime Wheelock had declared in 1980 that "the interests of small owners are radically different from those of large ones. We cannot ally ourselves with them because at any moment they could betray us, as they did to Sandino ... as they did in Chile" (*Bda* 5 January 1980). But by the mid-1980s, Wheelock painted Nicaraguan history in quite different terms. "We cannot throw in the same bag," he declared in 1986, the large owner who "persecuted and murdered peasants," and those, who might own as much as 400 hectares, but who "may well have fought alongside Sandino, may well have struggled against imperialism ... Neither from an economic nor a political point of view, and much less from the point of view of our revolutionary morality, can we throw into the same sack a *somocista* and a revolutionary, merely because the two own the same amount of land" (1986c, 29). Thus, class location no longer depended upon the "mere" question of ownership of means of production: "A bourgeois," Daniel Ortega argued, "is the one who says that we are worse off with the revolution." The bourgeois thus "can be very rich or can have no money" (FBIS 14 July 1987).[55]

In the countryside, responsibility for building bridges to the "patriotic producers" went to UNAG, which was shedding both its original identity as an essentially peasant organization and its class rhetoric. In a late 1984 interview, UNAG head Daniel Nuñez dismissed the question of whether "rich peasants," who employed up to 500 workers during harvest time, should be allowed to join UNAG: "Yes, why not? If he is a patriotic man he is in the UNAG ... The framework should not be philosophical questions, but rather the conduct of men" (1985, 370). UNAG's shift in orientation was effective in containing the influence of the opposition bourgeoisie in the countryside. Many rural producers found it more prudent to distance themselves from the strident and highly politicized path of COSEP and affiliate themselves with UNAG, which was increasingly becoming an effective "fixer" for broad sectors of the agrarian bourgeoisie.[56]

The contrast between the two options was highlighted whenever the two organizations participated in a public meeting with government officials. Thus, in an early 1987 meeting, called to discuss the economic plan, COSEP head Enrique Bolaños repeated his group's position that there would be no improvement in the economy until the FSLN agreed to dialogue with the contras, and told President Ortega: "All this is a total failure, a national tragedy. Your government has failed, the political project of the FSLN has failed ... What we must do now is begin anew." The UNAG representative, on the other hand, focused on a series of specific economic concerns of producers. He criticized, for example, the lack of availability of MIDINRA regional officials, who were too busy driving around in their "air-conditioned vehicles." When the UNAG official did touch on more "political" questions, he was careful that any criticism take the structure of revolutionary power as a given. Thus he criticized the government for convoking producers to discuss an already formulated economic plan, by pointing out that such a right of participation was provided for in the constitution passed by the FSLN-dominated National Assembly (D. Ortega et al., 1987a).

By early 1986, UNAG was claiming 124,000 members, and held that its membership was responsible for the bulk of agro-export production (*Bda* 23 January 1986). Whether or not these statistics are accurate, it is clear that a significant portion of what remained of the agrarian bourgeoisie was now affiliated with an organization established by the FSLN. Because UNAG did not make many demands on its members, however, one cannot say that membership in UNAG implied loyalty to the government. Nevertheless, UNAG at the very least appeared successful in closing some of the "organizational space" that might have been used by opposition groups.

A price had to be paid for the political success of UNAG: the FSLN gave far more autonomy to UNAG than to any other mass organization. As they integrated "patriotic producers" into the organization, UNAG officials essentially used their autonomy to bring some of the economic demands of the bourgeoisie into the revolutionary sector. An April 1987 meeting between the government cabinet and mass organization representatives highlights the special nature of UNAG. A series of officials from the CST "representing" urban workers rose to speak of the importance of productivity and of defeating the contras, while studiously ignoring the issue of the calamitous drop in the living standards of their constituency. The UNAG representatives, on the other hand, aggressively spoke to the immediate concerns of their constituency. One demanded that the mobilization of young men for defence be done in a way that was less disruptive of rural production. She attacked the ATC for trying to impose collective agreements on private producers by wielding the threat of expropriation. She noted that it was impossible to dialogue with government representatives in the rural regions, and that unjust expropriations of private producers were commonplace (D. Ortega et al. 1987b). These were many of the same concerns that had been articulated by the rural bourgeoisie in 1979–80, which had often provoked harsh reactions from FSLN leaders. Now, however, the concerns were being expressed from within one of the FSLN's own creations. Thus it was not clear whether a sector of the bourgeoisie was being "revolutionized," or whether part of the revolutionary bloc was being "bourgeoisified."

The shift in the FSLN's strategy towards the bourgeoisie was not without tension, however. We will see below that grass-roots pressure forced an intensification in the agrarian reform process in 1985–6, one that partly frustrated the FSLN's attempts to mollify the agrarian bourgeoisie.

The Esquipulas Accord

In early August 1987, the five Central American presidents signed the Esquipulas II accord, which would decisively influence political relations between the FSLN and the bourgeoisie for the remainder of the Sandinista decade. The accord presented both the FSLN and the bourgeoisie with new dilemmas. On the one hand, the Nicaraguan government pledged, along with its regional counterparts, to promote "an authentic pluralistic and participatory democratic process" (Presidents of Central America 1987). This included a commitment to "complete freedom" for media, including the right to run television stations (which would threaten the monopoly of Nicaragua's Sandinista Television System), and to other civil rights.

On the other hand, the accord accepted the legitimacy of the existing governments and constitutions in the region, and condemned armed opposition movements. The governments committed themselves only to hold future elections "in accordance with existing constitutions," and to "initiate a dialogue with all *unarmed* political opposition groups within the country" (emphasis added). Most significantly, the five governments promised to "prevent the use of their own territories" by movements seeking to "destabilize" any government in the region. This implied, among other things, a commitment by the Honduran government to evict the contras from its territory. The accord seemed certain to reduce the pressure the contras could exert upon the FSLN, and thus there was a sector of the Nicaraguan opposition dismayed that the accord would "oblige us to continue putting up with a Marxist government" (*Psa* 1 October 1987).

The months after the Esquipulas II agreement underlined the tensions among the opposition parties. Several parties felt that the accord had created an opening for fruitful negotiations on political questions, and took part in a "National Dialogue" with the government. The more intransigent parties, associated with the Democratic Coordinator, ignored the spirit and letter of the Esquipulas II accord, declaring that "the efforts of the civic opposition parties have failed" and demanding immediate elections supervised by the Organization of American States (*Psa* 7 December 1987). The conflict generated around this question led to the splintering of several of the opposition parties into pro- and anti-National-Dialogue factions.

This splintering of the opposition was related to a tension between the opposition parties and COSEP, which had hitherto coordinated the intransigent wing of the bourgeois opposition. The government, viewing COSEP as the most Reaganite segment of the opposition, refused to invite it to the National Dialogue.[57] The government argued that, as the FSLN was attending the dialogue as a political party, unaccompanied by its unions and mass organizations, so should the opposition channel its representation through existing parties. COSEP felt that a dialogue that excluded it was a dialogue that should not take place at all, and pressured those politicians closest to it not to participate.

The post-Esquipulas period also generated tensions within the FSLN leadership, however. These tensions centred on the question whether the government should begin to implement some aspects of the Esquipulas accord before the other Central American governments had begun to do so, even though the actual accord called for all measures to be implemented "publicly and simultaneously" in early November. The government originally held to the principle of simultaneity. Returning from the Guatemala summit, Daniel Ortega stressed that the accord was "indivisible, and the implementation of this document is simultaneous." Ortega also stated that Nicaragua would not lift the state of emergency until "the aggression stops" (FBIS 11 August 1987). But various factors led the National Directorate to give ground on the simultaneity question, a policy shift apparently spearheaded by Daniel Ortega. A major factor was the military situation. Though the government had been proclaiming the contras' "strategic defeat" since 1985, by late 1987 Humberto Ortega admitted that "the war is the fiercest it has ever been" (*NYT* 22 December 1987).[58]

Indeed, the war had taken an ominous turn. The government's acquisition of Soviet MI-24 helicopters had helped tilt the military situation in Nicaragua's favour. Though the contras acquired SAM-7s in 1985 (FBIS 30 April 1985; *NYT* 4 May 1985), prior to 1987 only one Nicaraguan helicopter had been downed (FBIS 5 December 1985).

After the U.S. Congress approved $100 million for the contras in June 1986, however, the contras asked for more sophisticated surface-to-air missiles (*NYT* 27 June 1986). The United States supplied the contras with Redeye missiles, creating the unusual situation of a "guerrilla" force possessing more advanced anti-aircraft technology than any government army in the region (FBIS 28 July 1987). From May 1987 on, the contras began downing Nicaraguan helicopters regularly. By November, the government acknowledged losing ten helicopters in the previous months (*NYT* 22 December 1987), and it was reported that the Sandinista army would not use its remaining helicopters in subsequent military actions (*Psa* 19 November 1987). This seriously hampered the effectiveness of an army "almost completely dependent on helicopters to ferry troops and supplies" (*NYT* 28 June 1987). By September, it was reported that for the first time in the war the contras were on the verge of establishing a foothold inside Nicaragua, in the Boaco-Chontales region east of Managua (*NYT* 13 September 1987).

A further concern for the Sandinista leadership was the fact that the Soviet Union was signalling a reduction in support for Nicaragua even while the United States was increasing its support for the contras. Of particular importance was Soviet oil aid. Through the 1985–7 period, the Soviet Union was directly or indirectly responsible for nearly all of Nicaragua's oil imports (Grayson 1985, 253; Bulmer-Thomas 1987, 256). In August 1986 a Soviet technical delegation that was expected to arrive with $50 million in aid came empty-handed, and warned that the Soviet Union would no longer be able to meet all Nicaragua's oil needs. By mid-1987 the government publicly admitted that only 40 per cent of its required oil supply had been guaranteed (FBIS 2 June 1987). From this point on, the government would be engaged in a constant scramble to maintain oil supplies.

There was thus great concern that the contra threat would continue indefinitely, and that the government would no longer receive the support needed to confront that threat and hold the economy together. These concerns were heightened by the Reagan administration's announced intention to seek a further $270 million in aid for the contras. Ortega and those who supported him calculated – correctly, as it turned out – that showing flexibility on the question of simultaneity would undercut congressional support for the contras.[59]

Thus, in late September 1987, the government permitted the reopening of *La Prensa*, which had been closed in June 1986 after the U.S. Congress' contra aid vote.[60] Despite government hopes that the opposition paper would adopt a more sober tone, the resurrected *La Prensa*, now free of prior censorship for the first time since March 1982, was more vitriolic than ever. The government also repealed the

1981 law that called for the confiscation of the assets of persons absent from the country for more than six months. In the coming months, the government would move farther beyond minimum compliance with the Esquipulas II agreement, agreeing to indirect negotiations with the contras, and then to direct negotiations. This decision reversed the long-standing pledge of the FSLN never to negotiate with the counterrevolutionary "beasts".[61]

Though seeking to promote "national reconciliation," these FSLN concessions convinced the more hard-line elements of the bourgeoisie that the Sandinistas were on their last legs. Nicaraguans, exulted COSEP head Enrique Bolaños, "are no longer afraid of the Sandinista Defence Committees, nor of listening to counterrevolutionary radio stations or the Voice of America at maximum volume ... Now we just have to strike the final blow and reverse the actions of Sandinism" (END 24 August 1987). The next phase of FSLN-bourgeois relations would be marked by the hard-line bourgeoisie's attempt to deal that final blow, and the FSLN's attempts to stave it off.

C. AGRARIAN REFORM

By late 1984 Minister of Agriculture Jaime Wheelock was promising private producers in different parts of the country that there would be no more expropriations in their regions, other than those to punish "counterrevolutionary" activity. Agrarian reform expropriations in 1984 were down by more than half in relation to the previous year, and the government believed it could meet the demands of those peasants still without land with a judicious transfer of land from the state sector, some expropriations of private producers, and the integration of the landless into existing production cooperatives. MIDINRA's planned land transfers for 1985 were well below the 1984 level. Thus, it was hoped that peasant land hunger could be met while guaranteeing the property rights of the "patriotic" agrarian bourgeoisie.

Peasant initiatives, however, dashed this hope in mid-1985. In early June, landless peasants seized several private estates in the Masaya area, near Managua. The department of Masaya, with the highest rural population density in the country, had been a focus of land tension since 1979. Both before and after the insurrection, peasants seized land that was then worked collectively until the end of 1979. In 1980, however, the state either turned the seized land into state farms or returned it to its former owners (M. Ortega 1985). Some land was seized in 1983 as unemployment in the department rose, but pressures continued as the deterioration of the department's artisan economy removed a traditional safety valve for the rural unemployed. Because large farms in the area were in general efficiently used, there was little land available for agrarian reform purposes.

Throughout early 1985, local UNAG activists were helping landless peasants organize themselves to present their demands for land to MIDINRA. But on 7 June, the peasants decided not to wait for the ministry's response, and seized several farms – including that of COSEP leader Enrique Bolaños. The peasants began to plant corn the same afternoon, and vowed not to give up the land.

Jaime Wheelock's first reaction to the seizure was negative, referring to the need to respect national unity. But a week later the government accepted the peasants' demands, and tried to reach compensation accords with the owners of the land. Accords were reached with all the owners except Bolaños.[62] In total, some 5,000 hectares were affected, including 1,400 belonging to Bolaños (*Envío*, September 1985). Significantly, the land was transferred to the peasants in individual form, signalling a relaxation of the government's policy of promoting cooperative development.[63]

In October a similar case occurred, as peasants seized over 400 hectares of land in the department of Matagalpa. Once again MIDINRA accepted the seizure, and ministry officials said that there were many similar situations developing throughout the Matagalpa-Jinotega region, which also happened to be one of the areas of intense contra activity (*END* 16 October 1985; *Bda* 14 October 1985).

Far from strengthening the security of bourgeois property rights, the government now seemed to be returning to the immediate post-triumph policy of offering *ex post* legalization of peasant land seizures. One COSEP leader complained: "Finally, it seemed that the [FSLN], after six years' of experience in administering the country, was becoming a bit more pragmatic ... We thought we were arriving at a real understanding. But suddenly we find them starting to stir people up" (Díaz 1985).

But the government's willingness to condone land seizures and accept the granting of land titles to individual peasants reflected the same "pragmatism" that had inspired many policy changes in 1985. Faced with a tension between two class demands – that of the rural bourgeoisie for security of property, and that of the landless peasantry for land – the FSLN decided in 1985 that the peasantry represented the more urgent problem. The events in Masaya brought on a rapid acceleration of the agrarian reform. The land transferred to cooperatives and individuals from June to the end of 1985 equalled nearly half the amount transferred from the beginning of the reform process to June 1985 (M. Ortega 1986). Total transfers to cooperatives for 1985 were nearly double their planned level, and 100,000 hectares were transferred to individual peasants (MIDINRA 1986), almost fourteen times the original plan (*Revolución y Desarrollo*, April-June 1984). Nearly all of the transfers to individuals occurred after the Masaya land seizures.

At the same time, the FSLN hoped that it could use the peasant land pressure to strengthen the "patriotic" inclinations of the agrarian bourgeoisie. A National Directorate document in late 1985 outlining strategy for 1986 stressed that strengthening the "alliance" with the peasantry should come at the expense of "enemy landowners" (Dirección Nacional 1985b).

The land problem was also exacerbated by the contra war, which by early 1986, had led to the transfer of some 40,000 families out of the war zones (Wheelock 1986c, 35). The transfer furthered military objectives, but also represented, as one observer wrote, "a gigantic reordering of population, and an important modification in the socio-economic structure of the affected regions, which will facilitate the promotion of works of progress and social services" (*Pensamiento Propio*, April 1985). Thus, the war was permitting the realization of an old Sandinista project: the gathering together of a dispersed peasantry in order to promote its modernization. While the FSLN was making concessions to "peasant backwardness" by increasing the transfer of land to individuals, it had not abandoned its project for the transformation of the peasantry.

In early 1986, the agrarian reform law was amended to give the government more flexibility in meeting peasant demands. The new law removed the lower size limits on expropriations. The law also gave the government the power to expropriate land "for reasons of public utility or social interest" (Law 14). This clause essentially created an all-purpose mechanism for expropriating specific land parcels, without having to declare an entire area an "agricultural development zone," as was necessary under the old law.

Despite the "tilt" to the peasantry in 1985, the FSLN tried to maintain an interclass balancing act in the countryside. The new agrarian reform law gave the government the legal right to expropriate land at will, but full recourse to this legality would have undermined the FSLN's efforts to consolidate the sector of "patriotic producers." Thus, though the new law appeared to weaken property security, Jaime Wheelock signalled the government's intention to use the "public interest" clause sparingly, to avoid hurting "the traditional reality of the countryside".[64] Where land was required that could not be expropriated under the abandonment or underuse clauses of the reform law, Wheelock promised, the government would seek to negotiate its purchase or exchange for other land. Further to reassure private producers, Wheelock noted that the majority of land transferred to peasants in 1986 would come from state farms or unused national lands (1986c, 59ff). Despite the use of state lands, however, total expropriations doubled in 1986 to 135,000 hectares, the highest level ever.

While the response to peasant land demands had to be coordinated with the project of building bridges to the "patriotic producers," it had to be balanced with other policy objectives as well. Agrarian reform policy had originally sought to protect the modern pole of Nicaragua's bimodal agricultural economy. The rapid transfer of land to cooperatives in late 1983 and 1984 had threatened that modern pole somewhat, and the 1985 acceptance of the need to transfer land to individual peasants represented a further sacrifice of modern agriculture to the goal of "strengthening the alliance with the Revolution in the countryside," as an internal FSLN document put it (Dirección Nacional y Asamblea Sandinista 1986).[65] The same document noted that the government had yet to find the correct "technical-economic structuring" to accompany changes that had been dictated by political objectives. There was thus great concern that the "alliance with the peasantry" was being purchased at the expense of long-term economic stagnation.[66]

The agrarian reform's weakening of the modern pole of the bimodal system also had implications for state dominance of the economy. This project had reinforced the FSLN's bias for large-scale agricultural production. The explosion of cooperatives not closely linked with MIDINRA from 1984 on, and the 1985 increase in land transfers to individual peasants made the types of rural economic relations envisioned in the state-dominant economy seem increasingly unrealistic. Jaime Wheelock would later comment that it was the growing role of the peasant economy, more than the survival of capitalist enterprise, that pushed the FSLN towards a "commodity economy, away from centralized planning" (1990, 18).

Concerns over the long-term implications of the agrarian reform, along with the FSLN's belief that the contras were now surviving more because of U.S. technology than peasant support, led to a slowing down of the agrarian reform in 1987. The SPP's 1987 economic plan called for changes in land tenancy to be subordinated to "the logic of the economic and social transformation" and to the needs of military defence. Land should be transferred, the plan urged, only under the condition that it improve in productivity, and emphasis should be placed on moving landless peasants into previously deserted war zones in which the contra presence had now been diminished. The plan also urged that alternatives to land transfers be sought for landless peasants (SPP 1987, 3–4). One such alternative was to join cooperatives that needed to replenish their membership. Voting with their feet on the FSLN's preference for collective agriculture, an estimated 25 per cent of members had deserted production cooperatives from 1983–4 onwards (*Bda*

30 January 1987).[67] This had led to a situation in which much land transferred to cooperatives was standing idle, and the 1987 economic plan called for one-quarter of transferred land to come *from* the cooperatives.

In 1987, only 38,500 hectares of land were expropriated under the agrarian reform, down over 70 per cent from the previous year. The MIDINRA vice-minister in charge of the agrarian reform declared that "the transformation of the countryside is fundamentally complete" (*END* 18 December 1987). This position would be maintained throughout the next two years.

D.   CONCLUSION

By late 1987, the FSLN leadership knew that it was entering a very difficult period. The Esquipulas accord would make it harder for the FSLN to control the domestic political space as thoroughly as before. Directorate member Bayardo Arce commented that the FSLN was "entering a period of acute ideological struggle" (*Bda* 6 September 1987). The accord also strengthened the FSLN's commitment to hold a presidential election in 1990.

Thus, the FSLN found itself three years away from presidential elections, and in the midst of a severe economic crisis. As Tomás Borge admitted, support for the revolution was being "worn out": there was now "discontent, not just among certain sectors, but I would say amidst the entire population of the country" (*Bda* 4 October 1987). The FSLN had to hope that, despite the economic crisis, a large part of the population would remain loyal to the party that had overthrown Somoza and stood up to the Yanqui empire, and that the rest would divide their support among a plethora of opposition parties. The first hope was fulfilled to a surprising degree. The second was not.

7 Triumph of the Market, 1988–9

In the 1988–9 period, economic reforms scuttled most key elements of the state-dominant economy project. Price controls were abandoned, and the market was allowed to determine ever more significant economic variables, including, by 1989, the exchange rate.

These reforms did not arrest Nicaragua's economic decline. Real gross domestic product (GDP) dropped a total of 13.5 per cent in 1988–9, ending the period 38 per cent below its 1977 level. GDP per capita dropped 19 per cent, to just 42 per cent of its 1977 level. Large economic imbalances persisted. Exports dropped by 20 per cent in 1988, to just $235 million, and the current account deficit reached $865 million. Exports recovered slightly in 1989, to $292 million.[1] This recovery and a drop in imports reduced the current account deficit to $571 million, its lowest level since 1982. Fiscal imbalance and inflation also persisted, as shall be seen.

Politically, the degree to which support for the FSLN had depended upon the containment of market forces became even clearer. The increase in tensions within the Sandinista camp provoked an erratic political strategy on the part of the leadership, with attempts at reconciliation with the bourgeoisie alternating with attacks on that same class.

In this chapter, as in chapter six, the questions of state organization and price policy will be combined in section A. The following two sections will examine relations with the bourgeoisie and the agrarian reform, respectively. Section D will examine the Sandinista revolution's "final act," the 1990 election.

A. ECONOMIC ADJUSTMENT: THE TRIUMPH OF THE MARKET

The "Valentine's Day Blow"

On 14 February 1988, President Ortega announced the most complete package of economic policies since the shift of direction of February 1985 (Ortega 1988a). In a speech to the nation, Ortega reminded Nicaraguans of the cost of the contra war, and of the economic policies implemented in 1985. These policies, Ortega stated, had failed to stem inflation, "which continues to grow, profoundly affecting the productive sector, and in particular formal sector workers." It was time to recognize, Ortega declared, that the 1985 measures were "exhausted," and new measures were required to "confront this critical situation."

After this preamble, Ortega announced a currency reform. Over the following three days, Nicaraguans would trade in their currency for "new *córdobas*," at a rate of 1000:1. After February 17, the old *córdoba* would cease to function as legal tender. After assuring Nicaraguans that "those who have obtained their money in a legal fashion" had nothing to fear from the reform, Ortega announced that no person could trade in more than 10 million old *córdobas* in cash. Amounts in excess of this would be frozen in special accounts for a time.

In a move aimed at recovering some of the resources lost by the state complex in previous years owing to negative real interest rates, Ortega announced that a "conversion factor" would be applied to monetary obligations before converting them into new *córdobas*. Thus, for example, a bank loan issued in the last trimester of 1986 would be multiplied by 19 before being converted into new *córdobas* (Presidential Decree 306). These conversion factors would also be applied to obligations such as unpaid taxes and fines.[2]

The new *córdoba* was pegged at ten to the dollar, which, Ortega promised, would serve as a unified exchange rate for all exports and imports. This represented a devaluation of from 2,700 per cent to 14,300 per cent, depending on the figure one used for the previous official exchange rate.

The monetary reform was to be accompanied by a realignment of relative prices. "We are giving work its true value," Ortega declared, "we are giving goods and services their true value".[3] Increases of official prices of consumer goods raised the total cost of various baskets of basic consumer items by 129 per cent (*Envío*, April 1988) to 273 per cent (Stahler-Sholk 1988a, 29). Basic salaries, however, were increased by an average of 385 per cent. These increases were skewed in favour of the upper levels of the national wage scale (SNOTS): the minimum wage was increased just 305 per cent, while the maximum increased 662 per cent. At the same time, however, the government sharply contracted the system of salary bonuses. The only bonuses retained were for seniority, a productivity bonus for agricultural workers, and bonuses that some companies could negotiate with their workers (*Bda* 15 February 1988).[4]

When the Employment and Salaries Department of the Secretariat for Planning and Budgeting (SPP) was asked to recommend a new salary scale to accompany the monetary reform, we were told to peg the salary of the average worker to the cost of the basic consumer basket. Thus, the February 1988 measures resurrected the notion that the basic salary should allow a worker to get by, albeit modestly. Ortega declared, echoing the language that had accompanied the February 1985 reforms, that "we are protecting the formal sector, and returning to wage labour part of the purchasing power it has lost in these past years" (Ortega 1988a). This commitment would vanish in the months following the reform, as it had in 1985.

The official presentation of the new measures stressed the need to "defend" the new prices and exchange rate. "We are all obliged," Ortega declared "to defend these measures, to demand respect for these new prices. No one in this country, none of you, fellow Nicaraguans, can yield to the pressure of the speculators. We must all demand, in a combative fashion, that the new schedule of prices and salaries be respected" (1988a). Thus, as in 1985, the new measures were accompanied by calls to crush "speculation." These calls were converted into a short-lived attempt at "social control."

Certain critical elements in the new economic package were not presented during Ortega's speech on 14 February , and were only made public through various announcements in the following weeks. In mid-March, the government announced that the banking system would finance only 80 per cent of the working costs of agricultural producers (*Bda* 19 March 1988). Similar announcements had been made in past years, but this time the government was actually prepared to put the policy into effect. Advocates of a "productionist" orientation within the government had suffered a significant set-back. In April, industrial sector managers were informed of the government's intention to reduce short-term credit to industry and commerce by 10 per cent, and long-term credit by 30 per cent (*Bda* 11 April 1988).

The new economic policy also sought to reduce the fiscal deficit to 8 per cent of GDP, from its 1987 level of 17 per cent (*Bda* 4 April 1988). This was to be achieved through an increase in the tax burden and a reduction in government spending. This latter goal was to be accomplished through the "compression" [*compactación*] of the central government, a strategy announced in March. The compression aimed at reducing employment in the central government bureaucracy by 10 per cent. It was hoped that jobs could be eliminated without hurting government performance by combining certain ministries, and restructuring others, such as the Ministry of Agriculture (MIDINRA).

More than just a fiscal measure, the compression reflected a more modest conception of the state's role in the economy. In announcing the compression at his ministry, Wheelock commented that MIDINRA "is letting go of its functions of administrator, entrepreneur, large investor and educator, and will take on a purely regulatory role" (*Bda* 18 March 1988).

In correspondence with this changing view of the state's role, public enterprises were to be granted more autonomy. In essence, administrators were told to undertake the shift from the state-enterprise relation typical of the socialist economy to the autonomy associated with a market system. Luís Carrión told state managers that the government would no longer act as their "godfather": "we will not be unconditional advocates of state entrepreneurs" (*Bda* 27 April 1988). In particular, Carrión warned, state companies, like their private counterparts, would have to meet their fiscal obligations and adapt to the new credit policy.

As they were promised more autonomy, state firms were also told to adapt their behaviour to the new economic thinking. SPP head Alejandro Martínez commented that "managers must be efficient and guarantee that their production has quality. They must learn marketing techniques. Economic criteria should determine decisions on the administration of resources" (*Bda* 24 May 1988).

In the words of the manager of FANATEX, one of the largest state industries, state companies had to confront a shift from "a centralized, directed economic model, with a closed market," to "an open market, that is, one governed by the capitalist laws of supply and demand, in which one must maximize the profitability of capital" (*Bda* 17 September 1988).[5] While state enterprises had been exhorted to be efficient in the past, concrete measures were now being demanded of them. One of these was to trim their payroll. In fact, the bulk of the 10,000 jobs lost in the 1988 "compression" were in the state enterprises, rather than the central government (Pérez and Somarriba 1989, 15).

In distinction to the 1985 measures, it is not clear whether any overall logic underlay the February 1988 package. Ortega's presentation gave the impression that a central goal of the measures was to end inflation. It should have been clear from the experiences of the 1985–7 period, however, that a devaluation and salary increase of the magnitude undertaken would intensify the "adjustment spiral." Nevertheless, the government projected that annual inflation rates would be reduced to

100 per cent after implementation of the measures (Arana 1990, 19). It was hoped that the reduction of the fiscal deficit and the reduction of the real money supply through the monetary reform would dampen "objective" inflationary pressures. In addition, the architects of the package apparently believed that the monetary reform and the "social control" campaign to "defend" the new official prices would be sufficient to break inflationary expectations, thus addressing the "subjective" component of inflation (Arana 1990, 19; Acevedo Volg 1989, 19). This hope may have been based on the "heterodox" anti-inflation strategies pursued in various Latin American countries. As Adolfo Acevedo Volg pointed out, however, key prices such as the exchange rate had already been realigned in these other cases before an attempt to stop inertial inflation was undertaken (1989, 20).

A similar ambiguity underlay the government's promise to "protect the formal sector." Had the policy of stabilizing real salaries been maintained, the measures would have addressed the labour supply problem that was hurting the formal sector. In general, however, the measures represented a sharp shift from a "productionist" to a "financial" orientation. As such, they could be expected to hurt certain productive sectors that had benefited from the "productionist" orientation. The agro-export sector is a case in point. The unification of the exchange rate, which sought to eliminate exchange-rate loss, essentially returned exporters to the pre-1982 situation, in which export prices were determined by world prices.[6] An analysis undertaken by MIDINRA suggested that "nearly all export products" would be unprofitable with the new structure of costs and official prices. The implication of MIDINRA's analysis was either that the 3,000-per-cent to 14,000-per-cent devaluation that accompanied the measures was insufficient, or that the government should abandon its hopes of unifying the exchange rate. The Central Bank, on the other hand, argued that profitability would be restored over time as producers shifted their production technique to adapt to the new relative prices (Stahler-Sholk 1988b, 45). What needed to be avoided, in the Central Bank analysis, was the establishment of producer prices on the basis of whatever costs happened to emerge from the current practices of producers: only a degree of pressure on producers would force them to address problems of "X-inefficiency" and adapt to realistically priced imported inputs. As the Central Bank won this argument for the time being, it appears that government decision-makers were willing to risk a temporary downturn in exports. Thus the overall degree of protection which the new measures afforded the formal sector was debatable.

Similar observations can be made with respect to the shift in credit policy. One may note, first of all, that the unilateral revaluation of outstanding loans, which essentially made real interest rates positive after the fact, left producers with dramatically higher payments owing to the banks. Oddly, however, the new measures left *current* interest rates practically untouched: the highest nominal interest rate for agricultural producers was just 30 per cent (*Bda* 19 March 1988). Instead of using higher interest rates to dampen demand for credit, the government tightened credit rationing. The difficulty with this strategy, as previously noted, is that many producers had few inflation-proof stores of value available that would allow them to meet their 20 per cent share of production costs with resources left over from the previous year.[7] Even had such inflation-proof savings mechanisms been available, it is probable that many peasants would not have been able to accumulate enough in previous years to make the contribution to their production costs that the banking system was demanding of them. It would quickly become clear that the new credit policy was endangering the spring planting.

If the likely impact of the new policies upon production was unpredictable, so too was their political impact. The monetary reform process itself does not appear to have been very significant in this regard. Though the Superior Council of Private Enterprise (COSEP) predictably attacked the freeze placed on old *córdoba* holdings in excess of c$10 million as yet another example of the "lack of security regarding the right to own property" (FBIS 7 March 1988), it appears that less than one in a thousand families was affected by the measure (*Bda* 3 March 1988).

More problematic was the "compression." Even in January Ortega had declared that the difference between Nicaragua's response to economic crisis and that of other Latin American countries was that jobs would not be eliminated in Nicaragua (FBIS 4 January 1988). Firing people had traditionally been viewed as a response to economic difficulties that was typical of capitalism and the tactics of the International Monetary Fund (IMF).[8] Now the government was declaring the need to "eliminate the conception that everyone has a right to a job independently of whether this job is indispensable," as Finance Minister William Hüpper put it (*Bda* 4 April 1988).

The government sought to soften the compression process by establishing a relocation service, and Labour Minister Benedicto Meneses promised that "efficient and disciplined" workers who had been fired would be eligible for unemployment insurance at 100 per cent of their salary for two months, and 75 per cent for the third month (*Bda* 20 March 1988). Nevertheless, there were many complaints about the handling of the lay-offs. It was charged, for example, that many managers were deciding who was to lose their jobs without consulting workers or their union. Some managers, anxious to cut payroll without actually reducing active staff, singled out women on maternity leave and men mobilized for defence tasks, in defiance of explicit government guidelines (*Bda* 17 April 1988). *La Prensa* claimed that the lay-offs were being used to purge those who did not proclaim their loyalty to the FSLN (FBIS 2 September 1988). In addition, the Ministry of Labour was repeatedly criticized for dragging its feet in establishing an effective relocation service (*Bda* 3 May 1988; 14 May 1988).

Another potential political cost of the new policies concerned the government's relationship with the peasantry. Already threatened by restrictions on credit, peasants were dismayed that the official price of beans, a key peasant crop, was not raised at all in the February package. While peasants were theoretically free to sell their beans to whomever they wished, the proclaimed objective of "social control," if successful, would reduce the prices that private traders could offer peasants, by increasing the risks of selling beans to consumers at higher-than-official prices (Zalkin 1988a, 51). Finally, the policy of "social control," had it been successful, could be expected to generate the same political challenge to the FSLN's relation with the urban popular *barrios* as did the 1985 economic package, a challenge that helped scuttle the 1985 reforms.

Any analysis of the political impact of the February package is highly speculative, as events in subsequent months bore so little resemblance to what decision-makers had expected, and the policies formulated in June to address these unexpected events bore so little resemblance to the February measures, that the February package must be viewed as a mere way-station on the road to the radical policy changes of June 1988. The most salient characteristics of the months following the February package were the collapse of the "social control" effort, the persistence of inflation, and the temporary paralysis of policy in the face of these phenomena.

An active policy of "social control" was launched in a rather spectacular fashion the week after the announcement of the new economic measures. In a speech on 20 February, Ortega called on citizens to take action against merchants who did not respect the new schedule of official prices. Those who refused to lower their prices, Ortega said, would go to jail, "even if the merchant hollers his head off ... at the CIA newspaper [La Prensa]." "We will see who is stronger," Ortega vowed, "the speculators or the Nicaraguan peasants, labourers and factory workers" (*NYT* 21 February 1988; FBIS 22 February 1988).

That same evening, 400 factory workers organized by the Sandinista Defence Committees (CDS) entered Managua's Eastern Market and forcibly expelled unlicensed merchants operating there (*Pensamiento Propio*, March 1988). Thus began a series of actions throughout late February and March. In mid-March, for example, 1,000 members of "ideological anti-speculation brigades" raided various markets in the city, confiscating hoarded goods and dislodging illegal merchants. Any merchants carrying more than 20 pounds of basic grains reportedly had their stores confiscated (JPRS LAM–88–015).

The strategy of focusing attacks on illegal merchants continued the post-1985 strategy of the Ministry of Internal Trade (MICOIN) of seeking to avoid a frontal confrontation with all merchants. In late February, Ortega commented that "the comrades who work in the markets work hard; they have been working there for years and have good experience as market vendors. They respect the law; they are legal merchants. We must get together with them". The problem, Ortega argued, was that "those other merchants have suddenly made an appearance in the market; they have shown up at the last minute ... They should leave the legal merchants alone" (FBIS 29 February 1988). There is no evidence, however, that the mere fact of holding a MICOIN licence made the "legal" merchants more willing to respect official prices than their "illegal" counterparts. Hence the attack on the "illegal" merchants seemed designed to keep "speculation" within limits rather than to eliminate it altogether.

The "social control" actions occasionally took a violent turn. It was reported that one person was knifed by a merchant in the February 20 action in the Eastern Market (*Pensamiento Propio,* March 1988). The *New York Times* reported on 28 February 1988 various "violent clashes" between police and market vendors. Bayardo Arce commended the practice of going shopping in groups of ten, so that consumers might defend themselves against the violence of the speculators (FBIS 26 February 1988). While the rhetoric of some National Directorate members may have fanned the flames during this period,[9] there were also calls from the directorate to remain within the limits of the law in the fight against speculation (FBIS 26 February 1988).

Most observers argue that the attack on speculation failed less for political reasons, as had been the case in 1985, than for technical ones: the new official prices established in the February 1988 package did not take full account of the cost increases sparked by the package itself, hence prices were often set below, not just their market-clearing levels, but their cost of production as well. The citizenry was mobilized to "defend" prices that simply could not be defended for long, without paralysing production (Acevedo Volg 1989, 20; Arana 1988, 18). As official prices began to be adjusted upwards, often in a quite anarchic fashion, the agents of "social control" were demoralized. Quietly, the social control campaign was abandoned. On 13 April 1988 *Barricada* carried a photo of the Eastern Market with the caption: "Once again, legal and illegal merchants have occupied the streets of the Eastern Market. What results did the Economic Brigades have? The prices of perishables are set by the illegal merchants, and there are no controls." The abandonment of the social control campaign effectively marked the end of the FSLN's long-standing attempts to control consumer prices. In April, directorate member Luís Carrión gave an indication of the direction of government policy when he commented that "there are a great number of prices, and when one wishes to set them administratively – to protect consumers – one just ends up complicating things." He added, "I think there is a conflict between the desire to keep a close eye on prices and the ability to fix them in an expeditious manner" (*Bda* 11 April 1988).

Increases in official prices and the failure to control unofficial prices implied the persistence of high levels of inflation. Prices rose almost 200 per cent in the March–May trimester. This led to a paralysis of policy similar to that which occurred when the inflation associated with the 1985 measures proved much greater than expected. Though the February 1988 measures had sought to re-establish realistic prices for labour and foreign exchange, both salaries and the exchange rate were frozen in the post-February period.

Since the government wished to maintain a unified exchange rate, the failure to devalue in the post-February period made export production increasingly unprofitable. Private coffee producers warned in April that their production costs would be at least c$2,025 per quintal, on the assumption that all necessary inputs were available at official prices. The official producer price for coffee, however, was just c$1,130 (*END* 16 April 1988).

If the failure to devalue in the face of persistent inflation provoked concerns, the post-February salary freeze was even more controversial. As in 1985, the government had abandoned its stated commitment to protect the real earnings of the formal sector. In response, labour shortages intensified. There were reports of convicts being used at the Chiltepe milk project just outside of Managua (*FBIS* 26 February 1988), and as maintenance workers in the capital, "in response to the lack of workers" (*END* 13 May 1988).

An important difference with respect to the 1985 situation, however, was that the post-Esquipulas political atmosphere permitted much clearer expressions of discontent with the government's policy. In late February, wildcat strikes broke out, even among workers belonging to FSLN unions (*NYT* 28 February 1988). The General Confederation of Labour affiliated with the Nicaraguan Socialist Party, launched a strike of construction workers. The workers were protesting the elimination of salary bonuses, and what they alleged were excessive work norms in the construction sector (*Bda* 1 March 1988). The workers demanded a 200 per cent increase in basic salaries, and repeated earlier demands for a suspension of the SNOTS. Though *Barricada* quickly claimed that the strike was losing strength, and affected only 1,200 of 32,000 construction workers (*Bda* 2 March 1988), the strike sparked similar actions in other sectors. By mid-March, workers at a Managua hospital, employees of MIDINRA's Chiltepe milk project, and auto mechanics had gone on strike (*Bda* 10 March 1988; 17 March 1988).

Officially, the FSLN was highly critical of the strikes. It was claimed that the strikers were being coordinated by the U.S. embassy (*Bda* 28 April 1988), and Daniel Ortega, in his May Day speech, said that the strikers' demands "have counterrevolutionary connotations" (FBIS 2 May 1988). When some of the strikers began a hunger strike at their headquarters, police cordoned them off, and briefly arrested opposition leaders who tried to visit the strikers (FBIS 3 May 1988; 5 May 1988). The government's response to the strike led the opposition parties to withdraw once more from the on-again-off-again national dialogue process (*Bda* 27 April 1988).

But while the FSLN and government maintained a hard line during the strikes, there were signs within the FSLN both of sympathy for some of the strikers' demands and of awareness of an urgent need to find a new salary policy. In mid-March, Wheelock suggested that the decision to eliminate most salary bonuses needed to be reconsidered (*Bda* 11 March 1988). In May, construction workers who had not joined the strike urged that work norms in the sector be "reviewed" (*END* 13 May 1988; 20 May 1988). Even the minister of construction called for more incentives for workers in the sector (*Bda* 12 May 1988).[10] Attacks on salary policy from within the FSLN bloc intensified in May. Workers at the national bus company, though affiliated with the Sandinista Workers' Central (CST), demanded a 100 per cent salary increase (*END* 13 May 1988). Even *Barricada*, traditionally a transmitter of FSLN and government policy, joined the campaign for salary increases (*Bda* 13 May 1988).

Publicly, the National Directorate was displaying little openness to concerns over salary policy. Asked in early June whether the working class was not carrying too much of the burden of economic adjustment, Victor Tirado, the directorate's liaison with unions, replied: "What is the thought behind that position? That we should attack the bourgeoisie? ... The workers should understand that the burden falls on them because this is their revolution" (*Barricada Internacional* 2 June 1988).

Apart from exchange rate and salary policy, a third controversial area of policy in the post-February period was that of credit. In April, the head of FANATEX, a state textile company, warned that the new credit policy was "drowning companies" (*Bda* 27 April 1988). The gravest concerns were expressed in the agricultural sector. As noted above, producers found themselves doubly squeezed by an increase in payments owing to the banks for past loans and by a reduction in bank financing. In April, the farmers' association (UNAG) warned that producers were confronting a "grave lack of liquidity," and predicted that many producers would not be able to cover 20 per cent of working costs themselves, as demanded by the new credit policy (*Bda* 13 April 1988). Bank officials, however, insisted that only 80 per cent of working costs could be financed (*Bda* 20 April 1988). According to one study of rural producers, peasants reacted to the liquidity crisis sparked by the new policy by reducing their use of inputs and turning to the informal credit mechanisms which were reappearing in the countryside (Stahler-Sholk 1990, 74).

The difficulties of producers were compounded by delays in the granting of credit for the new agricultural season. UNAG officials pointed out that such delays had occurred in previous years, but they had not had an impact upon production in the past because the banks gave advances to producers. In 1988 however, such advances were not available (*Bda* 2 May 1988). The change in policy led to repeated warnings that delays in granting credit would hurt production (*END* 16 April 1988; *Bda* 20 April 1988).

The June 1988 Measures

The paralysis that characterized government policy in the wake of the failure of the February 1988 economic measures was abruptly ended on 14 June, when President Ortega presented the broad lines of the new government strategy. In the following days, various ministries announced the concrete policies comprising the new strategy. Despite the greater openness to the market displayed in policy shifts throughout 1987 and in February 1988, the June package represents a key point of inflection in Sandinista policy, and the final abandonment of many of its cherished economic policies.

Throughout the speech, Ortega stressed that "we are facing an economy that has been profoundly, seriously, damaged".[11] This fact, Ortega argued, had not been sufficiently appreciated: "All sectors have difficulty believing that this country has accrued an economic deterioration in order to win the war." It was not a time to be "thinking of sectoral demands," rather "the fundamental task remains the defence of revolutionary power," which required above all the defence of production and the economy. There were even those in the revolutionary bloc, Ortega complained, who were not clear on this point. This was weakening "political and ideological cohesion," and "this weakness will be expressed throughout the society which we are trying to influence."

As in February, Ortega stressed the importance of controlling inflation. Now, however, the government's objectives appeared more modest: "We must take new measures to tame a horse that is running quickly, a horse that cannot be stopped, but which will not continue to run as fast ... To achieve this, we must contain salaries, and also demand more from producers." Specifically, producers would be required to pay the "true value" of bank loans. "The truth is," Ortega noted, "credit has been given away in real terms throughout these years." In this respect "we violated all economic rules applied under both socialism and capitalism." Henceforth, Ortega announced, producers would have to repay to the banks the real value they had borrowed from it. This would be achieved by tying interest rates to the rate of inflation. Such a policy, Ortega hoped, would lead producers to calculate more carefully before asking for credit.

On the question of salaries, Ortega began by noting that Nicaragua was a nation of 3.5 million people resting upon a "fragile base" of "real production" made up of just 205,000 workers in agriculture, industry, construction, and the banks. If this productive base had access to "much technology," its numerical size would not be a problem. But as it did not, the situation was "grave." "This means," Ortega argued, "that it is not possible to answer the *aggressions* of those workers [who demand] more salary, better supplies and better living conditions."[12] "Since 1985," Ortega went on, "we have been fighting a great battle against salary increases, a battle in which the Sandinista Workers' Central and the Association of Rural Workers have shone." Despite this battle, Nicaragua still had "sectors that are weak, in which sectoral demands repeatedly arise, demands that work against the very class interests that we are defending." Thus, Ortega argued, "salaries cannot be adjusted as workers might wish." Rather, there would be a "minimal" adjustment. At the same time, Ortega promised in an obscure passage, workers in the productive sector would receive incentives to productivity, because such incentives, unlike general salary increases, were not inflationary. The meaning of this promise only became clear with the ministerial announcements that accompanied Ortega's speech.

With respect to the exchange rate, Ortega argued that Nicaragua must cease to price imports in an "unreal" fashion. Henceforth, "the exchange rate will move whenever necessary" to keep prices aligned with world prices, because "Nicaragua cannot be an exception among economies, with different prices, subsidized prices."

These policies, Ortega recognized, would be costly for some sectors of production. Here he indicated that the government was contemplating a triage operation. Nicaragua must work, he argued, to re-establish production "in those sectors of greatest interest, because we cannot do this everywhere." Ortega went on to say that companies like MILCA, the soft-drink bottler, did not represent "real production." Such "real production" was to be found in the countryside, and its prime example was "coffee, the main source of foreign exchange." Hence, Ortega argued, the government should not maintain inefficient employment in urban industry, but should try to convince the urban unemployed to move to rural areas, in order to meet the countryside's need for 8,000 additional workers.

On the subject of price policy, Ortega stated that "it did not help us not to recognize the real cost of production in this country, which deformed our economy." Henceforth, products with prices "below their real level" would become more expensive. In a passage that said much more than it appeared to, Ortega declared that "in some cases, we will protect prices, influence them; in other cases, the products will circulate freely. We will influence prices that are very sensitive for the country. That is to say, this is not a typically capitalist free market, rather, it is a free market in a revolutionary State, with a clear socialist orientation." With this rather vague statement, Ortega had in fact announced "the liberation of all prices," as *Barricada*'s 15 June summary of the speech put it.[13]

Throughout his speech, Ortega was concerned to present an ideological defence of the measures. He gave repeated indications that the leadership was under pressure to take a different course. At various points, he defended the government's decision not to abolish private property. While Cuba had done this, Ortega argued, "our situation is not that of Cuba, where a reality was imposed upon the United States, a reality that they cannot easily attack ... as they do Nicaragua." But Nicaragua had not refrained from abolishing private property for merely "geopolitical" reasons, he said, but also because "we are living a stage of defence of revolutionary power."

As opposed to the radical course that some were apparently urging, the government was implementing measures that were "somewhat similar" to those that would be applied in any capitalist nation in crisis. Ortega noted that "the measures which we applied in February, sought to liberalize our economy and make it more flexible, and this may appear to be contrary to the class interests defended by this Revolution." But, he insisted, "Our revolution has a socialist orientation. This is a definite fact. But we are not in the stage in which the application of some socialist measures will contribute to the principal objective, which is the defence of revolutionary power." In an indication of the leadership's awareness of just how far economic policy had shifted, Ortega declared that "we are not applying International Monetary Fund policies, *in the strict sense of the word*" (emphasis added). Finally, to address concerns over the class orientation of the new measures, Ortega admitted that new incentives being offered to export producers might be "resented" by salaried workers, "who will ask how is it possible that we give producers incentives while the worker only receives appeals for consciousness and ideology. The truth is that there is no other way of stimulating the producer, who is motivated by economic incentives. Thus, there is a higher objective, to defend the workers' class power, which is a revolutionary power, based upon the revolutionary principles of Sandinism, which is unquestionably based upon Marxism, the ideology of the proletariat."

The new measures announced by various ministries clarified the meaning of various aspects of Ortega's speech. The Central Bank announced a 567 per cent devaluation, from c$12:$1 to c$80:$1, and declared that henceforth the exchange rate would be devalued in accordance with movements of a modified consumer price index (*Bda* 15 June 1988).[14] This modified consumer price index (CPI) would be used to determine interest rates on most bank loans. For loans used to buy imported inputs, the producer would take on the "exchange rate risk." That is, such loans would be indexed to the *córdoba* cost of the dollar. The banking system would provide loans to cover the full cost of such inputs, and would also cover the full costs of the harvest. Thus, government policy was shifting from rationing to something approximating market pricing of credit.

With respect to salaries, the SNOTS scale was adjusted upwards by just 30 per cent. But the government announced that the scale would henceforth be applied only to government workers. For production workers, the SNOTS scale would serve only as a "non-obligatory reference." Similarly, the government announced that it would limit itself to publishing "reference prices" for some basic goods. The consumer protection law, it was announced, was "still in force," but "its regulations will no longer be applied" (*Bda* 17 June 1988). The price of fuels was increased approximately tenfold (López 1989, 81), and it was announced that public service tariffs would be adjusted periodically to maintain realistic relative prices.

Some sectors expressed delight at the new measures. COSEP head Enrique Bolaños welcomed the elimination of wage and price controls, while the Socialist Party's General Confederation of Labour declared the limiting of SNOTS to government workers a victory for the working class. The head of CONAPRO-HM, the FSLN's association of professionals, praised the government for moving away from an "egalitarian" approach to salary increases (FBIS 16 June 1988).

Yet many FSLN supporters were troubled by the new economic policy. The monthly magazine *Envío*, which had traditionally sought to support every twist and turn of government policy, titled its article on the new measures "A package with the people left out."[15] Many shared the view of Adolfo Acevedo Volg, who argued that the measures represented a take-over of government policy by "monetarists" (1989). These monetarists, Acevedo Volg argued, sought at all costs to eliminate inflation, held that inflation was primarily caused by the "monetary mass," and believed that it was necessary to create market conditions in order for production to recover, which would involve the collapse of "inefficient" economic agents.

Apart from these broad issues, the new measures sparked several technical concerns. It was argued that the price liberalization was based upon a fictitious view of the market, one that ignored the monopolistic nature of the industrial sector (ibid., 23).[16] The government would react to this problem later in the year, re-imposing controls on some industries. The new credit policy was problematic in several respects. The banks apparently did not have the administrative capacity to handle the complex new interest rate system (Stahler-Sholk 1990, 74). Tying interest rates to a measure of inflation generated great uncertainty for producers, since they could have no assurance that the prices of their marketed produce would keep pace with the general price level. Whether for technical reasons, or because of concerns over the political implications of the new credit policy, the "inflation-proof" interest rates were not implemented until late in the year (ECLAC 1988, 448). At this point, the government was indicating that some sectors would be exempted from the new policy (FBIS 6 September 1988).

Concerns within the revolutionary bloc over the new economic strategy would continue to be expressed in the coming months, and the "political and ideological cohesion" for which Ortega had pleaded in his June speech was not achieved. Even National Directorate member Henry Ruiz expressed concern, noting that the "adjustment program is a good idea but inefficient. That is, it has failed to hit the main targets." Ruiz added that "if the deterioration continues, the entire economy will be disrupted and the class struggle will worsen" (FBIS 5 October 1988).

On 20 September 1988, *Barricada* published perhaps its most critical editorial ever, titled "A counterpart to the economic logic is missing." The editorial welcomed certain "encouraging signs" in the economy, such as "the recovery of managerial capacity within companies, the tendency to re-establish the relative price system, the stabilization of the black market for foreign exchange, and a better assignment and use of inputs and imported materials." At the same time, however, there had been a failure to analyse the "social and ideological repercussions" of the economic measures. A "set of concepts has lost validity," concepts that for years had been "slogans and guides for mass action. 'Social control,' 'secure channels,' 'price controls,' 'state subsidies,' 'preferential prices for the peasantry,' etc. are the banners of a vanished epoch." All this was "necessary," the editorial accepted, but the failure to articulate a "new code" to accompany the economic adjustment "has created the impression that a vacuum exists." The "reproduction of Sandinista hegemony" required that people grasp the links between current economic policy and the revolution's "socialist orientation."[17]

The editorial noted that much emphasis had been placed on the restoration of "entrepreneurial capacity," but little on the equally "unavoidable need" for working sectors to "recover their bargaining power." The FSLN unions must address the challenges facing workers: "The unions must act like unions now, or they will cease to exist."

The editorial's counterposition of a successful "economic" logic with a problematic "social and ideological" logic indicated the fear of many FSLN activists that government policy had been hijacked by technocrats. Stung by this criticism, Daniel Ortega told a meeting of peasants not to "believe that technicians tell us what to do, as some theoreticians claim. That is not so. We do not analyze things from a technical viewpoint, we analyze them from a political viewpoint" (FBIS 6 September 1988).

One of the problems that provoked great concern in the wake of the June measures was the situation of wage workers. Many workers were now freed from the SNOTS scale, but they had been freed in a very difficult moment: industrial firms were suffering a liquidity crunch, and generally faced a seriously weakened domestic market. The union head at a private soap company commented that employers, who had often claimed they would love to raise workers' salaries were it not for the SNOTS system, were now singing a quite different tune (*Bda* 19 September 1988).

Those companies not in dire straits were able to offer their workers large salary increases, hence wide differentials emerged between those doing similar tasks for different companies. Those firms that increased salaries more quickly were often able to do so because of a monopoly situation in the market. The abolition of SNOTS for part of the workforce contributed to inflation in those cases where employers and workers were not in a truly oppositional relation. Thus, salary increases were linked to monopolistic price increases, not to productivity improvements, as the leadership had hoped would occur. This practice would lead President Ortega to criticize companies who were simply concerned to "get along with their workers" by raising prices and salaries (1989b).

It appears that those state companies in a position to do so engaged in price increases in much the same fashion as their private sector counterparts (APEN 1989, 69). Leaders lamented this behaviour on various occasions (FBIS 8 July 1988; 6 September 1988), but the new economic strategy left the government with little capacity to influence enterprise behaviour. In September, the Ministry of the Economy announced that it would "negotiate" with industries enjoying a monopolistic market position, in order to prevent "anarchic" price increases. Those industries targeted generally produced intermediate goods. Officials stressed that this decision did not affect the general policy of price liberation (*Bda* 22 September 1988).

In the countryside, extensive conflicts arose around the salary question. As in the industrial sector, the abolition of SNOTS did not come at a propitious moment for most workers. The suspension of subsidies on food in the June measures had increased workers' subsistence costs, but many employers, faced with tighter and more expensive credit, were unwilling to meet workers' demands, or even to negotiate wages (Pérez and Somarriba 1989, 15; Stahler-Sholk 1990, 75).

Those whose salaries were still set by the SNOTS scale saw their real incomes continue to deteriorate. From July to November, nominal salaries were increased 477 per cent (López 1989, 82), while the CPI rose 1,017 per cent. For 1988 as a whole, observers estimate a drop of real salaries in the neighbourhood of 85 per cent (Acevedo Volg 1989, 27; *Análisis*, January 1990, 26).

Shortly after the introduction of the June measures, the government announced its "AFA" program,[18] under which those workers still under the SNOTS scale would receive a monthly package of 10 pounds each of beans and rice, and 5 pounds of sugar. The AFA program covered some 160,000 workers in all (*Bda* 12 July 1988; *END* 12 July 1988; FBIS 8 July 1988). Thus, even at a time when the market was being given greater sway over most aspects of economic life, the government preferred to rely on a "secure channel" strategy rather than nominal salary increases to address the concerns of government workers.[19]

While concerns over the earnings of salaried workers had previously focused upon the gap between these earnings and those of the informal sector, many observers now pointed to a deterioration of living conditions of popular sectors in general. The June measures had hurt not only salaried workers, but the freeing of markets, combined with a drop in demand, had squeezed much of the informal sector, deepening the crisis for families who had hitherto survived on the basis of their combined earnings from formal and informal employment.[20]

Concerns over the direction of policy were not allayed by the general economic results for 1988. GDP dropped 10.9 per cent, the sharpest drop in the FSLN's decade in power. Reflecting in part the triage operation intimated in Ortega's June speech on the economy, manufacturing value added had dropped by approximately 29 per cent (ECLAC 1989). The industrial collapse primarily affected small and medium production (Stahler-Sholk 1990, 72).

The acceleration of the GDP's slide occurred without clear progress in the government's stabilization program, thus undermining those who might argue that the economy was undergoing "short-term pain for long-term gain." The most dramatic indicator of the failure to stabilize the economy was the CPI, which more than doubled in each of November and December, rising during the two month period at an annual rate of over 1,200,000 per cent. Inflation for 1988 as a whole was 33,600 per cent.

Despite the hope that the fiscal deficit would be reduced to 8 per cent of GDP, it in fact rose to over 25 per cent, wiping out the slow progress that had been made in this area since 1985. One factor in this result was the failure of tax receipts to keep pace with inflation. Observers also pointed out that the reform process itself hurt fiscal revenues: the lack of liquidity experienced by many agents made it impossible for them to pay all taxes owing, and sales of tax products such as cigarettes and rum were hurt by the general economic downturn (Pilarte 1988, 7). These factors combined to reduce the tax burden from 25 per cent to 19 per cent of GDP (ECLAC 1989). On the expenditure side, hopes to reduce the ratio of government spending to GDP by 10 to 15 percentage points (*Bda* 4 April 1988) were dashed, as in fact the ratio rose slightly, to 46.4 per cent (ECLAC 1989). This rigidity of government spending would be the prime target of the next round of new economic measures, announced in January 1989.

By year's end, implementation of other aspects of the 1988 adjustment packages was only partially under way. The indexing of credit to inflation was implemented only in the final two months of 1988. Monthly interest rates for loans to the agricultural sector stood at 50 per cent at year's end (Arana 1990, 52), still negative in real terms when deflated by the CPI. The new *córdoba*, devalued to C$80:$1 in the June package, had undergone four further devaluations by year's end, and in late December stood at C$920:$1. Nevertheless, when deflated by the CPI, this represented a 120 per cent *revaluation* in the *córdoba* in the second half of the year.

Thus, it seemed at year's end that the policy shifts of 1988 had brought production to the point of collapse, without noticeably improving the economy's financial balance. This state of affairs promoted ongoing debate on economic strategy, a debate that appears to have influenced the National Directorate's own internal debate. One example of the critical tone of the debate could be seen in the economic proposals for 1989 of the Association of Economists (APEN) (1989).[21]

APEN urged that the global stabilization policies being pursued by the government be tempered by sectoral polices designed to stimulate production, and by policies aimed at "reproducing the class alliance."

The association criticized the "subordination of the general performance of the economy to financial objectives,"[22] and warned that the "costs of recovery should be distributed in a rational and evenhanded manner." Most importantly, the APEN document called for a re-centralization of the economy. The economists argued that "just as the emergency provoked by hurricane [Joan, which hit Nicaragua's Atlantic Coast in late October] led to an organized mobilization of all available resources and energies in pursuit of a single objective, so too in 1989, in the same organized way and with the same intensity, all political, institutional, and mass efforts, and all necessary resources, should be directed on one course: attaining the production targets set for each sector and sub-sector of production." APEN went on to suggest the formation of national and regional Economic Emergency Councils to assure the fulfilment of production targets "with all means at their disposal."

Other critics also warned the FSLN leadership that economic policy was threatening the party's base of support. An article in early January in *El Nuevo Diario* called for "drastic controls on new prices" in order to put an end to "not only irrational but false profits." Such controls, the paper stated, were necessary in order to avoid "the further political erosion of the revolutionary government" (FBIS 7 February 1989).

It appears that these warnings were being taken seriously by at least some members of the National Directorate. There were reports that the debate within the directorate was revolving around two stark alternatives: either holding the course and deepening the 1988 measures by applying more drastic budget cuts, or implementing a "war economy" (NYT 1 February 1989). On at least two occasions in 1989 Ortega indicated that the directorate was in fact thinking in terms of these alternatives. In his speech on economic policy of 30 January, Ortega commented that "if we are not able to make a qualitative leap under these difficult and complex conditions," then "we will definitely be obliged to implement a war economy." Ortega defined this as a situation of "total rationing and total intervention of the State in all production and in the distribution of all resources" (1989b).

It is not clear how seriously the National Directorate debated the possibility of implementing a war economy, nor which members advocated such a course. Nor is it clear whether the alternative was rejected primarily because of its political implications, or because the leadership doubted the state's capacity to manage such an undertaking. A key factor in the directorate's debate was probably the belief that the FSLN's base of support was strong enough to absorb the political costs of the current economic policies. This belief, which would persist until the final hours of 25 February 1990, would strongly influence the FSLN's actions in several respects through 1989. In any event, the advocates of "staying the course" won the day, and on 30 January Ortega delivered another speech to the nation announcing new economic measures (Ortega 1989b).

Ortega began by noting the costs of the counterrevolutionary war. The war had not only hurt the economy, he said, but had "hurt the construction of the mixed economy" and "polarized class positions." He repeated the theme first sounded in February 1985, that the government had erred in trying to do too much for the people. The government was now forced to implement new budget cuts, because January inflation could reach as high as 200 per cent, "and we cannot permit this to occur."[23]

To slow inflation, Ortega announced, the government would reduce the fiscal deficit to just 11 per cent of government spending in 1989, down from over 50 per cent in 1988. Since about half of the government budget was devoted to defence (FBIS 23 November 1988), this goal could not be accomplished without sharp cuts to the ministries of defence and the interior, which had been relatively immune to budgetary restraint.[24] Ortega noted that the new measures would generate unemployment, but added that there was a great demand for workers in rural areas. The head of the SPP estimated that a "minimum" of thirty thousand jobs would be lost, including 10,000 army officials and 13,000 employees of the Ministry of the Interior (FBIS 2 February 1989).

Ortega's speech also reiterated the government's determination to "give to things their true value." The policy of price liberation would not be changed. With respect to the exchange rate, Ortega indicated that the parallel rate would be brought closer to that prevailing in the unofficial market, thus restoring to the parallel market the role that had originally been foreseen for it in 1985. The speech contained no changes in salary policy which, Ortega said, "will have to be determined on the fly."

The FSLN leadership was aware of the political implications of this latest round of measures. Earlier in the month, Ortega had promised that the government would not undertake "IMF-type measures" (FBIS 19 January 1989), but in his speech of 30 January he commented that the budget cuts were a "typically capitalist" measure. In a speech to the National Assembly a year later, Ortega would comment that the 1989 measures could not have been applied earlier, because of the need for subsidies to "save the Nicaraguan economy, which was seriously threatened by the US-sponsored war ... We could not think of implementing a policy of unemployment and applying well-known IMF formulas." Ortega would add that he had originally opposed the January 1989 application of these "IMF formulas" as he found them "too harsh" (1990). Nevertheless, throughout 1989, the government would by and large hold to the adjustment policies, to a degree that was surprising given the imminence of elections. This again points to the FSLN's belief that it could absorb the political costs of adjustment and still win the 1990 elections.

In economic terms, the January measures signalled a willingness to aggravate the economic downturn as a necessary price for controlling inflation. Alejandro Martínez, minister of the SPP, would later estimate that the adjustment policies had been responsible for a 4 per cent to 6 per cent drop in GDP in 1988, and a further 4 per cent in 1989, but argued that in the absence of adjustment "the monetary and financial system would have collapsed, resulting in an incalculable decline in the GDP of as much as 20 per cent" (FBIS 5 October 1989). Another high SPP official argued that "it is impossible to control inflation and to revitalize the economy at the same time," hence "a partial economic recession will be unavoidable if prices are stabilized" (FBIS 22 March 1989).

In exchange rate policy, the government managed a real devaluation through the year. While the *córdoba* had been revalued by 120 per cent in real terms during the second half of 1988, by the second half of 1989 the "real" exchange rate had been returned roughly to its June 1988 level. The real devaluation brought the official rate closer to the unofficial-market rate than it had been at any time during the FSLN's decade in power. By September, the unofficial-market rate was just 15 per cent higher than its official counterpart (Arana 1990, 51), a gap reduced from 476 per cent at the end of 1988. The parallel market rate lagged behind the unofficial rate only in May. From June on, the parallel market rate was roughly equal to that of the unofficial market.

This near-unification in the economy's exchange rates was generally achieved through a policy of frequent minor devaluations, with the exception of a 117 per cent devaluation in the first days of the year, and a 110 per cent devaluation, from c$9,500:$1 to c$20,000:$1, in mid-June (FBIS 13 June 1989). The latter devaluation came after a period in which the gap between the official and unofficial exchange rates was allowed to widen, and devaluations were delayed for "political" reasons, as Daniel Ortega would later comment (1990). In general, the second trimester of the year was a period of great pressure on the government to soften its adjustment program, pressure that affected credit policy.

Thus, broadly speaking, the government kept its promise to "give foreign exchange its true price," as Henry Ruiz put it (Stahler-Sholk 1990, 65). Along with eliminating the fragmentation of prices between the official and unofficial import spheres, which had marked the economy for nearly a decade, the near-unification of exchange rates delivered a verdict of sorts on much of the government's investment strategy. Many major projects, such as the Contingency Plan for basic grains production, were now shown to be extremely costly, when relevant prices were aligned with their international equivalents (Stahler-Sholk 1990, 75; Arana 1990, 28). Peasant production of such products as milk now appeared more efficient than the high-technology production promoted by MIDINRA on the Pacific Coast (*Envío*, April 1988).

The policy of allowing world prices to express themselves inside the Nicaraguan economy via a liberalized exchange rate was not applied in an entirely uniform manner, however. For reasons that are not clear, the government decided to pay cotton growers a subsidy of 1.7 million *córdobas* per hectare (FBIS 25 April 1989). "We cannot abandon cotton production," Daniel Ortega argued, "just because current prices are less than those of the 50s or 60s" (FBIS 19 January 1989).

While the government generally held firm on its exchange rate policy, it had more difficulty doing so in the area of credit policy. To address the complaints of producers over the uncertainty generated by floating interest rates, Daniel Ortega announced in late April a policy of fixing the rates for four months (FBIS 25 April 1989). Since the rates were frozen at a moment when inflation was at its lowest level in several years, real interest rates would turn highly negative when inflation intensified in June and July. A loan to a peasant producer, for example, would lose 42 per cent of its value during those two months, when deflated by the CPI.

In general, real interest rates on loans were negative throughout the year. Rates on deposits, however, were positive in real terms for most of the year. Particularly from July on, the government sought to keep interest rates on deposits higher than the rate of devaluations, in order to eliminate speculative holdings of dollars. The fact that interest rates were higher on deposits than on loans meant that some disaccumulation of the banking system was still occurring. Banking system losses were also incurred as the government made political concessions "such as forgiving debts or restructuring them under favourable conditions" (R. Gutiérrez 1989). Peasant grain producers in particular were forgiven part of their debts from the 1988–9 agricultural cycle (Stahler-Sholk 1990, 77). Despite this softening of the government's credit policy, however, a broad change in orientation, from a "productionist" to a "financial" focus, had to a large extent been completed.

Salaries for those still on the SNOTS scale remained a contentious area of policy. When deflated by the CPI, these salaries improved in 1989, though the increase took place from such a depressed level that it did little to reduce tensions around the question.[25] These tensions were manifested in a fashion that particularly worried the FSLN, when a partial teachers' strike broke out in late May (FBIS 26 May 1989). Though the government claimed that few teachers had struck, the situation took a serious turn when the FSLN teachers' union and even the minister of education "demanded" a salary increase for teachers (Ortega 1989d).

This state of affairs led Ortega to meet with hundreds of teachers in early June. Ortega's speech to the meeting is of interest because he provided a defence of the government's economic policy, a defence aimed at answering criticisms that extended far beyond the teachers' union (1989d). "We do not promote," he argued, "a society of rich people and poor people, because we are defending the people's power, the power of workers. However, in the economic sphere, we do defend and promote a mixed economy that generates economic differences in which there are rich people and poor people." There were, Ortega insisted, only "two economic options to solve the economic problems Nicaragua is facing. The measure we are applying follows a liberal trend, an IMF trend." The other alternative would be "to implement a war economy ... the salary would no longer exist; the salary would disappear, and everyone would receive a ration of whatever food is available at the time."

Just because the government was following an "IMF trend," however, did not mean that it shared the objectives of the IMF. In a striking departure from the leadership's traditional rhetoric, Ortega argued that economic policies were analogous to rifles, which could be used either to oppress or to liberate the people. Economic policies had suddenly become politically neutral instruments.

Turning to the specific question of teachers, Ortega recognized that unrest was "logical and normal." The problem was not unrest, but the fact that the teachers' union and the minister of education were making wage demands, and the Ministry of Labour also "fostered the expectation that a wage increase was possible." Instead, Ortega said, "we have to do political work with teachers so they understand the economic situation." Nevertheless, he did promise the teachers a modest salary increase in June, to compensate for May's inflation. In addition, Ortega promised some non-salary benefits, such as tokens for free public transit, additional study materials, and scholarships for the children of teachers to study abroad.

The teachers' strike may have been one of the factors leading the government temporarily to soften its market-oriented policies in June. After the 110 per cent devaluation at the beginning of the month, the government ordered a temporary price freeze on nine basic products, in reaction to "indiscriminate price hikes" (FBIS 15 June 1989). The water and electrical utilities were also ordered not to increase their tariffs in the wake of the devaluation (FBIS 14 June 1989), and subsidies were announced for butane gas, diesel, and kerosene, the "fuel used by the people" (FBIS 13 June 1989). The government also renewed its appeals to public companies to restrain price increases. Public sector managers, argued Economy Minister Luís Carrión, "cannot make the same kind of financial decisions as would a private businessman." Yet Carrión stressed that he was not seeking a return to the days when the government sought to restrain inflation by sacrificing the financial health of the public companies. Public companies must eventually pass on any "true cost increase entailed by devaluation," he argued, and could not sell below cost "for an indefinite time" (FBIS 20 June 1989).

Despite concessions such as these, the government broadly held the line on its economic strategy, thus testing its base of support to an unprecedented degree. The shift in economic strategy was accompanied by a re-interpretation of the fundamental direction of the Sandinista revolution, a re-interpretation that sought to remain within a broad Marxist framework. Not surprisingly, the leadership relied heavily on Marxian determinism to understand and justify changes in strategy. Thus, Daniel Ortega commented that "socialism cannot be imposed on the minds of an unprepared people. Such an imposition will be determined by society's degree of development" (1989a). In an interview with a Mexican journalist, he argued that "we do not have a large proletariat, and there is no industrial development. Our society is basically agrarian. This clearly means that the implementation of revolutionary and Sandinist theories as well as the interpretation and implementation of Marxism under our true conditions have to be based on facts ... In Nicaragua, carrying out a revolution, being a Marxist, being a revolutionary means doing what we are doing now" (1989c).

Similarly, the turn to the market was legitimated through Marxist theory. Asked whether the turn to the market "could have ideological implications," Tomás Borge replied that "the theory of scientific socialism has always overcome the idea of associating commercial relations only with capitalism, as if these were unknown to socialism. It is [a question of] employing them in a conscious way and preventing them from operating blindly" (1989b).

Finally, as the new economic strategy carried Nicaragua farther away from the vision of socialism that the leadership had held, one noticed attempts to find a new model for the country's future. Abandoning the leadership's traditional distance from social democracy, Daniel Ortega made a number of references to the Nordic countries as a model for Nicaragua. These countries, he argued, were small, yet promoted social justice and stayed clear of military alliances (FBIS 11 May 1989). A Soviet magazine even cited Tomás Borge as appealing to the Nordic model (JPRS UIA–89–008).

In summary, though 1989 saw some flexibility in the application of the government's economic strategy, the consistency with which that strategy was applied is striking, particularly when compared to the stop-go adjustments of the 1985–7 period. By year's end, this strategy was yielding some results. After the high inflation of June and July, which reflected in part June's 110 per cent devaluation, the CPI increased in the August-December period at an annual rate of 439 per cent. As this drop in the rate of price increases was achieved without suppressing inflation through price controls or an overvalued exchange rate, the government had reason to hope that inflation in 1990 could be further reduced. The government had also come close to attaining its targeted deficit reduction: the deficit was just 13 per cent of government spending, down from 53 per cent in 1988, and represented just 5 per cent of GDP (*Análisis*, January 1990).

The government showed every sign of continuing its adjustment strategy through 1990. The 1990 budget called for a further 44 per cent reduction in spending, including a 49 per cent cut for the Ministry of the Interior and the army (FBIS 6 February 1990). A high economy ministry official promised that "no sharp turns in economic policy are foreseen for the coming year, only adjustments to consolidate the objectives laid out from February 1988 on. There will be some government resources to support the efforts of productive sectors, but to a large extent the possibility of survival will be determined by the capacity of producers and entrepreneurs to adapt to the new economic context, and by the results of their own managerial initiatives in achieving an efficient use of their resources and countering the recessive effects of the adjustment policy" (Elizondo 1990, 22).

This statement indicates the mood among government decision-makers at year's end. Despite the drop in the GDP and consumption levels in the second half of the decade, some things were looking up. The economy was being stabilized, export levels were finally improving, and the economy was slowly weaning itself from dependence upon Soviet bloc aid. And, most importantly, the FSLN was on the verge of winning another election, which would give it another six years to get the economic house back in order, and to try to give new meaning to the objectives of the Sandinista revolution.

B. RELATIONS WITH THE BOURGEOISIE

A reduction in the size of the Nicaraguan state and a consequent redefinition of its role accompanied the government's "turn to the market." A corollary of this strategy was the realization that economic recovery would in large part depend on the behaviour of private economic agents. In consequence, the FSLN made various attempts during the 1988–9 period to mend some fences with the bourgeoisie. These attempts, however, were often interrupted by periods of conflict.

Shortly after the announcement of the economic measures of February 1988, Jaime Wheelock ordered an end to all land expropriations in the Departments of Boaco and Juigalpa (Pilarte, Ubau, et al. 1988, 22). In May, a MIDINRA vice-minister announced that there would be no more expropriations anywhere in the country (*Bda* 23 May 1988). Also in May, the government announced the formation of a national cotton commission, made up of state and private sector representatives, and one member of the Association of Rural Workers. The commission, which was a prototype for those to be developed in other agricultural sectors, was to examine the problems facing cotton production, and recommend policies to the government. In announcing the commission's creation, MIDINRA Vice-Minister Salvador Mayorga noted that state organization in the agricultural sector had been "very vertical and inflexible," and had paid little attention to the needs of bourgeois producers. Mayorga also noted that private producers had learned that "the effort of some sectors to use production as a political weapon had negative results for themselves" (*Bda* 23 May 1988). It seemed that the FSLN was attaining its long-sought objective of channelling bourgeois demands in an economistic direction.

Indeed, the bourgeoisie, or at least broad sectors of it, was coming to terms with the idea that they might have to coexist with the Sandinistas for quite some time yet. There were both external and internal reasons for this. Jaime Wheelock remarked in March that many producers with whom he had recently met were much less hostile than on previous occasions, and attributed the change to their awareness that Reagan had lost control of U.S. foreign policy, and hence the Sandinista revolution had become a permanent fact of life (*Bda* 11 March 1988).

This shift in bourgeois attitudes was at least partly related to the increasing marginalization of the contras. Seeking to undercut U.S. Congressional support for the contras, the Nicaraguan government in mid-January abandoned its long-standing pledge never to negotiate directly with its armed opponents. In early February, the U.S. Congress rejected a bill providing additional "lethal" aid for the contras. This rejection brought the contras to the negotiating table, and a cease-fire agreement was reached at Sapoa, Nicaragua, in late March. Though the terms of the agreement were never fully implemented, the contras were henceforth generally perceived as a spent force, though they were still valued by some opposition figures for their ability to maintain low-level harassment of the Sandinistas.[26]

At the same time, the bourgeoisie now had more space for civic political activity. In January, the government ended the state of emergency implemented in 1987, and abolished the "Popular Anti-Somocista Tribunals." Some observers detected continued tensions within the National Directorate over the decision to allow more room to the civilian opposition, and over the decision to talk directly with the contras. The announcement on direct talks was followed closely by the arrest of several opposition leaders who had recently met with the contra leadership in Guatemala. Since the arrests occurred on the same day Daniel

Ortega arrived in Costa Rica for a regional summit meeting to discuss implementation of the Esquipulas II accords, some opposition figures argued that Tomás Borge, who headed the Ministry of the Interior and controlled the police force, was seeking to embarrass Ortega and signal his displeasure with the political opening (*NYT* 17 January 1988; 21 January 1988). Such speculation increased when FSLN demonstrators, allegedly following orders of National Directorate member Bayardo Arce, broke up an opposition meeting "without Mr. Ortega's knowledge" (*NYT* 24 January 1988). Borge, for his part, dismissed reports of tensions within the directorate as "dreams" of the opposition, and expressed his support for the government's political concessions, which were made, he said, "to revive peace and to allow the Sandinista project to live forever" (FBIS 26 January 1988).

Relations with the opposition deteriorated in mid-1988, however. One factor in the change was the new package of economic policies announced in mid-June. The FSLN was well aware of the unpopularity of the measures, and was concerned that the opposition could gain great political capital. In a speech given two days after the measures were announced, Daniel Ortega warned that the opposition would "act demagogically" around the question of high prices and low salaries, and promised that "I will not tolerate or allow people who once criticized the revolution's actions to question our efforts now that we are adopting measures to defend the economy in times of great difficulty." Ortega branded COSEP, *La Prensa*, and the right-wing parties "pro-Yankee fascists," and commented, "They are rabble rousers who are never satisfied. The only way to satisfy them is to bury them once and for all ... Peace is being offered to them ... But if they do not take advantage of this opportunity and do not act accordingly, let them be sure that we will wipe them out" (FBIS 17 June 1988).

In July, the government showed that these threats were more than mere rhetoric. On 10 July, the police broke up an opposition rally in Nandaime, near Managua, with "tear gas, rifle butts and truncheons" (*NYT* 11 July 1988).[27] An editorial in *Barricada* on 11 July warned that the entire population could rise up "rebelliously and justly, to defend their power, democracy and legality." Immediately after the events at Nandaime, the government expelled U.S. Ambassador Melton, claiming that he had masterminded a "Melton Plan" to destabilize the country. At the same time, an opposition leader was arrested for instigating violence at Nandaime, and both *La Prensa* and the Catholic radio station were temporarily closed for engaging in a "subversive campaign" (*Bda* 12 July 1988). A week later, Tomás Borge warned that the FSLN was ready to respond with "institutional violence" to those who provoked it (FBIS 19 July 1988).

Some observers expressed surprise that the government had reacted so strongly against the opposition, given that it seemed to have the political situation well in hand, with the contras in disarray and the civic opposition as divided as ever (*NYT* 18 July 1988). The government, on the other hand, pointed to an alleged coordination of subversive actions: contra attacks had stepped up, and Ambassador Melton had participated in a COSEP meeting in Estelí that allegedly called for the overthrow of the government (*Bda* 12 July 1988). The government's claim that a coordinated "Melton Plan" had sought to destabilize the country received confirmation from an unlikely source later in the year, when the Speaker of the U.S. House of Representatives revealed that the Central Intelligence Agency (CIA) "had deliberately provoked opposition activities in Nicaragua in hopes of prompting an overreaction by Nicaragua's Sandinista Government" (*NYT* 21 September 1988).

In the week after the Nandaime events, the government expropriated the San Antonio sugar mill, the nearly 3,000 hectares surrounding it, and its associated rum company, the largest remaining private concern in the country. The sugar complex, as opposition figures hastened to point out, had been the showpiece of Nicaragua's mixed economy: the apparently warm relations between the government and Alfredo Pellas, owner of the San Antonio mill, had often been offered as a sign of the "pragmatism" of the Sandinistas, and as proof that the bourgeoisie was not united in opposition to the revolution.[28]

Relations had in fact never been as friendly as they appeared to many observers. Charges of decapitalization were raised against the company as early as 1981 (JPRS 78617). In a letter to the National Directorate in late 1984, Tomás Borge complained that the Pellas family was shipping machinery from the San Antonio mill out of the country (1984c). In late 1985, some workers at the mill charged that the managers were trying to disrupt the harvest (*END* 6 November 1985). Such complaints became more frequent in 1987, when some workers called upon the state to "intervene" the company. They pointed out that the mill had produced only 60 per cent of its targeted sugar output, and charged that managers "spend only two days a week at the mill, and spend the rest of the time in Managua or outside the country" (*END* 14 April 1987). An article in *El Nuevo Diario* on 25 April 1987 on the "sordid history" of the San Antonio mill charged that executives there "have been enjoying long vacations in the US," where they were involved in "obvious counterrevolutionary confabulations."[29] After the 1987–8 harvest, it was noted that the mill had again fallen well short of its production target, producing only half of a planned two million quintals of sugar (*Bda* 22 May 1988).

The San Antonio concern was expropriated under the terms of the 1986 agrarian reform law. The justification officially adduced was the decline in production since 1979 and the deterioration of facilities (FBIS 14 July 1988), phenomena that in truth characterized most economic concerns in the country. The expropriation was clearly prompted by political factors. In his 1988 May Day speech, Jaime Wheelock charged that most of the participants in a rightist May Day march in Chinandega in north-west Nicaragua were workers of the San Antonio mill paid to march against the government (*Bda* 2 May 1988). Daniel Ortega claimed that the United States was using the San Antonio mill to distribute funds to the contras (FBIS 20 July 1988).[30]

Whatever the reasons for the expropriation, it clearly hurt the government's *rapprochement* with the bourgeoisie. The government could argue that the action was consistent with long-standing warnings to the bourgeoisie not to use their economic power to seek to destabilize the revolution. Opposition leaders, on the other hand, pointed out that the action, coming after government promises that expropriations had ended, showed once again that the FSLN was not to be trusted.

Nevertheless, with the National Directorate's decision in early 1989 to continue the economic adjustment strategy, new overtures were made to the bourgeoisie. In his speech of 31 January announcing new budget cuts, Daniel Ortega struck a conciliatory tone:

We are Sandinistas, we are Marxists, Marxist-Leninists, and whatever else one might wish to add. What we understand is that the application of the revolutionary project to the Nicaraguan reality must respect the characteristics of our society, and must be done in alliance with the fundamental forces of our society, and with all those social, economic, political and religious sectors that are willing to build a new Nicaragua ... .

Those who have another type of thought, another ideology, can keep thinking and working on the basis of that ideology: those who think that capitalism is best for Nicaragua can keep thinking that way; even those who think that subordination to U.S. policy is best for Nicaragua can keep thinking and working on the basis of this (1989b).

Those holding different ideologies could join in a "national *concertación*," or national "coming together" to solve the country's problems and ensure peace. As an inducement to participate in the *concertación*, Ortega declared that "there is no reason to take an inch of land away from anyone. Enough land has already been distributed ... We have enough land to give to peasants without land, without affecting one single producer *among those who are interested in entering into a real process of National Concertación*."[31] While criticizing agricultural producers who "have used the profits made during these years to buy farms in other Central American countries," Ortega said that the majority of producers "have reinvested, have made an effort along with the workers to increase production." This was true, he said, even of many producers affiliated with COSEP.

Thus began a renewed campaign to improve relations with the bourgeoisie. The *New York Times* reported on 2 February 1989 that "Sandinista leaders have declared that their top priority will be to revitalize the country's beleaguered private business sector."[32] The head of the Chamber of Commerce, after meeting with Economy Minister Luís Carrión, noted that the latter had "emphasized the need to guarantee the space of the private sector and define the ways in which the Government can exercise economic influence." Carrión also spoke of a plan to "define or delimit the mixed economy" (*Bda* 31 January 1989), for which the bourgeoisie had been asking for many years. In the coming months Carrión would undertake various *concertación* meetings with private sector groups (*Bda Internacional*, English ed., 11 March 1989).

The National Directorate's Victor Tirado turned once again to the orthodox Marxist theory of historical stages to explain the policy of national *concertación*: "The groundwork for economic development has to be laid so science and technology can contribute to production regardless of the economic sectors that are participating." Later on, Tirado said, when Nicaragua had reached the level of "the developed countries," Nicaraguans could "decide whether we want socialism, capitalism, or something else," because "socialism comes from wealth and development" (FBIS 6 February 1989).

COSEP viewed these developments with concern. Ramiro Gurdián, who at the time was head of both COSEP and the rightist Democratic Coordinator, criticized the government for meeting with producers on a "sectorial" basis. Gurdián stated that the groups belonging to COSEP and the Democratic Coordinator would only participate in a national *concertación* if the contras were also invited to participate (FBIS 13 February 1989).

The government did not look kindly upon COSEP's attempt to sabotage the *concertación* process. In his June 1989 meeting with teachers, Daniel Ortega referred to COSEP and other rightist forces: "We live with a scorpion on our shirt. We know that we have the scorpion on our shirt but [we] trust the people's strength, and if the scorpion turns violent we crush it" (1989d). Later in the month, the government expropriated the farms of three coffee farmers affiliated with COSEP in Matagalpa. The government stated that the action was a response to the "confrontational and anarchic attitudes" of the three producers, who had "assumed attitudes that go against the efforts to achieve the unity necessary to confront the crisis in Nicaragua." The vice-minister of the interior la-belled one of the three a "professional provocateur in the service of the CIA" (FBIS 23 June 1989). Jaime Wheelock warned that other proper-ties of those who plotted against the government would be seized (FBIS 28 June 1989), and former COSEP head Enrique Bolaños claimed that he had a list of thirty-six farms that would be expropriated before the end of the year (FBIS 11 July 1989).

Once again, the government was sending a nuanced, but not contradic-tory, message: a political opening existed, but it had limits; property rights would be respected, but they too had limits. However much economic and political policy had evolved, the government remained willing to act decisively against those who assumed too intransigent a position within the opposition.

This message appears to have been understood by many members of the bourgeoisie. Although COSEP's member organizations in the cotton and cattle sectors withdrew from their respective national commissions in response to the June expropriations (FBIS 23 June 1989), many pro-ducers who had been affiliated with COSEP continued to participate in the *concertación* process (FBIS 18 July 1989). This eclipsing of COSEP's influence would become more manifest in the electoral process, which brought about a significant realignment of bourgeois political repre-sentation.

C. THE AGRARIAN REFORM

Land expropriations for agrarian reform purposes were by and large suspended during 1988–9. Though statements to this effect were made in 1988, the shift in policy was made more explicit in early 1989. Fol-lowing up on Daniel Ortega's speech of 31 January, the government formally introduced before the National Assembly a law marking the end of land expropriation (FBIS 6 March 1989). "The Revolution has completed a cycle," declared Economy Minister Luís Carrión. Hence-forth emphasis would be placed upon "the consolidation of the mixed economy," on the basis of existing property relations (Carrión 1989).

The peasantry's demand for land, however, had not conveniently dis-appeared in accordance with the shift in agrarian reform policy. In fact, the deterioration in the situation of rural wage workers resulting from the economic adjustment strategy led to renewed demands for land. In his 1988 year-end speech, Daniel Ortega noted that 42,000 hectares had been distributed to over 3,000 families in 1988, and pledged that "we plan to maintain this agrarian reform policy" (FBIS 3 January 1989). In his June 1989 speech to teachers, Ortega expressed concern that cotton-sector workers had begun seizing land. Ortega estimated that there were some 7,000 unemployed rural workers demanding land (1989d). In that same month, speaking to peasants in Masaya, Ortega promised that the government would continue giving land out to peasants, "until no peasant is without land in Nicaragua" (FBIS 8 June 1989). Finally, during the election campaign, Ortega promised that a land bank would be formed to meet the needs of 25,000 peasant families (FBIS 15 December 1989). Thus, it was clear that, though the agrarian reform had delivered land to some 100,000 families, Nicaragua's economic deterioration continued to generate new land pressures, as families sought a small parcel as part of their survival strategy.

It was not clear, however, where the land needed to continue the reform program would come from. Throughout much of the decade, nationalized farms had been used as a pressure valve to meet land demands without increasing expropriations. But by the end of 1988, less than 12 per cent of agricultural land remained in state hands, down by nearly half from the early 1980s (Wheelock 1990, 115). State farms had generally divested themselves of their miscellaneous small parcels, and Jaime Wheelock declared that state lands should not be further divided (FBIS 28 June 1989).[33] In any case, further division of state lands would run counter to the emphasis being placed upon recovering export output.

A second possible source of land was constituted by the "enemies of the revolution" placed on notice by the June 1989 expropriations. But any extensive expropriations of this kind would undo the government's whole *concertación* policy. A third possibility was that virgin lands would be offered to peasants, marking a return to the pre-1979 "colonization" schemes. Daniel Ortega hinted at such a policy in the same speech in which he promised that no peasant would be left without land: Masaya peasants requiring land, he noted, might have to move to other parts of the country (FBIS 8 June 1989). While such a strategy was theoretically feasible, the investments required for colonization projects would be hard to finance given the fiscal austerity policy, which had already involved sharp reductions in public investments.

One hope, first articulated in 1986–7, was that peasant land demands could be met without distributing new lands by directing peasants to cooperatives needing new members. In his January 1989 speech on the economy, Daniel Ortega commented that "enough land has already been distributed. It is true that there are peasants who are demanding land, but we have an answer for them, in cooperatives, cooperatives that own 500 to 1,000 *manzanas* and who have seen their membership reduced, so that they do not have the people necessary to work their land" (1989b).

But the production cooperatives, which had never been the peasantry's preferred land solution, were looking ever more unattractive.

A member of one of UNAG's regional executive committees was cited as offering "harsh criticism" of the cooperatives in his region: apart from the problem of member desertion, the cooperatives were plagued with labour indiscipline and increasing alcoholism (JPRS LAM–88–015). An analysis in *Barricada* on 11 April 1988 commented that "the low cultural level of the peasants with regard to the management and control of goods and production plans constitutes an obstacle to the qualitative development of cooperatives." The article went on to cite cases of cooperatives that had received no technical assistance for over three months, and were unable to fill out requests for bank credit or maintain their own machinery.

After the state "compression" was announced in early 1988, there was much talk of inducing fired workers to move to cooperatives, where they could occupy administrative posts and raise the "cultural level" of the cooperatives (*Bda* 21 March 1988; 23 March 1988; 11 April 1988). Given the chasm between urban and rural living conditions, however, it was unlikely that many would respond to this invitation, despite worsening living conditions in the cities. UNAG head Daniel Nuñez commented that "we have never believed that professionals, accountants or secretaries will go *en masse* to the country." At best, he noted, the move to the country was an option for those who had moved into the cities relatively recently (*Bda Internacional,* February 1989). Such persons, however, were unlikely to possess the special skills thought lacking in the cooperatives.

Hence, just as the state sector had shrunk throughout the 1980s, the future held the prospect of a collapse of the cooperative sector. The Sandinista agrarian reform had transformed the face of the Nicaraguan countryside, and was viewed as one of the revolution's fundamental achievements, one that would be defended at all costs. But the transformation little resembled that which the FSLN leadership had originally envisioned. After an initial push to the "higher" forms of production, the countryside had been in the grip of a seemingly inexorable "historic regression" to "lower" forms of production, forms that seemed to answer some of the deepest aspirations of hundreds of thousands of Nicaraguans.

D. THE FINAL ACT: THE 1990 ELECTION

At a meeting in El Salvador in mid-February 1989, the Central American presidents reached another accord on implementation of the regional peace process. Nicaragua agreed to move the 1990 election, scheduled for November, up to 25 February. The Nicaraguan government also promised that 1,700 jailed former National Guardsmen would be released "almost immediately." Honduras, for its part, promised to close contra bases in its country (*NYT* 15 February 1989).[34] Daniel Ortega promised to hand over the reins of government within three months, should the FSLN be defeated (FBIS 21 February 1989), thus putting an end to the FSLN's traditional ambiguity on the meaning of elections, an ambiguity that had been maintained even after the 1987 signing of the Esquipulas Accord.[35]

The El Salvador agreement caught the political organizations of the bourgeoisie by surprise. The *New York Times* commented on 30 March 1989 that "opposition politicians have been forced to seek a quick consensus." Among the welter of opposition parties and organizations,[36] one can identify at least four broad tendencies. The first might be called the "moderate" opposition parties: those that had participated fully in the 1984 elections, and had consistently been willing to distance themselves from the contras.[37] The second tendency was made up of "hardline" domestic opposition groups, who had boycotted the 1984 election campaign and continually flirted with the contras.[38] The civilian leadership of the contra forces that had operated out of Honduras represented a third tendency. This group had maintained the closest links with the U.S. administration, which was now encouraging contra leaders to return to Nicaragua from their Miami combat centre, in order to participate in the elections.[39] A final tendency, small yet influential, was comprised of the civilian associates of the contra forces that had operated out of Costa Rica, under the occasional leadership of Edén Pastora. This group was generally believed to have maintained more distance from the U.S. government.[40]

Apart from the struggles for personal influence that had traditionally characterized the opposition, conflicts reflected bourgeois divisions on the degree to which the FSLN and the changes it had wrought had to be accepted as a fact of life in Nicaragua. The opposition's eventual campaign platform would manifest this tension.[41]

Ironically, in early 1989 the FSLN was calling upon the opposition to unite, so that it might become a coherent interlocutor in the process of national *concertación*, one that might serve to legitimate that process. Bayardo Arce commented that "a union of conservatives, liberals, and others would be favourable" (FBIS 3 January 1989).[42] A *Barricada* article called on the opposition to "get their act together".[43] Thus, in its certainty of being re-elected, the FSLN was neglecting the key condition for its continued hold on power: that the opposition remain divided.

But the opposition was driven to unite by a factor more potent than the pleas of the FSLN: dollars. In April, the National Endowment for Democracy of the U.S. Congress announced that it would spend $2 million on the opposition political campaign. In an excess of honesty, an Endowment official stated that "the whole thrust of this program is to help the opposition coalesce and overcome their historical differences and develop a national political structure" (*NYT* 25 April 1989). By most accounts, U.S. influence was crucial in the formation of the National Opposition Union (UNO) in early June.[44]

Tensions persisted in the opposition coalition, however. Various parties, complaining of the "extremist" elements within UNO, discussed the possibility of forming a centrist alliance. One of the concerns of this group was the attempt by returning contra leaders to displace local politicians (FBIS 1 June 1989; 17 July 1989).[45] Further tensions were generated around the selection of an opposition ticket. At least six parties supported the nomination of former COSEP head Enrique Bolaños (FBIS 30 August 1989). Other opposition parties felt that Bolaños, as a member of the traditional landed elite, would be a weak candidate (*NYT* 19 August 1989). There was thus recognition of the degree to which class awareness had developed in Nicaragua during the 1980s, and of the consequent need to find a candidate who could appear to transcend class divisions. A consensus also developed within UNO that the presidential candidate must be someone who had opposed the Somoza regime (ibid.).

In September, UNO chose Violeta Chamorro and Virgilio Godoy as its presidential and vice-presidential candidates. The selection of Chamorro, the widow of *La Prensa* editor Pedro Joaquín Chamorro, murdered in early 1978, was welcomed by "American officials," who felt she "would unify the opposition" (*NYT* 4 September 1989). One of Chamorro's assets was thought to be her lack of involvement in any particular political party.

The selection of Godoy was more controversial, however. Various parties threatened to withdraw from UNO: some opposed Godoy for his participation in the FSLN government from 1979 to 1984, others were concerned by the extremism of his opposition since that time. The U.S. embassy was reported to be working hard to maintain UNO unity (FBIS 11 September 1989), but COSEP, frustrated by UNO's rejection of Bolaños, maintained its opposition to Godoy.[46] That opposition had little impact, however, manifesting what one observer termed COSEP's "sharp loss in political influence" (*NYT* 10 September 1989).

Tensions would persist within UNO throughout the campaign, and would work to undermine the subsequent Chamorro government. Godoy spoke disparagingly of his running mate, saying she would help "draw the women's vote" and that of peasants. Chamorro's speeches, Godoy added, "are not very sophisticated" (FBIS 19 September 1989). When disagreements flared up within UNO over its slate of candidates for the National Assembly, Godoy threatened a repeat of his last-minute withdrawal from the 1984 election (FBIS 29 September 1989). In January, it was reported that Chamorro's advisors had stopped the flow of campaign funds to Godoy (FBIS 22 January 1990). Late in the campaign, the top advisors of Chamorro and Godoy engaged in a "boxing match" on the podium at a UNO rally (FBIS 8 February 1990).

Chamorro's presidential campaign was strong on symbolism, and avoided emphasizing UNO's contradictory program. She never failed to invoke the name of her slain husband. She asserted that she was "in God's hands" (FBIS 22 September 1989), and referred vaguely to occasional conversations with God and her husband (Watson 1989). Her criticisms of the Sandinistas were fairly broad: she promised to end "half a century of dictatorships and totalitarianism" (FBIS 5 September 1989) and pledged to end the military draft. Surprisingly, in light of the state of the economy, Chamorro's speeches did not stress economic problems, though she did promise to improve real wages (FBIS 20 February 1990).

Chamorro's greatest political asset may have been her image as a healer or reconciler of the nation. Her candidacy promised an end to conflict with the United States, and she pledged not to be vindictive against the FSLN and its supporters. Chamorro promised, for example, that "all of those [government workers] who do their duties professionally and with a sense of responsibility will stay in their jobs," and that army officials affected by cuts in the military budget would be provided with alternative employment (ibid.).

The FSLN, for its part, repeatedly sought to identify UNO with the contras and with Somoza's National Guard. The election, Daniel Ortega declared, was a choice "between the revolution and the counter-revolution, between Somozism and Sandinism" (FBIS 20 July 1989). The opposition were "mercenaries without weapons," he commented (FBIS 9 November 1989).

The FSLN's official campaign slogan was "Everything will be better." Asked at a press conference to explain the slogan, Ortega explained that "everything will be better" because a flow of international aid would enter the country after elections (FBIS 28 September 1989). Observers stressed the increasingly populist tone of Ortega's campaign.

On at least two occasions there were concerns that the FSLN might suspend the election campaign. The first was in late October, when the government announced the resumption of military action against the contras, ending the government's nineteen-month, unilateral cease-fire (NYT 28 October 1989). The second occasion came at year's end, when the United States invaded Panama. The government declared a state of "maximum military alert," leading to opposition complaints that the Sandinistas were creating an artificial war atmosphere.[47]

But the FSLN saw no reason to suspend the election, as it was convinced that it would win by a wide margin.[48] FSLN leaders repeatedly declared that an opposition victory was inconceivable,[49] and there has never been any suggestion that in making these statements the Sandinistas were whistling in the dark. Late in the campaign, Ortega mused that UNO might not even win second place (FBIS 15 February 1990).

On 21 February, the anniversary of Sandino's 1934 assassination, the FSLN held its final campaign rally. The *New York Times* commented the following day that the crowd may have been Nicaragua's largest ever, a remarkable statement given that the Sandinistas had often organized rallies attended by close to half a million people. "On 25 February," Ortega told the crowd, "we must crush Somozism. We must crush the contras. We must crush treason" (FBIS 22 February 1990). Gazing out on the crowd, Ortega, thirty years a political activist, seven years a political prisoner, ten years a head of state, declared, "We have already won the election."

E. CONCLUSION

In explaining the course of events, it is hard to know what weight to attribute to simple error. The Sandinistas erred gravely in their estimation of Nicaragua's political mood. The rigour with which they pursued economic adjustment throughout 1989; their willingness to allow the opposition more political space; their willingness to move the date of national elections up, without any commitment from the U.S. government that it would respect a Sandinista victory: all these speak to the confidence with which the Sandinistas viewed their political position. They marched happily to the revolution's funeral, convinced that they were celebrating a renewal of what Tomás Borge had once called "the perpetual wedding vows between the Nicaraguan people and the Sandinista Front" (1984a, 164).

Yet this error was not accidental, but the product of the FSLN's longstanding vanguardism. The FSLN could not lose the election because it was the very embodiment of the Nicaraguan people and its deepest aspirations. In a revealing comment, Daniel Ortega argued that it was not possible for the opposition to win elections, because "I trust in the political maturity of the Nicaraguan people" (FBIS 4 May 1989). After a decade of Sandinista guidance, the Nicaraguan people had begun the long climb to the level of political consciousness of its vanguard.

It became a commonplace after the election to criticize the FSLN for having "lost contact" with the people. As one official told me, "The fact that we could not imagine losing is the best proof that we deserved to lose."[50] But it is more precise to say that the FSLN lost contact with the people because its perceptions of the contact it did have were mediated by the certainty that it was the only legitimate representative of the people.

All of this may be read as a blanket condemnation of vanguardism, and such condemnations are certainly *de rigeur* at the moment. But if one blames vanguardism for the Sandinistas' loss of power, must one also recognize its contribution to their having seized power in the first place, and to their ability to weather a decade of remarkable challenges? Without the sense of self-confidence and certainty in their historical mission that their very vanguardism gave them, would the Sandinistas have held power for a single day? It is an expression of the maddening dialectic of history that the *élan* which sustained the FSLN through its grim years in the wilderness, which helped bring it to power and consolidate that power against great odds, which captivated so many of us and generated a loyalty that mere political logic could not explain, also played a large part in the loss of power in 1990.

8   Reflections on the Sandinista Decade

Max Weber ended his *Protestant Ethic* by insisting that "it is, of course, not my aim to substitute for a one-sided materialistic an equally one-sided spiritualistic causal explanation of culture and of history" (1958b, 183). At another point in the same work, Weber stressed that "we have no intention whatever of maintaining such a foolish and doctrinaire thesis as that the spirit of capitalism ... could only have arisen as the result of certain effects of the Reformation, or even that capitalism as an economic system is a creation of the Reformation" (91). To this last remark, Weber appended a plaintive footnote: "In spite of this and the following remarks, which in my opinion are clear enough, and have never been changed, I have again and again been accused of this" (217).

Despite this insistence, Weber's work came to be interpreted as the "response" of idealism to Marxian materialism. This misinterpretation is an interesting case of the interaction of ideas and ideologies. Despite Weber's pleas, his work was pressed into the service of Western academia's defence against Marxism. The perceived need for ideological instruments to combat Marxism was so great that it is not surprising that Weber's academic "disciples" ignored the nuances of his thought.

If even as lucid and influential a writer as Weber did not have complete control over the interpretation of his work, how can we lesser mortals hope to fare better? At a historical moment when state socialism is on the verge of extinction, when Western media and some academics celebrate the "New World Order," the "End of History," and the "Magic of the Market," it is perhaps inevitable that a study such as mine should be interpreted by some as yet another (superfluous) nail in the socialist coffin. Let me say once again, therefore, that I write as a socialist concerned for the future of socialism, a socialist who believes that we must come to terms both with the crisis of one model of socialism in the twentieth century, and with contradictions in the original Marxian socialist vision. This book is intended as a modest contribution towards that project.

Thus, examination of the difficulties of an anti-market and anti-capitalist development path should not be read as an endorsement of Third World capitalism. Though the Sandinista path failed, market-oriented regimes in Latin America did not fare very well through the 1980s either. The failure of the Sandinista model does not imply that market-centred development paths offer much hope to the millions of impoverished Latin Americans.

Let me recapitulate the main lines of argument. I have argued that the Sandinistas sought to do much more than merely take and hold state power. They gained state power as part of a broad project of social transformation. Contrary to much writing on the Sandinistas, this project had much in common, *mutatis mutandis*, with state socialist systems elsewhere. These common elements are not surprising in light of the relatively orthodox Marxism shared by the Sandinista leadership.

I have also argued that the Sandinista project of social transformation contributed to the severe economic and social crisis that began in the mid-1980s. In particular, there was an interaction between domestic policy and u.s. pressure: the former made the country more vulnerable, both economically and politically, to the latter. Thus, for example, Sandinista statism led to policies that alienated enough peasants to give the United States the human resources it needed to wage its war. In addition, the "productionist" bias of policy and the intensity of the state investment process stretched the government budget to the breaking point, which magnified the destabilizing effects of the increased defence spending needed to face the external threat.

Finally, I have argued that, despite attempts to change course, the Sandinistas never escaped constraints that developed in part from their early policy choices, choices that had generated both political and economic constraints. Thus, for example, price policy had been a means for increasing the popular legitimacy of the Sandinista project. Changes in that policy therefore eroded support in poor urban neighbourhoods at a time when the military service already represented a tough demand on people. At an economic level, attempts to close the gaps between official and unofficial prices, or to increase real salaries and achieve a real devaluation, triggered a hyper-inflationary "adjustment spiral."

A. SOCIALISM AND THE SANDINISTA EXPERIENCE

What is the value of the approach to the Sandinista decade offered here? Why relate the Sandinista experience to "catch-up socialism" at all? In exploring the difficulties of that path, are we not beating a horse that is already quite dead?

My working assumption is that Latin America, like much of the world, is not in a state of stable equilibrium. That is, current social and economic systems are probably not sustainable. If this assumption is valid, then the search for alternatives to Third World market systems will not die, whatever the fate of socialism in the 1980s. This makes it essential to study the experiences of previous alternatives to market development.

Thus, by stressing the links between Sandinista ideology and orthodox Marxism, by stressing the relation between many of their early policy choices and the catch-up socialist model, I have sought to show that the Sandinista decade was not an isolated idiosyncratic experience of no broad relevance.

I believe that this approach has also shed light in three general areas, which will be examined briefly here: (i) the relation between ideology and policy choices; (ii) the nature of catch-up socialism and the relation of Sandinista policy to this; and (iii) the dilemmas and challenges faced by the Sandinistas.

Ideology and Policy

First, we have explored the interrelation of Sandinista ideology and policy choices. We examined, for example, the manner in which the leaders' ideological outlook influenced their perceptions of the countryside. We also suggested the links between their ideological commitments and their initial policy choices, such as the preference for state farms, the statization of many key points in the economy, the attempt to limit the operation of the market mechanism, and the project of limiting the political projection of the bourgeoisie and channelling it in an "economistic" direction. A sense of the Sandinistas' ideological outlook helps clarify the rationality of these policy choices and their underlying unity.

One should not exaggerate the causal status being attributed to ideology here. I am not arguing that the Sandinistas came to power ready to implement a Marxist project "at any cost." They always displayed a clear sense that politics is a mediation between the desirable and the possible. Had they not had this sense, it is unlikely that they ever could have taken power in the first place. But to understand the concrete results of this mediation, one must examine its two "poles," the possible and the desirable. That is, while it is important to examine the constraints faced by the Sandinistas, constraints exist only in relation to objectives: had the Sandinistas sought merely to hold power, they would have met a very different set of constraints than they in fact faced.

Nor does the emphasis on ideology conflict with certain insights of "incrementalism," in particular with the view that "ad hoc-ery" plays a great role in state decision making. The argument does not presume that policy decisions emerge smoothly from pre-established interests, forged on the basis of ideology. Nor does it assume that, in the mediation between the possible and the desirable, the latter is given once and for all. The consideration of ideology is quite compatible with the view that interests evolve in the course of action. But in the complex interaction between hopes, constraints, actions, reactions, reformulation of hopes, and so on, ideology has its role to play.

The long-term impact of the Sandinistas' initial ideological commitments is best appreciated by bearing in mind the concept of *trajectory*. I have argued that, however much the Sandinista leadership might have undergone an ideological evolution once in power, such an evolution is always a movement from "somewhere" to "somewhere else." To say that the leadership is "flexible" does not mean that its initial outlook is somehow annihilated in the process of evolution. The weight of the starting point in this evolution is magnified when one considers that the leaders must to some extent carry the rest of the party with them as they evolve. It is in large part for this reason, I believe, that we find the leadership justifying the capitulation to the market in the late 1980s with the language of orthodox Marxism: changes must be legitimated through a language that bears some relation to the traditional language of the party.

But the concept of trajectory is important in another sense. The influence of orthodox Marxism, and of the catch-up socialist model associated with it, is seen most clearly in the initial period of Sandinista power. But this period will "weigh like a nightmare" on subsequent periods. The economic imbalances first sparked in this period were never overcome; nor were the confrontational relations with the organized bourgeoisie that arose at this time. Nor did the Sandinistas ever free themselves from the effects of the instruments of legitimacy wielded in this period, such as price controls and the rapid expansion of social services. Thus, even had the Sandinistas undergone a total ideological conversion in the mid-1980s, they would still have had to contend with the effects of early policy choices that were related to their initial ideological outlook.

This stress on trajectories is in no way deterministic: the constraints presented by the earlier moments of a trajectory are not absolute. But they are real, and they must be taken into account. To the extent possible, leaders must be aware that the decisions they make in the early days of revolutionary power are establishing a path, and reflect upon the possible limits of that path.

Catch-up Socialism and Initial Policy

A second general question on which I hope to have shed light concerns the nature of catch-up socialism and its relation to early Sandinista choices. In examining Soviet-type socialist economies, I have focused attention away from both the simple distinction between public and private ownership, and the alleged distinction between the *ex ante* rationality of socialism and the *ex post* rationality of capitalism. Rather, I have focused on the manner in which the catch-up socialist economy reorients the attention of firm managers from market signals to administrative ones, and the consequences of this reorientation for other aspects of the socialist economy.

This reorientation of attention is quite compatible with a "poly-cephalic" state. That is, the fundamental distinction between a capitalist market economy and catch-up socialism does not depend on the existence of an all-powerful planning bureau.

This approach to the socialist economy helps give us a sense of the key points of inflection in the Sandinista decade. I have argued that the eclipse of the Ministry of Planning from 1982 on did not imply an abandonment of key characteristics of the catch-up socialist project. The stress on state control of the economy and on output maximization, typical of catch-up socialist enterprises, continued despite the absence of a powerful planning ministry. Similarly, the change of direction introduced by the 1985 economic plan was not as fundamental as has been argued by many observers. The reality of the market was to be taken into account, but the 1985 plan clearly sought to consolidate the state-dominant sector of the economy.

The more decisive policy shifts began to appear at a point that has received less attention from observers: in the confusion that followed upon the failure of the 1985 strategy, the groundwork was laid for an overall "turn to the market." The first major symptom of this was the relaxation of controls on peasant grain trading. But this was a highly contradictory turn to the market and did not yield the economic stabilization. Had it done so, the thoroughgoing capitulation to the market in the 1988–9 period might have been avoided.

Dilemmas and Challenges

Prices and markets. Finally, the approach taken here has helped illuminate some of the dilemmas and challenges faced by the Sandinistas. We will recall some of those dilemmas here, beginning with questions related to prices and markets. A central dilemma for the FSLN was that captured in the Preobrazhensky-Bukharin debate: can a socialist government foster the process of state-centred accumulation without weakening its political alliances? This problem is an expression of the basic political challenge facing catch-up socialism which, by its nature, must emphasize the need for rapid accumulation, which tends not to be the most popular of policies. The Preobrazhensky-Bukharin dilemma is but one of those related to the tension between the economic project of the socialist state and its need for political consolidation. I have argued that this tension is heightened by the "statization" of economic decisions and the concomitant destruction of the "fetishes" bequeathed by capitalism. The salary "fan" between low-level workers and specialists, the prices paid to the export bourgeoisie, the mechanisms by which grain is acquired from the peasantry: suddenly, none of these is part of the "natural order of things."

The problem of accumulation is related to the state's general ability to capture resources, which brings us to the question of inflation and the "printing-press." Though a concern for financial discipline and stability is often associated with International Monetary Fund prescriptions, the Nicaraguan experience suggests that the problem of finances must be taken seriously within any project of social change. This is so for both political and administrative reasons. In seizing resources through monetary emission, the state has little control over who actually yields up those resources. The state's political alliances, therefore, may be left at the mercy of an inflationary struggle in the private economy. Worse, if party influence leads some sectors to hoist the white flag in that inflationary struggle, as occurred with salaried workers organized in the Sandinista unions, it is precisely the sectors most likely to support the revolution that are hardest hit by price increases. This is not a recipe for long-term political survival.

In addition, an inflationary situation can wreak havoc upon the state's attempts to administer the economy. The broad consultative mechanisms established to determine prices in the state sector, for example, were incompatible with a situation of rapid inflation. Similarly, the SNOTS system for standardizing jobs and wages, which might have been effective in ordering salaries in a situation of stable prices, broke down badly in the face of inflation.

There are important interrelations among the foregoing problems. In particular, a different approach to the accumulation versus alliances question might have changed state enterprises from fiscal liabilities into fiscal assets. This in turn would have reduced the salience of inflation. Because much of the inflation of the late 1980s reflected the effects of attempts to compensate for earlier inflation, an "accumulationist" orientation might have yielded significantly different results for the decade as a whole.

But there were many roots to the fiscal deficit and inflation. The fiscal impact of the defence effort, in particular, was decisive. The deficit and the inflation that resulted from it were also related to a type of accumulation distinct from that just discussed: we have seen that the Ministry of Agriculture, in particular, laid great stress on the rapid accumulation, not of financial resources, but of means of production, regardless of whether those means of production could lay the basis for future state surpluses. Major investment projects were launched in the early 1980s that relied heavily on external financing, yet still represented a serious claim on the state budget. When the war hit in full force, these projects were one of the factors that limited the state's ability to adapt. The catch-up socialist project thus faces a tension between the promotion of economic dynamism and the preservation of "slack" in the economy, which allows the society to confront external shocks, be they political or economic. The Nicaraguan experience suggests that, while decision-makers may seek to overcome underdevelopment with the same audacity with which they seized power, such a course may leave the economy extremely vulnerable.

A final dilemma related to prices and markets has to do with the "moral substratum" of the socialist economy. In the absence of an extremely authoritarian state, and maybe even then, the success of non-market distribution mechanisms will depend upon the generalized acceptance of certain norms of behaviour, norms that have often been termed "socialist morality." For example, the solidity of a rationing system, its immunity from "leaks," will vary with the degree to which people accept the system as fair and content themselves with the products available through the system. This acceptance, in turn, depends upon the degree to which people see each other as fellow members of society with an equal claim on that society's production.

The insurrection period may do much to create the attitudes that non-market structures require. Unfortunately, the Nicaraguan experience suggests that the manner in which price policy is handled may do much to erode the ethic required to sustain alternatives to the market. Thus, I argued that policies that led to an ever-greater gap between prices on the official and unofficial markets helped destroy the very moral substratum needed to maintain the official market, by making it too costly to obey the law, and too easy to do otherwise.

The implication of this analysis is that, while "socialist morality" might constitute an important resource for a revolutionary state, it is a resource that must be used judiciously. More concretely, there may be limits on the degree to which official prices can diverge from unofficial ones before provoking a whole range of unofficial-market phenomena that erode respect for non-market economic mechanisms.[1]

State organization. Moving to the question of state organization, the Nicaraguan experience illustrates the tension between increasing the state's role in the economy and containing "bureaucratism." Though the term was used quite loosely in Nicaragua, there was much validity to the oft-expressed frustrations with the growth of the state apparatus, and to the complaints that parts of the state had involuted, losing contact with the economic sectors they were supposed to be coordinating. While there is nothing inevitable about "bureaucratism," it is an entirely unsurprising result of the rapid expansion of the state's role.

A second type of dilemma related to state organization concerns the behaviour of state firms: how can the state profit from the social nature of property without subjecting firms to such a wide variety of demands that they either do nothing well, or do pretty much whatever they want? In particular, how can the state harvest the benefits of "internalizing externalities," without subjecting firms to the crude criterion of maximizing gross output? Neither the Nicaraguan nor other catch-up socialist experiences have solved such problems.

Finally, must the expansion of the formal, state-dominant sector be seen as an attack on the informal sector? Is it possible to formulate policies that would create strong "pull" factors drawing people out of the informal sector? Or does this suppose ideal conditions, unlikely to exist in a transitional situation? As we have seen, relations between the state and the informal sector generated serious problems for the Sandinistas, as the party's base of support overlapped significantly with an economic sector it was trying to subject to control.

The bourgeoisie. The analysis has also revealed a number of dilemmas related to the survival of the bourgeoisie. Any catch-up socialist project will probably have some need for the bourgeoisie's expertise, but the Nicaraguan case has shown that this expertise carries an extremely high price. Unless one can successfully atomize the bourgeoisie, converting it into a set of economistic "potatoes in a sack," one will be faced with an adversary with formidable internal and external political resources. Even should one be so fortunate as to develop an economistic bourgeoisie, there will be tensions between that bourgeoisie's desire to continue living in the style to which it is accustomed, and the state's need to capture as much of the economic surplus as possible. In the Nicaraguan case, this latter problem was most clearly expressed in the struggle for the "dollar surplus": despite the theoretical state monopoly on foreign trade, the bourgeois demand for luxury imports generated significant unofficial-import mechanisms, which drained an ever-greater share of foreign exchange from the official sector.

The peasantry. Finally, with respect to the peasantry, catch-up socialists must reconsider whether small-hold production is compatible with their project. This requires that the "organic" nature of various alternative models of socialism be examined anew: which components are truly vital? Which could be modified without greatly affecting the rest? Is the traditional resistance to peasant production one of the elements that could be relaxed? Under what conditions? If one concludes that peasant production is *not* compatible with one's project, then the wide range of political problems that ensue must be confronted. The Nicaraguan case is sadly eloquent on this point.

B. THE PATHS NOT CHOSEN

Given the long list of dilemmas and challenges enumerated above, was the Sandinista project doomed from the start? There can be no confident answer to such a question. Perhaps, had the flexibility that characterized Sandinista policy in the mid-1980s been present from the outset, the revolution would have avoided the crisis that undid it. Perhaps, had the Sandinistas initially delayed their project of economic transformation for the sake of consolidating political support, or had they given civil society time to "mature" according to its own rhythms, the counterrevolution would never have found supporters in Nicaragua.

But such conjectures are quite speculative. We can say little about the probable outcomes of the paths not chosen. That the path that the Sandinistas constructed through their choices proved so difficult does not mean that the paths not chosen would have been conflict-free. As was stressed at the outset, we must examine Sandinista choices within the context of concrete dilemmas, rather than jumping hastily to the conclusion that this or that choice was a simple "error."

Some Sandinistas have in fact begun to examine the Sandinista decade in terms of unambiguously mistaken choices. An examination of some of the problems with this line of analysis will illustrate the difficulties inherent in drawing simple lessons from the Nicaraguan experience. For example, in interviews given just before the 1990 election, Tomás Borge reflected upon "the greatest mistake made by the Sandinist government in its 10 years in power." He suggested that "the worst mistake was to try to artificially raise the people's living conditions" (FBIS 26 February 1990). "Another mistake," he noted elsewhere, "was not to make a massive redistribution of the land confiscated from

Somoza" (FBIS 16 February 1990). Let us review the dilemmas that led to these two perceived blunders.

Should the Sandinistas have avoided "artificial" attempts to raise living standards? We should recall that the FSLN felt it could not turn to the people with a language of economic austerity on the morrow of having promised it was ready and able to transform reality. The 1980 economic plan expressed this constraint when it noted that "the people will not accept paying for the economic recovery with their hunger, after having paid for the liberation with their blood" (MIPLAN 1980, 116).

Was this a false constraint? The Sandinistas at the time saw themselves engaged in an "open card game with the bourgeoisie" (H. Ortega 1981, 38), a game that included struggle for the loyalties of ordinary Nicaraguans. This was the context in which the choice was made to attempt an "artificial" increase in living standards. There is simply no way of knowing whether or not the Sandinistas' base of support could have survived an initial policy of economic austerity. This of course is not to say that the choices of 1980 were necessarily the wisest. I am merely arguing that an understanding of how alternatives appeared to decision-makers at the time they were making decisions should make one less ready to conclude that any given choice was a simple mistake.

The second perceived error concerns relations with the peasantry. Should the FSLN have followed a "peasant path" from the outset, distributing confiscated land to individual farmers? Should it have refrained from interference in the marketing of peasant products?

More than any other area of policy, relations with the peasantry led the Sandinista leadership into a profound self-criticism after the loss of power. In 1990, Sergio Ramírez wrote of the FSLN and the Nicaraguan peasant:

My dream of justice and modernity for his life clashed dramatically with the world that continued to surround him, a world of isolation, misery and backwardness, and it clashed with his own perception of this world ...

We wanted to take away his religion, separate him from his sons, oblige him to become organized in cooperatives, impose a price for his crops, recruit him to our side to fight in a war in which victory would forever strip him of his simple values, all the more encompassing for their simplicity. That was what was whispered in his ear, with mellifluous power of persuasion, while our message was often loud, rhetorical, imposing. And meanwhile the golden fruit of our dreams would take years, maybe decades, to ripen.

It was for no other reason that the counterrevolutionary war became converted over time into a peasant war and divided the peasants between those who understood the reasons for the revolution and those who rejected them (1991, 23).

One hears in these words, still, the old theme of peasant backwardness and its clash with modernity. But one also hears, finally, a note of doubt, a loss of the arrogant belief that modernity is necessarily in the right in its clash with backwardness. And one hears, above all, a frank recognition of the enormous cultural gulf that always separated the FSLN from one of the supposed "fundamental forces of the revolution."

In its 1991 report to the FSLN's first party congress, the National Directorate also paid great attention to perceived errors in the relation with the peasantry. The most important of these was the "initial tendency to distribute lands primarily in the form of state farms and cooperatives" (Dirección Nacional 1991, 18).[2]

The scope of the Sandinistas' self-critique with respect to the peasantry is impressive. But as Alvin Gouldner writes, "confession may be good for the soul, but it is no tonic to the mind" (1973, 54). Were policies towards the peasantry any more unambiguously in error than the "artificial" attempt to raise living standards?

We must remember that the original focus on state farms was perceived as an integral part of the overall project of a state-dominant economy. The shift to the cooperative phase of the agrarian reform in 1981–2 represented an attempt to adjust agrarian strategy at a minimum cost to the broad project, which was a project preparing the ground for socialism, *as the leadership understood socialism at the time.* Leaving aside such problematic motives as the desire to overcome peasant "backwardness," we cannot dismiss as simply mistaken the belief that state farms or cooperatives were essential to the Sandinista project. Certainly the events of the late 1980s did little to dispel the Sandinista belief that a strategy of transferring land to individuals was incompatible with socialized marketing structures. Nor can we doubt the tension between such an agrarian strategy and the labour needs of the export sector. Once again, therefore, the choices the Sandinistas had to make on agrarian questions were difficult ones, and it is not clear whether the paths not chosen would have yielded unambiguously superior outcomes.

C. CONCLUSION

To summarize, I believe it is more helpful to study the Sandinista decade as a dilemma-laden, rather than error-ridden, process. Consideration of the challenges faced by the Sandinistas should lead us to a more general reflection upon the dilemmas of the socialist project, however conceived, and to critical reflection on the Marxian socialist vision as a whole. These two needs overlap to some extent. It is important to recognize that the original Marxist vision of socialism was to a considerable extent dilemma-free. In Marx's original vision of "revolution in the fullness of time" (Schumpeter 1976, 58), socialism would simultaneously realize a number of human values. Socialism would be democratic, because the workers – who would be the vast majority of late capitalist society – would already have revolutionized themselves in the course of the struggle against capitalism; there would be no serious problem of accumulation, because the forces of production would already stand at an advanced level; and since the defeat of capitalism would eliminate a tremendous waste of social resources, it would even be possible to *accelerate* accumulation while humanizing work and increasing leisure. All this was possible in the *first* phase of socialism, prior to the overcoming of scarcity, the most utopian element of Marx's vision.

This all-encompassing harmony, this echo of ancient religious visions of a future in which "all manner of thing shall be well," as Julian of Norwich put it, is perhaps the best reason for being sceptical of the original Marxist vision. If one rejects the hope in a harmonious realization of a wide range of human values, then one must tackle the dilemmas of socialism, and must work to construct mechanisms by which people themselves may make intelligent choices in the face of those dilemmas.

At this point, it is woefully banal to say that socialists must reflect critically upon the Marxist vision of socialism. But it must be stressed that this critical reflection requires an identification of both what must evolve in that vision and, much more difficult today, what needs to be preserved. It is enormously tempting simply to abandon that vision, to turn to "post-Marxism" or to some other "post-" (many of which often seem more "pre-" or "anti-" than "post-"). The generalization of such a course may well sacrifice the theoretical wealth of Marxism and of the Marxist tradition. This could be a loss equivalent to the disappearance of Aristotle from European thought for a millennium.

Paralleling the danger of a general neglect of the Marxist vision is the danger that deeper study of the fate of twentieth-century socialism will likewise be neglected. It is tempting for both Marxist and "post-Marxist" progressives of whatever stripe to conclude that state socialism was nothing but a disaster best forgotten. This too would be tragic, because alternatives to capitalism will continue to be sought throughout the world, and it is vital to examine the fate of previous alternatives. Among these experiences is the Sandinista revolution which, I believe, will continue to be worthy of careful study. Certainly Nicaraguans themselves will continue to study that experience. And, almost as certainly, they will continue to grope for some new social model, as the situation in which they now find themselves is truly desperate.

Let us end where we began: a rural hilltop several years ago. Don Andrés and I met the boredom of guard duty by swapping visions of the future Nicaragua. Mine, the vision of an urban middle-class socialist from a wealthy country, focused on peace and the resumption of the Sandinista project of transformation, however modified. His, the vision of a poor rural Nicaraguan puzzled by the hurricane of history that had swept through his country and turned his own life upside down, focused on peace and a return to an individualistic peasant existence in which he could produce an adequate supply of beans and corn.

Neither of our visions has been fulfilled. Speaking on behalf of those who fell in love with the Nicaraguan people and with their Sandinista revolution, I can say that both the vision and the suffering of that people will always haunt our work for social transformation, wherever that work takes place.

Notes

1 By "orthodox Marxism" I mean the orthodoxy codified and maintained by the Soviet Union.

2 Throughout the book, the term "bourgeoisie" will be used to denote those who own means of production sufficient to sustain them without their own personal labour. It is used in preference to the more neutral "private sector," which would denote too broad a social sector in the Nicaraguan context, including peasants and artisans.

3 Thus, in 1980 Jaime Wheelock commented that "it would be very simple to tell you that we will implement all the laws of socialism, and expropriate everyone here" (JPRS 76378). Similarly, Tomás Borge wrote that "socialism was established in Cuba very soon after the victory – that is to say, the basic means of production are in the hands of the state" (1987, 58).

4 Though Downs deals specifically with electoral regimes, he clearly believes his analysis is generalizable: "Governors carry out their social function primarily in order to attain their private ends. Furthermore, those ends are probably the same in all societies: power, prestige, income, and the excitement of the political game" (1957, 291). The model may be termed "entrepreneurial" in that, just as economic entrepreneurs seek to maximize profit, Downs's political entrepreneurs seek "to maximize political support" (11). And just as the ideal-type entrepreneur aims to produce profit rather than any particular product for its own sake, so too the political entrepreneur is indifferent to the specific content of policy.

5 D. Ortega's speeches to a meeting of the non-aligned nations less than two
   months after taking power and to the UN General Assembly a month later
   are prime examples (Ortega 1988d).
6 Without exaggerating the similarities between situations, it is worth noting
   how quickly El Salvador's 1979 reformist regime degenerated into one of
   the most repressive governments in the hemisphere.
7 ECLAC data indicate that, during the ten complete years for which the Sandinistas held power (1980–9), GDP per capita dropped 34 per cent. The
   rest of Central America, by comparison, dropped 14 per cent. Latin America as a whole suffered a GDP per-capita drop of 7 per cent for the same period. The Nicaraguan result was the worst in Latin America: the second
   worst drop, 25 per cent, was suffered by Bolivia.
       The picture is grimmer still when one considers that the Sandinista de-
   cade began after two years of economic turmoil related to the insurrection.
   Thus, taking the 1978–9 period as a whole, Nicaragua's GDP per capita
   dropped *58 per cent.* Once again, this is by far the worst result in Latin
   America. The second-worst result for the period, a drop of 21 per cent, was
   suffered by Peru. The rest of Central America experienced a GDP per-
   capita drop of 15 per cent over the same twelve-year period. For Latin
   America as a whole, GDP per capita actually increased by 2 per cent.
       Turning to external debt figures: at the end of 1978, the last complete
   year before the Sandinistas took power, the Nicaraguan debt to export ratio
   (1.97) was slightly below the Latin American average (1.99). By 1989, the
   Nicaraguan ratio (22.07) was over seven times the Latin American average
   (2.99). Again, the Nicaraguan ratio was by far the worst in Latin America,
   over four times the second-worst ratio, that for Argentina (5.34).
8 There is no assumption here that markets need be price-equalizing, as is
   assumed in the neo-classical definition of the market (Stigler 1966,
   85).
9 This is important to keep in mind at the present time, when many Sandinistas are concluding that their economic policies were purely and simply
   mistaken. While a thoroughgoing self-critique is laudable from many
   points of view, it may not help prepare the Sandinistas to wield power anew,
   if it loses sight of the tough choices that had to be made through the 1980s.
   I will return to this point in the final chapter.
10 This term will be used in preference to "black market," which generally carries a connotation of illegality. The activities of Nicaragua's "unofficial market" straddled the none-too-clear line between legality and illegality. Thus,
   from 1984 on, the economy would be characterized by (i) official markets,
   run by the state or under state supervision, with goods sold at official
   prices; (ii) unofficial markets, which "escaped" state regulation (though
   whose prices and practices were greatly affected by the existence of such
   regulation); and (iii) "parallel" markets, established by the state with

higher-than-official prices, to compete with the unofficial marketeers. In practice, the line between (i) and (ii) was somewhat fuzzy.

11 Thus, organization theorist Herbert Simon stressed the importance of indoctrination, which will "enable [the employee] to make decisions, by himself, as the organization would like him to decide" (1965, 103). Training would replace the direct exercise of authority, giving the subordinate a frame of reference, and a set of "approved" solutions (15–16).

12 This statement is based on the comparison of speeches made in meetings that I attended with their *Barricada* coverage. For example, the *Barricada* coverage of a mid-1985 speech by Minister of Internal Trade Ramón Cabrales omitted Cabrales's outline of the government's long-term plan to take over wholesale trade (see chapter six). Coverage of an early 1987 speech by Daniel Ortega to workers at the SPP omitted remarks that were implicitly critical of fellow National Directorate member Henry Ruiz. Upon occasion, *Barricada* published two versions of the same speech, the second apparently aimed at "correcting" some statements in the first. In chapter seven, I will note some differences between two versions of a June 1988 speech by Daniel Ortega.

13 I will make the same assumptions regarding speeches and interviews published in books. Again, I do not wish to exaggerate the degree of filtering that took place as books were prepared. An interesting case is an early 1985 speech by National Directorate member Victor Tirado, parts of which drew a mild – yet extremely rare – public rebuke from Daniel Ortega (see chapter six). A collection of Tirado's speeches published by the FSLN's *Editorial Vanguardia* omitted the speech (1986). On the other hand, a collection published by the CST included the speech, with its controversial paragraphs intact (1985).

14 The most significant errors were the economic growth figures for 1980 and 1981, which were revised downwards only in 1985.

CHAPTER TWO

1 See *Barricada*, 13 August 1979; Nolan (1984, 34); *El Nuevo Diario*, 24 October 1987; Fonseca (1985, 1:262, 1:271); Rothschuh (1983, 33); Borge (1989a, 153, 194).

2 I was continually surprised by the willingness of total strangers to offer me all their complaints concerning the government. When we moved into a new neighbourhood in 1985, our next-door neighbour introduced herself saying, "Pleased to meet you. Isn't this the worst government you've ever seen?"

3 On another occasion, Borge commented that "the state coercive bodies – the Army, the Police and the state security bodies – are in the hands of the Sandinistas, who also have the support of the masses, the mass

organizations ... We can do whatever we want with the power we have. We can remove the government and replace it with another if we like" (1980b).

4 Even the final surrender of Somoza's National Guard was "drafted jointly" with a member of the directorate (OAS 1987, 201).

5 One sees here the danger of an overly broad conception of ideology. Booth lumps together, in his consideration of FSLN ideology: (i) rhetoric; (ii) political programs, which FSLN leaders acknowledge are adopted in large part as a political tactic (H. Ortega 1981); (iii) the beliefs of some of those who were brought to the door of the party in the mid-1970s (none of whom reached the highest level of the party); and (iv) the various compromises the FSLN had to accept in order to seize and maintain power (political pluralism, etc.). If all of this is ideology, then what is *not* ideology?

6 Though Nolan seeks to do a careful study of the Sandinistas, he merely proves that one cannot analyse a Marxist movement without understanding something of Marxism itself. In the key chapter of his book, in which he analyses the "major themes" of Sandinista ideology, one finds such statements as: "The Sandinistas fundamentally differ from Karl Marx and modern social scientists on the socioeconomic class theory of revolutionary causation. Objective class inequality is irrelevant. The fact that the poor are more numerous than the rich ... in all capitalist societies is not sufficient cause to assume that they will make a revolution" (1984, 119). It would be interesting to know of a single statement by Marx, or by any "modern social scientist," for that matter, suggesting that the numerical preponderance of the poor *is* sufficient cause for revolution.

7 In his interview with Belausteguigoitia (1985, 182ff), for example, Sandino remarked that: i) not having land was not a serious problem for Nicaraguans; ii) he had no "difficulties" with the idea of giving land to those who did not have it; iii) he thought land should belong to the state; and iv) land should be developed in cooperative form along the Coco River in the North. Elsewhere he expressed an interest in developing agrarian cooperatives (Román 1983, 108; Sandino 1984, 2:245).

8 Fonseca, like Borge and Daniel Ortega, was actively religious in his youth (Rothschuh 1983, 17; Borge 1989a, 41; D. Ortega 1987b). Like the Sandino story, Christian ideals may have helped prepare the psychological terrain for revolutionary activity. The Christian injunctions to love, to win one's life by laying it down, to give all one has to the poor, can all help nurture the generosity of spirit that will make a person open to a radical political involvement.

Directorate member Luís Carrión came to the FSLN in the early 1970s through involvement in a Christian community in a Managua neighbourhood. Ironically, however, those who entered the FSLN from this community formed the nucleus of Jaime Wheelock's "ultra-orthodox" FSLN faction, the "proletarian tendency." The fact that members of a Christian community should form the most pedantically Marxist branch of the FSLN exemplifies the dialectics of personal trajectories and the fact that ideological affinities are not constant over time.

9 In the 1930s, the bishop of Granada blessed the arms of U.S. Marines fighting against Sandino. The daughter of the first Somoza was crowned "Queen of the Armed Forces" in the Managua cathedral, in a ceremony presided over by the bishops of Managua and Granada (Gispert-Sauch 1981, 60). Even the contras were not ashamed to enlist God and the church for their cause. The contras' radio station began its broadcasts, "Without communism, without Somozism, with God and patriotism, this is Radio 15 September" (JPRS 78573). In a felicitous articulation of spiritual and material concerns, the same radio station defined Sandinista communism as denying "the existence of God, the soul, spirit and private property" (JPRS 78215). In 1983, the contras circulated posters claiming "The Pope is with us." Though ever sensitive to perceived FSLN manipulation of religion, the bishops did not criticize this practice. In a 1982 interview with the author, Bishop Salvador Schlaefer referred to the contras as "freedom fighters." In general, the bishops refused to comment on even the contras' most outrageous attacks on civilians.

10 Borge's November 1979 eulogy of Carlos Fonseca is typical: Borge speaks throughout as if Fonseca is still alive, and is now omnipresent (1982). Thus, Fonseca is identified with the Christian resurrection story. In the same vein, Borge's lyrics to the "hymn" to Carlos Fonseca refer to Fonseca as "conqueror of death" and "bridegroom" of the new Nicaragua. In Christian symbolism, Christ is the conqueror of death and the bridegroom of his church.

Borge also uses quasi-religious rhetoric in a more aggressive fashion. Answering the criticisms of an opposition figure, Borge exclaimed, "We expose these hypocrites, these Pharisees, those who yesterday sold Christ and today are willing even to sell their own mothers" (1980a, 13). When opposition figures charged the FSLN with weakening national unity, Borge proclaimed that there can be no unity with "the race of vipers of which Christ spoke" (*Psa* 11 January 1980).

11 See, for example, Arce's first response in (Ortega, Wheelock, and Arce 1986, 11), and Borge (1981b).

12 The concept of backwardness also influenced Sandinista relations with the Miskito people on the Atlantic Coast, who were, Tomás Borge commented in 1982, "still the victims of their own backwardness" (FBIS 24 February 1982).

13 Unless otherwise noted, all laws and decrees are cited from JGRN (1979–88). "Decrees" were issued by the Government Junta for National Reconstruction from 20 July 1979 to the end of 1984 (some had also been approved by the Council of State; in any case, a Decree required junta

approval to become law). "Presidential Decrees" were issued by President Daniel Ortega from January 1985 to early 1990. "Laws" were passed by the National Assembly from January 1985 on. All three types of laws are numbered consecutively.

14 In this, the Sandinistas clearly differed from their elitist opposition. Bishop Pablo Vega, an ardent opponent of the FSLN, commented in 1981 that "they want to make the working class believe that they should exercise power. But the opposite is true: the working class does not want power. Workers want only to produce in order to change their social life, and to be able quietly to eat a bit of rice and beans in their humble homes" (*Bda* 30 September 1981).

15 Thus, there were organizations for children, youth, women, neighbourhoods, rural workers, and peasants, among others.

16 Such views could be held simultaneously with the awareness that the very "backwardness" of the people precluded its real exercise of power. Thus, the same Tirado recognized in 1980 that "the slogan 'power to the workers and peasants' will be just a phrase so long as they live in the midst of spiritual backwardness. Without education [*cultura*], no social class can govern a country" (*Bda* 29 August 1980).

17 Just as the FSLN's vanguardism affected its view of democracy, so was the rightist opposition's view affected by its elitism. An interesting example of this is a 1981 declaration of the Democratic Conservative Party. The party proposed what it called a "planned democracy," in which all political parties would negotiate a plan of government. Elections would then be held, and the winning party would be bound to implement the plan. Thus, elections would merely determine the administrator of an elite-determined plan (JPRS 79928).

18 A declaration of the CST was more colourful: "Popular Democracy means tying up the hands of thieves, pulling out the tongues of demagogic politicians, repressing with a firm hand both opportunists and those who have infiltrated us, paid by imperialism in order to abort our process" (*Bda* 13 December 1979).

19 This argument is presented, for example, by Humberto Ortega (*Bda* 11 July 1980), Daniel Ortega (*Bda* 2 August 1979), and Borge (1985c, 173).

20 Tomás Borge ratified this point, arguing that the new democracy which the FSLN wished to form in Nicaragua could not exist "in a society in which social inequalities still exist, nor in a society which reproduces the irrationality of the exploitation of man by man" (1984a, 168).

21 Superstructuralism was also expressed with respect to other phenomena: "The political activity of people, as Marx noted, is nothing more than the concentrated expression of the economy in which we live" (Arce 1980, 9); "In my view, the world capitalist crisis can lead to victorious revolutions.

The Sandinista revolution in Nicaragua was nothing more than a response to this crisis" (Tirado 1986, 75); "War has existed since the apparition of private property and classes" (H. Ortega 1981, 5).

22 It is symptomatic of Borge's superstructural view of education that in *Barricada*'s version of this speech on 7 February 1983, the word "*conocimiento*" [knowledge] appears only near the end.

23 The exact meaning of the "fantasies and superstitions" to which Borge alludes is made clear from the speech as a whole, which returns repeatedly to the role of religion in keeping people ignorant and justifying domination.

24 One finds this equation of socialism with state ownership in Borge (1987, 58), Wheelock (1983, 101), and Wheelock (JPRS 76378).

25 Borge (1989a, 243ff) gives an interesting account of this period.

26 Fonseca (1985, 1:155); Morales (1983, 143); Humberto Ortega (1979, 92).

27 With regard to the materials used in this theoretical preparation, one clue is Omar Cabezas's comment that "I knew Marta Harnacker's *Elementary Concepts of Historical Materialism* by heart, from so much repetition" (1982, 32). Not only Marxist works were studied, however: the militants also studied Fonseca's compilation of Sandino's thought.

28 Borge may have had some doubts about all this. In a revealing 1983 interview with a Peruvian magazine, he was asked, "Do you think that an emphasis on ideology can take root among the Nicaraguan people?" Borge responded: "Well, I must confess, first off, that you are a fine journalist." After this compliment, Borge dodged the question (JPRS 84041).

29 Though Humberto Ortega was the main strategist of the victorious Sandinista revolution, his enemies always underestimated his intelligence. One U.S. ambassador to Nicaragua, Anthony Quainton, told me in 1983 that he had difficulty talking with Ortega, "because he hasn't received much education."

30 Through all this, the "proletarians" revealed their strong psychological conservatism. They proclaimed that the revolutionary movement should devote its energies, not to making revolution, but to "internal critique" (1979, 182). Wheelock claimed that he really did want to overthrow Somoza, but "without taking risks" (1979, 126). Fellow "proletarian" Carlos Núñez would later comment that their tendency's political work was proceeding at this point in an "orderly" fashion, "without brusque jumps" (Arias 1980, 141).

31 Indeed, after the "business strike" of early 1978, the *Wall Street Journal* reported on 23 February 1978 that "businessmen believe they have won considerable trust by leading the strike. Now, by playing up their old family names, their practical experience and education, and an increased concern for social and economic development, they hope to sell themselves as the answer to peaceful, moderate transition."

32 The dual military structure was also prolonged beyond 1979. A broad-based militia was formed, alongside the armed forces. Membership in the latter required not merely that one have a distinguished history in combat, but that one be "politically reliable" (H. Weber 1981, 104). In an interview with a Cuban magazine, Luís Carrión commented that "the hallmark of our popular army does not derive from its operational structure but from its political training and its objectives … It will be an army schooled in fidelity to the vanguard of our people" (JPRS 74338). Thus, the FSLN continued to respect Mao's dictum that "power grows out of the barrel of the gun. Our principle is that the party commands the gun and the gun shall never be allowed to command the party" (Nordlinger 1977, 16).

33 An example that will be discussed later in this chapter: a neo-classical ideology may lead one to assume that exploitation *cannot exist* in a voluntary market relation. Similarly, a Marxist ideology may lead one to assume that mutual satisfaction *cannot exist* in a relation between members of opposing classes.

34 The term "reproduction" is used here despite its inherent ambiguity (Barrett 1980, 19ff).

35 These figures are broadly consistent with those gathered in other Latin American societies (United Nations 1991, 101).

36 Caroline Moser defines practical gender needs as "those needs which are formulated from the concrete conditions women experience, in their engendered position within the sexual division of labour" (1991, 90). Thus, while one may argue from an abstract perspective that potable water is not a "women's issue," because both men and women should be responsible for the water supply, in practical terms easy access to clean water will be of more importance for those who actually do obtain that water, under the prevailing gender division of labour.

   Nothing in this discussion should be taken to suggest that Nicaraguan rural women were exclusively concerned with reproductive tasks, while men were in charge of "production." In fact, women's "directly" productive role had always been significant, and increased during the Sandinista decade, as many men shifted from production to defence tasks. The argument is rather that, being directly responsible for the reproductive sphere, women would be more directly affected by changes in this sphere than men.

37 There were efforts to organize rural women in the 1980s, but these developed after relations with the peasantry had reached a point of crisis, and remained a relatively marginal component of Sandinista strategy.

38 Moser defines these as "needs which are formulated from the analysis of women's subordination to men, and deriving out of this the strategic gender interest identified for an alternative, more equal and satisfactory organization of society" (1991, 89–90). Thus, while the identification of practical gender needs takes the gender division of labour as a given, the identification of strategic needs calls that division of labour into question.

This does not mean that there is a necessary contradiction between the pursuit of practical and strategic gender interests. Just as Marx saw trade unions as a "preparation for the overthrow of the whole old society" (Draper 1978, 95), the self-organization of women in response to their practical needs can nurture the capacity to identify and mobilize around their strategic needs.

39 Some evidence for the argument that women had an interest in the potential benefits of a rural modernization strategy is provided by a 1986 meeting of female farm workers, whose demands included various types of socialization of reproductive tasks, such as communal drinking water, washing places, and mills for corn grinding (Collinson 1990, 46).

40 Thus, Tomás Borge writes that when Gladys Baez, the only woman in his guerrilla column, hid a package of sensitive documents under her shirt, "she looked like she was pregnant. This was a perfect disguise, since this was the natural state of peasant women" (1989a, 309). Omar Cabezas relates how, upon entering the mountain, their squadron leader would shame them by telling them, among other things, that they were "little women" (1982, 112). Elsewhere, Cabezas recounts a long conversation with a rural woman, the main point of which seems to be to display the woman's ignorance (121).

41 It might also have helped ensure that the eventual make-up of the FSLN leadership displayed some gender balance.

CHAPTER THREE

1 Though we examine state organization and price policy as distinct issue-areas, for purposes of exposition it will sometimes be more fruitful to examine them together. This reflects the fact that, in the Nicaraguan case, changes in thinking on the two areas were often intimately interrelated. This will be seen in particular in the economic reforms of 1985 and 1988.

2 Calculations are based on the 1974 Central Bank input-output matrix (CEPAL 1983).

3 One important exception to this pattern was rice, much of which was produced in large, modern farms.

4 In the words of Eduardo Galeano, "the creation of barriers to *external foreign* competition, so to speak, allowed the *internal foreign* companies to sell at higher prices and earn greater profits" (1980, 426).

5 The phrase is Samir Amin's (1974, 166).

6 There were frequent rumours in Nicaragua in the mid-1980s that industrialists, particularly in Guatemala, were warning their governments not to participate in the destruction of the Nicaraguan economy. Even as the Reagan administration was seeking to isolate Nicaragua, the Guatemalan economy minister was emphasizing the need to bolster trade between the two countries

(FBIS 15 December 1983). The Guatemalan government also indicated its desire to mediate conflicts between Honduras and Nicaragua (JPRS 83446).

The Sandinistas regularly reminded other Central American leaders of their interdependence. Government junta member Sergio Ramírez pointed out in 1982 that "whoever thinks of Central America without Nicaragua is simply not realistic," and reminded people that "no merchandise can go from Guatemala to Costa Rica and vice versa without going through Nicaragua" (FBIS 7 July 1982). In a press conference in Mexico, Bayardo Arce and Henry Ruiz claimed that the isolation of Nicaragua from Central America would cost Guatemala 22,000 jobs (FBIS 7 December 1982).

While the Sandinistas stressed interdependence, they were also very ambivalent about it. Cabinet member Alejandro Martínez argues that the Sandinista leaders' distaste for some of the other regimes in the region led them to accept the demise of the CACM, though the common market was essential to the viability of the industrial sector (Martínez 1990, 77). Martínez's book, like most memoirs, must be taken with a grain of salt. One Sandinista official told me that Martínez should have subtitled the book "If only they had listened to me, everything would have worked out fine." Though Martínez suggests that he was a strong defender of the CACM against his more ideologically minded colleagues in the revolution's early years, he in fact commented in 1980 that the common market was obsolete, and had become an obstacle to development (JPRS 75278).

7 This conclusion is based on calculations that rely on BCN (1979) and Spoor (1987).

8 Industrial exports, however, were vulnerable to changes in the health of the CACM, as they were generally not competitive at world prices (Weeks 1985a, 138). Ironically, the triumph of the Sandinistas would itself do much to undermine the common market. With three-quarters of Nicaragua's industrial exports heading to the CACM (BCN 1978; Brundenius 1985), this factor would become important in the 1980s.

9 Jorge Alaniz, who worked for a time in the Nicaraguan ministry coordinating external aid, puts the actual debt total at $1.1 billion, and argues that the $500 million gap between this figure and the one cited by government officials represents loans contracted but not disbursed (1985, 227). At the end of 1978, the medium- and long-term external public debt stood at $961.3 million (BCN 1978, 188). But the picture is clouded by Nicaragua's accumulation of short-term debts prior to the FSLN's coming to power, as interest and principal payments on medium- and long-term debt fell due. In addition, the new government assumed responsibility for the $175 million in debts of the nationalized banking system (Decree 907), and $55 million in debts of other nationalized companies (Decree 998). Taking these figures into account, it is probable that the official government figure is more accurate than that of Alaniz. ECLA puts the external debt for which

the new government bore responsibility in one way or another at $1.53 billion as of August 1979 (1979, 48).

10 Throughout the period, $1.5 billion in capital goods were imported. Foreign loans appear to have been used to finance the economy's current operations only in the 1974–5 period (BCN 1979).

In general, the government's accounting of its use of the publicly contracted debt is typical of the regional experience: the public sector incurred external obligations in order to support private economic development (BCN 1978, 192–3). In Nicaragua, however, the Somoza family had consistently blurred the line between "public" and "private." For example, at the end of 1978, $174 million of the $961 in public external debt was listed as having been dedicated to "National Reconstruction." The category presumably refers to loans used to "rebuild" Managua after the 1972 earthquake. But observers agree that it was precisely in this reconstruction process that the corruption of the Somoza regime reached its height, and hence it is likely that a large portion of this $174 million was siphoned off by companies owned by the Somoza family. Bulmer-Thomas drily comments that "from 1972 to 1975 inclusive, and again in 1979, the public sector in Nicaragua under Somoza's rule borrowed far in excess of what was spent on public capital formation, and allegations of corruption by the borrower (together with incompetence or complicity by lenders) seem justified" (1987, 217–18).

11 "Price" will be understood here to include any charge for a good or service. The concept thus includes interest rates, salaries, etc.

12 To the best of my knowledge, Evgeny Preobrazhensky (1965) is responsible for the introduction of this concept. Though he did not provide an explicit definition of the state complex, his usage conforms with the definition provided here.

13 The last two components are separated as they represented, in Sandinista Nicaragua, two separate sources of state disaccumulation. See chapter five.

14 His argument is analogous to the "Laffer curve" upon which "Reaganomics" was based.

15 One of Marx's critiques of the market focused on its propensity to generate "fetishism," the confusion between social and "natural" phenomena (1954–9, 2:229). Capital earns a "going rate" of profit that seems to arise from the very nature of capital, basic labour earns a "natural" wage rate, etc. This "naturalness" of the outcomes of capitalist relations helps the capitalist state to appear as a "neutral" enforcer of the rules of the market game. Once the state of "primitive accumulation" is completed, and the majority of the population is well and truly separated from the means of production, the state can appear, not as a class state or as a dispenser of special favours, but as the guarantor of personal rights, including the right to own and profit from property.

Though Marx condemned fetishism, the "premature" loss of such fetishism may present serious obstacles on the path to socialism. If nothing is "natural," then everything can be "up for discussion." From the point of view of Marxist philosophy, this may seem to be an ideal: a society that debates everything, that takes nothing for granted, is a society that will become transparent to itself. But this is not a good recipe for establishing hegemony. As victorious revolutionaries have to make use of certain pre-existing mechanisms in order to pursue their own ends, they may wish to have people continue to take these mechanisms "for granted" for a time. While revolutionaries will want the people at large to question much of what has been seen as "natural," there are many fetishes they may wish to leave standing.

16 None of the most influential ministries promoted a consistent accumulationist perspective. We will see below that the Ministry of Planning's economic plans stressed the importance of state accumulation, yet combined that stress with a number of contradictory elements. Jaime Wheelock's agriculture ministry, for its part, seemed to be more interested in "accumulating" means of production, without regard to the financial performance of those means of production.

17 For Soviet examples, see Hewett (1988, 165–6) and Shmelev and Popov (1989, 123).

18 That is, the firm could maximize its profit, subject to hiring so many workers, meeting such and such a level of working conditions, etc.

19 The export products brought under state control represented about two-thirds of the value of Nicaragua's 1978 exports.

20 The Allende government's nationalization decree deducted $774 million "in alleged excess profits" from the compensation to be paid to the Anaconda and Kennecott mining companies (*NYT* 29 September 1971).

21 The "proponents" Collins is citing confuse two fundamentally different strategies here: volume-maximization and net foreign exchange maximization. In the former strategy inputs are increased until the marginal productivity of every input equals zero. In the latter case, the increase in imported inputs stops when the dollar value of their marginal productivity equals their dollar cost, a level below the volume-maximizing level.

Neither strategy is particularly rational. Each strategy holds that its particular objective function, be it production or foreign exchange, should be maximized "whatever the cost." These are simple strategies, but dangerous ones.

22 One opponent of the Sandinistas commented: "The Sandinistas seem to be waiting for the thousands of young boys and girls currently being trained in communist countries to return to Nicaragua. The government may then proceed to nationalize the whole economy" (Cruz 1987, 46).

23 It is reported that Wheelock's ministry was generally staffed with adherents of his "proletarian" tendency, and some "insurrectionals," while adherents

of Borge's GPP tendency were excluded (Gilbert 1990, 47). During the time I worked in the SPP, the successor to Ruiz's MIPLAN, I often heard strong attacks against Wheelock. No other member of the National Directorate came in for such treatment.

24 On another occasion, Ruiz commented that "the Planning Ministry is and expects to be the backbone of Nicaragua's planning system, that is, the governing agency of the Nicaraguan economy" (JPRS 75491).

25 Zinoviev complained in 1925 that creating jobs for 2,000 workers in the cities would draw another 10,000 peasants from the countryside. "You cannot empty this sea of unemployment with a teaspoon," he warned (Carr 1958, 366). This paradoxical effect of policies aimed to benefit the urban population was incorporated into Todaro's model of rural-urban migration (1969).

26 Upon the announcement of this last measure, a *Barricada* headline on 13 November 1979 proclaimed that ENABAS, the state agency charged with enforcing the controls, had "decreed an end to the exploitation of the people."

27 On the consequences of sellers' markets, see Kornai (1971). There were reports that Castro had warned the Sandinistas not to repeat Cuba's "error" of implementing a rationing system (*NYT* 31 January 1980; 9 July 1980).

28 No claim is made here that each stage is "inevitable" in any given situation.

29 This fact can be obscured by the abstractions of both Marxian value theory and neoclassical thought: overreliance on the assumptions that prices equal values, or that markets are in equilibrium, can cast a veil over the human activities that serve to establish these conditions (to the extent that they are established at all).

30 Analogously, Lenin defines the "whole essence of socialism" as the separation of "the working peasant from the peasant owner, the peasant worker from the peasant huckster, the peasant who labours from the peasant who profiteers" (1968, 278–9).

31 One attempt to outline empirical boundaries for the class estimates that just over 2,000 Nicaraguans remained in the "haute bourgeoisie" in 1980, after the wave of anti-Somozist expropriations had been completed. Most of these belonged to the agrarian bourgeoisie. A further 40,000 Nicaraguans were classified within the "middle bourgeoisie" (*Pensamiento Propio*, July-August 1983). The same analysis considered the "haute bourgeoisie" to include those owning industrial establishments with more than 100 workers, those owing more than 45 hectares of coffee land, or 140 hectares of cotton land, for example. These must be considered rough and ready boundaries, particularly in the agricultural sector, given the vast differences of yield per hectare for land of varying quality, and for different technological levels. Nevertheless, the calculations are useful in indicating the demographically minuscule size of Nicaragua's "haute bourgeoisie."

32 A leading Sandinista diplomat would later comment, "In 1979 we weighed the national, regional and the international balance of forces as best we could in making our major policy decisions. To put it cynically, the question was how much could we get away with without being clobbered on the head by the reactionary forces at large" (Bendaña 1991).

33 This is analogous to the situation in immediate postwar Czechoslovakia, where the property of Germans and Hungarians was expropriated without threatening property owners as a whole (Griffith-Jones 1981, 82).

34 An article in the *Wall Street Journal* on 23 February 1978 commented on this combination of non-regulation and arbitrariness. Nicaragua possessed "a laissez-faire legal structure that should draw outside capital like flies to honey." Yet this was not occurring, allegedly because the Somoza family demanded some share of the "action" on all foreign investments.

35 On the pre-1979 legal environment for business, see Tijerino and Palma (1978).

36 Government advisor E.V.K. Fitzgerald thus claims that the bourgeoisie did not make investments during the Sandinista decade because of an "irrational preoccupation with future property rights." The state was always open to "sectorial" negotiations with the bourgeoisie, Fitzgerald claimed, and in these negotiations it was always "generous" (1989, 33).

37 The plan was in large part drafted by Alfredo César, a former general manager of the largest sugar refinery in the country (Nolan 1984, 141), who had begun collaborating with the FSLN's insurrectional tendency in 1977.

38 The members of the government junta reportedly referred to the Plan of Government as "the Bible" (*NYT* 20 August 1979). For COSEP, the country's main bourgeois organization, the plan represented "the acceptable and apropriate framework to channel everyone's cooperation" (JPRS 74894). Note also the appeals to the Plan of Government in Bolaños (1984); Alaniz (1985); Christian (1985, 190); and the Social Christian Party's critique of the FSLN (*Psa* 24 January 1980).

39 For an English translation of the plan, see the appendix to ECLA (1979).

40 Other differences between the plan and Sandinista practice will be examined in the next chapter.

41 Orthodox socialist theory assumes that the centre has the information required to induce x-efficiency, for example by demanding greater efficiency in the use of inputs each year. In socialist administrative practice, however, the problem of efficiency and technological progress was never resolved.

42 An article on 3 June 1980 in *Barricada* complained that the private sector had rejected the idea of production agreements because of its "lack of trust" in the government.

43 As Carr notes, "The conception of the banks as the controlling lever in a planned and organized economy goes back to Saint-Simon, and had an honoured place in nineteenth-century socialist tradition" (1966, 136).

44 More generally, Stalin argued that "we do not need just any growth of productivity of the people's labour. We need a *definite* growth of productivity of
the people's labour, namely the growth which ensures a *systematic preponderance* of the socialist sector of the economy over the capitalist sector" (Ellman 1979, 16).

45 Years later, after the FSLN had effectively capitulated to both the peasantry
and the market, Daniel Ortega would comment that, had Nicaragua held
the resources needed to develop a high-tech agriculture, "we would not
have to take the broad economic measures that we took when we made up
our minds to leave to the free market the production of corn, basic grains,
and perishables" (FBIS 15 June 1988).

46 Though the modernist Wheelock tended to be more explicit in this view of
the peasantry, there is no evidence that other members of the National Directorate differed markedly from his view. This view of the peasantry was
not easily reconciled with the belief that it was one of the "fundamental
classes" of the revolution. The contradiction led to some interesting formu-
lations, as when Tomás Borge argued that "peasants constitute an objectively revolutionary social force, though because of their relations with
production and because of concrete historical elements they are more
backward than factory workers and the agrarian proletariat" (*Bda*
28 August 1984). In Marxist thought production relations are usually the
key determinant of "objective" class position. Thus Borge is in essence saying that peasants are "objectively" both revolutionary and backward.

47 Similarly, Henry Ruiz noted the importance of the political consciousness
raising that takes place on the state farms (*Bda* 20 April 1980), and an editorial in *Barricada* on 17 July 1980 supported cooperatives for their capacity to overcome the "traditional individualism of the peasant," because they
promote "the consolidation of the spirit of mutual cooperation amongst
members; the development of consciousness and political motivation; the
raising of the peasant's cultural level, and of his living and working conditions."

48 This mystique is not limited to Nicaragua. Debray held, for example, that
"any man, even a comrade, who spends his life in a city is unwittingly bourgeois in comparison with a *guerrillero* (1968, 68).

49 The hope, government advisor E.V.K. Fitzgerald would later note, was that
the "semi-proletariat," that large social sector "*disguised in the form of an impoverished peasantry,*" would be "absorbed in state employment and the
'true' proletariat would be constructed as a majority class" (1985a, 225;
1989, 33; emphasis added).

50 Biderman notes that the agrarian reform law passed in 1963 during the Somoza dynasty's mildly reformist phase led in effect to "a few colonization
projects and the provision of land titles in these and other remote areas to
which [peasants] migrated" (1983, 21).

51 The experience of Peru during the Velasco era would support this concern. Stepan notes that incomes of members of sugar cooperatives put them in the top quarter of the Peruvian population. Cooperative members sought to restrict membership, relying instead on part-time hired labour when their labour needs increased. Such part-time workers received only one-quarter the earnings of cooperative members (1978, 217ff).

52 This does not mean that the directorate ignored the need to develop its political support in the countryside. We will see in the next chapter that agricultural credit for peasant production rose rapidly after 1979. The government also hoped that improved working conditions for rural wage workers and an improvement in social services would solidify rural support.

CHAPTER FOUR

1 "Hegemony" is used here in one Gramscian sense, to denote a situation of "intellectual and moral unity," in which the values and interests of one social group are presented "not on a corporate but on a 'universal' plane" (1971, 181–2). Thus, a situation of hegemony is one in which the values and interests of the dominant political group enjoy the status of being taken for granted among large segments of the population.

2 While the 1980 plan was entitled "Programme of economic reactivation for the benefit of the people," the 1981 plan was more soberly called the "Economic programme for austerity and efficiency," symbolizing the FSLN's changing perception of the economic situation.

3 Post-insurrection credit policy was not merely expansive, but departed sharply from traditional financial principles. Large sums of credit were extended to the peasantry, for reasons that were essentially political. Credit policy was thus a key expression of an "alliance-building" as opposed to "accumulationist" orientation. Only one-quarter of this credit would be repaid (Enriquez and Spalding 1987, 117), and the credit was not translated into increased basic grains production. A precedent had been set, however, and the view became widespread that the government had an obligation to extend low-cost credit to the peasantry.

4 One possible reason for this decision is that the directorate members placed a high value on maintaining unity, and may have felt that the subordination of MIDINRA to MIPLAN would create serious tensions. Another possibility, discussed in the next chapter, is that MIDINRA's vision of how Nicaragua should be transformed seemed more viable than that of MIPLAN.

5 Forrest Colburn's study of agricultural state enterprises provides a graphic picture of the irrelevance of the planning process to state managers. Enterprise managers generally ignored requests for statistical information and refused to submit "required" statistical statements. It is unlikely that most firms

had the necessary literacy and numeracy skills to provide central government offices with all the information they requested. Colburn notes that MIDINRA "required" its firms to submit a plethora of statistical statements: "one daily, six monthly, sixteen quarterly, and one annually" (1990, 48).

MIPLAN officials recognized the problem. The November 1981 seminar concluded that the "national information system ... does not exist in practice," and complained that "information arrives late, and it is unreliable and even contradictory."

6 Some of the planners appear to have felt that their grasp of theory absolved them from the need to discuss the plan with others: Plan 81 declared itself "nothing but the scientific expression of the historic aspirations of the Nicaraguan people for this phase of the Popular Sandinista Revolution" (MIPLAN 1981a, 15).

7 These figures include the central bureaucracy only, and exclude employment in state enterprises. Despite repeated attempts to freeze government employment, the bureaucracy would continue to grow, reaching 77,000 in 1986–7 (SPP data). Defence and interior ministry personnel are omitted from these figures. In a mid-1988 speech, Daniel Ortega (1988c) indicated that there were 130,000 permanent positions in the two armed ministries.

8 "*Yoquepierdismo*," one of many "isms" coined to describe behaviour within the new state.

9 Thus, for example, the International Fund for Reconstruction was set up to channel all foreign aid, but Decree 308 allowed organizers of the 1980 literacy crusade to ignore this mechanism.

10 Arce went on to complain that "often the plan is submitted to discussion with *compañeros* who do not have an adequate level of training or preparation needed to be able to make a real contribution to the discussion."

11 One, and only one, member of the National Directorate, criticized this aspect of the new state. The increasingly technocratic Wheelock criticized the growth of political activities within the state apparatus, condemning the "ideologists" with their "revolutionoid posturing" who always wanted to hold political meetings in his ministry (Wheelock 1986a, 61). Other FSLN leaders considered such political activities essential to the development of politically reliable experts.

12 For an account of life in the new state by an opponent of the FSLN, see Alaniz (1985, 67ff).

13 Henry Ruiz recognized the problem of the exodus of specialists, but suggested it was owing to "their petty bourgeois sensibility, since the workers no longer call them 'sir,' and question them." Nevertheless, Ruiz argued, it was important to keep specialists in Nicaragua, since "a whole generation must pass before we have specialists with a new mentality" (*Bda* 11 September 1981). Once again, one sees the hope that the revolution could create specialists made in its own image.

14 Thus, it was not merely the peasantry that was turning out to be a bad credit risk. Biondi-Morra notes that a 1981 MIDINRA study "indicated that out of 49 enterprises for which updated financial statements existed, 38 were operating at a loss" (1988, 32).

15 For advocates of the accumulationist approach, Colburn's study paints a grim picture indeed. He writes of one accountant who answered requests for cost information with an impatient "I am not a magician" (1990, 110). Another enterprise ran up debts of c$99 million, though no one could explain how the debt had been accumulated (87). An official at another farm stated that no control was maintained over inventory, because no one at MIDINRA ever asked for inventory reports (67). Biondi-Morra cites a manager who argued that "we were so short of administrative personnel that we had to make choices. It was better for us to plant one acre of rice without keeping a record of it, than to write on a piece of paper that no acre was planted" (1988, 277).

16 December to December inflation, as registered by the unreliable CPI, was 25 per cent in 1980 and 23 per cent in 1981. While this was an improvement over 1979's figure of 70 per cent, the drop partly reflected price-control policies that created a situation of "repressed inflation."

17 The decree also made MICOIN responsible for "ensuring an adequate supply of such goods," though the ministry was given no powers that would have allowed it to fulfil this responsibility.

18 In general, fear of the consequences of consumption austerity made a significant contribution to the trade deficit in this period. The maintenance of domestic beef consumption led to a total shortfall of $52 million in beef exports during the period, relative to planned levels. In addition, consumer-goods imports were allowed to exceed planned levels by a total of $152 million in the biennium. Together, lowered beef exports and increased consumer-goods imports account for half of the difference between planned and actual trade deficits. Overall, the 1980 and 1981 trade deficits were 100 per cent and 115 per cent above their planned levels, respectively. Part of this outcome reflected the evolution of terms of trade, which deteriorated 30 per cent from 1977 to 1981, according to ECLAC data.

It is important to keep in mind that we are comparing the *actual* trade figures with their *planned* level, rather than with the previous year's data. The planned trade deficit was already substantially larger than the deficits of the 1970s, not to compare it to 1979, when there was in fact a trade surplus. So the plan already allowed for an increase in consumption goods imports, reflecting the government's sense of the political risks of an austerity program. But the actual increase went well beyond this.

19 Included were sugar, rice, beans, maize, salt, laundry soap, cooking oil, eggs, and "any other product that might subsequently be added." The fluctuations in this list throughout the 1980s, as state channels gained and lost

control over the distribution of various products, provide a window on the condition of at least one aspect of the non-market economy. Similarly, the ongoing shifts of the "secure channels" from workplace to neighbourhood and back again reflect the FSLN's attempts to meet political challenges from various quarters.

20 The law, conflicts with ENABAS, and the anti-speculation rhetoric of the FSLN leadership led private merchants to hold a rally in Managua, replete with banners declaring "We are not exploiters," "We want freedom of trade," and "We want to be free, in a free country" (*Psa* 10 March 1980). The sprawling Eastern Market, where many private merchants were concentrated, became a centre of anti-Sandinista sentiment, and was quite impervious to government attempts at control. A MICOIN official told me in 1983 that price inspectors were refusing to enter the market after one of their colleagues was murdered there.

21 This warning echoed those issued in the Soviet Union during the New Economic Policy period (Carr 1958, 424).

22 Biondi-Morra cites a state milk plant manager who describes the long process for approving new prices. The manager complained that "the last time we made a price proposal, it took more than six months to get it approved. By then, the new price was inadequate due to its erosion by inflation" (1988, 235).

23 Official prices also lagged behind the general price level. Bearing in mind the weaknesses of the CPI, by the end of 1981, deflated producer prices for beans and maize were 14 per cent and 39 per cent lower, respectively, than their 1977 levels (BCN 1979; Medal 1985; Spoor 1987). Kaimowitz offers the interesting hypothesis that the low prices paid by ENABAS to producers reflected, not just consumer interests, but the goal of preserving a labour supply for the agro-export harvests by limiting peasant income from food sales (1989, 58).

24 Internal Trade Minister Ramón Cabrales would later comment that "One of the most notable mistakes of this period was the fact that we were forcing peasants to sell us their production every agricultural cycle, at prices set officially and in a coercive manner" (1987, 42; Wheelock 1983, 117). Colburn notes that "in some rural areas peasants caught selling their crops to private middlemen have their entire harvests seized without any compensation" (1989, 192). What is not entirely clear is whether such pressures on the peasantry reflected law, administrative regulation, or the initiatives of local officials. Kaimowitz places responsibility on "local party officials" who engaged in "directly repressive actions" (1989, 56). This interpretation was, not surprisingly, also advanced by Daniel Ortega, who would later comment that "the incorrect *application* of some measures" led to the government's "giving the counterrevolution a peasant social base" (1988c; emphasis added).

But if local officials who punished peasants for selling to private traders were not following specific instructions, their interpretation of government policy was certainly a reasonable one. ENABAS was clearly trying to establish itself as a monopsony, and, to this end, was seeking to eliminate private traders (Kaimowitz 1989, 56; Zalkin 1988b, 82). In addition, since the private grain network *had to* sell to consumers at higher-than-official prices in order to be able to pay peasants the prices it did, local officials could reasonably conclude that private trading was ipso facto an illegal activity, and treat it accordingly.

25 Ironically, the government was creating administrative pressures on the peasantry at the same time that it was removing other long-standing pressure mechanisms. As Zalkin points out, the government's easy credit policy, and the fact that the state banking system would not seize land as payment for delinquent loans, eliminated a mechanism that had traditionally fostered grain marketing (1988b, 80).

26 The idea of paying isolated peasants with cheques demonstrates the problems generated by the interaction of the state-dominant economy and peasant production. Cheques were used, of course, to maintain controls on the individuals acting as state buyers. Private traders were free from this encumbrance.

27 With its growing influence, MIDINRA could have been a forceful advocate for the peasantry, had it been oriented towards the promotion of peasant production, which it was not.

28 Calculations based on SPP data.

29 Arce was referring to opposition in the Congress to the Carter administration's proposal to loan Nicaragua $75 million.

30 Calculations based on ECLA data.

31 As noted in ([Ryan] 1983): "For the first time, large coffee and cotton producers must respect minimum-wage laws. They must also provide better meals for their workers and, in many cases, pay their health costs. Some producers say that workers are not as productive as they used to be and that they have shortened their work day. Edgardo García of the ATC ... suggests that, if some workers are not producing as much as before, it is because they are now working at a more humane pace."

32 A document of the International Fund for Reconstruction (FIR 1982) is typical. It outlines the generous debt-restructuring policies provided for the private sector in the post-insurrection period, including the cancelling of delinquent interest payments, the easy credit made available to the private sector, the high rates of profit being realized in the 1980–1 period, etc.

33 The FSLN tried unsuccessfully to channel the bourgeoisie in an economistic direction, and members of the National Directorate repeatedly expressed their displeasure at bourgeois demands that were "political in nature, going beyond the framework of financial demands," as Henry Ruiz put it (*Bda* 14 March 1980).

34 Written from a Reaganite perspective, Christian (1985) provides an interesting account of Washington's efforts to do just this.

35 Key declarations of COSEP and its member organizations, which accord with the analysis presented here, are published in (*Psa* 2 March 1980; 26 May 1980; 11 November 1980; JPRS 74894).

36 See the declarations in (JPRS 74894; *Psa* 26 May 1980; 11 November 1980).

37 In the Nicaraguan case, this corollary was strengthened by the fact that, as FSLN-opponent Jorge Alaníz recognizes, "law practically never ruled" in Nicaragua (1985, 50). Thus, FSLN leaders wondered aloud how the bourgeoisie had suddenly become allergic to arbitrary government practice, when it had by and large tolerated that practice under Somoza. In all fairness, the bourgeoisie could answer that, to the extent that it had opposed Somoza, it had done so precisely to put an end to arbitrary practices.

38 An example pertinent to the Nicaraguan case is freedom of expression. Many foreign observers deplored Sandinista controls on opposition media as attacks on the sacred freedom of the press. I know of no foreign protest, however, against the common practice of the owners of those opposition media of firing staff members for political reasons. It appears to be a common assumption that the capitalist property rights of the owner of a medium should take precedence over the freedom of expression of mere employees.

39 Though opponents of the FSLN saw these organizations as pure "transmission belts," their actual role was more complex, often to the chagrin of the FSLN leadership. A September 1979 internal party document criticized mass organization leaders who "have practically nullified the authority of government representatives and are demanding measures that have nothing to do with the guidelines that have been charted," thereby seeking to make the mass organizations the "sole judges of how things should be run" (FSLN 1987, 224). Another reflection of the relative autonomy between the FSLN and its mass organizations is Decree 388, which stripped the Council of State of its power to veto decrees passed by the government junta. Since the FSLN and its mass organizations together comprised a majority in the council, this decree would have no reason for being had the organizations been purely passive transmission belts. The mass organizations were thus neither simple reflections of the classes they claimed to represent, nor pure instruments of the FSLN. As the war progressed in the 1980s, this dialectic would be weakened, and some of the mass organizations would increasingly take on the characteristics of "transmission belts." Others, such as UNAG, would retain a high degree of autonomy.

40 Even when it respected property rights, however, the FSLN could put a scare into the bourgeoisie. Hassan's speech to workers went on to state: "We have lots of time ahead, and the measures we take will be taken in the necessary and opportune moment."

41 This vanguardist theme had previously been developed by other members of the directorate. In May 1980, Daniel Ortega commented that elections would have to be preceded by the development of "a higher political consciousness, a higher vision of society," and by the eradication of illiteracy (*Bda* 13 May 1980).

42 The plan had not set a date for elections. Article 1.2 mandated the government junta to hold power "for whatever period of time is required to lay the bases for a genuine democratic development in Nicaragua." The preamble to the document suggests that the entire Plan of Government, with its ambitious vision of social transformation, can be read as a gloss on the meaning of the phrase "the bases for a genuine democratic development."

43 Ironically, Arce's comment echoed the declaration of the Brazilian military junta upon seizing power in a 1964 coup: "The successful Revolution ... is legitimized by itself" (Roett 1989, 382).

44 *La Prensa* published one of the most complete presentations of this alternate version on 2 January 1980.

45 Carlos Nuñez, cited in *Barricada* (9 October 1979) See also the comments of Wheelock (*Bda* 5 October 1979), D. Ortega (*Bda* 16 August 1979), and Borge (*Bda* 24 April 1980).

46 A *Barricada* headline on 25 September 1979 announced: "New TV show will combat bourgeois influence."

47 Nichols (1988) alleges that the paper began receiving covert CIA funding around this time. In January 1984 I did a content analysis of one month of *La Prensa*'s international news. The results were summarized in an article published under a pseudonym in *Barricada* (21 June 1984) and in Ramírez (1987, 248). I found that over half of the paper's U.S.-centred news was "official," that is, stories of the form "U.S. officials stated today. ..." This type of news, essentially press releases of the Reagan administration, made up fully one-sixth of all international news in *La Prensa*. U.S. official statements on Central America outweighed those from Nicaraguan officials by a 15:1 ratio. The bulk of U.S. official news on Central America consisted of direct attacks against the Nicaraguan government. I also found that the paper routinely suppressed information that might cast doubts on the Reaganite analysis of events in Nicaragua.

48 Robelo's rhetoric led Eden Pastora to comment: "If I had Robelo's $125 million, Jesus' comment about the camel and the eye of the needle would make me tremble with fear" (*Bda* 28 April 1980). Even from exile, Robelo's Nicaraguan Democratic Movement would continue to woo Obando y Bravo, referring to him as "the most beloved figure of the Nicaraguan people; his flawless conduct constitutes an extraordinary moral support" (*La Nación*, 22 August 1982).

49 In 1989–90, the organizers of Violeta Chamorro's campaign for the presidency would continue the long national tradition of saturating politics with

religious imagery. Chamorro, portrayed by her campaign as the "Mother of Nicaragua," made her campaign appearances dressed completely in white, evoking the "Most Pure" Virgin Mary, who is at the heart of popular religiosity in Nicaragua. A reporter commented that Chamorro "sometimes makes airy references to 'conversations' with God and her martyred husband" (Watson 1989). Chamorro's daughter, editor of *La Prensa*, spoke of her father, Violeta Chamorro's murdered husband, in distinctly religious terms, referring to "his bullet-ridden body, like the Crucified Christ" (*Psa* 21 August 1990).

50 Sergio Ramírez referred to the decree as "a preventative and exemplary measure," a "warning" against decapitalization (*Bda* 22 July 1981). Critics, however, said that one of the confiscated firms, the *Prego* soap company, had "money in the bank, rising production, a three-year supply of spare parts and a stockpile of imported raw materials" (*Wall Street Journal,* 15 September 1981). Sholk notes that the private sector was also particularly disturbed by the expropriation of the *La Perfecta* milk company, as it had a Law of Protection appeal before the Supreme Court at the time. Expropriation of the company was thus interpreted as a sign that no real judicial recourse existed (1984, 265).

51 See *La Prensa*, 26 May 1980, for COSEP's list of its demands. Ramírez gives quite a different picture, claiming that COSEP demanded three key cabinet positions during the negotiations (1987, 163).

52 The *Wall Street Journal* commented on 29 February 1980 that "international banking sources say approval of as much as $500 million in additional international aid to Nicaragua may have been awaiting passage of the U.S. aid bill as a reassuring signal of U.S. confidence in the stability of Nicaragua. 'With a yes vote from the U.S., world money ought almost to pour into Nicaragua,' says one London development banker."

53 Cruz had worked for several years at the Inter-American Development Bank. Córdova Rivas was a leading figure in the Conservative Democratic Party.

54 Specifically, the Republicans declared that "we will support the efforts of the Nicaraguan people to establish a free and independent government." On the intended interpretation of this clause as a declaration of support for an armed overthrow, see Gutman (1988, 20).

55 This point is not disputed, though there is dispute over the details surrounding Salazar's death (*Bda* 18 November 1980; 26 November 1980; Christian 1985, 175ff).

56 In late January 1981, Arce commented that "our enemies ... say that our project of pluralism, mixed economy, and freedom is interesting. But we have been very clear: this project continues only so long as there is support from all the different sectors. Can you imagine that in a situation in which we have a shortage of foreign exchange and of food, and military aggres-

sion, we can allow reactionary groups to survive, saying and doing whatever they want, that we can permit business people to rob and exploit as they wish? We will simply put an end to the problem and be done with it" (1981b). See also Arce (1981a), and Borge's comments in JPRS (78200).

57 Alfonso Robelo suggested in late 1981 that "the Reagan Administration should keep quiet because this way they are just giving the Sandinists someone to blame for all their problems" (NYT 30 December 1981). Robelo would eventually reconcile himself to U.S. strategy, however, and become a contra leader.

58 "Speculation" was a common term of opprobrium among the FSLN leaders, though it was never clearly defined. Typical of the confusion is Victor Tirado's definition: a speculator, said Tirado, is "a merchant who constantly acquires goods in order to speculate, without participating in production" (1986, 238). The first part of the definition is circular, the second part seems to embrace all merchants, who by definition are not "directly productive." In general, "speculation" seemed to denote commercial activity that flouted official prices or other regulations. Aslund notes the similarly imprecise nature of the term in the Soviet Union, where speculation "can mean any gainful private activity" (1989, 154).

59 Fiscal deficits in 1980 and 1981 hovered around 10 per cent of GDP. While these deficits were consistent with planned levels, they did indicate a trend in the fiscal situation that would soon become problematic. From 1970 to 1977, deficits had averaged just 4 per cent of GDP. The jump to the 10 per cent level occurred though the tax burden had nearly doubled, from a 1970-7 average of 10.2 per cent, to 18.7 per cent in 1980-1. Government spending, having averaged 16.6 per cent of GDP in the 1970-7 period, rose to 32 per cent of GDP during the 1980-1 period. Monetary emissions to cover the fiscal deficit became substantial: while internal financing of the deficit had averaged 0.4 per cent of GDP in the 1970-7 period (BCN 1979), by 1981 it had reached 8 per cent (ECLAC 1983), and was rising.

60 The Wall Street Journal also commented on 15 September 1981 that the emergency measures "are viewed as generally beneficial to business."

61 COSEP cited Ortega as telling people to prepare lists of "potentially counterrevolutionary elements," and promised that "those who consciously or unconsciously support the plans of imperialism ... if they do not take part in defence, will be the first, when the aggression comes, to be found hanging alongside all the country's roads and highways" (Psa 20 October 1981).

62 It appears that communist union leaders were demanding salary increases, and were accused of fomenting unrest in factories (Bda 24 October 1981). This simultaneous crack-down on Right and Left led Tomás Borge to comment that "political pluralism in Nicaragua is demonstrated even in the jails" (Bda 26 November 1981).

63 The COSEP leaders were freed in February 1982 (*Bda* 15 February 1982), and those of the Communist Party in September 1982 (*Bda* 9 September 1982).

64 It would become commonplace among FSLN supporters to argue that COSEP in fact represented only a fraction of the private sector. Thus, Xabier Gorostiaga argued that COSEP members accounted for but a sixth of private sector output (1986, 58). But in analysing the bourgeoisie as a politically active class, this argument is neither here nor there: COSEP, and the right-wing parties that joined it in opposition to the FSLN, constituted the only visible face of the organized bourgeoisie. Generally, non-COSEP bourgeois were as politically active as "potatoes in a sack," to borrow a metaphor. Unlike many observers, the FSLN itself would recognize this fact (Dirección Nacional 1991, 14; FBIS 13 April 1982).

65 The FSLN had originally tried to incorporate peasants in the ATC. The acceptance of a separate peasant organization suggests a retreat within the FSLN from the Wheelock argument that the countryside had been, and should continue to be, substantially proletarianized.

66 Collins estimates that the new maximum rents were 85 per cent below existing market rates (1982, 37).

67 The ATC's argument is interesting: the land seizures that the bourgeoisie routinely denounced as arbitrary are here presented as a response to the state's inability or unwillingness to enforce its legally mandated intervention in the market. This non-enforcement of law is as "arbitrary" as the types of government action that so enraged the bourgeoisie, but it is a form of arbitrariness that is quite common in the capitalist "state of law," a form about which the bourgeoisie rarely complains.

68 This was a perennial argument of MIDINRA officials. In a late 1983 interview, a "pro-peasant" activist commented to me that "if we wait for the MIDINRA bureaucrats to get 'ready' for an agrarian reform, we will wait until the next century."

69 Even COSEP's Enrique Dreyfus expressed support for the law (Keesing's Contemporary Archives 31290).

70 There are indications that Wheelock at this point saw the agrarian reform process as a strictly temporary retreat from his statist agricultural project. He commented that "we cannot transform an idle large estate from the seigniorial period of national independence – which has to go through a phase of capitalization – we cannot initially transform this into an estate appropriate for the APP. What we perhaps can do there is create an agricultural base by forming a cooperative and gathering together peasants, who have been more or less dispersed – like an archipelago – throughout the area, and unite them on the estate, associating them in a higher form of production (1981b, 16).

71 "In practice," Kaimowitz adds, "the State had little capacity to ensure fulfilment of these plans."

CHAPTER FIVE

1 Economic performance in 1982 was affected by a combination of flooding in May and drought later in the year. Towards the end of the period, the contra war came to have a significant impact upon overall economic performance. The government asserted that during 1984 there was $24.4 million in physical damage and $159.6 million in lost production as a direct result of the war (Fitzgerald 1985b). Much of the lost production was destined for export, including some $69 million of coffee in war zones that could not be harvested (ECLAC 1984).

2 Stagnant export prices contributed in part to this outcome, but there had also been significant drops in the volume of Nicaragua's traditional agro-exports. The volume of cotton, beef, and seafood exports dropped 35 per cent, 74 per cent, and 75 per cent, respectively, between 1978 and 1984 (INEC 1984; BCN 1978). The drop in exports in the 1982–4 period would have led to an even bleaker trade balance had not the government imposed an import austerity program in 1982, which led to a $223 million drop in imports. Consumer goods imports declined 34 per cent between 1981 and 1982. The industrial sector also felt the effects of import compression: raw material imports for the sector were cut back by 29 per cent (Spoor 1987).

3 During 1983, Nicaragua was able to pay only $5 million of the $90 million that fell due on its private bank debt, and renegotiated the rest (Figueroa 1983).

4 In 1984, defence spending accounted for 23 per cent of total government spending. This represented 14 per cent of GDP, up from just 3.5 per cent in 1980, and accounts for the bulk of the deficit increase. Apart from the war, the most significant factor in the expansion of the fiscal deficit was the increased financing of investment projects from the budget. From 1982 to 1983, capital spending's share of total government expenditures doubled, as work began on several major projects (Argüello, Croes, and Kleiterp 1987, 31). While government capital spending had averaged 7 per cent of GDP in the 1970–7 period, it represented 23 per cent in 1983 and 17 per cent in 1984 (ECLAC 1985). Apart from their high immediate costs, the investment decisions made during this period implied significant future costs for the budget, as the government locked itself into a series of large projects with long maturation periods.

5 Several years later, Ortega would comment to a meeting of SPP officials that the SPP had added "competence" to the "enthusiasm" that had characterized Ruiz's MIPLAN. In a private 1983 interview with a group of visiting Canadians, even pro-planner Tomás Borge indicated his impatience with the MIPLAN technocrats (Borge 1985c, 177).

6 Though high external financing continued, the nature of that financing was shifting: the U.S. administration was urging its allies not to lend to Nic-

aragua, and politicized multilateral lending institutions. On 21 January 1985, the *New York Times* reported that the U.S. government had gone so far as to threaten to paralyse the operations of the Inter-American Development Bank if a $60 million loan to Nicaragua was approved. These efforts of the Reagan administration bore much fruit. Gradually, Western bilateral aid would come to be overshadowed by credit from CMEA countries.

7 This attitude is captured nicely in a book by Carlos Alemán, who was my supervisor in early 1984. Alemán worked on a dam being built near Managua to supply the TIMAL sugar project, and offers a rhapsody of praise for those who had the vision to build the dam. At one point he excoriates the bureaucrats who had the temerity to question such profane matters as cost overruns and double or triple shifts: "Suddenly it seemed as if, from the heart of the bureaucracy another dam had arisen, a dam of paper that blocked the flow of money" (1985, 36). In the end, Alemán recounts, the people of "vision" overcame the unbelievers, and the dam was finished. All visions carry a cost: the dam displaced thousands of peasants, whom the government sought to move into new villages. "Some people say we have destroyed their culture," Alemán commented to me, "but the only culture they ever had was a culture of misery."

8 The Chiltepe milk project near Managua provides a good example of this logic: by all accounts, costs per litre were much higher than anywhere else in the country, but MIDINRA considered the project a great success, as it provided milk that was immediately transferred to the state dairies in Managua, thus obviating the need to chase after privately produced milk.

9 Partly as a result, while overall agricultural and livestock production in 1985 was down 10.6 per cent relative to 1983, imports for the agricultural sector were up 33.9 per cent (SPP 1986b; INEC 1986).

10 Thus, the January 1982 meeting of the Sandinista Assembly numbered among the residual "vices of Somocism": "inefficiency, over-staffing, bureaucratism, administrative corruption, abuse of the assets of the Revolutionary State, [and] waste in public institutions" (*Bda* 1 February 1982). Jaime Wheelock decried the fact that "changes in society are proceeding more quickly than the formation of new state officials, and there is the bureaucratism of those who do not yet understand that their duty, and the *raison d'etre* of their jobs, is to resolve the problems of the people" (1985a, 110).

11 On regionalization, see Wilson (1987) and Bernales (1985).

12 This is not to say that output-maximization was the only goal of state firms, merely that it overshadowed financial goals. Colburn notes that, as the war intensified, state firms in war zones found themselves responsible for housing and feeding soldiers, maintaining a militia, etc. (1990, 117).

13 Alejandro Martínez later commmented that concerns expressed in the cabinet over APP inefficiency were repeatedly met with the response that "that is a political matter" (1990, 127).

14 Thus, Biondi-Morra argues that a recalculation of state farm financial results using a shadow exchange rate yields profits instead of losses (1988,
161–2). Such recalculation can cut both ways however. A recalculation of
textile sector financial results using shadow exchange rates, interest rates,
and salaries, transformed profits into losses (Avilés and Amaya 1987).

15 There also appears to have been debate on how far to extend the powers of
MICOIN. *Barricada* reported on 4 June 1982 that a law had been drafted
giving MICOIN "total control of Nicaraguan commerce," but in fact the
ministry's powers were not substantially beefed up until mid-1984.

16 Interestingly, *La Prensa* commented that the decision to ration sugar was
"good because it enables all the population to obtain sugar." The paper,
however, protested the fact that the neighbourhood CDS would be handling the rationing cards, as the use of a "partisan organization" to perform
a state task suggested a "sweetened totalitarian project of creating a single
party" (FBIS 5 February 1982). It appears that some local CDS officials did
use the ration cards as a lever to force people to participate in neighbourhood activities, a practice that government officials expressly forbade (FBIS
16 November 1983).

17 Minister of Internal Trade Ramón Cabrales estimated that between 1982
and 1984 the number of merchants working in the Eastern Market rose
from 4,000 to 27,000 (*END* 18 July 1987).

18 The majority of Canadians working in Nicaragua continued to convert
their dollars into córdobas at the legal parallel rate of C$28:$1, even while
the unofficial-market rate passed the 500:1 mark. Though I worked in
some of the most "revolutionary" institutions in the state apparatus, this behaviour amused rather than impressed our colleagues. It was regularly necessary to defend oneself from the charge of being a complete fool
["*pendejo*"] on this matter.

19 In mid-1983, interest rates to producers ranged from 8 per cent on long-
term loans for the cattle sector, to 18 per cent on short-term loans for industry (*Bda* 20 May 1983). As has been noted, inflation for 1983 was 33
per cent. Nominal interest rates would rise little in subsequent years, despite the rapid acceleration of inflation.

20 Many state companies were unable or unwilling to repay their loans, as
were many peasants. In 1983 in particular, the government was driven to
forgive much of the peasant debt, in order to address the effects of contra
propaganda, which was telling peasants the Sandinistas would use debts as
a pretext for seizing their land (*Bda* 19 June 1983). Overall, by 1984 21 per
cent of production loans were frozen, compared to 6 per cent in 1977
(INEC 1984, 52; BCN 1978, 41).

21 These private agents can be either merchants, if the state firm is producing
final goods, or producers, in the case of intermediate goods. Aburto's study
of the urban informal sector concluded that many "producers" earned

their profits by a thinly disguised process of reselling on the unofficial market inputs purchased at official prices. Aburto considers these agents "distributing houses" of state inputs, rather than producers (1988). Thus the distinction between "productive" and "unproductive" economic activities breaks down for much of the informal sector: many activities were "productive" in appearance, yet yielded incomes which were essentially identical to arbitrageur profits.

22 For the same reason, agro-export farms that had traditionally planted some basic grains in order to feed their labour force stopped doing so.

23 To be more precise, the cost-plus logic was applied to producers who had greater alternatives available to them. Thus, cotton producers, who made year-to-year decisions on whether and what to produce, were favoured with an increase of 194 per cent in the producer price for the 1982–3 cycle, while coffee producers, who were pretty much stuck with their coffee plants, saw their producer price rise by only 20 per cent (Spoor 1987). They reacted by spending less on plant maintenance, which led to a gradual decline in yields (Colburn 1984, 510).

24 The creation of a series of implicit rates of exchange had interesting side effects: in his study of state farms, Colburn found that "since the exchange rate is set by the government and not by the market, everyone perceives that the government can change the prices it pays whenever and however it likes" (1990, 64). This exacerbated the firms' already considerable lack of concern over financial performance. We see once again the side-effects of destroying the "fetishes" of the market.

25 These transactions were affected by conditions in the official market. A report in *Barricada* on 30 September 1985 suggested that private traders were paying peasants just slightly above the official price for beans, then reselling those beans in Managua with a mark-up of 400 per cent. The traders, who often enjoyed a near-monopsonist position vis à vis isolated peasants, could use the official price as a benchmark upon which they only had to improve marginally. Thus, low official prices hurt peasants both when they sold to the state and when they sold in the unofficial market.

26 By which Wheelock meant simply the supply-demand mechanism.

27 The gap remained substantial however. On 3 August 1984, *Barricada* recorded unofficial-market mark-ups over the new official prices: 300 per cent for beans, 110 per cent for rice, and 267 per cent for cooking oil.

28 Calculations based on SPP data.

29 The link between salaries and productivity was common in official statements, and reflects a profound confusion: Tirado was arguing that *nominal* salaries should only be adjusted for increases in *real* productivity. In an inflationary situation, such a demand implies that real salaries must fall. And fall they did through the coming years, reaching remarkably low levels in the late 1980s, as shall be seen. The rhetorical link between salaries and

productivity was analogous to the view that state firms should earn profits "through productivity, not through price increases." Both views assume an inflation-free situation, and provide no direction for policy in inflationary situations.

30 For reasons that are not clear, high officials in the government and FSLN seemed better to understand, or to be more interested in, cost-push inflation rather than demand-pull inflation. While working in the SPP, I was often asked to prepare an estimate of the inflation "because of increased costs" that would result from a forthcoming salary increase. Should I also try to estimate *actual* inflation, I would ask? No, just inflation "via costs."

31 Ernest Mandel argues that "the theory of payment 'in accordance with the quantity and quality of labour performed' is nothing but a crude justification of the differences in wages which exist *de facto* in the USSR and in other societies in transition from capitalism to socialism under a marked degree of bureaucratic domination." The authentically Marxist formula for distribution during the transition, Mandel insists, is that put forth by Marx in his "Critique of the Gotha Programme": "the producers will be paid only in accordance with the *quantity* of labour performed" (1968, 725, 724).

The SNOTS definitions of work "complexity" provide support for Mandel's critique. It was stipulated that those in directive positions should always be paid more than the highest-paid person under their responsibility (MIPLAN and MITRAB 1984). Hierarchical position, therefore, was better rewarded than expertise.

32 As early as 1980, MIPLAN had advocated the payment of workers according to "work accomplished," rather than hours worked (*Bda* 17 October 1980). But the legitimacy of piece-work payment depends on the worker's output being linked to her own efforts. In the coming years, Nicaraguan workers would complain that the SNOTS scheme penalized them for factors beyond their control, such as power failures in their plants and raw materials shortages. Thus, during a wild-cat strike at a Managua textile factory in 1986, workers complained that they could not meet their production quotas because 466 of the company's 842 machines were broken (*Bda* 19 April 1986). While advocating piece-work, FSLN policy was resolutely opposed to profit sharing. A 1980 party statement dismissed profit sharing as a form of manipulation of workers (Secretaría Nacional 1980). Students of mine were strongly rebuked by members of their examining board during the defence of their honours thesis for having recommended profit sharing, since Marx had condemned the practice in some writing or other.

33 This last type of bonus implied an increase in workers' dependence upon their immediate supervisors. It could also provide yet another cover for hierarchical privileges. In August 1987 I studied the performance evaluations of 181 workers at the SPP. The evaluations revealed an interesting "hierarchy bias": while 19 per cent of personnel received an overall evalua-

tion of "very good," this figure rose to 32 per cent for directors, and dropped to 10 per cent for lower-level personnel.

34 Thus, Bayardo Arce commented in June 1982 that if Nicaragua were pushed "to a situation in which we have only whatever we may produce and only a little foreign aid from countries that do not yield to pressure from the Reagan administration, then it will be difficult to maintain a mixed economy" (FBIS 23 June 1982).

35 Such votes of confidence were most frequently expressed by Jaime Wheelock (e.g., 1983, 35–6). But Wheelock seems to have been articulating the view of at least part of the National Directorate during this time. Carlos Nuñez commented in 1983 that the Reaganites "think that we Sandinistas are going to lose the patience and realism that has characterized us through the last twenty-two years of revolutionary struggle. They want this counterrevolutionary offensive to make us desperate, to oblige us to take measures that they will use to justify their aggression ... But we are committed to maintaining our revolutionary model. National unity, the mixed economy and political pluralism are the best instruments for the defence of the revolution and we will not destroy those instruments" (*Bda* 24 April 1983).

36 Asked about the coincidences between her party's line and that of Reagan, Azucena Ferry of the Social Christian Party commented that "maybe those gentlemen have studied the Nicaraguan problem so well that they are quite knowledgeable, and that is why they say the same things we do" (*Bda* 16 December 1983). Within a few months, she had joined the contra executive.

37 COSEP would appear to have been the only component of the Coordinator that had a clear constituency. An observer comments that the Coordinator's "parties were weak, some existing only on paper, others compromised by their performance under the old regime. Sandinista restrictions had limited their development under the revolution. A Western ambassador gave this assessment of them in 1983: 'They have no leaders, no program, and so few members that they would have a hard time coming up with poll watchers in an election'" (Gilbert 1990, 122).

The *New York Times* noted on 29 July 1988 that "Nicaraguan political parties are traditionally weak and divided, but business groups are remarkably united."

38 A branch of the Democratic Conservative Party had split off to field candidate Clemente Guido, and the Independent Liberal Party, which had been allied with the FSLN, moved into opposition and ran Virgilio Godoy, who quickly adopted a strident rightist rhetoric.

39 The leftist parties other than the FSLN, whose influence had so worried the FSLN in 1979–80, in total won a mere 4 per cent of the vote.

40 It is a near-impossible task to evaluate the degree of internal support for the various opposition tendencies. Part of the problem is that *La Prensa* was

the central communication medium of the opposition, and it resolutely suppressed news about the doings of opposition parties that did not toe the abstentionist line during the election campaign.

41 See for example the comments of Adolfo Calero, head of the local Coca-Cola factory, political secretary of the Conservative Party, and future contra leader (FBIS 19 February 1982).

42 Agrarian reform played some role in this shift: medium and large private producers lost approximately 16 per cent of their land. Lands under the control of the state sector, however, did not grow during this period.

43 The analysis has remained at a "neo-classical" level, arguing that the price signals given to the bourgeoisie did not encourage production. The argument is strengthened by taking into account the overall social situation of the bourgeoisie. As Carlos Vilas put it: "Politically subordinated, militarily disarmed, facing the possibility of total confiscation if he joins the counter-revolution or leaves the country, surreptitiously sending his sons out of the country to avoid military service, the Nicaraguan bourgeois is living a true hell, a situation that certainly does not encourage productive investment or the calculus based on entrepreneurial profits" (1986, 88).

   Life described the bourgeoisie's "life on the edge": "Their Mercedes are locked in garages; their yachts are in dry dock. When they venture out to restaurants, they suspect the waiters are spies ... 'How do I stand it?' says one businessman. 'I leave the country every four weeks and live like an aristocrat'" (Dougherty 1983).

44 Calculations based on (Wheelock 1990; *Envío*, September 1985; *Bda* 16 July 1987).

45 Without specifically mentioning Grenada, both Borge (1984b, 159) and Wheelock (1985b, 90; 1990, 72) recognize that the acceleration of the reform was a response to U.S. aggression.

46 This generally affected those who had settled on idle national lands along the agricultural frontier. Under the Somoza regime, such squatters had often been displaced by the export agriculture booms.

47 The 1981 agrarian reform law called for the expropriation of all lands involved in non-monetary renting, such as share-cropping. CIERA condemned such rental arrangements as "proper to the Middle Ages" (1983a, 41). While share-cropping relations are often highly exploitative, the assumption that they are necessarily so is problematic. In the Nicaraguan context, peasants who received access to a plot of land and a modest working capital in exchange for half of their crop [*mediería*] might have been no worse off than many who were paying a money rent and relying on usurers for working capital. In any case, they certainly did not feel themselves worse off than those who had no access to land at all. But under the terms of the agrarian reform law, peasants could find themselves liberated from their exploitative share-cropping arrangements, only to find that they now had

no access to land at all, unless they were willing to join a production cooperative.

As Vilas notes, "The revolutionary outlook correctly sees the exploitative content of [paternalistic landlord-peasant relations]. But it does not always see that this relation also addresses some basic needs of people" (1987, 11). Ironically, even some state farms were leasing land to peasants under these "super-exploitative" forms (*Bda* 30 January 1983). Kaimowitz argues, however, that in general the state farms abandoned the non-monetary rental relations maintained by the farms' previous owners (1989, 62). This aggravated the land problem for local peasants.

The state's actions in "liberating" peasants from nonmonetary rental arrangements was similar in effect to its attempted liberation of peasants from private rural merchants who, it eventually became clear, had linked the peasantry with the city in a much more complex fashion than state trading organizations understood.

48 This statement is typical of the vague sense of disquiet running through much official discourse on the peasantry at this time: if the "will" of the peasantry was to socialize production, why were "thousands of cadres" required "to provide political and ideological support" for something the peasantry already wanted?

49 The discussion here focuses on the production cooperatives. There were other forms of cooperative organization that did not involve collective production. The "credit and service cooperatives," for example, were groups of individual producers organized for purposes of receiving credit and other agricultural services.

50 In many cases, the cooperatives did develop an *esprit de corps*, however. On one occasion, I sat on the sidelines of a rather bloody brawl between members of two neighbouring cooperatives of the Matagalpa department, in which the participants displayed very little of that peasant individualism that so worried the FSLN, and a high degree of collective spirit, though not in the fashion that the advocates of the cooperatives had hoped.

51 M. Ortega states that 61 per cent of those killed in the war up to 1987 were cooperative members. He adds that peasants also stayed away from the cooperatives as they were seen as a prime site of recruitment for the Sandinista Popular Army (1989, 204).

52 Kaimowitz points out that, since many peasants were also seasonal wage workers, they were also hurt by declining real wages (1989, 65).

CHAPTER SIX

1 This extreme external imbalance fundamentally reflected the collapse of export volumes, not problems with terms of trade. According to ECLAC data, Nicaragua's terms of trade in 1986 were 14 per cent lower than in

1977. The drop in export volumes for coffee, cotton, sugar and beef, on the other hand, were 38 per cent, 58 per cent, 29 per cent, and 90 per cent, respectively (ECLA data). Coffee output continued to be affected by the war situation, as the country's main coffee producing area of Jinotega-Matagalpa was also a zone of intense contra activity. Production was also hurt by a drop in yields reflecting the lack of care of plants in previous years. Cotton production was reduced as cotton land was converted to other uses, reflecting the squeeze between low world prices and increased prices for inputs. The near-total disappearance of beef exports during the period reflected the twin pressures of declining cattle herds and the government's decision to sustain high levels of domestic consumption in some sectors. In the case of sugar, total output was actually comparable to the best levels reached in the 1970s. But as with beef, domestic consumption pressures affected exports.

2 This position enjoyed much support at other levels of the FSLN. The Trade Union Coordinator, made up of the leadership of the various FSLN union federations, also called for a strengthening of MIPLAN's position, and argued that the economy needed, not flexibility, but stricter control (Coordinadora Sindical 1985).

3 Perhaps to soften the blow of his loss of MIPLAN, Henry Ruiz was made minister of the new Ministry for External Cooperation (formerly the International Fund for Reconstruction).

4 The council had three National Directorate members: Ortega, as president, Wheelock, as head of MIDINRA, and Ruiz, representing the Ministry for External Cooperation. Other members were the vice-president, the minister of industry, and the heads of the SPP and the Central Bank (FBIS 8 January 1985).

5 The plan had called for an elimination of all subsidies (SPP 1985, 11). We will see below that subsidies in fact lingered until mid-1988.

6 In an implicit critique of investment policy prior to 1985, the plan gave priority to projects that could come on stream quickly and not use capital-intensive technology (SPP 1985, 58). Given the tremendous backlog in the investment program, however, it proved quite difficult to change the orientation of investment. By 1987, nearly the entire investment program was made up of backlogged projects.

7 The basic exchange rate for exports was to be c$28:$1, while import exchange rates would vary from c$20:$1 for essential consumer goods to c$40:$1 for capital goods (Cuadra 1985).

8 Asked by an interviewer in 1990 why the 1985 plan did not address the problem of interest rates, Alejandro Martínez, one of the architects of the plan, commented that "one must take into account that in both the agricultural and industrial sectors, there were institutional interests, and a lot of political power. The question of interest rates touched on those sectoral

ministries." Martínez went on to comment that "it was not prudent to have Commanders of the Revolution in charge of State ministries" (1990, 125–6). The comment seems to indicate that a change in interest rate policies was blocked above all by the minister of agriculture, Jaime Wheelock, who was the only National Directorate member in charge of a "sectoral" ministry at the time. Wheelock's opposition may simply have reflected the traditional productionist orientation of MIDINRA.

9 Wheelock (1985c); Meneses (1985); Hüpper (1985); and Dirección Nacional (1985a).

10 There were attempts to prepare urban Nicaraguans for this shock prior to the announcement of the measures. In late January, my neighbourhood was convoked for a CDS meeting, similar to ones taking place throughout the city. A CDS representative from the Managua regional office told us that "measures must be taken because we cannot continue in this desperate situation," and warned the neighbourhood that "tough days are ahead."

11 SPP (1985, 8); Dirección Nacional (1985a); Wheelock (1985c); and Hüpper (1985).

12 It was also hoped that these virtues would be promoted through the state reorganization. "Political competence," Daniel Ortega declared in January 1985, "must give way to administrative and technical competence" (FBIS 4 January 1985). Ortega expressed the hope that the reorganization would allow the executive branch to "exert overall control over Nicaragua's economy" (FBIS 4 February 1985).

13 There was a widespread view in Nicaragua that a society bound for socialism had no need to study such things as price theory. The first class I gave in Microeconomics in the National Autonomous University of Nicaragua in April 1984 was marked by a long discussion of whether concepts such as supply and demand should be taught at all. Upon the announcement of the 1985 measures, some microeconomics teachers, who had long laboured under the opprobrium of teaching an obsolete and reactionary course – a course originally titled "Bourgeois Economics 1" – were exultant. "And they said microeconomics was garbage, that it was bourgeois economics," crowed one colleague. "Now look what's happening: even the leaders are talking about supply and demand."

14 Daniel Ortega himself declared that the main difference between the government's approach and the typical IMF package was the existence of "initiatives to guarantee the workers' real salaries" (FBIS 19 March 1985). The comment is ironic, as these guarantees broke down within months. But it is suggestive that the president should have reduced the difference between two fundamentally distinct adjustment strategies to this one point.

15 The bias of the CPI towards official prices led to a probable overstatement of inflation during this period.

16 By April 1986, the gap had widened to 72 per cent.

17 Rather than replacing the unofficial exchange market, the exchange houses created a new informal sector activity: "liners-up" [*fileros*]. As the parallel market rate was increasingly below that of the unofficial market, it was an easy matter to sell one's dollars at the exchange houses. Buying them there was rather more difficult; hence the "liners-up." By July 1987, these enterprising individuals would line up in front of the exchange houses, then sell their place in line for c$500,000, the equivalent of seven months average salary at the time. The "liners-up" claimed that lines were as long as two weeks (*END* 9 July 1987). The "liners-up" exemplify the capacity of the informal sector to commodify pretty well anything.

18 The CPI increased by over 40 per cent in both March and April. Overall, the CPI increased more in the first half of 1986 than in all of 1985.

19 It also meant that the inflation actually experienced by the peasantry in 1985 and subsequent years was probably lower than that registered by the CPI, since the peasantry was enjoying improved access to goods at official prices.

20 Carlos Zamora, chief representative of the government and the FSLN in the Matagalpa-Jinotega region, recognized that the liberation of peasant products was undertaken because "it was necessary to begin by stopping the deterioration in the rural sector that was threatening our power" (JPRS LAM–87–059).

21 In a confidential speech in July 1985, Internal Trade Minister Ramón Cabrales complained that the policy had left the state unable to buy enough basic grains to keep the urban "secure channels" supplied. ENABAS, the state grain marketing company, was authorized to buy beans at c$2,500 per quintal, Cabrales said, while the unofficial-market price was between c$5,000 and c$6,000.

In the same speech, Cabrales complained that "there is no price policy." MICOIN, he said, was only finding out about new prices for producers when MIDINRA announced them in the newspaper. Hence, consumer prices had become "nothing more than the resultant of the various ministerial and enterprise decisions" (1985b).

22 Thus, in speeches to an UNAG assembly in early 1986, National Directorate members spoke of the peasantry's moral responsibility to "sell the State part of your production at official prices, so that we can offer it cheaply to the workers" (Carrión 1986, 20; Wheelock 1986c, 54).

23 Maize had already generally been assigned to urban tortilla makers, rather than being sold directly to consumers.

24 This analysis applies specifically to maize and beans, the two basic grains traditionally produced by the peasantry. It was easier for the state to control rice, the bulk of which was produced by large state and private producers. It was even easier to control wheat distribution, since all wheat was entering the country through official donations.

25 The two peasant crops were a vital "input" for the agro-export sector. When I picked coffee in early 1987, our daily diet invariably consisted of three servings of beans and tortilla, with rice added only at lunch.

26 Humberto Ortega (1985) defined this defeat in terms of the "impossibility of the mercenary forces developing themselves as a military threat to the Revolution," and compared the weakened contras to "parasites," with which "one can live for a long time without dying."

This "strategic defeat" was perceived by foreign observers as well. The *New York Times* noted in early 1986 that the contras had retreated to their camps in Honduras, that their activity "has declined sharply in recent months," and that the government was "in its strongest military position since it took power" (30 January 1986; 21 February 1986).

If new policies towards the peasantry contributed to this outcome, so too did strictly military factors such as the consolidation of military service and the introduction of Soviet MI-24 helicopters in late 1984. The latter gave Sandinista troops much greater mobility, and led the contra leadership to press the United States for anti-aircraft missiles (*NYT* 21 February 1986). It is important to note this technological factor in the war's evolution, since the contras' acquisition of advanced surface-to-air missiles in 1987 would lead to another shift in the military situation.

27 Some officials in the SPP's External Sector division reasoned that, since over half of Nicaragua's imports now came from CMEA countries, it was both possible and necessary to impose CMEA-style planning.

28 The published "summary" of the 1987 plan omitted this reference to the National Directorate, as well as references to the FSLN's August 1986 document on production and distribution, perhaps to veil the 1987 plan's quite explicit fusion of party and state roles (INIES 1987).

29 In the highly inflationary situation that was developing, these results could change quickly. In late 1987, an official with the state power company claimed that the consumer price of electricity covered only one-sixth the cost (*END* 20 October 1987).

30 As the minister responsible for getting production into the "secure channels," Cabrales was acutely aware of the breakdown in relations between state enterprises and the government. He commented in early 1987 that "in reality, there is no ministerial control. We turn the raw materials over to the enterprises and the producers, but no agreements are established as to what they in turn will supply to the state ... We do not know for certain how much is produced; we do not know if all that is produced is delivered to us" (JPRS LAM–87–027).

31 *Barricada* reported on 3 January 1986 that Wheelock was "responsible for production, employment and salaries within the National Planning Council." This would seem to make Wheelock, after Daniel Ortega, the National Directorate's most powerful voice on economic questions.

32 If the rate of profit is lower than the rate of inflation during the cycle of production, the enterprise is losing real purchasing power, rather than generating it. If it borrows money from state banks, this real loss can be transferred to another part of the state complex, yet still represents a loss for the state as a whole.

33 Thus, a cooking oil factory gave its workers one and a half gallons of oil per month (*Bda* 29 October 1987). A rice processor sold its workers 100 pounds of rice per month at the official price (*END* 28 January 1987). A state chicken enterprise gave its workers forty eggs and 7 pounds of chicken each month, while a private firm gave workers 10 pounds of chicken each week (*Bda* 9 February 1987). A state slaughterhouse sold its workers 20 pounds of beef each month at the wholesale price, while a private counterpart gave its workers 20 pounds per week (*Bda* 10 February 1987). One example of the importance of the practice is the case of a state textile company that ended payment in kind, and immediately lost 20 per cent of its work force (JPRS LAM–87–025).

34 It was also easier to administrate roadblocks on the relatively few interregional roads than to control trade within regions.

35 The effect of market liberalization on the actual output of peasant products is unclear. Bean production continued to stagnate, declining a total of 7 per cent in 1986 and 1987 (ECLAC 1989). On the other hand, it was reported that in 1986 the peasantry had substantially increased the amount of land it planted with corn (*Bda* 27 April 1987).

36 For several years, the government had tried to regulate taxi fares. Its efforts had done little more than turn the bulk of taxi drivers into resolute enemies of the FSLN. At one point, Tomás Borge had suggested that the government should jail "reactionary" taxi drivers and confiscate their licence plates (*Bda* 4 June 1984). In early April 1987, the government adopted a new tack, announcing that any private car could operate as a taxi without acquiring a licence.

37 Thus, an article on a new upscale supermarket in Managua boasted that "there one can buy whatever quantity of products one desires, according to one's monetary capacity. Prices are the only limitation, just as in any other non-revolutionary capitalist country" (*END* 25 July 1987). In late April, two SPP economists were interviewed on the problems of the economy. One criticized state "subsidies" of health care, while the other called for banks to be run on a for-profit basis (*END* 27 April 1987). It had hitherto been unheard of for government officials publicly to attack two such central government policies as public health care and the administered banking system.

38 On the question of corruption, see also (JPRS LAM–87–021; LAM–87–025).

39 In late April, Victor Tirado commented that "the problem is not just a drop in production, but that our working class could be weakened, disorganized,

that it could lose its cohesiveness, its organization, its identity as a class. We must be clear that economic development is linked to the development of the working class" (1987).

40 In the case of productive firms, I have referred to this phenomenon as a "productionist" bias, but it existed in the central government ministries as well. During the mid-1980s, the "at any cost" attitude was most pronounced in the defence and internal security sectors. Martínez would later comment that government ministers were "afraid" to question defence spending, "as it might be interpreted that we were not giving sufficient priority to defence" (1990, 120).

41 The complicated mechanism for assigning scarce foreign exchange often hurt exports. The mechanism, as Pizarro argued, worked better for large items than for what might be termed "odds and ends" (1987). Thus, Pizarro noted, a state textile firm failed to fulfil a $1 million export agreement because of an inability to acquire imported spare parts worth $38,000. Similarly, shrimp exports were hurt by the lack of a relatively inexpensive imported chemical needed to keep the shrimp from being discoloured (*END* 29 September 1985). There is a parallel here with the difficulties of several socialist economies. Shmelev and Popov note the chronic shortages of "trifles" in the Soviet economy (1989, 82, 117).

42 The precise figures are questionable, as many of the weaknesses of the CPI became particularly prominent during this period. A price index calculated by the Employment and Salary Department of the SPP told a somewhat different story. While the CPI jumped 897 per cent in the April-October period, the SPP's basket increased 284 per cent. The SPP's basket, on the other hand, registered higher inflation than the CPI during the pre-adjustment period.

43 We are adapting Hodgson's (1988) notion of price norms to an inflationary situation. I believe that, by 1987, norms concerning absolute or relative prices had been weakened or destroyed by years of inflation and shifting relative prices, yet norms concerning price *increases* remained.

44 The "signals" given off by the official announcements of salary increases were exacerbated by the practice of announcing various types of official price increases at the same time. Thus, the minister of tourism for some reason chose to announce 200 per cent increases in the prices of luxury restaurant meals simultaneously with the announcement of the April salary increase. Though luxury restaurant prices were irrelevant for Nicaraguans in general, the combination of announcements suggested that a major upward move in prices was under way, and unofficial-market prices jumped accordingly. Similarly, the July salary increase of 20 per cent was accompanied by an 82 per cent increase in official consumer prices.

45 E.H. Carr reports a similar phenomenon in the Soviet Union in the 1922–3 period (1960, 78).

46 Brus and Laski have noted the difficulty for socialist reforms presented by the lack of an oppositional relation between managers and workers on salary questions (1989, 85).

47 The task of cultivating this new generation began at an early age. Across the street from the house where we lived in 1984 was a grade school. Every morning, the student body would gather outside before classes began for a short assembly. One morning, the principal told her students: "You must study hard. Some of you are going to grow up to be doctors. But you won't be like those doctors who fill their pockets with money. You're going to be doctors who care about your country, about the people, about making people healthy."

48 Jimenez thus represented the curious phenomenon of a workers' leader who opposed salary increases for workers in general, but supported them for specialists.

49 The suffix "HM" stands for "Heroes and Martyrs," and was meant to distinguish the FSLN's professional organization from that belonging to COSEP.

50 Thus, *Economía Política* (1982, 482–3) notes that Article 14 of the Soviet Constitution enshrines the principle of "from each according to his capacity; to each according to his labour." But labour, the textbook goes on, refers to both "quantity and quality." The book also attacks the "egalitarianism" of such "revisionist leftists" as Trotskyists and Maoists, which "impedes social production" and blocks "the development of human capacities."

51 This point is the "negative infinity" of banking: as real interest rates approach -100 per cent, "loans" effectively become "donations." Deflating by the CPI, real interest rates in 1987 were approximately -91 per cent.

52 Ortega too, however, recognized the political delicacy of seeking *rapprochement* with the bourgeoisie. Perhaps because of this, he maintained a class rhetoric even in his attempts to build bridges to the bourgeoisie. In his meeting with the private producers, he commented: "With respect to what the gentleman ... said, about the entrepreneurs being the workhorses pulling the cart, there are different interpretations. There are some who understand that in fact the feet, the heart, the lungs, the muscles of the workhorses are the workers. The horse walks thanks basically to the efforts of the workers, and can survive without entrepreneurs. I think we're clear on this, I think that any company here can survive without its owners" (*Bda* 18 February 1985).

53 Bolaños declared that the new economic measures could not succeed without an "adequate socio-political climate," and commented that the measures were "tactical, transitory, conjunctural, as the communists say." He also repeated COSEP's demand that the government negotiate with the contras (*END* 17 February 1985).

    Bolaños at this point was as much as pleading for a U.S. invasion. In a March 1985 speech in Panama, he warned business people there that they must wake up to the threat of communist enslavement in Central America. "Soviet penetration into the area is already a reality," he warned, and insisted that containment was not "the appropriate response to communism's objectives." At the end of the meeting, a local business leader collected funds to help "expel the communist regime in a final offensive" (FBIS 27 March 1985).

Months later, Bolaños argued that the Sandinistas had no right to speak of Nicaragua's right to self-determination, since, in their own struggle against Somoza, they had called for "hemispheric solidarity." Again, Bolaños called for a fight against "Soviet expansionism" (FBIS 12 June 1985).

54 The adjective "patriotic," while useful in political terms, was perhaps not as accurate as "economistic" for describing this segment of the bourgeoisie. Apparently unaware of the irony of his words, Xabier Gorostiaga classified "a good part of the transnational companies" operating in Nicaragua as "patriotic producers" (1986, 55).

55 Simultaneous innovations in class language were also being applied to the state sector. The government was seeking to "strengthen the authority of enterprise managers" (Dirección Nacional y Asamblea Sandinista 1986), and was apparently concerned that the use of class language at the grass-roots level could undermine the attempt. Victor Tirado thus argued in this period that enterprise directors were as much members of the working class as anyone else, and that the working class includes anyone who is "part of one production process" (1986, 119). Daniel Ortega also stressed that "the manager of a company is a worker," and warned that "the enemy will also instill mistrust between the union and the management, between the union and the [specialist]" (JPRS LAM–86–075). What had once been a normal expression of class tension was now the work of the "enemy."

There were many symbols of this integration of upper administrative echelons into the "working class": at the end of union elections in my ministry in early 1987, the ballots were counted by the minister.

56 Luciak notes that "UNAG members will be affected [by the agrarian reform] only in truly exceptional cases, considering the enormous political and economic power of the organization" (1987, 138). This created a great incentive to join the organization. Luciak notes that many local affiliates of UPANIC, COSEP's organization of agricultural producers, were also members of UNAG, and refrained from echoing the hard-line position of the UPANIC national leadership.

57 COSEP did little during this period to dispel this impression. Ramiro Gurdián of COSEP thanked Reagan, who is "looking after the problem of Nicaragua," for his "solidarity" with the country (*Psa* 2 October 1987).

58 Official data on deaths in the Sandinista armed forces provide an index of this intensity. Some 300 soldiers were said to have died in all 1983 (*Bda* 28 December 1983). "Approximately 1,000" died in 1984 (FBIS

27 December 1984). In 1985 and 1986, just under 100 soldiers were being killed monthly (*NYT* 31 December 1985; FBIS 2 January 1987). In 1987, over 1,700 soldiers and reservists were killed, almost 150 per month (FBIS 31 December 1987).

59 Indeed, it was reported that U.S. officials were counting on Sandinista inflexibility to create momentum for the contra aid bill (*NYT* 15 October 1987). Ortega was acutely aware of the double standard on the whole question of compliance with the regional peace accord: "Everyone is watching what Nicaragua will do. No one is aware of what Honduras, El Salvador, and Guatemala are doing" (FBIS 6 October 1987).

60 The decision was not to the liking of all National Directorate members. Just twelve days before *La Prensa* was given permission to reopen, Jaime Wheelock promised a meeting of FSLN militants that the paper would only reopen "when it is no longer an instrument of the CIA" (*Bda* 7 September 1987).

61 Tomás Borge's 1985 assertion that "dialogue with the contras would mean abandoning all our revolutionary principles" was typical of the Sandinistas' long-standing position (FBIS 23 April 1985). As recently as August 1987, Daniel Ortega had declared that "we maintain the principle of not negotiating" with the contras, who are "nothing more than paid U.S. government employees" (FBIS 11 August 1987). The November 1987 rally at which Ortega announced indirect negotiations with the contras was the first time I had ever heard people at a Sandinista rally express disagreement with a leadership announcement.

62 Bolaños was offered two hectares of state land for every one he lost in the land seizure, but rejected the offer because state land was "illegitimately obtained" (FBIS 9 July 1985).

63 Jaime Wheelock presented this shift as a response to the same peasant backwardness that cooperatives and state farms were to have overcome. Cooperatives remained, Wheelock noted, "the most appropriate form of organization because they raise the social and economic level in the rural sector," but they were "complex," and required a "certain level of cultural understanding," which the peasantry lacked (JPRS LAM–85–086).

64 Bulmer-Thomas argues that the 1986 agrarian reform law represented "an end to the state's efforts to reach an accommodation with the rural bourgeoisie" (1987, 258). But Bulmer-Thomas has focused too much on the difference between the 1986 and 1981 laws, and too little on the actual application of the laws. The Agrarian Tribunal almost never overturned expropriations in the early years of the reform. In April 1982, the tribunal reported that it had confirmed the expropriations in all sixty-two cases it had heard to that point (FBIS 29 April 1982). Later in the decade, however, landowners were able to win appeals against expropriation. It was reported in 1987 that 40 per cent of the land expropriated for idleness in the previ-

ous two years had been returned to owners after investigation (*END* 15 July 1987). Thus, while the 1986 law may have been more severe for large producers than the earlier one, the overall agrarian reform process was milder.

65 Land transfers to individuals represented 47 per cent of all transfers in the 1985–7 period, up from just 18 per cent in the 1981–4 period (I. Gutiérrez 1989, 119).

66 An associate of Henry Ruiz told me in mid-1987 that he had been urging Ruiz for some time to "attack" the agrarian reform process, which he felt was leading agricultural production to ruin. Similar concerns were also expressed at an internal SPP seminar in January 1987.

67 Collective production was being eroded even within the production cooperatives. Land devoted to family plots was expanding inside most cooperatives, and many cooperatives had undergone a *de facto* transformation into "idle furrow" cooperatives [*cooperativas de surco muerto*] (*Envío*, June 1987). In this form, the land was divided up among members, but instead of marking the division lines with fences or other obstacles, a furrow-width of land was left idle. This allowed continued enjoyment of economies of scale from mechanization.

CHAPTER SEVEN

1 At the end of 1989, according to ECLAC data, the external public debt stood at $7.57 billion, twenty-six times the value of exports.

2 A more generous set of conversion factors was established for state obligations to private citizens, though such obligations were generally of little importance.

3 Such references to the "true value" of things would become frequent in the 1988–9 period. One gets the impression that the FSLN leadership had identified a need to reconstruct the "fetishes" that years of topsy-turvy prices had destroyed.

4 The latter bonuses were highly restricted: they could total no more than 20 per cent of the collective payroll of a company, they had to be paid from company profits (*Bda* 17 February 1988), and they could only be granted by companies that did not exceed planned costs (*Bda* 9 March 1988). Under the difficult conditions facing companies after the monetary reform, such restrictions made these bonuses exceedingly rare.

5 As in early periods, the FSLN leadership would continue to give companies conflicting signals. Thus, in the same speech in which he cut the apron strings of state companies, Luis Carrión declared that "entrepreneurial decisions cannot be based upon maximizing profits, but must take the interests of society into account, even when they go against the company, especially in the case of essential products" (*Bda* 27 April 1988). In actual practice, however, enterprise decisions were increasingly governed by the

profit motive, leading to behaviour that irritated the government, and in some cases led to a resumption of controls.

6 Thus, for example, the new producer price for coffee was c$1,130, representing a world price of $133 times the c$10:$1 exchange rate, with c$200 deducted for processing costs (*END* 16 April 1988).

7 While some producers would have regularly bought dollars through the 1980s as a store of value, this option was not readily available to all rural producers. In addition, small producers did not have the storage facilities necessary to use their own grain production as a store of value.

8 In a 1986 speech to workers, Ortega had declared that "we will never allow ourselves to influenced by the philosophy of exploitation, by the philosophy of the IMF, which solves economic problems in other places to the detriment of the workers, by putting workers on the street" (1986, 13).

9 As, for example, when Tomás Borge denounced speculation as "counter-revolutionary, because [it] attacks the essence of the revolution" (FBIS 1 March 1988).

10 The various strikes wound down in mid-May, in response to informal promises that salary policy would be adjusted, as occurred in June.

11 There are at least three printed versions of the speech (FBIS 15 June 1988; D. Ortega 1988b, 1988c). Unless otherwise noted, citations are from the last of these three sources, which is the most complete.

12 Emphasis added; this statement was printed in (1988b), but omitted in the (1988c) version.

13 Though there had been repeated declarations of the government's intent to eliminate subsidies on food, these had continually reappeared as the government sought to cushion the political effects of its adjustment policies. Even in March 1988 MIDINRA had announced that consumers would pay only c$4.10 per pound of rice, though producers were receiving c$6 per pound (*Bda* 9 March 1988). Food subsidies finally disappeared in the wake of the June 1988 measures.

14 For the purpose of devaluation, taxed products such as rum, cigarettes and soft drinks would be omitted from the CPI.

15 "*Paquete sin pueblo*" (*Envío*, August 1988).

16 There are indications that the leadership was not entirely clear on the consequences of price liberalization. Ortega commented that "the product must be sold at its real cost. If it is worth 100 then it should be sold for 100, leaving no room for the speculator to move in and make a profit" (FBIS 17 June 1988). But it is only under ideal market conditions that market-clearing prices, those that "leave no room for the speculator," equal cost-plus prices, ones that represent the "real cost" of a product plus a reasonable profit margin. Ortega's comment, and many similar comments made in the following months, indicate that the leadership had not decided what to do about "excessive profits" when it decided to liberalize prices.

17 A phrase which *Barricada* put in quotation marks, perhaps for the first time.

18 "*Arroz, frijol, azúcar*" [Rice, beans, sugar].

19 The "territorial network," however, through which ENABAS had supplied neighbourhoods with basic goods at official prices throughout the 1980s, was formally abolished in November 1988 (López 1989, 81).

20 Aburto (1988) provides an interesting study of various informal sector agents who suffered a sharp drop in real earnings through 1988.

21 The fact that those concerned by government policy used APEN as a vehicle for their complaints indicates the degree to which the FSLN was and was not open to debate on fundamental questions of economic strategy. APEN was a member of CONAPRO-HM, the FSLN's umbrella organization of professionals. One could thus suppose that many of those who participated in drafting the APEN statement were FSLN militants or at least associated with the party. It seems therefore that they were allowed to express their concerns, on the condition that they use a relatively marginal medium such as APEN, which to my knowledge had no previous public participation in policy debates.

22 There were repeated complaints at this time that the government was placing too much emphasis upon restraining demand, and too little upon encouraging supply. Economy Minister Luís Carrión responded that "the government spent eight and a half years dealing only with supply. All our speeches, all our economic actions, were directed towards increasing national production" (1989).

23 In fact the CPI rose "only" 91.8 per cent in January, representing an annual rate of inflation of 247,000 per cent.

24 The 1989 budget provided for a 40 per cent cut in interior ministry spending, and 29 per cent in that of the army (FBIS 3 January 1989).

25 Thus, the December 1989 base salary of central government workers was 76 per cent higher than the previous December, when deflated by the CPI. But December 1988 had been an exceptionally poor month, in which deflated salaries had dropped by more than half. Thus, despite the modest improvement in 1989, the December 1989 real salary was just 27 per cent of the December 1987 level (*Análisis*, January 1990).

26 A leader of the Conservative Party would comment in 1989 that "I think that the Sandinistas are bound to do a better job with the contras in existence than without them" (*NYT* 30 March 1989).

27 The *New York Times* stated that this was the first time the Sandinista government had ever used tear gas against civilians, a remarkable record in Latin America.

28 See, for example, *Le Monde*, 3 April 1981, and Austin and Ickis (1986a, 783). The Pellas family had founded Nicaragua's *Banco de América* in 1952, and had thus led one of the country's main economic groups during the Somoza era (Strachan 1976). A 1980 radio report commented that "during 45 years of

death and destruction, there was only one man whose wealth could be compared to Somoza's money and investments. That man was Alfredo Pellas" (JPRS 75278). In 1979 Humberto Ortega allegedly asked a member of the family to join the government junta (Christian 1985, 156).

29 The mill's administrator responded to the charge of inefficiency by arguing that the mill had received little more than a third of the foreign exchange it required for the year. He also noted that the mill's specialists were "frustrated because the quality of life has been standardized, and they do not enjoy the fringe benefits they did before" (*Bda* 21 April 1987).

30 This is a rather improbable accusation, unless by "contras" Ortega meant the rightist opposition that had traditionally been tacitly allied with the armed contras.

31 Emphasis added. The article on 31 January in the *New York Times* covering the speech omitted this crucial qualifier, the importance of which would become clear in June.

32 As part of the new campaign, the government reached a compensation agreement with the owners of the San Antonio sugar mill, and retroactively exempted the Pellas family's rum company from the expropriation (FBIS 2 February 1989).

33 Whatever the difficulties faced by the state farms, at least part of the National Directorate continued to believe that they represented "the most advanced form of production," as Luís Carrión put it (1989).

34 Of the three key provisions of the pact, two were fulfilled: the Nicaraguan government released 1,900 guardsmen in March (NYT 17 March 1989), and held elections on schedule. Honduras, however, bowed to U.S. pressure and announced, just one month after the El Salvador accords, that it would not expel the contras (NYT 14 March 1989; 23 March 1989).

35 In December 1987, Ortega declared that "in the hypothetical case that we should lose elections, we would hand over the government, but not power," just as, he argued, the "capitalist class [in Chile] never gave power to Allende, only the government." Ortega went on, "All Latin American governments must very much take into account the armed forces as part of the power reality that exists in each country" (*Bda* 14–15 December 1987).

In January 1988, the *New York Times* reported that Ortega had written a letter to Reagan promising to give up power if he lost the elections. On the same day the letter was made public, however, Bayardo Arce told a Managua rally that the FSLN would never give up power, because it could not "usurp the right of the people" (NYT 25 January 1988).

After the 1989 El Salvador accords, however, there was no hint from the FSLN leadership that executive and legislative power was not at stake in the upcoming elections. Tomás Borge commented in June that "there will be no alternative to accepting the results" should the FSLN lose. The only alternative, he said, would be a military coup, which would inevitably lead to a u.s. invasion (FBIS 1 June 1989). In any case, Borge added, the FSLN "cannot conceive of the possibility of defeat."

36 There were thought to be some twenty-five opposition parties and "splinter groups of parties" in existence in early 1989 (*Bda Internacional*, English ed., 25 March 1989).

37 Most notable in this tendency were the Popular Social Christian Party, and factions of the Conservative and Independent Liberal parties.

38 Key elements in this tendency were COSEP, *La Prensa*, and various rightist parties and fractions thereof. This group would be represented on the eventual opposition ticket by Virgilio Godoy, who had run for president in the 1984 election, only to withdraw at the last minute, after the ballots had been printed.

39 As an added inducement to return, the u.s. government halved the living stipends of contra leaders in Miami in March, and in July eliminated funding for the contras' Miami office altogether (*NYT* 29 March 1989; 17 July 1989).

40 The central representative of this tendency was Alfredo César, who had participated in the drafting of the 1979 junta's Program of Government, and had served as Central Bank head before abandoning the government in 1982. In November 1989, Violeta Chamorro appointed César her main campaign advisor, just days after the opposition coalition had thrown him off its campaign committee (FBIS 24 November 1989).

41 Thus, the UNO program promised to respect the property of peasants, including that which had been granted through the agrarian reform. But it also held that all land expropriations since 1979 would be subject to review, with the exception of the land expropriated from the Somozas by Decree 3.

42 The opposition, Arce generously admitted, played an important role, allowing the FSLN to know "the opinion of the bourgeoisie, the petite bourgeoisie, etc."

43 Sofía Montenegro, a *Barricada* editor, wrote: "Why don't they follow the example of the government ministries and consolidate themselves as a first big step in the struggle against the disorder and chaos prevailing among their ranks?" This would save the opposition money and eliminate the need for external U.S. funding, Montenegro went on, "besides being proof of the opposition's political willingness to seek a way out of the problems that are besieging us and giving them back a certain credibility, even with the government" (*Bda Internacional*, English ed., 25 March 1989).

44 In total, the United States was to commit at least $17.5 million to UNO. It was reported in October that "so far this year Washington has given opposition groups $3.5 million in overt aid, and intelligence sources say the CIA has covertly provided $5 million for opposition 'housekeeping' costs" (Watson 1989). Later in October, the u.s. Congress agreed to send an additional $9 million (*NYT* 18 October 1989).

45 Eventually, the Social Christian parties would leave UNO and form an alliance. Despite the active support of Edén Pastora, who returned to Nicaragua in December, the Social Christians won a negligible portion of the vote (FBIS 29 September 1989; NYT 4 December 1989).

46 Former COSEP head Bolaños claimed that UNO had rejected him as its presidential candidate because it had been infiltrated by the FSLN. "Within UNO," Bolaños claimed, "there are people who are opposition during the day and then at night they sleep with the Sandinista Front" (FBIS 25 September 1989).

47 In the wake of the invasion, the Ministry of Defence issued a bulletin promising to "carry out plans for the neutralization, trial and execution of all the most recalcitrant, traitorous elements that openly or covertly have incited the Yankee intervention," in the event of a U.S. invasion of Nicaragua (NYT 28 December 1989).

48 Indeed, reliable polls confirmed the FSLN in this expectation.

49 See, e.g., FBIS 2 May 1989, 4 May 1989, 28 September 1989; Ramírez (1991).

50 The National Directorate's report to the FSLN party congress in 1991 admitted that "our ability to communicate with important sectors of the population declined over the years" (Dirección Nacional 1991, 27).

CHAPTER EIGHT

1 These limits would vary product by product, depending, for example, upon the structure of production. Thus, from the outset the Sandinistas had more room to manoeuvre with industrial goods than with peasant grains, given the dispersed production of the latter. By the late 1980s, however, even state industrial firms had ceased to respect the norms of the state economy.

2 Among other perceived errors, the directorate also expressed regret over the early monopolization of material and human resources by the state farms, expropriations of some "medium-scale producers of peasant origin and of efficient producers," and the "imposing style that characterized our political and administrative behaviour, which was resented by the peasantry" (Dirección Nacional 1991, 19). Controls on rural trade, military service, and declining urban-rural terms of trade were also noted by the directorate, though not explicitly acknowledged as errors (20).

Works Cited

Some Spanish language publishers use "edition" numbers to refer to printings. In such cases, only those "editions" that are explicitly identified as having been revised are counted as new editions for purposes of giving the publication date.

Some frequently cited newspapers have been given abbreviated citations in the text. The following abbreviations have been used:

Bda: *Barricada (Managua)*
END: *El Nuevo Diario (Managua)*
NYT: *New York Times*
Psa: *La Prensa (Managua)*

Aburto, Róger. 1988. Impacto de la reforma económica en el sector informal urbano. *Boletín Socioeconómico* (Managua), no. 9 (September–October): 31–43.

Acevedo Volg, Adolfo José. 1989. 1988: del shock "heterodoxo" de febrero al super "ortodoxo" de junio. *Boletín Socioeconómico* (Managua), no. 11 (January–February): 18–31.

Alaniz Pinell, Jorge. 1985. *Nicaragua: Una revolución reaccionaria.* Mexico City: Kosmos.

Alemán Ocampo, Carlos. 1985. ...*y se hizo la presa.* Managua: MIDINRA.

Allison, Graham. 1971. *Essence of decision.* Boston: Little, Brown and Co.

Althusser, Louis. 1971. Ideology and ideological state apparatuses. In *Lenin and philosophy,* trans. Ben Brewster. New York: Monthly Review Press.

Amin, Samir. 1974. *Accumulation on a world scale.* New York: Monthly Review Press.

Análisis (Managua).

APEN (Asociación de Profesionales de la Economía). 1989. Evaluación de las políticas de 1988 y propuesta para 1989. *Revolución y Desarrollo* (Managua), no. 4 (January-March): 65–74.

Arana, Mario. 1988. Reforma económica 1988: Notas comparativas con los paquetes de "choque heterodóxo." *Boletín Socioeconómico* (Managua), no. 7 (May): 17–21.

– 1990. Nicaragua: estabilización, ajuste y estrategia económica, 1988–1989. In *Políticas de ajuste en Nicaragua: Reflexiones sobre sus implicaciones estratégicas.* Managua: CRIES.

Arana, Mario, Richard Stahler-Shock, Gerardo Timossi, and Carmen López. 1987. *Deuda, estabilización y ajuste: La transformación en Nicaragua, 1979–1986.* Managua: CRIES.

Arce, Bayardo. 1980. *El papel de las fuerzas motrices antes y después del triunfo.* Managua: Secretaría Nacional de Propaganda y Educación Política del FSLN.

– 1981a. Estamos en pie de lucha y confiamos en la solidaridad internacional. *Barricada,* 28 January.

– 1981b. La defensa: no solo con las armas sino con el trabajo. *Barricada,* 25 January.

– 1985. *Sandinismo y política imperialista.* Managua: Editorial Nueva Nicaragua.

– 1986. La cara de Carlos, la cara de Sandino. *Nicaráuac* (Managua), no. 13 (December): 39–48.

Argüello, A., E. Croes, and N. Kleiterp. 1987. *Nicaragua: Acumulación y transformación.* Managua: SPP.

Arias, Pilar. 1980. *Nicaragua: Revolución.* Mexico City: Siglo XXI.

Asamblea Nacional de Sindicatos. 1985. Acuerdos del segundo balance. Managua: Mimeographed.

Aslund, Anders. 1989. *Gorbachev's struggle for economic reform.* London: Pinter Publishers.

Austin, James E., and John C. Ickis. 1986a. Management, managers, and revolution. *World Development* 14: 775–90.

– 1986b. Managing after the revolutionaries have won. *Harvard Business Review,* no. 64 (May–June): 103–9.

Avilés, Isabel Cristina, and Ana Lissette Amaya. 1987. Problemas en la política de precios: El caso de las empresas de tejido plano. Honours thesis, Universidad Nacional Autónoma de Nicaragua (Managua).

Barraclough, Solon. 1984. *Un análisis preliminar del sistema alimentario en Nicaragua.* Gineva: UNRISD.

Barrett, Michele. 1980. *Women's oppression today.* London: Verso.

Barricada Internacional (Managua).

Baumeister, Eduardo. 1989. El problema agrario y los sujetos del desarrollo nicaragüense. In *El debate sobre la reforma agraria en Nicaragua,* ed. Raúl Ruben and J.P. De Groot. Managua: Editorial Ciencias Sociales.

Baumeister, Eduardo, and Oscar Neira. 1986. La conformación de una economía mixta: Estructura de clases y política estatal en la transición nicaragüense. In *La transición difícil: La autodeterminación de los pequeños países periféricos*, ed. José Luis Corragio and Carmen Diana Deere. Mexico City: Siglo XXI.

BCN (Banco Central de Nicaragua). 1970–8. *Informe anual.* 9 vols. Managua: BCN.

– 1979. *Indicadores económicos.* Managua: BCN.

Belausteguigoitia, Ramón de. 1985. *Con Sandino en Nicaragua.* 2d ed. Managua: Editorial Nueva Nicaragua.

Belli, Humberto. 1982. Interview. *National Catholic Register* (28 November).

Bendaña, Alejandro. 1991. Many lessons to learn from Nicaragua. *The New African* (Johannesburg, South Africa). 27 June.

Berger, Peter L., and Thomas Luckmann. 1967. *The social construction of reality.* Garden City: Doubleday.

Bernales Alvarado, Manuel. 1985. La transformación del estado: problemas y perspectivas. In *La revolución en Nicaragua*, ed. Richard Harris and Carlos Vilas. Mexico City: Ediciones Era.

Biderman, Jaime. 1983. The development of capitalism in Nicaragua: A political economic history. *Latin American Perspectives* 10, no. 1: 7–32.

Biondi-Morra, Brizio Nico. 1988. Managing food policy implementation in developing countries: The case of the Nicaraguan state-owned agrobusiness enterprises. PH.D. dissertation, Harvard University.

Bloch, Marc. 1989. *La société féodale.* Paris: Albin Michel.

Bolaños, Enrique. 1984. *Linea directa.* Managua: COSEP.

Booth, John A. 1985. *The end and the beginning.* 2d ed. Boulder: Westview Press.

Borge, Tomás. 1979. Interview by Daniel Waksman Schinca. In *La batalla de Nicaragua*, ed. Gabriel García Márquez, G. Selser, and D. Waksman. Mexico City: Bruguera Mexicana de Ediciones.

– 1980a. *Nuestros niños lo van a entender.* Managua: Secretaría Nacional de Propaganda y Educación Política del FSLN.

– 1980b. Borge on threats to revolution, third world unity. JPRS 76513.

– 1981a. Debemos ir a las masas. *Barricada*, 20 July.

– 1981b. Minister of Interior discusses foreign relations, revolutionary process. JPRS 78200.

– 1982. Carlos es el tejedor de nuestros sueños. In *Carlos Fonseca siempre.* Managua: Departamento de Propaganda y Educación Política del FSLN.

– 1984a. *El axioma de la esperanza.* Bilbao: Desclée de Brouwer.

– 1984b. Interview by Iosu Perales. In *Nicaragua: Valientamente libre.* Madrid: Editorial Revolución.

– 1984c. [Letter to the National Directorate]. Managua: Mimeographed.

– 1985a. The new education in the new Nicaragua. In *Nicaragua: The Sandinista people's revolution*, ed. Bruce Marcus. New York: Pathfinder Press.

– 1985b. The organized people are the backbone of the Sandinista police. In *Nicaragua: The Sandinista people's revolution*, ed. Bruce Marcus. New York: Pathfinder Press.

– 1985c. This is a revolution of working people. In *Nicaragua: The Sandinista people's revolution*, ed. Bruce Marcus. New York: Pathfinder Press.

– 1985d. This revolution was made to create a new society. In *Nicaragua: The Sandinista people's revolution*, ed. Bruce Marcus. New York: Pathfinder Press.

– 1985e. El nuestro es un proyecto enredado. *Pensamiento Propio*, no. 24 (June–July): 7–15.

– 1987. Tomás Borge on the Nicaraguan revolution. Interview by Fredric Jameson. *New Left Review*, no. 164 (July–August): 53–64.

– 1989a. *La paciente impaciencia*. Managua: Editorial Vanguardia.

– 1989b. Overcoming years of distrust: The challenge of *concertación*. *Barricada Internacional* (English ed.), 25 March.

Braybrooke, David. 1967. Ideology. In *The encyclopedia of philosophy*, 8 vols., ed. Paul Edwards. N.Y.: Macmillan & Free Press.

Brundenius, Claes. 1985. *Estrategia del desarrollo industrial en Nicaragua, 1979–1984*. Managua: CRIES.

Brus, Wlodzimierz. 1972. *The market in a socialist economy*. London: Routledge.

Brus, Wlodzimierz, and Kazimierz Laski. 1989. *From Marx to the market: Socialism in search of an economic system*. Oxford: Clarendon.

Bukharin, N.I. 1982. A new revelation concerning the Soviet economy or how to destroy the worker-peasant bloc (on the question of the economic basis of Trotskyism). In *Selected writings on the state and the transition to socialism*, trans. Richard B. Day. Armonk, New York: M.E. Sharpe.

Bulmer-Thomas, Victor. 1987. *The political economy of Central America since 1920*. Cambridge: Cambridge University Press.

Cabezas, Omar. 1982. *La montaña es algo más que una inmensa estepa verde*. 2d ed. Managua: Editorial Nueva Nicaragua.

Cabieses, Hugo. 1986. *Economía y política económica en Nicaragua, 1979–1985*. Managua: Mimeographed.

Cabrales, Ramón. 1985a. Garantizar abastecimiento y frenar especulación. *Barricada*, 8 February.

– 1985b. [Speech to CONAPRO-HM]. Managua: author's notes, 27 July.

– 1985c. [Speech to MICOIN congress on distribution]. El Crucero: author's notes, 19 October.

– 1987. El abastecimiento en ocho años de revolución. *Revista Nicaragüense de Ciencias Sociales*, no. 3 (December): 41–7.

Carl, Beverly May. 1984. How Marxist is Nicaragua? A look at the laws. *Crime and Social Justice*, nos. 21–2: 116–27.

Carr, E.H. 1958. *Socialism in one country, 1924–1926*. New York: Macmillan.

– 1960. *The Interregnum, 1923–1924*. London: Macmillan.

– 1966. *The Bolshevik revolution, 1917–1923*, vol. 2. Harmondsworth: Penguin.

Carrión, Luis. 1986. Ser patriota, no es 'quedarse', sino trabajar para el pueblo. In *La Dirección Nacional y la organización campesina*. Managua: Ediciones Tierra Arada.

– 1989. Consolidating the mixed economy. *Barricada Internacional*, 25 February.

CEPAL (Comisión Económica para América Latina). 1983. Tablas de insumo-producto en América Latina. Santiago: CEPAL.

– 1985. *Balance preliminar de la economía latinoamericana*. Santiago: CEPAL.

Christian, Shirley. 1985. *Nicaragua: Revolution in the family*. New York: Random House.

CIERA (Centro de Investigaciones y Estudios de la Reforma Agraria). 1983a. Agrarian reform in Nicaragua: The first three years. *International Journal of Sociology* 13, no. 2: 3–91.

– 1983b. *Distribución y consumo popular de alimentos en Managua*. Managua: CIERA.

– 1984. *El funcionamiento del sistema alimentario*. Managua: CIERA.

Colburn, Forrest D. 1984. Class, state, and revolution in rural Nicaragua: The case of *los cafetaleros*. *The Journal of Developing Areas* 18 (July): 501–18.

– 1986. *Post-revolutionary Nicaragua: State, class and the dilemmas of agrarian policy*. Berkeley: University of California Press.

– 1989. Foot dragging and other peasant responses to the Nicaraguan Revolution. In *Everyday forms of peasant resistance*, ed. Forrest D. Colburn. London: M.E. Sharpe.

– 1990. *Managing the commanding heights: Nicaragua's state enterprises*. Berkeley: University of California Press.

Collins, Joseph. 1982. *What difference could a revolution make?* San Francisco: Institute for Food and Development Policy.

Collinson, Helen, ed. 1990. *Women and revolution in Nicaragua*. London: Zed Press.

Conferencia Episcopal de Nicaragua. 1981. Compromiso cristiano para una Nicaragua nueva. In *Nicaragua: la hora de los desafíos*, ed. Ana Gispert-Sauch. Lima: Centro de Estudios y Publicaciones.

Coordinadora Sindical. 1985. [Statement on the 1985 economic plan]. Managua: Mimeographed.

COSEP (Consejo Superior de la Empresa Privada). 1987. Analysis of the government's performance (November 1980). In *The Central American crisis reader*, ed. Robert Leiken and Barry Rubin. New York: Summit Books.

Cruz, Arturo J. Sr. 1987. Leninism in Nicaragua. In *Conflict in Nicaragua: A multidimensional perspective*, ed. Jiri Valenta and Esperanza Durán. Boston: Allen and Unwin.

Cruz, Arturo Jr. 1989. *Memoirs of a counter-revolutionary*. New York: Doubleday.

Cuadra, Joaquín. 1985. Las nuevas medidas en política cambiaria y crediticia. *Barricada*, 8 February.

Debray, Régis. 1968. *Revolution in the revolution?* Trans. Bobbye Ortiz. Harmondsworth: Penguin.

Deere, Carmen Diana, and Peter Marchetti. 1981. The worker-peasant alliance in the first year of the Nicaraguan agrarian reform. *Latin American Perspectives* 8, no. 2: 40–73.

Desai, Padma. 1989. *Perestroika in perspective: The design and dilemmas of Soviet reform.* Princeton: Princeton University Press.

Deutscher, Isaac. 1966. *Stalin.* Rev. ed. Harmondsworth: Penguin Books.

Díaz, Rosendo. 1985. Las relaciones han mejorado pero ... *Pensamiento Propio,* no. 24 (June–July).

Dijkstra, Geske. 1987. *La industria en la economía mixta de Nicaragua.* Managua: CRIES.

Dirección Nacional del Frente Sandinista de Liberación Nacional. 1985a. Conquistamos la luz y vamos a defenderla con sangre, sudor y confianza en el futuro. *Barricada,* 8 February.

– 1985b. Orientaciones para 1986. Managua: Mimeographed.

– 1991. Informe central. Managua: n.p.

Dirección Nacional y Asamblea Sandinista del Frente Sandinista de Liberación Nacional. 1986. Producción y abastecimiento. Managua: Mimeographed.

Dougherty, Margot. 1983. Living on the edge: In Communist Nicaragua, a fearful upper class hangs on. *Life* (September).

Downs, Anthony. 1957. *An economic theory of democracy.* New York: Harper and Row.

Draper, Hal. 1978. *Karl Marx's theory of revolution,* vol. 2. New York: Monthly Review Press.

ECLA (United Nations Economic Commission for Latin America). 1979. *Nicaragua: Economic repercussions of recent political events.* Santiago: ECLA.

– 1979–1982. *Economic survey of Latin America.* Santiago: ECLA.

ECLAC (United Nations Economic Commission for Latin America and the Caribbean). 1983–1988. *Economic survey of Latin America and the Caribbean.* Santiago: ECLAC.

– 1990. *Preliminary overview of the economy of Latin America and the Caribbean, 1990.* Santiago: ECLAC.

Economía Política. 1982. Moscow: Editorial Progreso.

Elizondo, Ligia. 1990. 1990: un reto para productores y empresarios. *Análisis* (Managua), no. 5 (January): 19–22.

Ellman, Michael. 1979. *Socialist planning.* Cambridge: Cambridge University Press.

Enriquez, Laura, and Rose Spalding. 1987. Banking systems and revolutionary change: The politics of agricultural credit in Nicaragua. In *The political economy of revolutionary Nicaragua,* ed. Rose J. Spalding. Boston: Allen & Unwin.

Envío (Managua).

Facts on File. 1975. *Latin America, 1974.* New York: Facts on File.

FBIS (Foreign Broadcast Information Service). *Daily report: Latin America.*

Figueroa, Luis Enrique. 1983. [Report to the Council of State]. Author's notes.

FIR (Fondo Internacional para la Recontrucción). 1982. The economic policy of the Government of National Reconstruction towards the private sector. Managua: FIR.

First FSLN congress set to begin. 1991. *Weekly News Update on Nicaragua and the Americas*, no. 76 (14 July).

Fitzgerald, E.V.K. 1985a. Agrarian reform as a model of accumulation: The case of Nicaragua since 1979. *The Journal of Development Studies* 22, no. 1: 208–26.

– 1985b. Una evaluación del costo económico de la agresión del gobierno estadounidense contra el pueblo de Nicaragua. Paper presented at the Congress of the Latin American Studies Association, Albuquerque, New Mexico, April.

– 1989. Estado y economía en Nicaragua. In *El debate sobre la reforma agraria en Nicaragua*, ed. Raúl Ruben and J.P. De Groot. Managua: Editorial Ciencias Sociales.

Fonseca, Carlos. 1985. *Obras*. 3d ed. 2 vols. Managua: Editorial Nueva Nicaragua.

Frenkel, María Verónica. 1987. The evolution of food and agricultural policies during economic crisis and war. In *Nicaragua: Profiles of the revolutionary public sector*, ed. Michael E. Conroy. Boulder: Westview Press.

FSLN. 1981. Programa histórico del FSLN. Managua: DEPEP.

– 1985. Plan of struggle. In *Nicaragua: The Sandinista people's revolution*, ed. Bruce Marcus. New York: Pathfinder Press.

– 1987. Seventy-two hours document. In *The Central American crisis reader*, ed. Robert Leiken and Barry Rubin. New York: Summit Books.

[FSLN – Insurrectional tendency]. 1979a. In *Los sandinistas*, ed. Gabriel García Márquez. Bogotá: Editorial La Oveja Negra.

– 1979b. La situación general del FSLN. In *Los sandinistas*, ed. Gabriel García Márquez. Bogotá: Editorial La Oveja Negra.

[FSLN – Proletarian Tendency]. 1979. No al diálogo burgués, derrocar a la dictadura es la tarea. In *Los sandinistas*, ed. Gabriel García Márquez. Bogotá: Editorial La Oveja Negra.

– 1987. The internal crisis. In *The Central American crisis reader*, ed. Robert Leiken and Barry Rubin. New York: Summit Books.

Galeano, Eduardo. 1980. *Las venas abiertas de América Latina*. 3d ed. Mexico City: Siglo XXI.

Gibson, Bill. 1986. (de)Stabilization policy in Nicaragua. Burlington: Mimeographed.

Gilbert, Dennis. 1990. *Sandinistas*. Cambridge: Basil Blackwell.

Gispert-Sauch, Ana, ed. 1981. *Nicaragua: la hora de los desafíos*. Lima: Centro de Estudios y Publicaciones.

Goldman, Josef. 1964. Fluctuations and trend in the rate of economic growth in some socialist countries. *Economics of Planning* 4, no. 2: 88–98.

Gorostiaga, Xabier. 1986. Economía mixta y revolución sandinista. In *La economía mixta en Nicaragua: Proyecto o realidad*, ed. María Hurtado de Vigil. Managua: CINASE.

Gouldner, Alvin. 1973. *For sociology: Renewal and critique in sociology today.* New York: Basic Books.

[Governments of Central America]. 1962. *Convenio centroamericano de incentivos fiscales al desarrollo industrial.* Guatemala: SIECA.

Graham, Lawrence. 1987. The impact of the revolution on the state apparatus. In *Nicaragua: Profiles of the revolutionary public sector*, ed. Michael E. Conroy. Boulder: Westview Press.

Gramsci, Antonio. 1971. *Selections from the prison notebooks.* Trans. Quinton Hoare and Geoffrey Nowell Smith. New York: International Publishers.

Grayson, George W. 1985. Soviets aid with oil supplies. *Petroleum economist* 52 (July): 251–3.

Griffith-Jones, Stephany. 1981. *The role of finance in the transition to socialism.* London: Frances Pinter.

– 1983. El papel de la política financiera en la transición al socialismo. *Comercio Exterior* (Mexico) 33, no. 7: 591–6.

Guadamuz, Carlos José. 1982. *Y ... "las casas quedaron llenas de humo."* Managua: Editorial Nueva Nicaragua.

Guevara, Ernesto. 1985. *Obras escogidas, 1957–1967.* 2 vols. Havana: Editorial de Ciencias Sociales

Gutiérrez, Ivan. 1989. La política de tierras de la reforma agraria sandinista. In *El debate sobre la reforma agraria en Nicaragua*, ed. Raúl Ruben and J.P. De Groot. Managua: Editorial Ciencias Sociales.

Gutiérrez, Roberto. 1989. La política económica de la revolución. *Revolución y Desarrollo* (Managua), no. 5 (April-June): 37–61.

Gutman, Roy. 1988. *Banana diplomacy.* New York: Simon and Schuster.

Habla el Frente Sandinista: Cada día somos más fuertes. 1979. In *Los sandinistas*, ed. Gabriel García Márquez. Bogotá: Editorial La Oveja Negra.

Hewett, Ed. 1988. *Reforming the Soviet economy.* Washington: The Brookings Institution.

Hodges, Donald C. 1986. *Intellectual foundations of the Nicaraguan revolution.* Austin: University of Texas Press.

Hodgson, Geoffrey M. 1988. *Economics and institutions.* Cambridge: Polity Press.

Hüpper, William. 1985. Racionalizar el gasto en función de la defensa. *Barricada*, 8 February.

– 1987. Informe: Valoración [de las] medidas iniciadas en 1985 [y de la] situación actual, y propuestas. Managua: Mimeographed.

Iglesias, Enrique. 1983. La evolución económica de América Latina en 1982. *Comercio Exterior* (Mexico) 33 (February): 162–85.

IMF (International Monetary Fund). 1955–78. *Balance of payments yearbook.* Vols. 13 and 29. Washington: IMF.

INEC (Instituto Nacional de Estadísticas y Censos). 1980–1987. *Indice de precios al consumidor.* Managua: INEC.

– 1984. *Anuario estadístico de Nicaragua, 1984.* Managua: INEC.

– 1986. *Nicaragua en cifras, 1985.* Managua: INEC.

INIES (Instituto Nicaragüense de Investigaciones Económicas y Sociales). 1987. *Plan económico 1987.* Managua: INIES.

JGRN (Junta de Gobierno de Reconstrucción Nacional). 1979–88. *Decretos-leyes para gobierno de un país.* 15 vols. Ed. Rolando Lacayo and Martha Lacayo de Arauz. Managua: Editorial Unión.

– 1980. Programa de gobierno. *Encuentro* (Managua), no. 17: 31–46.

Johnston, B.F., and P. Kilby. 1975. *Agriculture and structural transformation.* New York: Oxford University Press.

JPRS (Joint Publications Research Service). *Latin America Report.*

Kaimowitz, David. 1989. La planificación agropecuaria en Nicaragua: De un proceso de acumulación basado en el estado a la alianza estratégica con el campesinado. In *El debate sobre la reforma agraria en Nicaragua,* ed. Raúl Ruben and J.P. De Groot. Managua: Editorial Ciencias Sociales.

Kaimowitz, David, and Joseph R. Thome. 1982. Nicaragua's agrarian reform: The first year. In *Nicaragua in revolution,* ed. Thomas Walker. New York: Praeger.

Kaser, Michael, and Janusz Zielinsky. 1970. *Planning in East Europe: industrial management by the state.* London: Bodley Head.

Keesing's Contemporary Archives.

Kleiterp, Nanno. 1989. El model de acumulación: un problema de balances. In *El debate sobre la reforma agraria en Nicaragua,* ed. Raúl Ruben and J.P. De Groot. Managua: Editorial Ciencias Sociales.

Kornai, Janos. 1971. Pressure and suction on the market. Working paper, International Development Research Center, Bloomington.

– 1990. *The road to a free economy.* New York: W.W. Norton.

Kuhn, Thomas. 1970. *The structure of scientific revolutions.* 2d ed. Chicago: University of Chicago Press.

Lang, Edgard. 1979. [Parting letter to his parents]. Lima: n.p.

Lange, Oscar. 1965. Political economy of socialism. In *Problems of political economy of socialism,* ed. Oscar Lange. 2d Indian edition. New Delhi: People's Publishing House.

Lenin, V.I. 1968. *Lenin on politics and revolution.* Ed. James E. Conner. Indianapolis: Bobbs-Merrill.

– 1969. *On religion.* 3d ed. Moscow: Progress Publishers.

– 1971. *Speeches at party congresses, 1918–1922.* Moscow: Progress Publishers.

Liebenstein, H. 1966. Allocative efficiency versus X-efficiency. *American Economic Review* 56, no. 3 (June): 392–415.

López, Carmen. 1989. Cronología de la política económica de Nicaragua. In *La política económica en Nicaragua, 1979–1988*. Managua: CRIES.

Luciak, Ilja. 1987. National unity and popular hegemony: The dialectics of Sandinista agrarian reform. *Journal of Latin American Studies* 19: 113–40.

Lukacs, Georg. 1971. *History and class consciousness*. Trans. Rodney Livingstone. London: Merlin Press.

Machiavelli, Niccolo. 1950. *The prince and the discourses*. Trans. Luigi Ricci. New York: Modern Library.

Mandel, Ernest. 1968. *Marxist economic theory*. Trans. Brian Pearce. London: Merlin Press.

Marchetti, Peter. 1982. Interview. *Working Papers* (March-April): 46–55.

Marenco, Dionisio. 1984. A enfrentar los problemas del abastecimiento. *Barricada*, 2 June.

Martínez Cuenca, Alejandro. 1990. *Nicaragua: Una década de retos*. Interview by Roberto Pizarro. Managua: Editorial Nueva Nicaragua.

Marx, Karl. 1954–9. *Capital*. 3 vols. Moscow: Progress Publishers.

– 1964. *Early writings*. Trans. T.B. Bottomore. New York: McGraw-Hill.

– 1973. *Grundrisse*. Trans. Martin Nicolaus. Harmondsworth: Penguin.

Marx, Karl, and F. Engels. 1969. *Selected works*. 3 vols. Moscow: Progress Publishers.

– 1942. *Selected Correspondence, 1846–1895*. Trans. Dona Torr. New York: International Publishers.

Maxfield, Sylvia and Richard Stahler-Sholk. 1985. External constraints. In *Nicaragua: The first five years*, ed. Thomas Walker. New York: Praeger.

Mayorga, Fransisco José. 1986. The Nicaraguan economic experience, 1950–1984: Development and exhaustion of an agroindustrial model. PH.D. dissertation, Yale University.

Medal, José Luís. 1985. *La revolución Nicaragüense: Balance económico y alternativas futuras*. Managua: Ediciones Nicaragua Hoy.

Meneses, Benedicto. 1985. Vincular salario y trabajo. *Barricada*, 8 February.

MIDINRA (Ministerio de Desarrollo Agropecuario y Reforma Agraria). 1984. *Informe de la gestión estatal de MIDINRA para la JGRN, 1979–84*. Managua: MIDINRA.

– 1986. *Plan de trabajo: Balance y perspectivas, 1986*. Managua: MIDINRA.

MIPLAN (Ministerio de Planificación). 1980. *Programa de reactivación económica en beneficio del pueblo*. Managua: MIPLAN.

– 1981a. *Programa económica de austeridad y eficiencia*. Managua: MIPLAN.

– 1981b. Conclusiones y recomendaciones del II seminario de MIPLAN. Managua: Mimeographed.

– 1983. Programa económico 1983. Managua: Mimeographed.

– 1984a. Programa económico 1984. Managua: Mimeographed.

– 1984b. Programa economica 1985: Cifras directivas. Managua: Mimeographed.

MIPLAN and MITRAB (Ministry of Labour). 1984. Organización del salario: Bases metodológicas. Managua: Mimeographed.

Le Monde (Paris).

Morales Avilés, Ricardo. 1983. *Obras.* Managua: Editorial Nueva Nicaragua.

Moser, Caroline. 1991. Gender planning in the Third World: Meeting practical and strategic needs. In *Gender and international relations*, ed. Rebecca Grant and Kathleen Newland. Bloomington: Indiana University Press.

La Nación (San José).

Nichols, John Spicer. 1982. The news media in the Nicaraguan revolution. In *Nicaragua in revolution*, ed. Thomas Walker. New York: Praeger.

– 1988. *La Prensa*: the CIA connection. *Columbia Journalism Review* (July–August): 34–5.

Nolan, David. 1984. *The ideology of the Sandinistas and the Nicaraguan revolution.* Coral Gables, Florida: Institute of Interamerican Studies.

Nordlinger, Eric. 1977. *Soldiers in politics.* Englewood Cliffs: Prentice-Hall.

Norsworthy, Kent, and Bill Robinson. 1990. Letter to the Editor. *NACLA Report on the Americas* 24, no. 2 (August): 2–3.

Nove, Alec. 1969. *An economic history of the U.S.S.R.* London: Allen Lane.

Núñez, Carlos. 1981. La unidad es imprescindible para perpetuar la victoria. *Barricada*, 14 June.

Núñez, Carlos, Joaquín Cuadra, and William Ramírez. 1985. Nicaragua: donde se aprendió luchando. In *Pueblos en armas*, ed. Marta Harnacker. Managua: Editorial Nueva Nicaragua.

Núñez, Daniel. 1985. If the peasantry did not trust the revolution, we would be through. In *Nicaragua: The Sandinista people's revolution*, ed. Bruce Marcus. New York: Pathfinder Press.

O'Brien, Conor Cruise. 1986. God and man in Nicaragua. *Atlantic* (August), 50–72.

OAS (Organization of American States). 1987. Report on human rights. In *The Central American crisis reader*, ed. Robert Leiken and Barry Rubin. New York: Summit Books.

OEDEC (Oficina Ejecutiva de Encuestas y Censos). 1977. *Anuario estadístico, 1977.* Managua: OEDEC.

Ortega, Daniel. 1981. Establecidas las reglas del juego. *Barricada*, 20 July.

– 1985. The Sandinista people's revolution is an irreversible political reality. In *Nicaragua: The Sandinista people's revolution*, ed. Bruce Marcus. New York: Pathfinder Press.

– 1986. *Con trabajadores de COMPANIC.* Managua: Dirección de Información y Prensa de la Presidencia de la República.

– 1987a. *El sandinismo: El más alto grado de organización del pueblo.* Managua: Editorial Nueva Nicaragua.

– 1987b. Interview with *El Nuevo Diario*, October 24–7.

– 1988a. Un paso al frente para defender la economía. *Barricada*, 15 February.

– 1988b. Defender la economía es defender el poder. *Barricada*, 15 June.
– 1988c. La primera demanda: Defender el poder. *Barricada*, 17 June.
– 1988d. *Combatiendo por la paz.* Mexico City: Siglo XXI.
– 1989a. Ortega discusses foreign, domestic issues. Interview with Carlos Fernando Chamorro. FBIS, 6 January.
– 1989b. Esfuerzo nacional por la paz y la reconstrucción. *Barricada*, 31 January.
– 1989c. More on U.S. relations, economy. Interview with Pilmeno Ibarra. FBIS, 13 February.
– 1989d. Ortega addresses teachers at Olaf Palme. FBIS, 5 June.
– 1990. Ortega opens sixth session of National Assembly. FBIS, 24 January.
Ortega, Daniel, et al. 1987a. De Cara al Pueblo. Managua: author's notes (29 January).
– 1987b. De Cara al Pueblo. Managua: author's notes (7 April).
Ortega, Humberto. 1979. *50 años de lucha sandinista.* Managua: Ministerio del Interior.
– 1980. Aplastar la contrarrevolución. *Barricada*, 24 August.
– 1981. *Sobre la insurrección.* Havana: Editorial de Ciencias Sociales.
– 1985. Nos tiene sin cuidado la política estúpida de Reagan. Interview with Joanne Omang. *Barricada*, 10 October.
[–] 1987. General political-military platform of the FSLN for the triumph of the popular Sandinista revolution (May 1977). In *Conflict in Nicaragua: A multidimensional perspective*, ed. Jiri Valenta and Esperanza Durán. Boston: Allen and Unwin.
– 1991. Es más difícil ser revolucionario en las actuales circunstancias. *N.Y. Transfer News Service*, 7 August.
Ortega, Humberto, Jaime Wheelock, and Bayardo Arce. 1986. *Sandinistas.* Interviews with Gabriele Invernizzi, Francis Pisani, and Jesús Ceberio. Managua: Editorial Vanguardia.
Ortega, Marvin. 1985. Tierra y lucha de clases. Paper presented to the Fourth Congress of the Asociación Nicaragüense de Científicos Sociales, Managua.
– 1986. La reforma agraria sandinista. *Nueva Sociedad* (Caracas), no. 83 (May-June): 17–23.
– 1989. Las cooperativas Sandinistas: Entre la democracia y el verticalismo. In *El debate sobre la reforma agraria en Nicaragua*, ed. Raúl Ruben and J.P. De Groot. Managua: Editorial Ciencias Sociales.
Pensamiento Propio (Managua).
Pérez, Daniel, and J. Antonio Somarriba. 1989. Impacto de la reforma económica en la fuerza de trabajo. *Boletín Socioeconómico* (Managua), no. 11 (January-February): 10–17.
Petras, James. 1979. Whither the Nicaraguan revolution? *Monthly Review* 31, no. 5 (October): 1–22.
Pilarte, René. 1988. Reforma económica: Hacia nuevas contradicciones. *Boletín Socioeconómico* (Managua), no. 9 (September-October): 3–12.

Pilarte, René, Vilma Ubau, and Elías Guevara. 1988. Medidas económicas y reforma monetaria: Tácticas por la sobrevivencia. *Boletín Socioeconómico* (Managua), no. 7 (May): 22–5.

Pizarro, Roberto. 1987. Situación del comercio exterior de Nicaragua. Managua: Mimeographed.

Polanyi, Karl. 1957. *The great transformation.* Boston: Beacon Press.

Preobrazhensky, Evgeny. 1965. *The new economics.* Trans. Brian Pearce. London: Oxford University Press.

Presidents of Central America. 1987. Esquipulas II accord: Plan to establish a firm and lasting peace in Central America. *Central America Report,* 14 August.

Ramírez, Sergio. 1987. *Las armas del futuro.* Managua: Editorial Nueva Nicaragua.

– 1991. Nicaragua: Confession of love. *This Magazine* 24, no. 8 (May), 21–8.

República de Nicaragua. 1955. *Ley de inversiones extranjeras.* Managua: Gobierno de Nicaragua.

Revolución y Desarrollo (Managua).

Rodríguez, Carlos Rafael. 1978. *Cuba en el tránsito al socialismo, 1959–1963.* Mexico City: Siglo XXI.

Roett, Riordan. 1989. The post-1964 military republic in Brazil. In *The politics of anti-politics,* ed. Brian Loveman and Thomas M. Davies, Jr. Lincoln, Nebraska: University of Nebraska Press.

Román, José. 1983. *Maldito país.* Managua: Editorial Unión.

Rothschuh, Guillermo. 1983. *Los guerrilleros vencen a los generales.* Managua: Ediciones Distribuidora Cultural.

Ruccio, David. 1987. The state and planning in Nicaragua. In *The political economy of revolutionary Nicaragua,* ed. Rose J. Spalding. Boston: Allen & Unwin.

Ruiz, Henry. 1980. La dirección única de la economía también depende de la voluntad política de los hombres. *Barricada,* 24 November.

– 1981. Los trabajadores y el plan 81. *Barricada,* 14 January.

– 1982. El legado de Sandino vive en Carlos. In *Carlos Fonseca siempre.* Managua: Departamento de Propaganda y Educación Política del FSLN.

[Ryan, Phil]. 1982. Nicaragua's economy. *Central America Update* (February).

[–] 1983. Coffee and cotton: Heart of the economy, symbol of determination. *Envío,* no. 29 (November).

[–] 1984. Nicaragua's agrarian reform. *Central American Historical Institute Update* 3, no. 2 (13 January).

– 1986. Nicaragua's mixed economy: Problems and prospects. Working paper, University of Toronto Development Studies Program, Toronto.

– 1987. Teoría y política de precios en Nicaragua. Working paper, Departamento de Economía Agrícola de la Universidad Nacional Autónoma de Nicaragua, Managua.

Sandino, Augusto Cesar. 1984. *El pensamiento vivo.* 2 vols. Ed. Sergio Ramírez. Managua: Editorial Nueva Nicaragua.

Saul, John. 1986. El papel de la ideología en la transición al socialismo. In *La transición difícil: La autodeterminación de los pequeños países periféricos*, ed. José Luis Corragio and Carmen Diana Deere. Mexico City: Siglo XXI.

Saulniers, Alfred H. 1987. State trading organizations in expansion: A case study of ENABAS. In *Nicaragua: Profiles of the revolutionary public sector*, ed. Michael E. Conroy. Boulder: Westview Press.

Schumpeter, Joseph. 1976. *Capitalism, socialism and democracy.* 3d ed. New York: Harper Torchbooks.

Schutz, Alfred. 1970. *On phenomenology and social relations.* Chicago: University of Chicago Press.

Secretaría Nacional de Propaganda y Educación Política del FSLN. 1980. Sandinismo no es democratismo. *Barricada,* 14 March.

Selucky, Radoslav. 1972. *Economic reforms in Eastern Europe.* New York: Praeger.

Shmelev, Nikolai, and Vladimir Popov. 1989. *The turning point: Revitalizing the Soviet economy.* Trans. Michele A. Berdy. New York: Doubleday.

Sholk, Richard. 1984. The national bourgeoisie in post-revolutionary Nicaragua. *Comparative Politics* 16, no. 3 (April): 253–76.

Simon, Herbert. 1965. *Administrative behavior.* 2d ed. New York: Free Press.

Spoor, Max, ed. 1987. Datos macro-económicos de Nicaragua. Working paper, Departamento de Economía Agrícola de la Universidad Nacional Autónoma de Nicaragua, Managua.

SPP (Secretaría de Planificación y Presupuesto). 1985. Plan económico 1985. Managua: Mimeographed.

– 1986a. Plan económico nacional 1986. Managua: Mimeographed.

– 1986b. Evaluación de 1985. Managua: Mimeographed.

– 1987. Plan económico nacional 1987. Managua: Mimeographed.

Stahler-Sholk, Richard. 1988a. Ajuste y estabilización en Nicaragua. *Boletín Socioeconómico* (Managua), no. 7 (May): 26–9.

– 1988b. Un tratamiento "shock" para la economía. *Pensamiento Propio* 6, no. 49 (March): 45–8.

– 1990. Ajuste y el sector agropecuario en Nicaragua en los 80: una evaluación preliminar. In *Políticas de ajuste en Nicaragua: Reflexiones sobre sus implicaciones estratégicas.* Managua: CRIES.

Stepan, Alfred. 1978. *The state and society: Peru in comparative perspective.* Princeton: Princeton University Press.

Stigler, George. 1966. *The theory of price.* 3d ed. New York: Macmillan.

Strachan, Harry W. 1976. *Family and other business groups in economic development: The case of Nicaragua.* New York: Praeger.

Sullivan, Wendy, and Felix Delgado. 1988. La reforma monetaria y su repercusión en las unidades económicas. *Boletín Socio-Económico* (Managua), no. 7 (May): 30–5.

Thompson, E.P. 1975. *Whigs and hunters.* London: Allen Lane.

Thucydides. 1954. *The Peloponnesian war.* Trans. Rex Warner. Harmondsworth: Penguin.

Tijerino Medrano, José Antonio, and Mario Palma Ibarra. 1978. *A statement of the laws of Nicaragua in matters affecting business.* 4th ed. Washington: OAS.

Tirado, Victor. 1985. *La primera gran conquista: La toma del poder político.* Managua: CST.

– 1986. *Nicaragua: Una nueva democracia en el tercer mundo.* Managua: Editorial Vanguardia.

– 1987. El objetivo estratégico de la clase obrera es la defensa y gestión del poder revolucionario. *Nuevo Amanecer Cultural* (Managua), 25 April.

Todaro, Michael. 1969. A model of labor migration and urban unemployment in less developed countries. *The American Economic Review* 59, no. 1 (March): 138–47.

Trotsky, Leon. 1971. *Lessons of October.* Trans. John G. Wright. London: New Park Publications.

United Nations. 1991. *The world's women, 1970–1990: Trends and statistics.* New York: United Nations.

UNO (Unión Nacional Opositora). 1989. *Programa de gobierno.* Managua: UNO.

Valenta, Jiri, and Virginia Valenta. 1987. The FSLN in power. In *Conflict in Nicaragua: A multidimensional perspective,* ed. Jiri Valenta and Esperanza Durán. Boston: Allen and Unwin.

Vargas, Oscar René. 1981. Nicaragua: Economía y revolución II. Managua: Mimeographed.

Vilas, Carlos. 1984. *Perfiles de la revolución Sandinista.* Havana: Casa de las Américas.

– 1985. Unidad nacional y contradicciones sociales en una economía mixta: Nicaragua, 1979–1984. In *La revolución en Nicaragua,* ed. Richard Harris and Carlos Vilas. Mexico City: Ediciones Era.

– 1986. La economía mixta y la transición desde el subdesarrollo. In *La economía mixta en Nicaragua: Proyecto o realidad,* ed. María Hurtado de Vigil. Managua: CINASE.

– 1987. El impacto de la guerra de agresión en la revolución sandinista. *Revista Nicaragüense de Ciencias Sociales* 2, no. 2 (March).

– 1990. What went wrong? *NACLA Report on the Americas* 24, no. 1 (June): 10–18.

Wall Street Journal.

Watson, Russell. 1989. Money isn't everything. *Newsweek,* 9 October, 47.

Weber, Henri. 1981. *Nicaragua: La révolution sandiniste.* Paris: Francois Maspero.

Weber, Max. 1949. *The methodology of the social sciences.* Ed. Edward A. Shils and Henry A. Finch. New York: Free Press of Glencoe.

– 1958a. *From Max Weber: Essays in sociology.* Trans. H.H. Gerth and C. Wright Mills. New York: Oxford University Press.

– 1958b. *The Protestant ethic and the spirit of capitalism*. Trans. Talcott Parsons. New York: Charles Scribner's Sons.

– 1978. *Economy and society*. 2 vols. Ed. Guenther Roth and Claus Wittich. Berkeley: University of California Press.

Weeks, John. 1985a. *The economies of Central America*. New York: Holmes & Meier.

– 1985b. The industrial sector. In *Nicaragua: The first five years*, ed. Thomas Walker. New York: Praeger.

Wheelock, Jaime. 1978. *Imperialismo y dictadura*. Rev. ed. Mexico City: Siglo XXI.

– 1979. Interview. *Latin American Perspectives* 6, no. 1: 121–6.

– 1981a. Logros y perspectivas de la economía sandinista. *Barricada*, 1 February.

– 1981b. *Marco estratégico de la reforma agraria*. Managua: DEPEP.

– 1981c. Solo queremos la soberanía para trabajar por nuestro pueblo. *Barricada*, 5 December.

– 1983. *El gran desafío*. Managua: Editorial Nueva Nicaragua.

– 1984a. El FSLN es la organización de los trabajadores. *Barricada*, 2 May.

– 1984b. El sector agropecuario en la transformación revolucionaria. *Revolución y Desarrollo*, no. 1 (April–June).

– 1985a. *Entre la crisis y la agresión*. Managua: Editorial Nueva Nicaragua.

– 1985b. Discurso de Jaime Wheelock ante el Consejo Superior de MIDINRA. In *MIDINRA: Plan de trabajo, balance y perspectivas*. Managua: MIDINRA.

– 1985c. Medidas económicas forman parte de la defensa patria. *Barricada*, 13 February.

– 1986a. Carlos Fonseca: Esencia de su legado. *Nicaráuac*, no. 13 (December): 56–65.

– 1986b. *Vanguardia y revolución en las sociedades periféricas*. Interview with Marta Harnacker. Mexico City: Siglo XXI.

– 1986c. Balance y perspectivas de las políticas de la revolución en el campo. In *La Dirección Nacional y la organización campesina*. Managua: Ediciones Tierra Arada.

– 1990. *La reforma agraria sandinista*. Managua: Editorial Vanguardia.

Wilson, Patricia A. 1987. A comparative evaluation of regionalization and decentralization. In *Nicaragua: Profiles of the revolutionary public sector*, ed. Michael E. Conroy. Boulder: Westview Press.

World Bank. 1982. *World development report, 1982*. Washington: World Bank.

Woroniuk, Beth. 1987. Women's oppression and revolution: The Nicaraguan debate. Occasional paper, CUSO Latin America Program, Ottawa.

Zalkin, Michael. 1987. Food policy and class transformation in revolutionary Nicaragua. *World Development* 15, no. 7: 961–84.

– 1988a. Una proyección sobre los efectos de las medidas. *Pensamiento Propio* 6, no. 49 (March): 49–52.

– 1988b. Nicaragua: The peasantry, grain policy, and the state. *Latin American Perspectives* 15 no. 4: 71–91.

Index

Accumulation focus, 13, 67, 105, 170, 248
Adjustment spiral, 171, 186–8, 208, 244
Agrarian reform, 90–6, 128–30, 155–8, 200–4, 235–7; acceleration, 156; expropriations, 130, 156, 158, 203, 204, 229, 235; FSLN promise of, 92; transfers to individuals, 202–3
Agrarian Reform Law, 52, 115, 128–30, 155, 202
Agrarian Reform Research Centre, 134, 159, 288
Agrarian Tribunals, 115, 298
Agriculture: agricultural strategy, 57, 58; as percentage of GDP, 56; pre-1979 agro-export dominance, 56; as proportion of exports, 56
Agro-export sector: danger of land redistribution, 95; declining volume, 282, 289; producer prices, 144; Sandinista decision to preserve, 77

Alemán, Carlos, 283
Alliance-building focus, 13, 67, 170, 248
Alternation in power, 36
APP. See People's Property Area
Arce, Bayardo: on FSLN and power, 302; on limits to mixed economy, 287; on limits to pluralism, 125; on post-Esquipulas period, 204; on "psychosis of scarcity," 105; on role of opposition, 303
Armed forces, Sandinista control of, 111, 259, 264
Association of Economists, 222
ATC. See Rural Workers' Union

Backwardness, concept of, 33, 51, 159, 261
Banking system, 72, 90. See also Credit policy
Barni, Julian, 122
Barricada, 19, 120, 259
Barrios de Chamorro, Violeta. See Chamorro, Violeta Barrios de

Beef exports, 274, 290
Black market. See Unofficial market
Bolaños, Enrique, 200, 218, 235, 239; call for dialogue with contras, 196; call for u.s. invasion, 296; and Masaya land seizures, 201; and 1990 election, 239, 304
Booth, John, 26
Borge, Tomás: acquiescence to 1985 policies, 168; attack on speculation, 300; on dialogue with the contras, 298; on economism, 148; on evolution of Sandinista ideology, 24; on ideology, 42; imprisonment of, 45; on inconceivability of FSLN defeat, 303; on the Inquisition, 122; on the mixed economy, 194; on peasant politics, 271; on popular discontent, 204; on problem of specialists, 74; on the rationality of socialist planning, 39; religious permeation of